CONDITIONING AND LEARNING

THE CENTURY
PSYCHOLOGY SERIES

EDITED BY

RICHARD M. ELLIOTT, PH.D., *University of Minnesota*

EXPERIMENTAL CHILD STUDY, by Florence L. Goodenough and John E. Anderson.

HUMAN LEARNING, by Edward L. Thorndike.

HISTORY OF EXPERIMENTAL PSYCHOLOGY, by Edwin G. Boring.

EFFECTIVE STUDY HABITS, by Charles Bird.

GREAT EXPERIMENTS IN PSYCHOLOGY, by Henry E. Garrett.

PHYSIQUE AND INTELLECT, by Donald G. Paterson.

PURPOSIVE BEHAVIOR IN ANIMALS AND MEN, by Edward C. Tolman.

ASSOCIATION THEORY TO-DAY, by Edward S. Robinson.

DIAGNOSING PERSONALITY AND CONDUCT, by P. M. Symonds.

THE WILD BOY OF AVEYRON, by Jean-Marc-Gaspard Itard, translated by George and Muriel Humphrey.

THE PHYSICAL DIMENSIONS OF CONSCIOUSNESS, by Edwin G. Boring.

SEVEN PSYCHOLOGIES, by Edna Heidbreder.

HYPNOSIS AND SUGGESTIBILITY, by Clark L. Hull.

DEVELOPMENTAL PSYCHOLOGY, by Florence L. Goodenough.

BEAUTY AND HUMAN NATURE, by Albert R. Chandler.

THE PSYCHOLOGY OF WANTS, INTERESTS, AND ATTITUDES, by Edward L. Thorndike.

GROWTH: A STUDY OF JOHNNY AND JIMMY, by Myrtle B. McGraw.

THE DEFINITION OF PSYCHOLOGY, by Fred S. Keller.

CHILD GUIDANCE PROCEDURES, by Members of the Staff of the Institute for Juvenile Research, Chicago.

THE BEHAVIOR OF ORGANISMS: AN EXPERIMENTAL ANALYSIS, by B. F. Skinner.

INTRODUCTION TO METHODS IN EXPERIMENTAL PSYCHOLOGY, by Miles A. Tinker and Kenneth H. Baker.

THE PSYCHOLOGY OF PARENT-CHILD RELATIONSHIPS, by Percival M. Symonds.

CONDITIONING AND LEARNING, by Ernest R. Hilgard and Donald G. Marquis.

SOCIAL PSYCHOLOGY, by Charles Bird.

OTHER VOLUMES ARRANGED

The Century Psychology Series
Richard M. Elliott, *Editor*

CONDITIONING AND LEARNING

By

ERNEST R. HILGARD
Stanford University

and

DONALD G. MARQUIS
Yale University

D. APPLETON-CENTURY COMPANY
Incorporated

NEW YORK   LONDON

PREFACE

THEORIES of learning which make use of conditioning principles are not related in a simple manner to the facts from conditioning experiments. This book represents an effort to place the facts and theories into some sort of order through critical exposition. The net result is not a finished theory; in many instances we have found it necessary to point to several alternative conceptions. The examination of the relation of conditioning to other basic learning experiments has at other points revealed serious gaps in our knowledge which future experimentation must fill.

Although conditioning has sometimes been proposed as a basic concept for the fields of cerebral physiology, of mental hygiene and personality, and of the higher thought processes, we have found it desirable to place greatest emphasis upon the relation of conditioning to learning theory. In the later chapters we have surveyed the possibilities of applying conditioning concepts within some of the other fields.

Our own experimental work in conditioning was first undertaken in the laboratories of Professors Raymond Dodge, Harold S. Burr, and John F. Fulton of Yale University, and to these and other teachers, colleagues, and collaborators, we owe much. We have profited greatly from the reading and criticism of the entire manuscript by Professor R. M. Elliott, editor of this series. The manuscript was improved through suggestions following critical reading of different portions by R. L. French, V. E. Hall, G. L. Heathers, W. T. Heron, C. I. Hovland, C. L. Hull, J. L. Kennedy, A. A. Lumsdaine, T. L. McCulloch, N. E. Miller, Helen Peak, T. C. Ruch,

R. R. Sears, B. F. Skinner, K. W. Spence, E. C. Tolman, and S. B. Williams. That their suggestions were all useful to us does not mean that they have approved the use which we made of them. The kindness of Dr. G. H. S. Razran in furnishing us an advance copy of his bibliography is gratefully acknowledged. He and several other authors kindly placed in our hands manuscripts prior to publication. Material has been drawn upon from personal communications received from the following: W. H. Burnham, W. H. Gantt, K. S. Lashley, R. B. Loucks, Florence Mateer, J. J. B. Morgan, Richard Parmenter, J. B. Watson, and R. M. Yerkes.

Acknowledgment is made to D. Appleton-Century Co., The Macmillan Company, Oxford University Press, and Prentice-Hall, Inc., from whose publications figures or quotations are reproduced, and to the editors and publishers of the following journals for similar reproductions: *American Journal of Psychology, Archives of Psychology, Journal of Comparative Psychology, Journal of Experimental Psychology, Journal of General Psychology, Journal of Genetic Psychology, Proceedings of the National Academy of Sciences, Psychological Monographs, Psychological Review,* and *Psychosomatic Medicine*. Citation to the original source is given in each case.

E. R. H.
D. G. M.

CONTENTS

FIGURES

CONDITIONING
AND LEARNING

Chapter 1

THE PLACE OF CONDITIONING IN PSYCHOLOGY

THE CLASSICAL conditioning experiment is known to every student of physiology and psychology. When meat powder is placed in a dog's mouth, saliva flows. This natural and relatively automatic behavior is known as an *unconditioned reflex*. An incidental stimulus, such as the sound of a ringing bell, does not at first result in the flow of saliva. If the bell sounds each time just before the food is presented, however, it will eventually elicit salivation. The new response to the bell is known as a *conditioned response,* and the bell is called a *conditioned stimulus*. A relationship has been established between the bell and food, so that a response originally made to the food is now made to the bell.

This simple experiment, with its superstructure of theory, has had a profound influence within the fields of physiology, psychology, and mental hygiene. Despite the fact that it provided a new technique for the investigation of many important problems, the influence of conditioning on experimental study was preceded and greatly overshadowed by its influence on broader problems of theory. For many persons, conditioning seemed to promise a completely objective science of the so-called higher mental functions. Biology and physiology, which had made great strides in the study of simple reflex activity, had been unable to use the same methods in the investigation of the complex functions of the brain. Except for a few experiments in localization, the study of higher processes had remained in the province of psychology, and physiology textbooks were forced to discuss cortical functions in mentalistic terms such as volition, attention, and

memory. Conditioning, it was now declared, provided a
method for the investigation of the higher brain functions
which was just as physiological as the methods for studying
spinal reflexes. Psychology too wanted to become an objective science like other sciences, and conditioning was offered
as evidence of advance in this direction. The conditioned response was called the unit of habit by psychologists to whom
habit was the most important concept in psychology; conditioning method was proclaimed as a substitute for introspection, once the chief method of psychology; the conditioning
process, said a distinguished psychologist-philosopher, brings
mind into being (Holt, 1931, p. 28).

Today uncritical enthusiasm for conditioning has decreased sufficiently to make a sober historical estimate possible. For this appraisal, it is essential to reconstruct the scientific temper at the time of the great ardor for conditioning
and so reveal the reasons for its acceptance. The data of experimental psychology gathered by other methods in the
fields of both perception and learning have always been far
richer in content than those gathered by the conditioning
method. Because this was especially true during the time that
conditioning was at the height of popularity, an interesting
problem confronts the historian. Why was a new method
hailed as a sign of the birth of an objective science of psychology before that method had been thoroughly tried out?
The answer to this question will place conditioning in proper
perspective and aid us in assigning it a rôle in psychology
more nearly in proportion to its potential service.

Preparation within Psychology for the Acceptance of Conditioning

When new concepts are incorporated into a scientific system prior to the experimental demonstration of their ade-

quacy, it is apparent that there has arisen within the system some kind of preparation or readiness for their assimilation. When such preparation is lacking, important discoveries and new methods are often refused admittance. The time must somehow have been ripe for conditioning. Otherwise it would not have been proposed as a method for measuring thresholds until it had been compared with the highly refined threshold methods already available, nor as a basis for learning theory before some effort had been made to compare what it accomplished with well-established findings from other types of experiments using problem-boxes, mazes, skilled tasks, and nonsense syllables. It was accepted, however, without such tests.

The fundamental facts of conditioning were known for many years before their exploitation took place. Twitmyer had independently discovered the phenomenon in an American psychological laboratory in 1902. Pavlov had published reports in English in 1906; Yerkes and Morgulis had reviewed his work and recommended his method to animal psychologists in 1909. In Watson's first book championing behaviorism (1914) the methods of Pavlov are discussed as somewhat inferior to other methods. It cannot be said that the conditioned response won its way into psychology because it was hailed immediately as a great discovery, or because psychologists were greatly impressed by the new methodology.

Three factors in the history of psychology are important in understanding the emphasis which was subsequently given to conditioning in psychological theory. These were, first, the tradition of association, second, the growing importance of habit as a psychological category, and third, the trend toward objectivity.

Association. Modern experimental psychology developed under the influence of association theory, inherited (with modifications) from English empiricism. Emphasis upon the experiential basis of ideas had led to the formulation of laws of association to account for the learned relations between ideas. The set of laws as conventionally stated included three primary ones (contiguity, similarity, and contrast) and numerous secondary or quantitative laws which regulated the effectiveness of the primary ones. These laws, especially the secondary ones, are the antecedents of laws of learning formulated by Thorndike and others. The laws of association underwent many changes, and no one list was ever officially canonized. There was a noticeable tendency, however, to subjugate the laws of similarity and contrast to that of contiguity. The law of contiguity states that an association is formed between experiences that occur close together in space or in time. It is the one law which was found in all the lists.

In an effort to find a physiological basis for association, the principle of contiguous excitation was proposed. As expressed by William James the principle reads:

When two elementary brain-processes have been active together or in immediate succession, one of them, on reoccurring, tends to propagate its excitement into the other. (W. James, 1890, I, p. 566.)

With association reduced to contiguous events and stated as a relation between brain states, the transition to a physiological doctrine of conditioning is straightforward and does no violence to established modes of thought.

Habit. Although psychology was prepared by association theory both for the elementarism of the conditioned response and for its brain physiology, association theory had placed no emphasis on habit and learning as important psychological concepts. Titchener, writing in 1909, preferred not to use the word 'learning' in his chapter on association, excusing himself on the grounds that learning was such a complex affair. In the following chapter (on memory and imagination) he devoted two pages to a discussion of slow and rapid learners, and to cramming. The word 'habit' was mentioned once in relation to the habit of introspection, and again in the chapter on attention. That is all. While Titchener was in some sense an associationist, it is evident from his writings that affiliation with association is not enough to force habit and learning into the foreground of a psychological system.

It was another development, Darwinian biology, which brought habit into focus as a psychological concept. An organism's struggle to adapt to its environment involves muscular movements of locomotion and the like, which resist description in purely conscious terms. Indeed, one characteristic of habitual acts appears to be that the more skillful they become, the less their details are represented in consciousness. The concept of habit breaks over the boundaries of an association theory limited to conscious processes.

William James gave prominence to habit in his *Principles*, not only by writing an important and readable chapter, but by placing it early in his book (Vol. I, Chapter 4) among other chapters dealing with the fundamental characteristics of psychological and brain processes. The usual introductory discussions of sensation and perception he postponed until later chapters. James R. Angell at the University of Chicago gave habit a central place in his systematic psychology which came to be known as functionalism. Earlier association theories had been essentially physiological; in functionalism, association was given a biological flavor. While consciousness remained the primary subject-matter of psychology, investigation of adaptive behavior could not be confined to introspective studies. Animals came to be used increasingly in studies of habit. Introspection in animal experiments was impossible; yet the experiments were producing significant information regarding the learning process.

Objectivity. The study of habit contributed to a general trend in psychology away from so-called subjective methods to more objective types of observation. When psychology became a laboratory science it was on the road to objectivity. Laboratories meant control and measurement, and the formulation of problems amenable to study in quantitative terms. From biology came the voices of the mechanists calling for an objective study of life sciences, without recourse to mentalistic concepts. The famous paper by Beer, Bethe, and v. Uexküll (1899) suggested new terms for the usual psychological ones, substituting, for example, *reception* for *sensation*. Jacques Loeb, the leader of the movement, who resided in America from 1891 until his death, taught for some years at the University of Chicago, where the influence of biology on psychology was strong.

Not without influence was a movement among philosophers to dispense with both dualism and subjective idealism, and to give a more objective account of mind. James entertained doubts about the need for a concept of consciousness in psychology, and Holt (1914) attempted a physiological account of the phenomena associated with the term. The movement was not confined to Harvard philosophers like James, Holt, and Perry. At Pennsylvania, for example, Singer (1911) lectured on *Mind as an observable object*.

Within psychology an increasing number of experiments were performed without the use of introspection. Cattell called attention to this in 1904 in an address at the time of the World's Fair in St. Louis. Thorndike's (1898) animal experiments had opened up a new field, quickly entered by others. Yerkes was developing animal experimentation at Harvard while his colleagues were laying a philosophical justification for objectivism. Although it had not yet reached the experimental stage, child study was being recommended by Hall and Baldwin. The fields of psychopathology and applied psychology, in which introspection is also not a satisfactory method, were growing in importance, and the case in favor of objective methods was becoming steadily stronger.

The convergence of the three historical developments outlined above gave rise in America to behaviorism. The leader of this movement, John B. Watson, had been a student under Angell at Chicago at the time that the concept of habit formation was receiving more stress. Watson, approaching psychology through animal study, was impressed by the need for objectivity. His behaviorism, launched in 1913, epitomized all three trends: it was an objective association psychology with an emphasis upon habit. It is noteworthy that behaviorism was fully flowered before it assimilated the conditioned response. In recounting his relation to Pavlov, Watson writes:

. . . I had worked the thing out in terms of HABIT formation. It was only later, when I began to dig into the vague word HABIT that I saw the enormous contribution Pavlov had made, and how easily the conditioned response could be looked upon as the unit of what we had been calling HABIT. I certainly, from that point on, gave the master his due credit.

The Entrance of Conditioning into Psychology

In spite of the anticipations of conditioning in the writings of the Greek philosophers, in Locke, James, and others, the history of conditioning as such is dominated by the figures of Pavlov and Bekhterev.

Ivan Petrovitch Pavlov (1849–1936) encountered the phenomenon of conditioning in the course of his studies of the digestive glands, for which he was awarded the Nobel Prize. The first report from his laboratory dealing with the newly discovered acquired reflexes was published in 1899 by Wolf-son as a thesis entitled "Observations upon salivary secretion" (Pavlov, 1927, p. 412). These reflexes were called "psychic" secretions to distinguish them from the unlearned physiological secretions. The term *conditioned reflex* was first used in print by Tolochinov, one of Pavlov's associates, who communicated his results at the Congress of Natural Sciences in Helsingfors in 1903. The experiments were performed in 1901. Pavlov continued to the time of his death to carry on research on conditioned responses of dogs, working almost exclusively with salivation to food and with salivation to acid placed in the mouth. Because of the precision of his methods and his full regard for the complexity of the process, Pavlov's reports, collected in two books available to English readers, provide a mine of information for experimenters. The facts are integrated by a conceptual system, which, although in many respects not acceptable, gives relevance to the experimental data, and poses many problems. Application of his findings to man was distinctly secondary for Pavlov, not because of any lack of concern for human problems, but because he conceived his task to be that of brain study. Furthermore, he thought of his work as only in its early stages, and he recognized its many unsolved problems. At the close of a chapter concerned with the applications to man he says:

At first, not to lose sight of the main issue, we were compelled to simplify, and, so to speak, schematize the subject. At present, after having acquired some knowledge of its general principles, we feel surrounded, nay crushed, by the mass of details, all calling for elucidation. (Pavlov, *Conditioned Reflexes,* Oxford University Press, 1927, p. 411.)

While the experimental findings of Pavlov were limited to the salivary responses of dogs, the concepts which he used in dealing with his data are those currently found in discussions of all types of conditioning: conditioned and unconditioned stimuli, reinforcement, extinction, irradiation, discrimination, and so on. His work has the great merit of providing a clearly stated and thoroughly studied reference experiment by which terms may be defined and to which other experiments may be compared. In spite of the broad uses made of his work, Pavlov continued to think of it as belonging to physiology, and he made no attempt to formulate a system of psychology. In fact, he distinguished between his work and that of the American animal psychologists because he was always interested in the physiology of the nervous system, whereas they appeared to him to be concerned with essentially human problems even though they worked with data from animals.

Vladimir M. Bekhterev (1857–1927) as early as 1886 had studied the localized representation in the dog's cortex of learned movements such as giving the paw, but his systematic study of *association-reflexes* began in the winter of 1906–1907. In his experimental investigations, which used first dogs and later human subjects, he studied the withdrawal and respiratory responses evoked by electrical shock stimulation. Unlike Pavlov, Bekhterev was very much interested in creating a new psychology. As early as 1904, before his work on association-reflexes began, he delivered a lecture on "Objective Psychology and its Subject-Matter." He had studied for a time in Wundt's laboratory, and his writings reflect his familiarity with the problems of psychology. It is probably to him more than to Pavlov that we owe the bold acceptance of conditioning by psychologists, although the details of conditioning which came to be accepted were Pavlov's. Bekhterev's *Objective Psychology* appeared serially from 1907 to 1912, and was translated into both French and German in 1913. The German translation carried the sub-title *Psycho-Reflexologie,* and Bekhterev's position gradually became known as reflexology. In 1932 the translators of a later book were able to declare: "Reflexology is the dominant note in Russian psychology today, and the late Bekhterev is the guiding light of humanistic science in the U.S.S.R." The range of Bekhterev's interests was enormous. He wrote widely on neurology, psychiatry, infancy, education, social psychology, judicial psychology, and aesthetics, and he founded a number of institutes for the study of problems in varied fields of neuropsychiatry and child study.

The 1913 translations of Bekhterev's book were very important in arousing the interest of American psychologists, and most of the American experimenters preferred to use his motor conditioning methods rather than the salivary method of Pavlov. Nevertheless, both Pavlov's terminology and his conceptual system have been more widely adopted than Bekhterev's. It may be that Bekhterev's term 'association-reflex' carried with it too much of the flavor of the association of ideas, and thus seemed to continue a tradition against which behaviorism was revolting. This might be one reason why Pavlov's term 'conditioned reflex' was more acceptable. Moreover, Pavlov's careful working out of one variety of experiment with great precision gave his results greater usefulness to laboratory workers than Bekhterev's more general applications.

Early Interest in Conditioning in America. Pavlov's 1906 Huxley lecture, delivered at Charing Cross Hospital, on "The scientific investigation of the psychical faculties or processes in the higher animals" appeared in *Science* and was thus made available to the American public. Details of the experiments from his laboratory were summarized for presentation to psychologists in a thorough review by Yerkes and Morgulis in 1909. The review, however, did not lead to any immediate repetitions of Pavlov's work in America, so far as published records reveal.

Krasnogorski, a student of Pavlov, performed some conditioning experiments on children, reported in German in 1909 and in 1913. These came to the attention of W. H. Burnham at Clark University, who incorporated the material into the lectures in his course on the mental hygiene of the school child. Among his students in 1913–1914 was Florence Mateer, who became interested in repeating Krasnogorski's work. She devoted the next two years to work in this field which was accepted as a doctoral dissertation in 1916 and published in book form in 1918. Mateer's experiments constitute the pioneer study of conditioning in this country. She used the ingenious method of placing a bandage over the eyes of the child just before food was placed in his mouth. The bandage came to serve as the conditioned stimulus, eventually evoking chewing and swallowing movements before the food was presented. The movements were recorded kymographically from tambours fastened under the chin and on the throat. The use of the bandage as a conditioned stimulus was discovered more or less accidentally. Mateer writes:

The great significance of the method came to me all at once about the fourth or fifth day of my first experiments with Phil, in 1914. I learned that even acceptance of a test posture, or entrance into the experimental laboratory, was a conditioning factor and that these and other casual environmental factors had to be unconditioned through disuse before any arbitrary conditioning factor might be used as predetermined in a planned procedure. Even with babies who could not sit up, the bandage was a conditioning factor, as valuable as other stimuli in evoking response. Neither Bekhterev nor Krasnogorski prepared me for this, and, though I had read Pavlov, it took personal experience to show how significant the minutiae of an experimental setting must be.

Mateer's successful conditioning of children furthered the case which Burnham made for the place of the conditioned reflex in mental hygiene (1917, 1921, 1924).

The appearance of the translations of Bekhterev's *Objective Psychology* brought conditioning strongly to the attention of psychologists, and references to it began to appear in 1916.

H. C. Brown (1916) pointed out a possible connection between language and the association-reflex, and F. L. Wells (1916) suggested that the association-reflex could supply a convenient account of affective transference.

Watson's Influence. Watson was very largely responsible for the enthusiastic incorporation of conditioning into American psychology. Prior to his presidential address entitled "The place of the conditioned reflex in psychology" (1916a), which was delivered in 1915 before the American Psychological Association, the conditioned reflex was not an important feature of American psychology. After this date, it began to have a prominent place in the textbooks, if not, for a time, in the research laboratory.

During the winter of 1914–1915, while Mateer was working independently at Clark University, Watson's seminar at Johns Hopkins was devoted to the translation and discussion of the French edition of Bekhterev's book. While Watson thought that Bekhterev was at heart a parallelist, rather than an objectivist, he did not deny the importance of his work. In the spring of 1915 a number of Bekhterev's experiments were repeated, chiefly by Lashley who was then working with Watson. The experiments on finger-withdrawal, respiration, and heart-rate were the factual substance of Watson's address. Watson used Pavlov's expression 'conditioned reflex' thereby stamping it upon the Bekhterev type of experiment. The esteem in which Bekhterev was held is evidenced by the fact that arrangements were made for Lashley to go for a time to work with Bekhterev, but the World War interfered with this plan.

Watson exploited conditioning in his presidential address primarily as a substitute for introspection. He sensed its importance, however, in relation to emotion, mental disease, language, and habit, and wrote about these matters within the next year. Its central position as the unit of habit was not emphasized until later.

With one exception, Watson reported no further experiments on conditioning. In 1920 he published (with Rosalie Rayner) a study of the conditioning of an infant's fear. An experiment with the boy Albert, whose fear of a loud sound was conditioned to a white rat and then to other furry objects, probably provides the most famous single case in conditioning literature. The way had already been paved for the introduction of conditioning into mental hygiene (Heilbronner, 1912; Watson, 1916b; Wells, 1916; Watson and J. J. B. Morgan, 1917; Burnham, 1917), and this experimental illustration of a learned fear fixed a place for conditioning in later discussions of mental hygiene and experimental education.

The conditioned response was prominent in Watson's textbook (1919), but it had not yet displaced the chapter on instinct. By the time of his *Behaviorism* (1925), conditioning was his central theoretical concept. He had espoused a radical environmentalism, and had discarded instincts and other forms of inherited tendencies. The remaining unit of native behavior was the reflex; the unit of habit was the conditioned reflex.

Conditioning: 1916–1926. During the first ten years after Watson launched the conditioned reflex, and while he and others were steering it to ever greater systematic importance, we find very few psychologists performing experiments on conditioning. Lashley (1916a, 1916b) gave up as unsuccessful his attempts to condition the salivary response in man. Mateer's experiments had already been completed, although her book did not appear until 1918. Hamel (1919) concluded from his studies of finger withdrawal that conditioning in man was confused by voluntary processes, but his monograph did not stem the rising tide of popularity of the conditioned reflex.

Cason (1922a) reported that an involuntary response, not represented in consciousness, can be conditioned. In his experiment, the constriction of the pupil which is reflexly evoked by a strong light, was conditioned to a bell stimulus. He also conditioned eyelid reactions in human subjects (1922b) and his results were given a prominent place in the textbooks. Of the few experiments performed, several questioned the current broad generalizations concerning conditioning, but it had already been too firmly established to be dislodged by an appeal to the detailed data of experiments.

The first general textbook to use a conditioning concept throughout was that of S. Smith and Guthrie (1921). They subordinated the reflex problem, and adopted the term 'conditioned response' instead of 'conditioned reflex,' broadening the conditioning concept to include all that had formerly been treated as associative learning. Allport (1924) first gave prominence to the conditioned reflex in a textbook of social psychology at a time when social psychology was seeking desperately for a substitute for instincts. Burnham's *Normal Mind* (1924) presented an extended review of conditioning literature in a textbook on mental hygiene. In the later '20's, textbook writers in psychology, sociology, and education allotted increasing space and prominence to the subject.

Conditioning: 1926–1936. In the next ten years the conditioned response lapsed into a less conspicuous rôle in textbooks, and at the same time began to receive more attention in psychological laboratories.

The lessening of the textbook importance of conditioning reflected a waning confidence in a narrowly formulated behaviorism during these years. Köhler's *Mentality of Apes,* appearing in English in 1925, brought the concept of insight dramatically before animal experimenters. Yerkes had already been promoting similar concepts, and had never accepted behaviorism. In spite of his great respect for Pavlov, he had always thought of the conditioned reflex as one among many methods of experimentation, and had never, strictly speaking, used the method himself. With animal psychology, the stronghold of behaviorism, becoming more skeptical of this system, it was natural for the other fields in which behaviorism had been strong, such as child psychology, to become more eclectic. Koffka's *Growth of the Mind* (1924) emphasized maturation, which, as a kind of substitute for certain aspects of growth formerly included in instinct, now became a formidable competitor of conditioning as a factor in the development of the child's behavior.

As already indicated, the importance of conditioning in research investigation was increasing while its theoretical importance was decreasing. Several reasons for this may be found. The early experiments, such as those of Watson, had been concerned with the question: Can conditioned responses be formed? An affirmative answer was all that was necessary to sanction the theoretical use of conditioning. A few experimental examples sufficed. After the initial wave of theorizing experimenters began to ask: Just what are the detailed facts about conditioning which we can legitimately use in psychology? This was a question that required experimental answer.

A second reason for the renewed interest in experimentation was the appearance in 1927 of a translation of Pavlov's book. The Pavlov volume made available in rich detail the facts discovered by Pavlov and his coworkers during more than a quarter of a century devoted to the study of conditioned salivation in dogs. Pavlov's experiments and theories called for repetition and confirmation using other organisms and other responses. Many laboratories now followed the example of the pioneering few which had already begun programs of experimentation. Liddell initiated in 1926 a series of conditioning experiments on several different animals. Kleitman and Crisler's important study of conditioned salivation to morphine injection appeared in 1927; Schlosberg's study of the conditioned knee jerk was published in 1928; and Upton's study of hearing in the guinea pig (1929) was followed by a series of investigations by others on the sensory capacities of animals. In the next few years, experimental reports on conditioned responses appeared in rapidly increasing numbers, and the usefulness of the method for the study of learning, sensory acuity and related problems was clearly demonstrated.

Clark L. Hull at Yale University began in 1929 a highly provocative series of articles in the *Psychological Review* making use of the findings of Pavlov and of other workers with the conditioned response in a detailed manner not previously attempted. His presidential address before the American Psychological Association in 1936 (Hull, 1937), two decades after Watson's, shows the changes which have come in the use of the conditioning experiment. Hull, like Watson, stressed the conditioning process, but, in the light of the newer detailed knowledge of conditioned responses, he presented a system of definitions, postulates, and theorems, by which to bridge the gap from conditioned responses to more complex forms of learning. Hull's systematic formulations have led to numerous experiments by his own students and others.

Because they contributed to the maturing of psychology as an experimental science, the developments within the years 1926–1936 were more wholesome than those of the previous decade. The period was marked by a significant shift from the broad theoretical and speculative exploitation of conditioning to a type of theory sensitive to laboratory data. The earlier promotional stage may have been a necessary and useful one, since it drew attention to the field in which experiments were eventually to be performed, and gave the experiments a systematic relevance.

Present Conceptions of the Place of Conditioning in Psychology

After abandonment of the early, extravagant claims that conditioning provided an immediate solution of the philosophical problems of a psychology seeking objective, scientific status, it became clearer that conditioning was significant chiefly in relation to learning theory. At the present time, however, there is a great diversity of opinion concerning its exact place in such theory.

Largely as a result of the attacks upon associationism by Gestalt psychologists, contemporary learning theories tend to be classified into two broad groups, association theories on the one hand, and field theories on the other. Theories using concepts such as redintegration, trial-and-error, and conditioning, are assigned to the first group; those using concepts such as insight, sign-learning, and least action, are assigned to the second group (e.g., Tolman, 1934). Field theories differ from conditioning and other association theories in two important respects. In the first place, through emphasis on the priority of the whole over the part, they are opposed to the analysis into part activities implied in conditioning theories. In the second place, according to field theories the dynamics of behavior are said to depend on the present structure of the force field in which the organism is imbedded, and not on the previous history of the organism. Previous history may be useful in giving an understanding of the present, but if the present were completely understood, the history would be irrelevant. Association and conditioning theories, on the contrary, have always stressed prior experience as primary for the understanding of present behavior. The cleavage between association and field theories, and attempted compromises, will be discussed later (Chapter 10); for the present the distinction is important to the extent that accepting one or the other positions affects the attitude taken towards the conditioned response in relation to learning.

At least five different views may be found among those who accept the conditioning experiment as an example of learning. The conditioned response has been proposed as (1) a substitute for association, (2) the unit of habit, (3) representative of other forms of learning, (4) a source of deductive principles, (5) a subordinate and restricted form of learning. Not all authorities endorse specifically just one of these proposals. Some indeed accept two or more of them, but each of the proposals has been selected for separate emphasis by someone (Hilgard, 1937).

(1) *Conditioning as a substitute for association.* Association in its more objective form, in which the association occurs between stimuli and movements rather than between ideas, often goes by the name of conditioning. S. Smith and Guthrie gave the initial impetus to this usage in their textbook (1921). They extended the language of conditioning to the whole range of psychological phenomena. Conditioning became in their hands a general formula—a modern substitute for *contiguity,* the primary law of association.

This usage differs from all the others in one significant respect: conditioning according to it is a *single* principle of learning, rather than a *set* of principles. The conditioning experiment is not important as a source of new principles, but is merely one of many instances in which the single principle may be applied to explain the observed modifications of behavior. The other four theories agree in directing more attention to the empirical facts discovered in conditioning experiments, but differ in their conceptions of the relation of the conditioned response to learning in general.

(2) *The conditioned response as the unit of habit.* The orthodox statement of the conditioning theory of learning

maintains that the conditioned response is the unit of all learned activity. Thus Pavlov states:

> It is obvious that the different kinds of habits based on training, education and discipline of any sort are nothing but a long chain of conditioned reflexes. (Pavlov, *Conditioned Reflexes*, Oxford University Press, 1927, p. 395.)

This is the position which Watson promulgated, and it enjoyed a great vogue in America for some years.

The doctrine that complex habits are simply compounds of conditioned responses should have led to a definite program of experimental work to discover the principles governing the chaining of component responses. Such a program did not follow; even the first stage of it, the development of chain conditioned responses, was not studied in the laboratory. Why Watson or his followers did not undertake the experimental investigations which followed so naturally from the theory requires an understanding of the place of the conditioned response in Watson's system of behaviorism.

The elementarism of Watson's behaviorism was rooted in the scientific tradition prevailing at the time that he wrote. In 1916 he was combatting an introspective and sensationistic analysis, but he did this within the same orthodox logical framework by substituting the reflex as the element in place of sensation, thus avoiding subjectivism, but leaving the current elementarism unchallenged. Sensation and attribute were analytic, not synthetic concepts, and the inadequacy of conditioning theory in its synthetic aspects was no greater than that of structuralism. It was not an important criticism at the time to point out that complex habits could not be completely reproduced by conditioning; to defend the position it sufficed to indicate the possibility that component conditioned responses could be detected when the habits were analyzed.

A second root of Watson's conditioning theory is found in his extreme emphasis upon the rôle of environment, as opposed to instinct, in determining human behavior. Since habits cannot arise from nothing, and reflexes are the only innate endowment, habits must arise out of reflexes. Conditioning conveniently provides the principle by which reflexes become habits. Thus the conception of the conditioned reflex as the unit of habit harmonized Watson's theoretical structure, and he accepted it without feeling any necessity to wait for detailed experimental verification.

Attacks on Watson's statement of conditioning theory have been numerous and vigorous. It is now clear on both theoretical and experimental grounds that simple chaining of conditioned responses will not predict the characteristics of complex habits. The component responses are greatly altered by virtue of their combination with other responses, and the influence of combination must be experimentally determined. Watson's simple conception of the conditioned response as the unit of habit has not proved serviceable and is now chiefly of historical interest.

(3) *Conditioning experiments as representative of other forms of learning.* If the conditioning experiment proves to exhibit in sharp focus all the essential characteristics of other learning, it is a useful place to look for 'laws of learning.' It is obviously under better control than many of the more practical learning situations, and to the extent that it is a 'pure case' of learning, it is a good source for the determination of the principles which hold true for all learning. Symonds (1927) has given a detailed exposition of this possibility. He listed 23 laws of conditioning and showed the analogies between them and learning in practical situations. The limitations of his position are those common to all arguments from analogy: a superficial similarity convenient for expository purposes may be misinterpreted as indicating identity of

underlying process. Symonds' analogies show many unjusti-
fiable leaps from conditioning to more familiar behavior.

All learning cannot be epitomized in conditioning, because
the conditioning experiment does not have within it all the
richness of patterning of stimuli and of coordination of movement found in other learning situations. To point out an analogy with conditioned finger retraction can never suffice to
account for the most favorable method of learning even a
manual skill such as typing, much less for more varied instances of problem-solving. This use of the conditioned response as representative of other forms of learning is properly
limited to situations in which the identity is very apparent or
is susceptible to demonstration.

(4) *Conditioning as a source of deductive principles.* The
relationships within conditioning experiments do not in themselves provide analogies to account for the backward order
of elimination of blind alleys in rat mazes or for the excess of
errors in the middle of a memorized series of nonsense syllables. Yet it may be possible to deduce facts such as these from
principles discovered in conditioning experiments, if the procedure advocated most prominently by Hull is followed. This
position differs from the previous ones in that the deduced
behavior may be superficially very unlike the conditioned response behavior which serves as the source of the principles
used in the deduction. In the hands of Hull and others, the
conditioning experiment has become the tool for harmonizing
many facts already known about learning, and for predicting
a variety of new facts.

This use of conditioning does not carry the implication that
all habits are compounded of simple conditioned responses or
that the principles discovered in conditioning experiments are
directly applicable to complex habit situations. The conditioning experiment, because of its simple and well controlled
structure, is a fruitful source of postulates from which deduc-

tions can be made concerning complex learning. The postulates must be verified in their new application; it is not enough to know that they were found true in simple conditioning.

(5) *Conditioning as a subordinate and restricted form of learning.* Psychologists who believe that each of the preceding points of view is either wrong or premature fall into two classes: first, those who are opposed to all association theories of learning, and second, those who are not opposed to association theories, but who believe that the conditioned response has been overemphasized. In the former group would fall the Gestalt psychologists, who have been most vigorous in their denunciation of associationism. They very naturally include the conditioned response among the targets of their attack, because it seems to possess the vices both of association theories of learning and of atomistic-mechanistic theories of science. Even they need not deny some minor place to conditioning as a laboratory curiosity, but they cannot be expected to endorse a conditioning theory of learning. Others, such as Robinson (1932), who defend an associationist account of learning believe that the conditioned response experiment is too limited to provide all of the principles needed to deal with more complicated learning. They would also be skeptical about a theory of learning based solely on the maze experiment or solely on serial memorizing. There is good reason to expect a richness of empirical learning principles commensurate with the variety of situations in which learning occurs.

No attempt has been made here to evaluate the theories summarized above, or to do more than place them in the perspective of the historical trends from which they arose. The time now appears to be ripe for a more critical assessment of conditioning. The abundant experimentation of the last few years has provided data by which to test and correct theories, and the theories themselves have become more precise. The first wave of enthusiasm has passed; assuredly the conditioned response is taking a more modest place than it filled ten years ago.

Notes

Preparation within Psychology for the Acceptance of Conditioning

Early illustrations of concepts anticipating the conditioned response may be found in reviews by Cason (1925a) and Hull (1934c).

The development and influence of association psychology is comprehensively traced in H. C. Warren's *A History of Association Psychology* (1921). The rise of objectivism is treated in the standard histories of psychology, such as Boring's *History of Experimental Psychology* (1929) and Murphy's *An Historical Introduction to Modern Psychology* (1929).

Acknowledgment is made to Dr. Watson for permission to quote from a personal communication regarding his relationship to Pavlov. It is interesting to note that in Russia, as well as in America, objectivism gained a strong position prior to the advent of conditioning. Russian objectivism is largely derived from Sechenov, a distinguished physiologist, who published his *Reflexes of the Brain* in 1863. In this book he outlined a comprehensive reflex theory of all behavior, including cerebral processes. Sechenov's conceptions were never well known outside Russia, but both Pavlov and Bekhterev acknowledge his great influ-

ence on their work. Recently a translation of the most important works of Sechenov has been made available in a volume (1935) issued at the time of the International Congress of Physiology in Moscow.

The Entrance of Conditioning into Psychology

Pavlov's work is summarized in two books available in English translation (1927, 1928). A biography is included in the second of these. Frolov's more recent book (1937) is useful chiefly for its characterizations of Pavlov as a man.

Bekhterev's work is summarized in his *Objective Psychology*, which appeared simultaneously in French and German (1913a, 1913b), and in his *General Principles of Reflexology*, which appeared in English in 1932. This contains a biographical statement, and a bibliography of his writings.

It is difficult to estimate the extent to which the lagging interest in experimental work on conditioning in America may be attributed to inaccessibility of the Russian publications. Yerkes, having been early interested in Pavlov's work, and having himself done independently some experiments on the frog (1905, 1906) which Pavlov considered pioneering work along the lines of conditioning, had urged Pavlov as early as 1909 to prepare a book for the Animal Behavior Series which Yerkes edited. Pavlov's reply (published here with Dr. Yerkes' permission) is characteristic:

"For a long time I have written unwillingly and rarely, and the proposed writing for you would not be easy for me. Frankly, I am planning to write a book on the conditioned reflexes, but only later when the subject shall have been carried farther and entirely worked over. The physiology of the conditioned reflexes is for me only a half of the story. Already, we work over the cord reflexes in connection with most varied destructions of the hemispheres. The objective of the whole work, as I understand it, is a foundation for the physiology of the brain."

Dr. Mateer kindly consented to the publication of a private communication regarding her early work under Burnham. In the course of preparation for her dissertation, she borrowed the Russian edition of Sechenov's *Reflexes of the Brain* from the Surgeon General's Office, and had significant passages translated. The interest at Clark University was serious, and quite independent of that at Johns Hopkins. Baird, who supervised the experimental portions of Mateer's study, arranged for her to meet Watson in 1914 because of their common interest in conditioning, but it is her recollection that at the time Watson did not mention experiments in progress. Lashley (private communication) agrees in the priority of the Clark experiments.

The account of the introduction of the conditioned reflex at Johns Hopkins is based upon communications from Watson and Lashley. Watson credits Lashley with most of the early experimentation; Lashley states that the initiative was Watson's in all that was done. Dr. Lashley writes, in part:

"We accumulated a considerable amount of experimental material on the conditioned reflex which has never been published. Watson saw it as the basis for a systematic psychology and was not greatly concerned with the mechanism of the reflex, which he regarded as a problem for the physiologist. I got interested in the possibility of tracing conditioned reflex paths through the cortex and this started my program of cerebral work."

Present Conceptions of the Place of Conditioning in Psychology

The use of conditioning as a substitute for the law of contiguity has received further treatment by Wilson (1924) and by Guthrie (1930, 1935, 1938). A somewhat similar proposal was made by Frank (1923) and promptly criticized by Peterson (1923). Analogous statements of an objective associationism have been proposed, such as Meyer's principle of double stimulation (1908, 1934), Washburn's principle of the association of movements (1916), and Hollingworth's principle of redintegration (1928). Pavlov (1932b) has castigated the use of a single principle such as this to account for all learning, because it results in overlooking many important concrete facts of conditioning. For a reply to Pavlov, see Guthrie (1934).

The statement that the conditioned reflex is the unit into which habits may be resolved was made in 1917 by Watson and J. J. B. Morgan. It was frequently reiterated by Watson (1919, 1926), and quoted with approval by others, e.g., Burnham (1924). Allport (1924) introduced essentially the same notion into social psychology. The infiltration of this point of view into the literature of education, sociology, and mental hygiene may be traced largely to these sources.

Symonds' exposition of conditioning as representative of all forms of learning became widely known through Sandiford's (1928) textbook on educational psychology. A number of other authors have favored a similar conception, e.g., Hunter (1933), Rexroad (1932, 1933), and Stagner (1931).

The laws of behavior recently proposed by Skinner (1938) are based on the detailed experimental study of a particular type of representative behavior, to be discussed later (Chapter 3). Skinner has made so few extensions of his principles to other situations, however, that it is not quite clear to which of the five positions his point of view should be assigned.

Hull's numerous papers in which he details the deductive approach from conditioning to learning theory may be located from the list of references. The most useful single presentation of his program may be found in his presidential address before the American Psychological Association (1937), and the most extensive application to the phenomena of rote memorizing is contained in a recent monograph by Hull, Hovland, Ross, M. Hall, D. T. Perkins, and F. B. Fitch (1940).

Illustrations of the criticisms of the association position in learning may be found in Köhler (1929), Peterson (1935), Tolman (1932), Wheeler (1929). Many accept the conditioning experiment as an interesting but limited situation, distinctly not representative of all learning. Among these are writers representing widely diverse theoretical points of view, e.g., Adams (1931), Dodge (1933), Finch and Culler (1935), Harlow (1936), Humphrey (1928a, 1933), Lashley (1916a, 1934), Stephens (1931b), Thorndike (1932a, 1935), Warner (1932b), K. A. Williams (1929b), Gustav and Wolf (1937).

Chapter 2

CLASSICAL CONDITIONING EXPERIMENTS

B EFORE a consideration of the principles of conditioning is
undertaken, the results of the experiments upon which
those principles are based must be surveyed. The basic relationships of any learning theory are derived from experiments
which have been designed to display in relatively simple and
uncomplicated fashion the fundamental processes which are
involved. Since learning is essentially a change in an individual's behavior which depends upon his previous experience
in the same situation, it is apparent that in any learning experiment the individual must be observed at least twice. The
progress of learning is usually followed by recording the behavior during successive trials, or discrete presentations of the
situation. The most serviceable experiments for the demonstration of the fundamental principles of learning will be
those in which all the factors influencing behavior are well
controlled or measured, and in which simplicity is secured by
studying a single response rather than a complicated series of
responses. The conditioning experiment fulfills these requirements. In this respect it may be considered a basic experiment.
There are, of course, a number of more complicated learning
situations not readily reducible to the pattern of conditioning.
Among them are serial performances such as maze-learning
and verbal memorization, experiments involving tools and de-
tours, other problem-solving and reasoning experiments, and
skilled acts involving precision and patterning of voluntary

movements. The relation of conditioning to these further situations will be considered later (Chapters 8–10), after the problems involved in the simpler situations have been more fully analyzed.

The body of data accumulated through years of study of conditioned salivation in the dog by Pavlov and his coworkers serves today as the point of departure for a description of conditioning experiments. Pavlov's work defines the type of situation to be considered as conditioning, and provides a terminology for its description. It is obvious that conditioning is not, however, restricted to the salivary responses of dogs, for it is entirely feasible to use other organisms and other responses without departing widely from the Pavlovian tradition. The essential features of the conditioning experiment are the following: (1) an unconditioned stimulus which, in the experimental situation, evokes a regular and measurable unconditioned response, (2) a conditioned stimulus which originally does not evoke the unconditioned response, (3) repeated presentation of the conditioned and unconditioned stimuli in a controlled and specified manner. Any new or altered response to the conditioned stimulus whose occurrence depends upon the repeated double stimulation is called a conditioned response.

Within this general structure, however, certain important differences in procedure may be found among various conditioning experiments. Two general types of experiment will be discussed: (1) classical conditioning, and (2) instrumental conditioning. The first type is the experiment of Pavlov, but the other type has also been studied by his students and has come to be designated as conditioning. The distinction between the two training procedures is based on the consequences of the conditioned response. In the first type the occurrence of the conditioned response results in no change in the procedure; the unconditioned stimulus is presented invariably at a fixed interval after the conditioned stimulus. In the instrumental training, however, the conditioned stimulus is followed by a reward (or an avoidance of punishment) only when the appropriate response is made to it. Many learning situations represent a combination of these types. Discussion of situations other than classical conditioning is postponed to the next chapter.

The reference experiment for classical conditioning is the study of conditioned salivation in dogs. The essential features of the procedure may be seen from a description of a typical experiment in Pavlov's laboratory (Anrep, 1920). In order to make possible the recording of the magnitude of the salivary response, the dog was first subjected to a minor operation in which the duct of the parotid gland was diverted so that the saliva flowed through an opening on the outside of the cheek. A small glass funnel was firmly cemented over the opening to collect the saliva, which could be measured with an accuracy of one-tenth drop by suitable devices. The dog was trained to stand quietly in a loose harness on a table in a room which was insulated against any distracting noises or vibrations. The experimenter occupied an adjoining room, observing the dog through a small window, and presenting the stimuli by means of automatic devices. A tuning fork was sounded and 7 or 8 seconds after the beginning of this conditioned stimulus a plate containing a small measured quantity of dry powdered food was moved within reach of the dog's mouth. No salivation was evoked by the tone, but during the eating there was a copious flow of saliva. Combinations of the tone and food were presented 3 times during a daily session, separated by intervals of from 5 to 35 minutes. The strength of the conditioned response was determined by presenting the tone alone for 30 seconds and measuring the amount of salivation. After 10 double stimulations there was a slight conditioned salivation, and after 30 combinations the tone evoked a salivation of 60 drops. On the early tests the conditioned salivation did not begin until the tone had sounded for 18 seconds; on later tests the salivation commenced after only 1 or 2 seconds.

Another example of classical conditioning which employs a motor rather than a secretory response may be selected from Liddell's (1934) studies on sheep. A metronome was set beating once per second for five seconds and then a shock was delivered from an inductorium through electrodes attached to the left foreleg of the animal. The metronome had no apparent effect upon the sheep's behavior, whereas the shock evoked a definite brief flexion of the limb, accompanied by changes in respiration and in electrical resistance of the skin. After 4 presentations of the metronome and shock in combination, the conditioned stimulus caused a definite change in breathing and skin resistance, and on the 6th trial there was a slight movement of the leg. By the 11th trial the conditioned leg flexion was fully established, and with further training was quite constant and stable. The reactions of the 11th trial are illustrated in Figure 1. Since the conditioned response occurred at a latency of 3 or 4 seconds following the onset of the metronome, it was not necessary to change the training procedure in any way to measure the strength of response on each trial.

Conditioning has been successfully carried out on many different organisms, using a large number of different unconditioned responses and conditioned stimuli. Its apparent universality supports the use of conditioning by many psychologists as a sort of common denominator of all learning situations. An enumeration of the various organisms and responses which have been studied will suggest both the generality and the limitations of conditioning phenomena.

Organisms Which Have Been Conditioned. Simple associations, which may be called conditioned, have been formed by protozoa, worms, snails, crabs, fish, reptiles, pigeons, chickens, rats, sheep, dogs, monkeys, and many other species. A few illustrations will serve to indicate the kinds of experiments done with animals differing widely in anatomical and behavioral characteristics.

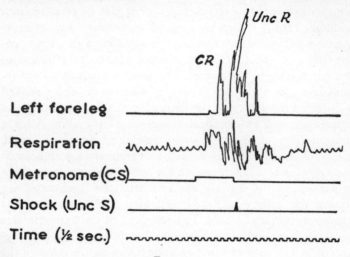

FIGURE I

CONDITIONED RESPONSES IN THE SHEEP

The diagram represents a tracing from a kymograph record of the eleventh presentation of a metronome (conditioned stimulus, CS) combined with a shock (unconditioned stimulus, UncS) delivered to the left foreleg. The metronome beat once a second for 5 seconds prior to the shock. Both the conditioned leg movements and respiratory changes began while the metronome was sounding, anticipating the shock. These conditioned responses (CR) may be distinguished from the unconditioned responses (UncR) following shock. After Liddell (1934, p. 268).

Experiments on colonies of infusoria, *Carchesi lachmani,* were performed by Plavilstchikov (1928) and summarized statistically by Razran (1933a). Tactile stimulation with a glass filament induced contraction of the colony (the unconditioned response). A filtered light, to which no original responses were observed, served as the conditioned stimulus.

Reactions were observed through a binocular microscope. Conditioned responses were established in all 82 colonies observed. The first response appeared after 79 to 284 repetitions. Parts of the conditioned colony were in several cases transplanted to hosts not previously used in the experiment. The new colony developed contractions after 1 to 3 trials. When the transplanted parts were removed after a few more trials, the remaining parts of the host continued to show conditioned responses after 1 to 3 additional trials.

Movements of the mouth region of the snail, *Physa Gyrina Say,* were conditioned by E. L. Thompson (1917). After the snails were adapted to the circumstances of experimentation a piece of lettuce pressed against the mouth region resulted frequently in mouth movements. Pressure applied to the ventral surface of the foot, not originally eliciting mouth movements, served as the conditioned stimulus. After frequent combinations of the pressure with the lettuce, mouth movements to pressure were elicited as conditioned responses. Experimental extinction was demonstrated when the pressure was applied a number of times without being followed by the lettuce leaf.

A number of experimenters have established conditioned responses in fish. Frolov (1925a), a student of Pavlov's, designed a method for transmitting the unconditioned stimulus (electric shock) to the fish by a wire clamped to the dorsal fin. This wire, attached to a Marey tambour, also recorded the movements of the fish on a kymograph. Conditioned stimuli were presented by the use of lamps, a submerged telephone, and an electric bell and tuning fork suspended above the aquarium. Conditioned motor responses appeared after 5 to 30 combinations of conditioned and unconditioned stimuli, best results being secured with the submerged telephone.

When similar sensory and muscular processes are chosen

in different species, it is possible to perform experiments which are useful for comparative purposes. Thus eyelid reactions have been conditioned in rats (Hughes and Schlosberg, 1938), dogs (Hilgard and D. G. Marquis, 1935), monkeys (Hilgard and D. G. Marquis, 1936), and men (Hilgard and A. A. Campbell, 1936). In each of these studies, the unconditioned response was lid closure to a puff of air directed at the eye. When the conditioned stimulus (a buzz in the case of the rat, a light in each of the other studies) preceded the air-puff regularly by a fraction of a second, the conditioned response developed in each case as a lid movement following the on-set of the conditioned stimulus but anticipating the air-puff. Records from dog, monkey, and man are reproduced in Figure 2. The gross similarity of the results in different species must not be permitted to obscure the differences. Although the air-puff is delivered to one eye only, the response tends to be equal in both eyelids in the monkey, more nearly confined to the puffed eye in the dog, and intermediate in man. In the human record illustrated, the conditioned response is similar in both eyelids, although the unconditioned response has habituated somewhat in the non-puffed eye and is of less amplitude than that of the puffed eye.

Reactions Used as Unconditioned Responses. In order to carry out a conditioning experiment it is first necessary to discover in the repertory of the organism some dependable unconditioned response on which to base the conditioning. Table 1 lists the responses which have been most used, and the unconditioned stimuli employed to elicit them.

It is obvious that the classificatory scheme is not a rigid one, for responses of an intact organism are too complicated to be assigned with assurance to reflex or voluntary categories. The responses in the first group are under the control of the autonomic nervous system. These may be expected to show certain differences, such as greater latency, when com-

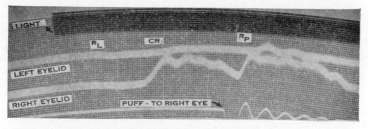

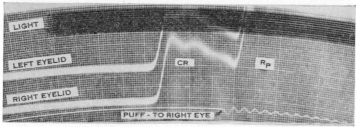

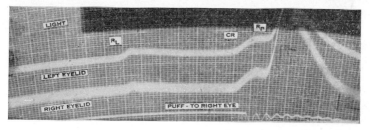

FIGURE 2

SPECIMEN RECORDS OF CONDITIONED EYELID RESPONSES IN DOG, MONKEY, AND MAN

The onset of the light (the conditioned stimulus) is shown by the darkening at the top of each record. The air-puff to the right eye (the unconditioned stimulus) shows as a break in the line at the bottom of each record. The three responses are, successively, the reflex to light (R_L), the conditioned response to the light (CR), and the unconditioned reflex to the air-puff (R_P). Time lines are spaced at 5 msec. in dog and monkey records, 10 msec. in record from man; emphasized lines in all cases, 50 msec. Interval between light and puff is 375 msec. for dog, 400 msec. for monkey, 450 msec. for man. Dog record from Hilgard and D. G. Marquis (1935); monkey, Hilgard and D. G. Marquis (1936); man, Hilgard and A. A. Campbell (1936). Records 1 and 2 were previously published; record 3 is an unpublished specimen. Since the responses are of insufficient amplitude to avoid the air-puff, at this stage the process qualifies as classical conditioning. If the air-puff were completely avoided, the conditioned responses might be considered instrumental avoidance responses, to be discussed in Chapter 3.

pared with responses of the second group, which are under the control of the somatic nervous system. In man, the awareness of the responses may also differ. The human subject is not ordinarily as conscious of his pupillary changes or salivary secretions as he is of his overt muscular movements. On the other hand, the autonomic responses are affected by states of apprehension and emotion of which the subject is clearly aware. There is not, therefore, a sharp dividing line between smooth muscle and striped muscle responses so far as psychological determination of response is concerned.

TABLE I

UNCONDITIONED RESPONSES AND THE STIMULI USED TO ELICIT THEM

1. *Glandular, smooth muscle, and blood responses:*

Salivation	Dry food; acid
Change in skin resistance	Electric shock
Pupillary reflex	Change in illumination
Gastro-intestinal secretions	Food
Vasomotor reactions	Shock; thermal stimuli
Nausea, vomiting, etc.	Morphine
Immunity reactions	Injection of toxin, antigen
Diuresis	Increased water intake

2. *Relatively involuntary responses in striate muscle:*

Flexion reflex	Electric shock
Knee jerk	Patellar blow
Eyelid reflex	Shock; sound; air-puff
Eye movements	Rotation
Change in respiration	Electric shock
Change in pitch of voice	Electric shock

3. *Semi-voluntary and voluntary responses:*

Withdrawal movements	Electric shock
Mouth opening, swallowing	Food
Locomotion	Shock
Instructed responses	Various
Previously conditioned responses	Various

The difference between responses of the second and third groups is likewise one of degree. To state that a response is voluntary means that its elicitation is highly dependent upon the instructions given to the subject, whether by command or by previous training. Thus the instruction to press a telegraph key at a signal yields a voluntary response, although the response may become relatively automatic with practice. A less voluntary response such as the knee jerk depends more upon the eliciting stimulus than on prior instructions. Even the most involuntary responses are subject to facilitation or interference by voluntary sets and attitudes of the organism, and, conversely, the most voluntary responses are influenced by the characteristics of the stimuli which set them off. The difference is primarily one of degree. In most conditioning experiments a relatively involuntary reaction is selected as the unconditioned response because it is more directly under experimental control. When an instructed reaction is employed additional factors, difficult to measure precisely, must be taken into consideration. The basic principles of conditioning can best be discovered in the simpler situation, and the data of voluntary conditioning are postponed for later discussion (Chapter 11).

The use of previously conditioned responses as unconditioned responses is designated *higher-order conditioning*. An experiment from Pavlov's laboratory illustrates the sequence of events. A metronome was combined with food until conditioned salivation to the metronome was established. Then a black square was held before the dog for 10 seconds, and after an interval of 15 seconds the metronome was sounded for 30 seconds. At the tenth repetition the dog began to salivate to the black square. The metronome had served as the unconditioned stimulus. Special precautions are needed in establishing such second order conditioned responses because the response to the metronome tends to be extinguished if it is not followed by the unconditioned food stimulus, and because a new stimulus (black square) presented along with the metronome under these conditions tends to become a conditioned inhibitor. The most effective procedure, according to

Pavlov (1927, p. 33), is to withdraw the new stimulus some seconds before the primary stimulus (metronome) is presented.

Extreme difficulty or failure has been encountered in the attempt to condition certain responses. These failures appear to fall into three classes. (1) Conditioning has been shown to be unsuccessful in vertebrates if the unconditioned response is evoked otherwise than by way of the central nervous system. Passive flexion of a limb, or direct electrical or chemical stimulation of a muscle or its motor nerve are ineffective as unconditioned responses (see p. 322, Chapter 13). (2) Certain simple reflexes appear to be extremely difficult to condition. The abdominal, patellar, Achilles, and plantar reflexes fall in this category. When successful conditioning does occur, as in the case of the knee jerk (Schlosberg, 1932), it appears that voluntary habitual facilitation is an important factor. (3) Some conditioning experiments are unsuccessful because of the presence in the situation of strong antagonistic tendencies which interfere with the performance of the conditioned responses. Several experimenters have reported failure to secure conditioned finger retraction based on unconditioned shock stimulation because of a competing tendency which is established by general instructions to hold the fingers on the electrodes. Further illustrations of this phenomenon will be presented in other connections.

Conditioned Stimuli. While unconditioned stimuli are chosen in reference to the response to be elicited, any environmental change to which the organism is sensitive may serve as a conditioned stimulus. Visual stimuli have included lights of various colors, papers, geometrical forms, rotating objects. Auditory stimuli have included pure tones, horns, buzzers, bubbling water, metronomes. Various thermal, tactual, olfactory, and proprioceptive stimuli have been used. Stimulus patterns may be presented in temporal as well as in spatial arrangements. Pavlov tended to prefer continuing stimuli, such as metronomes, electric fans, rotating disks. Experimenters using reflexes in striate muscles have tended to prefer stimuli with sharp onset, such as flashes of light, clicks, contact stimuli. The effectiveness of some stimuli may depend on their sudden onset, while others may depend for their effectiveness on summation. Pavlov has shown that a change in the intensity of a stimulus or the termination of a stimulus may serve as well as the appearance of a stimulus.

Internal stimuli are not as frequently employed in conditioning experiments as external stimuli because they are not so susceptible to precise control and measurement. They are important, however, in many types of experiment, as the technique of temporal conditioning illustrates. If a dog is given food regularly every thirtieth minute, it comes to salivate regularly at that interval. If the food is omitted the dog will salivate approximately 30 minutes after the last feeding. Although their nature has not been determined, it is apparent that internal stimuli of some sort are functioning as signals for the response.

The Nature of the Conditioned Response

The conditioned response has traditionally been assumed to be the response originally elicited by the unconditioned stimulus, evoked after learning by the conditioned stimulus. This assumption requires that the dog which formerly salivated only to the food should salivate in the same way to the metronome; the human subject who gave a galvanic reaction to an electric shock should respond similarly to a flash of light after conditioning. It is now recognized, however, that conditioned and unconditioned responses are seldom, if ever, identical, and that the conditioned response is not simply a duplicate of the unconditioned response. Some of the differences are illustrated in Figure 3. Many experiments offer little critical evidence on the nature of the conditioned responses, because the only responses measured are those similar to the unconditioned response. Thus Pavlov measured only salivary secretion, and neglected any precise measurement of the motor concomitants. When attention is directed to the differences between conditioned and unconditioned behavior, as well as to similarities, the conditioned response is found to be very complex, and to display significant variations from one experiment to another. Four different kinds of conditioned response will be described.

Redintegrative Responses. In some experiments, the conditioned response does appear to be almost an exact replica of the unconditioned response. Thus in the early stages of conditioned leg withdrawal, dogs act in the presence of the conditioned stimulus as though they were being shocked (Culler, Finch, Girden, and Brogden, 1935; Kellogg, 1938a). The mouth-opening, sucking, and swallowing of infants conditioned in the first 10 days of life (D. P. Marquis, 1931) appear to duplicate the unconditioned responses to the nursing bottle. One of the more dramatic illustrations is provided by the conditioned reactions based on morphine injection. The conditioned responses, in the absence of morphine, may include profuse salivation, vomiting, and other reactions characteristic of the nausea produced by morphine itself (Kleitman and Crisler, 1927).

Fractional Component Responses. In many experiments it is found that the conditioned response is merely a component of the unconditioned response. Thus conditioned salivation may appear without chewing, or conditioned chewing movements without swallowing, although the complex unconditioned response included salivation, chewing, and swallowing. A dog which has received a shock on the leg together with a buzzer may give a conditioned withdrawal response

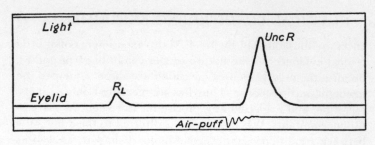

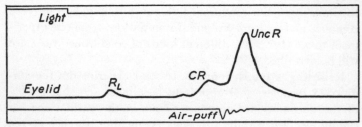

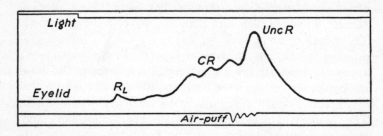

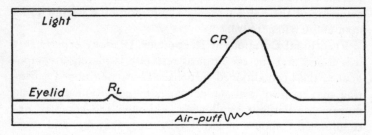

FIGURE 3

DEGREE OF RESEMBLANCE OF CONDITIONED AND UNCONDITIONED RESPONSES

The four records are tracings from photographic records of the eyelid responses of a single human subject. The top record shows the reflex to

without the vocalization which was part of the reaction to shock. The most characteristic finding of conditioning experiments is that the conditioned response resembles, but does not completely duplicate, the unconditioned response.

Preparatory Responses. A number of writers have called attention to the function of the conditioned response as a preparation for the unconditioned stimulus. In certain cases the conditioned response does not resemble the unconditioned response at all. It seems that the subject is getting ready for the forthcoming stimulation, and acting as if he were expecting it. The preparatory character of conditioned behavior in the Pavlov situation has been described by Zener (1937). Salivary responses were conditioned to a bell which preceded feeding in the usual manner. The total behavior was recorded by motion pictures, and the differences between conditioned and unconditioned behavior were summarized as follows:

Except for the component of salivary secretion the conditioned and unconditioned behavior is not identical. (a) During most of the time in which the bell is reinforced by the presence of food, chewing generally occurs with the head raised out of the food-pan but not directed either at the bell or into the food-pan, or at any definite environmental object. Yet this posture practically never, even chewing only occasionally, occurs to the conditioned stimulus alone. Despite Pavlov's assertions, the dog does not appear to be eating an imaginary food. (b) Nor is the behavior that does appear an arrested or partial unconditioned reaction consisting of those response elements not conflicting with other actions. It is a

---

light (R_L) and the unconditioned response to the air-puff (UncR) before conditioning. In the second record the slight anticipatory conditioned response (CR) might be considered a reduced replica of the unconditioned response. In the third record, the irregularity and recruitment of the conditioned response differ markedly from the characteristics of the unconditioned response. In the final record, the complete lid closure prevents the air-puff from reaching the eye. At this stage, the response may be classified as an avoidance reaction, as described more fully in Chapter 3. The original records were reproduced by Hilgard (1936a).

different reaction, anthropomorphically describable as a looking for, expecting, the fall of food with a readiness to perform the eating behavior which will occur when the food falls. The effector pattern is not identical with the unconditioned. (c) Movements frequently occur which do not appear as part of the unconditioned response to food: all the restless behavior of stamping, yawning, panting. (Zener, 1937, p. 393.)

When the restraining straps were removed, so that the range of the dog's activity was increased, the preparatory character of the behavior became more evident. At the conditioned signal for food, the dog would approach the food pan; at another signal which had been associated with the release of acid into the mouth, the dog would either do nothing (since the acid delivering tube was not attached), or it would walk away from the neighborhood of the stimulating devices. Furthermore, when the dog was satiated with food, the reactions to the conditioned stimulus were not only decreased in amount but qualitatively altered.

Even when the conditioned response appears in the same effectors as those of the unconditioned response, the form of response is often sufficiently different to make an interpretation as a fractional component response inappropriate. Thus conditioned respiration appeared in guinea pigs as restrained breathing, while the unconditioned response to the shock was a sharp inspiration (Upton, 1929).

To call a conditioned response a preparatory or expectation response is not to explain it. It means merely that the experimenter considers the response to be an appropriate reaction in the total situation. The origin of the appropriate behavior remains undescribed and unexplained. It must be assumed that the animal can somehow select from its potential behavior those responses which are suitable to the occasion. While something of the sort happens in conditioning experiments, many difficult problems of explanation are raised.

Modifications not Depending upon Double Stimulation. Within a conditioning experiment there are some progressive changes in response not qualifying strictly as conditioning, yet easily confused with it. In young organisms, for example, changes during a few days of experimenting may be due to the maturing of sensory and response mechanisms, and not to the circumstances of experimentation. In other cases, repetitive stimulation produces decrements commonly described in terms of adaptation or fatigue. To the extent that these changes would have occurred through the repeated presentation of single stimuli (not depending, therefore, upon the relationship between conditioned and unconditioned stimuli) they are not to be considered as changes truly representative of conditioning. Since such changes occur within conditioning experiments, control observations are necessary to determine the extent to which the changes are dependent upon the particular arrangements of the conditioning experiment.

There are certain phenomena, even more closely allied to those of conditioning, which occur in experiments in which the pairing of conditioned and unconditioned stimuli has been deliberately avoided, so that the requirements of true conditioning are not met. After a reflex to light had been adapted in fish, so that the light no longer evoked a response, the fish were shocked repeatedly, no illumination change accompanying the shock. After this regimen, both light and a vibratory stimulus produced reactions, which might have been interpreted as conditioned if the light and vibration had been combined with the shock (R. R. Sears, 1934). Similarly, monkeys were frightened several times by a powder flash (or a "snake" blow-out). Following this series of experiences, a bell was sounded, and fright responses were evoked which the bell had not previously elicited (Grether, 1938). The process has been described as *pseudo-conditioning*, since results similar to conditioning are obtained without following a strict conditioning procedure. The pseudo-conditioning consists in a heightened state of excitement, so that the animal is sensitized to stimuli not normally arousing the response.

The augmentation of an original response to the conditioned stimulus through a conditioning procedure may be described as *sensitization*. This is merely a form of pseudo-conditioning, unless it can be demonstrated that the sensitization is a function of the repetition of conditioned and unconditioned stimuli in precise relationship. Wendt (1930) was able to detect by a facilitation technique that there was a subthreshold tendency to give a bilateral knee jerk at a latency of 120 to 180 msec. after a tap on one leg. This is longer than the latency of the usual knee jerk (30 to 50 msec.). Subsequently a tap on the tendon of one leg was followed after 200 msec. by a tap on the other, and the bilateral reflex detected in the facilitation experiment appeared as a conditioned response, and increased in magnitude as training was continued. This response alteration, termed sensitization, depends for its nature on an original subthreshold tendency to react in that manner to the conditioned stimulus. Another illustration is provided by the startle response as conditioned in the rat by Prosser and Hunter (1936). Auditory stimuli just too weak to elicit startle responses were paired with an electric shock. This procedure increased the excitability to a point at which the reflex response was elicited by the previously ineffective sound. The authors doubted that true conditioning had occurred, since the latency of the 'conditioned' response was the same as that of the unconditioned response to more intense sounds. In a later experiment, Hunter (1937) showed that true conditioned startle reactions differed in latency and in other characteristics from the unconditioned startle response. Sensitization is encountered only very rarely and is probably mediated through gross postural and attitudinal changes, rather than through specific conditioning processes. There is no direct evidence that the phenomenon depends upon the temporal relation of the stimuli as the usual conditioned response does (Bernstein, 1934). Wendt found, for example, that instructions to kick voluntarily to the tendon tap also sensitized the bilateral reflex. A state of apprehension or excitement is common enough in conditioning situations, and if such a state produces exaggerated reflexes they may be thought of as accessory to conditioning, rather than as illustrations of ordinary conditioning.

From the foregoing account of types of responses occurring within the classical conditioning experiment, including redintegrative responses, fractional component responses, preparatory responses and responses not classifying strictly as conditioning (including pseudo-conditioning and sensitization) it is evident enough that there is a rich diversity. The range of behavioral changes within experiments similar to Pavlov's means that learning in these experiments has not been reduced to the level of simplicity sometimes attributed to conditioned response learning. The fact that the behavioral changes range widely does not destroy the usefulness of Pavlov's experiment as a convenient reference situation; it means, however, that several alternative theoretical interpretations are possible, even within the somewhat restricted sphere of these experiments.

Some Relationships within Classical Conditioning as Described by Pavlov

The ordering of stimuli in experiments on simple conditioning, and the arrangements of discrimination experiments, have given rise to a number of terms descriptive of these relationships as they were used in Pavlov's laboratory, and these terms are now rather generally used by those who do conditioning experiments. In order to introduce these terms in the context in which they were first used, some of the chief relationships will be summarized here, without any effort to report the supporting quantitative evidence. Many of the situations will be discussed again in later chapters, when they will be examined more critically.

Temporal Relationships within Conditioning. In typical experiments, the conditioned stimulus begins a few seconds before the unconditioned stimulus, and the two stimuli overlap in time. With different temporal relations the resulting conditioned response shows certain characteristics which Pavlov has summarized as follows:

A. Conditioned and unconditioned stimuli overlap temporally.
  1. *Simultaneous conditioned response.* The conditioned stimulus begins from a fraction of a second to 5 seconds before the unconditioned stimulus, and continues until the latter occurs. The conditioned response tends to follow the beginning of the conditioned stimulus almost immediately.
  2. *Delayed conditioned response.* The conditioned stimulus begins from 5 seconds to several minutes before the unconditioned stimulus, and continues until the latter occurs. Although the conditioned response begins before the unconditioned stimulus, it follows the onset of the conditioned stimulus by a delay proportional to the length of the interval between the two stimuli. Delayed conditioned responses are difficult to form unless a simultaneous conditioned response has already been established.

B. Conditioned and unconditioned stimuli do not overlap temporally.
  3. *Short-trace conditioned response.* The conditioned stimulus is removed for a few seconds before the unconditioned stimulus begins.
  4. *Long-trace conditioned response.* The interval between the cessation of the conditioned stimulus and the beginning of the unconditioned stimulus is 1 min-

ute or more. The conditioned response does not begin at the onset of the conditioned stimulus, nor at its cessation, but after an interval proportional to the time elapsing before the presentation of the unconditioned stimulus. Long-trace conditioned responses are formed with greater difficulty than delayed conditioned responses.

5. *Backward conditioned response.* The conditioned stimulus does not begin to act until after the cessation of the unconditioned stimulus.

C. Time interval functions as the conditioned stimulus.

6. *Temporal conditioned response.* An unconditioned stimulus is presented at regular intervals of time. If it is now omitted, a conditioned response will occur at approximately the usual interval. Intervals as long as 30 minutes have been used successfully with dogs.

Inhibitory Characteristics of Conditioned Responses. When the conditioned stimulus is followed by the unconditioned stimulus at an effective interval, it is said to be *reinforced.* Repetition of reinforcement is thus the essential procedure for establishing and strengthening a conditioned response. Once the conditioned response has been established, repetition of the conditioned stimulus without reinforcement results in a gradual *inhibition* of response. The procedure is known as *experimental extinction.* In a typical experiment, as described by Pavlov, a conditioned salivary response in a dog might be extinguished by the presentation of from 5 to 20 applications of the conditioned stimulus without the subsequent feeding. After an interval of hours following extinction the conditioned response can again be elicited. This return of excitability, without further training, is known as *spontaneous recovery.* The sudden presentation of a novel, distracting stimulus may result in a brief temporary restoration of an extinguished response. This restoration is known as *disinhibition.* The same kind of extra stimulus presented when the conditioned response is well established may cause a temporary reduction or abolition of the response, called *external inhibition.*

After a conditioned response has been developed to one stimulus, other similar stimuli may elicit the response without any specific reinforcement. This fact is known as *generalization.* Following such generalization it is possible to secure *discrimination,* which means that the individual responds to one stimulus but not to another stimulus which at some previous time did elicit the response. Discrimination may be accomplished in part through continued reinforcement of one stimulus, but more satisfactorily by reinforcing one of a pair of similar stimuli and never reinforcing the other. The latter procedure is known as the method of contrasts, and is used to determine the limits of sensory discrimination. Thus by reinforcing a tone of 800 cycles and not reinforcing one of 812 cycles, it has been shown that a dog can discriminate between the two tones because it reacts differentially to them. The neural process underlying generalization was called *irradiation* by Pavlov, and the neural counterpart of discrimination was called *concentration.* Since irradiation and concentration refer to hypothetical cortical processes, they should not be used as behavioral terms unless qualified to prevent misunderstanding.

The term *inhibition* is used to denote a decrease or absence of a response which is the result of some form of positive stimulation. The decrease resulting from an extraneous stimulus is called *external inhibition,* while the decrease resulting from the repeated presentation of the conditioned stimulus itself is called *internal inhibition.* Pavlov used the word inhibition also in the sense of a neural process or mechanism underlying the observed decrease in strength of response. Much confusion has unfortunately resulted from this dual use of the term. Inhibition will refer here only to the experimentally measured decrement in strength of response.

A stimulus whose conditioned response has been inhibited by extinction or differentiation is called a *conditioned inhibitory stimulus* because of its functional properties. It does not itself elicit any observable response, but it is capable of producing an inhibition of the response to another stimulus with which it is presented. For example, Pavlov (1927, p. 77) describes an experiment in which a whistle stimulus to which the salivary response had been extinguished, produced a decrease in the salivation to a tactile stimulus from 8 drops to 1 drop on the first occasion on which the two stimuli were presented together.

The types of behavioral situation to which the different varieties of inhibition apply were classified by Pavlov as follows:

A. External inhibition.
   Temporary decrement of a conditioned response due to an extraneous stimulus.

B. Internal inhibition.
   Internal inhibition develops slowly and progressively, when a conditioned stimulus is repeatedly presented under one of the following conditions:
   1. *Experimental extinction.* The weakening of response to a conditioned stimulus which is repeated a number of times without reinforcement.
   2. *Differential inhibition.* A conditioned response given originally to either of two stimuli is restricted to one of them through the reinforcement of one and the non-reinforcement of the other. The non-reinforced negative stimulus becomes inhibitory.
   3. *Conditioned inhibition.* A combination of stimuli is rendered ineffective through non-reinforcement, although the combination includes a stimulus which alone continues to evoke the conditioned response. The

other stimuli in the combination are conditioned inhibitors.

4. *Inhibition of delay*. If a regular interval of sufficient duration elapses between the commencement of a conditioned stimulus and its reinforcement, during the early portion of its isolated action the conditioned stimulus becomes not only ineffective, but actively inhibitory of other intercurrent activities. (There may be temporary disinhibition at the onset of the conditioned stimulus, so that there is a slight conditioned response before the inhibition is manifested.)

C. Disinhibition.

Temporary increment of an inhibited conditioned response due to an extraneous stimulus. This may be considered as an external inhibition of an internal inhibition.

This brief summary of the principal descriptive characteristics of conditioning may serve as an introduction to the more detailed consideration of the phenomena in later chapters. Conditioning is defined as an experimental procedure for the establishment of simple associative connections between definite stimuli and responses. The Pavlovian reference experiment represents one procedure which has been extensively used. The other training methods will be discussed in the next chapter.

Notes

The terminology adopted for the description of classical conditioning is that of Pavlov's translators, with a few minor alterations such as the substitution of the word response for reflex. Pavlov's terms are already so familiar, that, in spite of a certain awkwardness, it is more serviceable to accept them than to substitute the terminologies proposed by other writers, none of which has won wide acceptance. The adoption of conditioned response instead of conditioned reflex follows the practice common among psychologists, a practice based on the desire to avoid the identification of the behavior with the spinal reflexes of Sherrington. Some of the more common alternatives to Pavlov's terms are given in the *Glossary*.

Organisms and Responses Conditioned

For a catalog of organisms and responses conditioned, the bibliography of Razran (1937) is most helpful. Hull (1934c) describes a large number of specific experiments involving different stimuli. His chapter is probably the best source for gaining acquaintance with the concrete problems confronting those who perform conditioned response experiments and with the techniques which have been used. Razran's reviews are helpful: animals other than dogs, Razran (1933a); children, Razran (1933b). Cf. also Wolff (1937).

Apparatus and Technique

Details regarding the construction of Pavlov's sound-proof laboratory and the preparation of dogs for salivary experimentation are given by Podkopaev (1926). The laboratory care of dogs, and techniques used in motor conditioning, are described by Kellogg, R. C. Davis, and V. B. Scott (1939). A number of arrangements of apparatus for use with animals and children are pictured by Razran (1933a, 1933b). Animal holders suitable for different species, and types of photokymographic equipment, are illustrated by Wendt and Dodge (1938). The most useful general treatment of recording equipment is by Wendt (1938). Other devices useful in connection with various problems of condition-

ing are described by Brogden and Culler (1936), Culler, Finch and Girden (1934), Hanford and C. T. Morgan (1939), Loucks (1932, 1934, 1938a), Shastin (1938).

The Nature of the Conditioned Response

The question of the descriptive similarities and differences between conditioned and unconditioned responses is discussed more fully by Culler (1938b), Grant (1939b), Hilgard (1936a, 1936b), Kellogg (1938a), Liddell, W. T. James, and O. D. Anderson (1934), Razran (1939i), Schlosberg (1936, 1937), Warner (1932b), Woodworth (1938), Zener (1937).

The modification called sensitization in the text was designated 'alpha' conditioning by Hull (1934c) to distinguish it from the more usual conditioning ('beta'). The existence of 'alpha' conditioning was inferred from experiments by Wendt (1930) and Hilgard (1931). Later attempts to secure 'alpha' conditioning of eyelid reflexes have been unsuccessful (Bernstein, 1934, Hilgard and Biel, 1937). Bernstein made the suggestion, concurred in by Hilgard and Biel, that alterations in set, not necessarily related to the precise repetition of conditioned and unconditioned stimuli, probably account for whatever slight sensitization of the 'alpha' type that occurs. Hence, sensitization becomes a form of pseudo-conditioning.

Although pseudo-conditioning does not qualify as a form of classical conditioning, it may occur within classical conditioning experiments, and hence, in its interaction with other processes, it may be important as a factor in the observed modification (Harlow, 1939). The phenomenon is closely allied to the physiological principle of *dominance* described by Ukhtomski (1926, 1938). According to this principle, any reaction which has been elicited repeatedly by strong stimulation may become dominant over other reactions, so that it becomes elicitable by a range of stimuli much wider than is normally the case. One illustration of the applicability of this principle to classical conditioning is found in the restoration of extinguished conditioned responses. Following extinction, the response to the conditioned stimulus is completely restored by a few reinforcements. The restoration may be produced, however, by presenting the unconditioned stimulus alone for several times. In this case, the principle illustrated is that of dominance, rather than of true reconditioning, for the restoration of sensitivity to the conditioned stimulus takes place without its combination with the unconditioned stimulus.

Sensory Conditioning

Association in its traditional forms was concerned with associations among ideas and sensory processes. While conditioning has tended to emphasize the association between stimuli and movements, several investigators have attempted to apply the arrangements of the conditioning experiment to the investigation of sensory processes. An unconditioned stimulus elicits a sensory process reported, for example, as the color red. If a tone is repeatedly presented together with the unconditioned stimulus, will the tone come to elicit a corresponding experience of redness, i.e., a hallucinatory experience? The appearance of synesthesias in some individuals suggests a possible conditioned origin. The findings of Kelly (1934) and of Cason (1936) were negative, although some success is reported by Bogoslovski (1937). Bogoslovski measured conditioning by the electrical sensitivity of the eye. A metronome combined with a visual stimulus was found after conditioning to have raised the threshold of the dark adapted eye as measured by the amount of current which had to be passed through the eye to produce a visual experience. Because of the fragmentary nature of the results to date, these experiments were not included in the text as representative of varieties of responses conditioned.

Chapter 3

INSTRUMENTAL CONDITIONING EXPERIMENTS

THE METHODS of establishing simple conditioned responses are not exhausted by the classical training procedure of Pavlov. Several other important procedures which have come to be known as conditioning will be described in this chapter. These training methods are distinguished from classical conditioning by the fact that the reinforcement is presented only after the conditioned response has been made. When the occurrence of the reinforcement is contingent upon the organism's behavior the procedure may be termed *instrumental conditioning,* since the conditioned response is instrumental in bringing about the reinforcement. Various types of reinforcement have been employed in instrumental conditioning experiments, and illustrative examples of four types of procedure will be described below. These four are (1) *reward training,* in which the conditioned response is followed by the presentation of a positive incentive stimulus such as food, (2) *escape training,* in which the conditioned response is followed by the termination of a noxious stimulus such as electric shock, (3) *avoidance training,* in which the conditioned response prevents the occurrence of a noxious stimulus, and (4) *secondary reward training,* in which the conditioned response is followed by a stimulus such as a token which has acquired reward value in previous learning. The differences will be more evident as the four varieties of instrumental conditioning are described in more detail.

Reward Training

As a reference experiment for instrumental reward training we may select a study by Grindley (1932), who taught guinea pigs to secure carrots by turning the head to one side at the sound of a buzzer. The relevant stimuli and responses were kept simple and made as nearly repetitive as possible. The guinea pig was held in a stand in a sound-proof room. Head movements were recorded kymographically and observed through a telescope from another room. A buzzer was sounded as the conditioned stimulus. If the animal turned its head to the right side while the buzzer sounded, a carrot was automatically presented on a lever in front of the guinea pig. After the animal had nibbled it, the carrot was removed by means of a string controlled by the experimenter. The arrangement differs from the Pavlov experiment in that the reinforcement (carrot) is not presented at a fixed constant interval following the conditioned stimulus, but only after the animal has performed the head turning. In this procedure the conditioned response may properly be said to be instrumental in securing the reward. The head turning is not evoked by the reinforcing stimulus but must occur before the reinforcement is presented.

Preliminary adaptation trials on 8 to 15 days were needed before the animals would eat promptly when food was presented in the stand. When regular training began, learning was evidenced by a gradual decrease in the time between the onset of the buzzer and the appropriate head movement, a decrease from 100 seconds to 1 second. In the later trials, when the buzzer sounded, the animals often showed food responses, such as nibbling movements and sniffing, which were followed by prompt head movements to the right side. There was very little turning to the wrong side. Between trials some of the animals were quiescent or asleep; others were active, moving the head or nibbling.

It is evident that in an instrumental situation of this kind the measured conditioned response may not resemble at all the response to the reward stimulus. The sharp head movement to one side was not a part of the eating behavior, yet it was the response conspicuously strengthened. This reaction was selected out of the repertory of behavior which the animal exhibited in the presence of the buzzer; behavior which included a slight startle, rigidity, widening of the eyes, rapid and regular respiration, struggling and investigatory responses, as well as head movements. The responses to the buzzer were gradually reduced, except for the appropriate head movement rewarded by the carrot.

Instrumental reward training has been studied extensively in many different animals and with various responses. It is not a new training procedure; it is the same as that described by C. L. Morgan in 1894 and designated a few years later by Thorndike (1898) as "trial, error, and accidental success." Thorndike carried out a series of experiments in which cats were trained to escape from problem boxes to secure food outside. The boxes were constructed with sides of vertical slats so that the food was visible to the cat. A door in the box opened as soon as the cat performed a certain movement, such as pulling a string hanging from the top, or pressing a latch. A hungry cat when first placed in such a box shows a continued but variable activity, reaching between the slats toward the food, scratching at the sides, moving all about the box. In the course of this activity the cat eventually hits the release mechanism and immediately secures the food. The first successful response appears to be largely a matter of chance. On successive trials the cat's activity becomes concentrated in the region of the release mechanism and other activities gradually drop out until eventually the animal performs the correct act as soon as it is placed in the box.

The conception of an instrumental act must not be understood too narrowly. In the illustrations which have been given, what the organism does produces the reward in some mechanical fashion, either by bringing the organism into the presence of the reward through its own movements, or by bringing the reward to it through some release mechanism. The act which precedes the reward need not be mechanically related to the delivery of the reward, but instead may be purely arbitrary. For example, in one experiment Thorndike taught the cat to lick itself in order to be released from the cage. Training the dog to "shake hands" by rewarding is another illustration of an arbitrary act of this sort. The essential aspect of instrumental training is that the reward depends on what the organism does and follows the response in some systematic fashion.

It is entirely a question of terminological definition whether instrumental reward training is to be considered a type of learning different from conditioning or as a separate type of conditioning. There is a certain convenience served by adopting the latter point of view, and historical precedent for it is readily found. Students in Pavlov's laboratory have described instrumental training in the terminology of conditioning. For example, Ivanov-Smolensky (1927c) carried out a series of experiments in which children were taught to obtain food or other rewards by pressing a bulb when certain conditioned stimuli were presented. S. Miller and Konorski (1928) designated as a second type of conditioning their experiments in which dogs were trained to lift the paw. Following the conditioned stimulus, the experimenter flexed the dog's leg passively and then gave the dog a food reward. The dog soon learned to flex its leg at the signal. In some of their experiments, of which the later ones were performed in Pav-

lov's laboratory, Konorski and Miller also measured salivation, and hence secured classical and instrumental conditioning at the same time (Figure 4). When hydrochloric acid was

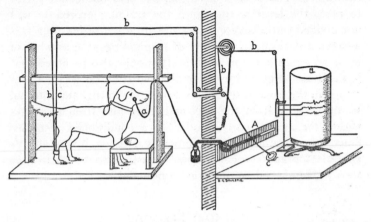

FIGURE 4

DIAGRAM OF ONE OF THE KONORSKI AND MILLER EXPERIMENTAL
ARRANGEMENTS USED IN PAVLOV'S LABORATORY

a—system to measure dog's salivation; *b*—system to measure the flexion
of the dog's leg; *c*—system to produce the passive flexion. After Konorski
and S. Miller, from Razran (1939i)

substituted for food, however, the conditioned leg flexion
was abolished, although conditioned salivation was maintained at full strength. Instead of flexion to the conditioned
stimulus, as with food reward, the leg was stiffened and could
be flexed only by applying excessive force.

The most extensive program of research on instrumental
training has been carried on by Skinner (1938) who considers
it a distinct type of conditioning. In his procedure a rat was
placed in a sound-proofed box containing a small lever which
when pressed, automatically released a pellet of food into a
tray. When first placed in the box a hungry rat would move

about, exploring the various parts of the box and in the course of minutes chance to press the lever, after which it ate the food. The rat was not removed from the box as in the case of Thorndike's situation, but was immediately free to press the lever again. Since the training procedure was not divided into discrete trials, the progress of learning was measured in terms of the *rate* of responding—the number of lever pressings per unit of time. It should also be noted that in this training procedure a conditioned stimulus was not presented in the usual way. The complex of external and internal stimuli arising from the box and lever and from processes within the animal corresponded to a conditioned stimulus. Since these stimuli were continuously present, it was always possible for another conditioned response to be elicited as soon as the preceding one was terminated.

Escape Training

Instrumental conditioning can be carried out by employing in place of a positive reward the cessation of a persisting disagreeable or noxious stimulus such as electric shock, immersion in water, or excessive temperature. This type of training procedure has seldom been used in laboratory conditioning experiments, although numerous examples are found in the learning of animals in their natural environment. An experiment reported by Mowrer (1940) may serve as the paradigm of instrumental escape training. A rat was placed in a box with a metal grille floor through which an electric shock could be administered to the animal. The shock was gradually increased during 2.25 minutes from zero to a stable intense value. At one end of the box was a pedal arrangement which would turn off the shock whenever pushed. The shock remained off as long as the pedal was depressed but when the pedal was released the shock would automatically start to build up again.

Rats in this situation began to show agitated behavior about 60 seconds after the beginning of the shock. As the shock became more intense the rats engaged in vigorous undirected activity characterized by jumping, running, squealing, biting at the grille and random thrashing about. In the course of this activity the rat always chanced to hit the pedal and thus terminated the shock. The pedal response occurred on the first trial only after from 3 to 6 minutes of activity, but by the tenth trial the rats pressed the pedal as soon as they began to feel the shock.

Many of the essential features of escape training are similar to reward training. In both procedures the correct response is not elicited by the reinforcing stimulus (i.e., the reward or escape) but must occur spontaneously on the first trial before the reinforcement is presented. The nature of the conditioned response is therefore not determined by the reinforcement. Rats might be trained to terminate a shock by pulling a loop, pushing a hanging rod, sitting up on their hind legs, or indeed by any response which is already in their repertory of behavior and likely to occur in the experimental situation. Perhaps the most frequent example of escape learning is that in which the organism moves from a region of noxious stimulation to a neutral region.

It should be carefully noted that instrumental escape training is not the same sort of training as that in the typical punishment situation. In the latter, shock is administered following incorrect response and may produce a decreased tendency to perform that response. In escape training, the shock is present before the conditioned response occurs, and escape from the shock produces an increased tendency to perform the response which immediately preceded the escape.

Avoidance Training

Differing from both instrumental reward and instrumental escape is that variety of training procedure in which the learned reaction prevents the appearance of a noxious stimulus. The reference experiment is the classical one by Bekhterev on conditioned withdrawal responses of hand or foot, in which the electric shock may be avoided by the performance of the conditioned response. If the electrodes are attached to the subject and the shock is delivered on every trial, the experiment is reduced to the classical Pavlov procedure. In some cases results appear to be very similar whether or not the conditioned response prevents the shock (Schlosberg, 1934, 1936; Hilden, 1937; Munn, 1939). In other cases there is a distinct difference. This is well shown in an experiment performed by Brogden, Lipman and Culler (1938). A guinea pig was placed in a revolving cage and after a conditioned stimulus (buzzer) it was given a shock which evoked running behavior. One group of animals, trained according to the Pavlov procedure, were shocked whether or not they ran. Another group, trained according to the arrangements of avoidance learning, were not shocked if they ran. Learning began similarly in both groups, but reached a much higher level of performance in the second group. The results are plotted in Figure 5. Guinea pigs which were shocked whether or not they ran continued to show anticipatory agitation at the sound of the buzzer, but after the first few trials the tendency to run did not increase; those shocked only if they did not run developed the habit of running promptly at the sound of the buzzer. Learning in this situation appears to be based in a real sense on the avoidance of the shock. It differs clearly from other types of instrumental training in which the conditioned response is followed by a definite stimulus change—food or the cessation of shock. In instrumental avoid-

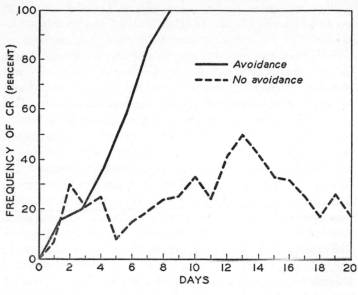

FIGURE 5

COMPARISON OF LEARNING PERFORMANCE WITH INSTRUMENTAL AVOIDANCE
TRAINING AND CLASSICAL CONDITIONING

The solid line represents the frequency of conditioned responses (running)
of 4 guinea pigs during the two seconds that a buzzer sounds, when running
prevents the appearance of a shock which occurs on those trials in which
the animal does not run. The broken line represents the corresponding values
for another group of 4 animals when the buzzer is invariably followed by
shock whether or not the animal runs. The greater learning under circumstances of shock-avoidance than of regular shock indicates that the shock
is not itself to be considered the reinforcement. (Brogden, Lipman, and Culler,
1938.)

ance training the new response is strengthened in the absence
of any such stimulus; indeed, it is strengthened because of
the absence of such a stimulus. Absence of stimulation can
obviously have an influence on behavior only if there exists
some sort of preparation for or expectation of the stimulation. This strengthening through absence of stimulation is im-

portant enough to make it desirable to consider avoidance training separately from the other kinds of instrumental training.

Since the organism must receive a certain number of shocks before it learns to avoid the shock following the conditioned stimulus, the first few trials of instrumental avoidance training are identical in procedure with classical conditioning. This is clear in the results shown in Figure 5 and is further illustrated in experiments on dogs by Culler, Finch, Girden and Brogden (1935). The conditioned stimulus was a tone which was followed by a shock to one paw whenever the dog failed to withdraw its leg. On the first few trials the dog received a shock every time. A conditioned response to the tone rapidly developed which was at first a "reduced replica" of the original reaction to the shock, and included generalized struggling movements of the body as well as retraction of the leg. In the course of further training trials the conditioned response became restricted to a precise and adaptive flexion of one leg by which the shock was avoided. Thus the experiment progressed from a preliminary stage of classical conditioning to a later stage of instrumental avoidance training. The similarity to the eyelid series presented in Figure 3 (Chapter 2, p. 38) may be noted.

It is apparent that the shock cannot be considered an unconditioned stimulus during the later stages of avoidance training. Omission of the shock on trials in which the conditioned flexion occurs does not produce extinction but instead strengthens the conditioned response. Extinction can be secured only if the dog fails to respond for some reason and thereby "discovers" that the tone is no longer followed by shock. After several trials of this sort extinction progresses rapidly. Further evidence that the shock is not an unconditioned stimulus is derived from experiments by Finch and

Culler (1934), who showed that the shock need not be delivered to the leg. After the conditioned withdrawal response had once been firmly established, the shock to the leg was disconnected, and a shock to the chest was administered whenever the dog failed to react to the tone. No extinction occurred and the conditioned response could be maintained at maximum strength for indefinite periods under these conditions. It was observed that the shock to the chest never itself evoked the leg withdrawal response.

An important clue to the understanding of instrumental avoidance learning is provided in a further experiment by Finch and Culler (1935). A buzzer was connected with the shock circuit, so that the buzzer would sound whenever the shock was turned on. Conditioned leg withdrawal avoided the shock, but the buzzer continued to sound. With conditioning well established extinction was undertaken, in one case by omitting both the shock and the buzzer following the tone, in the other case by omitting the shock but continuing the buzzer. Three dogs, each extinguished under both conditions, showed a mean time of extinction without the buzzer of 100 trials, with the buzzer of 372 trials. The difference, which is statistically significant, must be attributed to the reinforcing effect of the buzzer. The buzzer, however, cannot be considered an unconditioned stimulus for it did not by itself elicit leg withdrawal even after its repeated combination with the shock.

Far from being a stimulus to foot-withdrawal, the buzzer becomes the cue to *foot-replacement*. The buzzer, when it stops sounding, makes known that the trial is over and that the grid again is safe. Just as the tone announces that the grid will soon be 'hot' so the buzzer announces that it will soon be 'cold.'

By omitting the shock and continuing the buzzer, which has throughout the training period been coterminous with it, we are in a way tricking or deceiving the animal. The buzzer has come to symbolize charge-on-the-grid; it continues now to do so, even though it has become a false symbol. (Finch and Culler, 1935, p. 659.)

The buzzer is not a usual reinforcing agent. It derives whatever reinforcing significance it has from its association with shock, so that it maintains the animal's avoidance reactions originally based on shock. The stimuli which serve the rôle of secondary or derivative reinforcing agents in ordinary avoidance training are not always as apparent as the buzzer in this experiment. In the absence of the buzzer, the sight of the shock electrodes, the general experimental situation, and the perception of the time interval following the conditioned stimulus may operate in the same manner.

Secondary Reward Training

In avoidance training, as has been indicated, some feature of the experimental situation other than the punishment itself becomes capable of reinforcement as a result of its association with punishment. There is a parallel case in certain experiments with rewards, in which a neutral stimulus object may acquire the reinforcing properties of a reward if it has been repeatedly associated with a primary reward. The problem of explanation is essentially the same in avoidance learning and in secondary reward learning: how indifferent stimuli come to reinforce responses appropriate to punishment or to reward. Because of this common problem of explanation, as a representative experiment secondary reward training belongs logically with avoidance training rather than with simple instrumental reward and escape.

Illustrative of this type of training is Wolfe's (1936) study of token incentives in the behavior of chimpanzees. The tokens were small disks similar to poker chips to which the animals were originally quite indifferent. Preliminary training consisted of teaching the chimpanzees to insert tokens in the slot of a vending apparatus which automatically released a grape to the animal. Differential reward values were established for different colored tokens. For example, a blue token secured one grape, a red token, two grapes, and a brass token no food at all. From a heterogeneous collection of tokens a trained chimpanzee would first select the red tokens for deposit in the vending apparatus, and then the blue ones, leaving the brass untouched.

After having learned the reward value of tokens, chimpanzees were trained to perform simple instrumental responses to secure the tokens. One task required the lifting of a lever; another involved pulling in a small sliding tray by means of a cord. The animals would continue to work at these tasks for a number of tokens which could not be exchanged for food until later. In an extension of these experiments, Cowles (1937) found that token rewards were effective as incentives for the acquisition of simple position habits, of complex five-choice position habits, of visual size and color pattern discriminations, and of delayed responses. A position habit requiring as many as 20 trials could be completely learned in one session with tokens as the sole reinforcing agent and therefore prior to any reception of food reward.

Secondary rewards such as approval, money, prestige and so forth are of unquestioned importance in directing most learning by adult human individuals. In customary experiments with college students on the learning of rote verbal material, mirror drawing, or code substitution the only reward necessary is the knowledge of which responses are correct and which incorrect.

The mechanism of secondary reward training is difficult to analyze in the case of human learning because of the complexities introduced by the use of verbal language. The essential features of the procedure have, however, been successfully demonstrated with animals such as rats, cats and dogs as well as with chimpanzees. The results in general indicate that a secondary reward is only slightly less effective in the establishment of new learned responses than the primary reward with which it has been associated. The secondary reward loses its reinforcing value, however, if it is not itself repeatedly followed by the primary reward. In the chimpanzee experiments it was found that a token which was immediately exchangeable for food was more effective as an incentive than tokens which were exchangeable only at the end of a series of trials. And if the secondary reward was frequently presented without the subsequent primary reward the response became extinguished and its incentive value disappeared.

From a consideration of these characteristics of secondary rewards it is apparent that in the typical food-reward training situation, any stimulus occurring after the conditioned response and prior to the securing of food may take on the properties of a secondary reward in the course of training. Because of its position in the sequence of activities, such a stimulus has sometimes been designated a *sub-goal*. The sight of food or of the food container thus becomes an incentive in itself. Grindley (1929) studied the behavior of chickens which were placed in a narrow runway at the other end of which were grains of rice under a piece of glass, such that the chickens could see the rice but could not reach it. During the first 4 or 5 trials there was a gradual increase in running speed down the alley toward the food, indicating that the sight of food induced learning even when the eating was prevented. On subsequent trials the running speed became progressively slower.

The reinforcing action of a sub-goal in the learning by rats to press a lever to secure food has been clearly demonstrated by Skinner (1938) and by Bugelski (1938). The apparatus used was so constructed that when the lever was pressed there was a clearly audible click occasioned by the release of a pellet of food into the food receptacle. After the habit had been firmly established extinction was carried out in two ways (Bugelski, 1938). For half of the rats, pressing the bar resulted in the click but no food was delivered; for the other half the response was not followed by either the click or the food. The former group made 30 percent more responses during extinction than the latter group, indicating that the click had maintained the conditioned response for a short time until its reinforcing value was itself extinguished by the absence of subsequent food. The function of the click here parallels very closely that of the buzzer in the experiment of Finch and Culler (1935) described on p. 61. An explanation of the reinforcing effect of sub-goals will therefore go far toward an explanation of avoidance learning. Attempted explanations are postponed until Chapter 4.

The Nature of Conditioned Instrumental Responses

Since in all types of instrumental learning the response which is strengthened may be entirely unlike the response to the reinforcing stimulus, the origin of the conditioned response is not accounted for by the nature of the reinforcement. The training procedure itself is such that the conditioned response must occur before it can be reinforced. The conditioned response is therefore already in the behavior repertory of the subject, and the learning process consists only in strengthening the response so that it occurs promptly and with dependable frequency in the presence of the conditioned stimulus. The reinforcing stimulus differs from the unconditioned stimulus of the Pavlov procedure in that it can never be the original stimulus for the new response. The conditioned response first occurs as a random or spontaneous movement, a movement selected under the influence of a drive, a previously learned movement elicited as a generalized reaction to some feature of the environmental situation, or an appropriate movement which has been encouraged by some special means. The problem of the source of the conditioned response merits further consideration.

Random or Spontaneous Movements. Trial-and-error theories imply that the original success occurs by chance. That is, the organism in a restless state varies its behavior throughout a wide range of movements which appear to be random or spontaneous because they cannot be accounted for by recognized stimuli. They are not random, however, in the sense that their nature is a matter of chance, and they are not spontaneous in the sense that antecedent conditions do not determine their occurrence. They are acts which are organized and released by the central nervous system independently of identifiable external stimuli, and might more appropriately be named self-initiated acts. Such movements have recently been given much emphasis by Skinner (1938), who calls them *operants* to distinguish them from *respondents,* which are movements elicited by recognized stimuli.

The behavior of an animal in a new situation is not entirely random and spontaneous. Although the activity may not be directed specifically toward the correct solution of the problem, it is not completely undirected. The cats in Thorndike's puzzle box spent much time on the first trial reaching through the slats toward the food, and the rats in Skinner's situation explored the corners and projecting portions of the box. In some cases, as indicated below, it is possible to stipulate fairly definitely the original stimulus which occasions the conditioned response.

Responses Determined by the Drive. The problem situation is characterized by the presence of a drive which increases the restless behavior. Since drives have been associated in the animal's past with certain acts leading to reward, the responses likely to appear in a new experimental situation may include those which have occurred previously while the particular drive was active. Several recent experiments have demonstrated that animals can discriminate among their own drives; i.e., that a drive may be a conditioned stimulus evoking specific behavior (Hull, 1933, Leeper, 1935).

Generalized Responses to External Stimuli. When an organism is in a novel situation, it reacts to features of the environment bearing some marks of familiarity. In conditioning terms this is known as generalization; that is, previously conditioned responses are evoked by stimuli similar to the original learning situation. A rat which has secured food by digging in one box with a sawdust floor is more likely to begin digging when in a new box with a sawdust floor than is an animal without this previous experience.

Special Training. The appropriate response in instrumental learning may be encouraged in many artificial ways, depending upon the ingenuity of the experimenter or animal trainer. The response may be suggested by passive movement. This is common practice in animal training, as in teaching a dog to "shake hands." Or the leg movement which is rewarded may be originally produced by shock to the foot. Lever-pressing is sometimes enhanced by placing a bit of food on the lever to direct the animal's exploratory activity to that region. String-pulling behavior is facilitated by smearing food on the string, jiggling the string, and so on (T. L. McCulloch, 1934). Mechanically restricting the possibilities of movement, as in Grindley's experiment, is another method of assuring the appearance of the appropriate reaction. The experiment proper consists in the strengthening of the response after it has once appeared. This is an important difference from Pavlov's experiment. The difference is illustrated by the question: How many trials are needed before the first conditioned response appears? This may be asked with respect to Pavlov's experiment, but is meaningless with respect to instrumental training in which the conditioned response must always occur before the first trial is completed.

Comparison of Classical and Instrumental Conditioning

Classical and instrumental conditioning are similar in many basic respects and different in others. All conditioning experiments involve the presentation of a conditioned stimulus together with a stimulus situation which originally evokes a response, and with such additional features as will produce a strengthening of the new response to the conditioned stimulus. The various types of training will be examined with respect to these characteristics.

Conditioned Stimulus. In many experiments there is no specific conditioned stimulus which is turned on and off under the control of the experimenter. In these instances, the total situation confronting the subject may be considered as the analogue of the conditioned stimulus. The particular aspects of the situation to which the subject is responding can be discovered only by experimental variation of the situation. In this respect there are no differences between the classical and instrumental training procedures. Examples have been given of the use of a definite conditioned stimulus in both types; other examples are readily found in which the total situation served as a conditioned stimulus. Kleitman and Crisler (1927) found that the conditioned salivation based on administration of morphine was evoked when the dogs were brought to the experimental room and placed in the restraining stand. Skinner's instrumental reward training contained no conditioned stimulus; the rats pushed the lever to obtain food whenever they were in the experimental box.

This procedure was modified in some instances so that the conditioned response was evoked only when a light in the box was turned on (Skinner, 1935a). Measures of latency and of the effect of changes in the intensity of stimulus can of course be made only when the conditioned stimulus is a controlled feature of the training situation.

Original Stimulus for the Conditioned Response. Before a response can become associated with the conditioned stimulus, the response must be made to occur. The various training procedures employ different means for the original elicitation of the response to be conditioned. In classical conditioning an unconditioned stimulus is presented which invariably evokes the response. In instrumental training of all types the experimenter depends upon the occurrence of the response in the course of random spontaneous activity, although the chances of occurrence are increased if the subject has previously learned to perform the response under similar conditions of drive or of external stimulation. The response which occurs is then punished or rewarded, but the punishment or reward, unlike an unconditioned stimulus, does not produce the response in the first place.

Reinforcement. That feature of the training situation which is necessary for the strengthening of the new response to the conditioned stimulus is designated as the reinforcement. The reinforcement is identified by the fact that when it is present on successive training trials the conditioned response increases in strength; when it is omitted, the conditioned response decreases in strength; i.e., it is extinguished. While the nature of the conditioned response is determined by its original stimulus, its strength is determined by the intensity and the number of repetitions of the reinforcement. The particular reinforcement operating in any training situation is discovered experimentally in terms of its influence upon the strength of the conditioned response. This definition is circular; the following chapter presents a discussion of the possibilities of defining reinforcement independently of its strengthening effect on conditioned responses.

There are important differences in the nature of the reinforcement operating in the various types of training. In the classical situation the activity produced by the unconditioned stimulus supplies the reinforcement, and if the unconditioned stimulus is omitted on a series of trials the conditioned response undergoes extinction. It is important to note that the unconditioned stimulus is both the original stimulus determining the form of the conditioned response, and the source of the reinforcement. In instrumental training the reinforcement occurs by way of a reward, an escape, or an avoidance of punishment. In this situation the original stimulus determining the nature of the conditioned response is entirely distinct from the reinforcement.

The difference in reinforcement among the various types of training may be described in another way. If the conditioned response resembles the behavior evoked by the reinforcing agent, the reinforcement may be spoken of as *homogeneous*. This is the typical observation of classical conditioning. In instrumental reward and escape training the conditioned response bears no essential resemblance to the behavior evoked by the reinforcing agent, and the reinforcement may be designated as *heterogeneous*. Manipulating the latch in the Thorndike problem box, for example, has nothing in common with the response of eating food. If this terminology is extended to instrumental training based on avoidance of punishment or on secondary reward, the reinforcement may be designated as *derived*. In these cases it is clear that the conditioned response is not strengthened by the punishment or the primary reward, but by substitutes for them. The reinforcement is therefore carried by some process within the subject instigated by an agent which depends for its reinforcing power upon the previously experienced punishments and rewards. The designation 'derived reinforcement' has been chosen to imply the dependent nature of the reinforcement in avoidance and secondary reward training.

The differences among the several types of conditioning procedure with respect to the original stimulus for the conditioned response and with respect to the nature of the reinforcement demand more extended consideration. In the following chapter the analysis of this problem will be carried further in order to see whether a single set of principles can successfully account for the variety of relationships which have been pointed out.

Notes

Types of Conditioning Procedure

The suggestion that instrumental conditioning be considered a type distinct from classical conditioning was made by S. Miller and Konorski (1928), and later by Skinner (1935b). The differences in their viewpoints have been discussed in several papers (Konorski and S. Miller, 1937a, 1937b; Skinner, 1937). Two-fold classifications of learning situations, corresponding roughly to the distinction between classical conditioning and instrumental conditioning, have been proposed by other writers. Thorndike's distinction between associative shifting and learning by trial-and-error (1911, 1935) is of this sort, as is also Finch and Culler's (1935) differentiation between ordinary conditioning and motivated learning. Schlosberg (1937) distinguishes between conditioning and success learning. Razran (1939i) redefines the problem in terms of differences between specific or quantitative conditioning and more general or qualitative conditioning. He believes that ordinary conditioning is primarily of the specific sort, while learning under the 'law of effect' is characterized by the conditioning of "a general organismic adient quality or tendency."

The different varieties of training do not represent pure types of learning requiring necessarily different principles of explanation. This is evident from the interpenetration of the principles used to account for various forms of learning as analyzed by Dashiell (1935), Kellogg (1938b), Tolman (1934). The various types of conditioning differ in important aspects, however, which explanatory theories must take into consideration.

Skinner's Type S and Type R

Skinner's distinction between two types of conditioning, mentioned above, has been made by him the basis for an extended treatment of behavioral laws differing for each type (1938). Since his types correspond roughly to our distinctions in Chapters 2 and 3 between classical and instrumental conditioning, the differences between his classifications and ours should be clarified in order to avoid misunderstanding. He designates Pavlov's experiment Type S, since the conditioned *stimulus* is important as an experimental variable, and he calls the instrumental variety Type R, since it is the conditioned *response*, rather than its stimulus, which enters as the significant variable. This distinction is based in turn on the difference between respondent and operant behavior. Respondent behavior, like ordinary spinal reflexes, is elicited by specified stimuli. In Type S it is respondent behavior which is conditioned. Operant behavior, on the other hand, is emitted by the organism, and its stimuli cannot be specified. In Type R, operant behavior is conditioned. In situations involving discrimination operant behavior may become correlated with a differential cue, but such a cue is not to be confused with an eliciting stimulus. When an operant response becomes correlated in this way with a stimulus, so that the response appears superficially to be elicited by the stimulus, the relationship is that of a 'pseudo-reflex.' The laws of respondent behavior do not apply to pseudo-reflexes.

Confusion arises because Skinner appears to fit actual experiments into types based on abstract features of the experiment. No actual experiment is a pure case. Skinner's types correspond more nearly to our distinctions between homogeneous and heterogeneous reinforcement than to our classifications of experiments. Type S really represents that abstracted feature of Pavlov's experiment which may be described in terms of homogeneous reinforcement; Type R represents that aspect of reward training which can be described in terms of heterogeneous reinforcement. Skinner recognizes that Pavlov's experiment is not a pure case of Type S, but strictly speaking must be formulated as a pseudo-reflex (1935b, p. 73). His own experiment represents a complicated chain of events (1938, pp. 52–55), from which the principles of Type R must be abstracted by appropriate analysis.

The classifications in Chapters 2 and 3 are based on what happens in representative experiments, so that the behavioral changes included are broader than Skinner's abstracted Types S and R. It was recognized in Chapter 2 that classical conditioning experiments are much more complicated than Type S suggests, and the various types of response (redintegrative, fractional component, preparatory) were summarized. Similarly, the examples of instrumental learning in Chapter 3 are not pure cases of Type R. The example of reward training chosen from Grindley involved a discriminated conditioned stimulus (buzzer) which was the occasion for the operant (head-turning) leading to the reward (carrot). This is a discriminated operant according to Skinner, and is classified as pseudo-reflex. Therefore classical conditioning is not limited to Type S and instrumental conditioning is not confined to Type R. The task of coordinating empirical data from a wide variety of situations made it evident that a classification based on experimental arrangements was more feasible than a classification based on logical abstractions or idealized experiments. While for our purposes we have rejected Skinner's classification of conditioning types, we shall have further occasion to discuss aspects of his classification useful in understanding processes inferred to be going on during conditioning.

Because of the prominence in our discussion of what Skinner would call discriminated operants or pseudoreflexes, a comment is in order regarding our use of the word 'stimulus.' It must be clear from context that we refer to a stimulus as an instigator in the sense familiar in the psychological laboratory, as, for example, in the conventional reaction-time experiment. In this experiment, the stimulus is that event from which the latent time of the response is measured. It is in Skinner's terminology a discriminated stimulus, and the response is a discriminated operant. Most of the correlations between stimuli and responses with which we deal are of this kind. While responses are said to be evoked or elicited, this is a matter of convenience, and no more is intended than that the stimulus is in some sense the occasion for the response.

Reward Training

Rewarded learning has often been studied in conditioning laboratories, e.g., Eroféeva (1916), Beritov (1932), Dworkin (1934a), Wendt (1934). The lever-pressing situation introduced by Skinner and extensively studied by him has also been used by a number of workers in other laboratories who are quantifying the relationships within rewarded learning which correspond to the descriptive characteristics of classical conditioning, e.g., Arakelian (1939), Ellson (1938), S. B. Williams (1938), Youtz (1938a, 1938b, 1939).

Escape Training

Termination or reduction of a continuous noxious stimulus has been employed more frequently in establishing complex habits than in conditioning. Muenzinger and Fletcher (1936) trained rats in a visual brightness discrimination by delivering a continuous electric shock through the floor of the apparatus. By making the correct choice response the rats escaped into a goal box which was not electrified. Escape from water has been used as motivation for rats in maze learning by O. C. Glaser (1910), McDougall (1927), F. L. Ruch (1930) and Macfarlane (1930).

Avoidance Training

The distinction between classical conditioning based on noxious unconditioned stimuli and instrumental avoidance training has been made by several writers. Wood-worth (1938, pp. 101–107), for example, divides experiments into three classes: those in which the conditioned response neither produces nor avoids the unconditioned stimulus, those in which it produces the unconditioned stimulus, and those in which it escapes a noxious stimulus. He accepts the first two of these as conditioning, but rejects "stable and successful avoidance reactions" on the basis of Schlosberg's (1937) argument that the noxious stimulus is not really a reinforcing agent. If derived reinforcement is accepted, avoidance training may also be considered a variety of conditioning.

Shock, or other noxious stimuli, may be used in a variety of training procedures which are not always clearly distinguished. The following list is a condensed summary of the more important usages. (1) Shock may be used as the unconditioned stimulus in classical conditioning. In this procedure the shock always follows the conditioned stimulus regularly, whether or not any conditioned response has been made. (2) Shock may be terminated by the appropriate response, as in instrumental escape training. (3) Shock may be given whenever the subject makes a particular response. This is the typical punishment situation, and leads to reduction in strength of the punished response but does not guarantee the positive learning of any other response. It is a method for the elimination rather than the acquisition of a response. (4) Shock may be prevented by an appropriate response, as in instrumental avoidance training. (5) Shock may be given in such a way that it provides no specific reinforcement for correct response but modifies the learning in some general way. Muenzinger and A. Wood (1935) found that shock for both right and wrong choices in a visual discrimination habit by rats produced more rapid learning. The animals spent more time at the choice point and apparently were more "deliberate" in their selection of pathways.

Secondary Reward Training

Token reward has been studied with rats by Skinner (1938), with cats by M. F. Smith (1939), with dogs by Ellson (1937), with chimpanzees by Wolfe (1936), Nissen and Crawford (1936), and Cowles (1937), and in a comparable situation with children by Mitrano (1939). A secondary reward was used with rats by K. A. Williams (1929a). The reward value of the sight of food has been demonstrated by Grindley (1929) with chickens, and by Bruce (1932) with rats in the maze problem.

Chapter 4

THE NATURE OF REINFORCEMENT

THE STRENGTH of a conditioned response is increased by reinforcement and decreased by non-reinforcement. This is the basic statement of the conditioning process. Any theory about the conditioned response must concern itself with the concept of reinforcement; indeed, so central is its place in comprehending the functional relationships within a conditioning experiment that a theory may be judged by its success in handling this concept.

A survey of the different kinds of conditioning experiments demonstrates clearly that the reinforcement is not described in the same way for the various situations. The attempt to formulate a single explanation of the reinforcement process which will encompass the diverse examples discussed in the previous two chapters has claimed the attention of many writers. Such theories have found their origin in an emphasis upon one or another of the fundamental reference experiments. The three outstanding principles are *substitution, effect,* and *expectancy*. Substitution, the orthodox conditioning theory, is most appropriate as an explanation of learning by homogeneous reinforcement as it is studied in the classical conditioning procedure. The principle of effect applies most directly to learning by heterogeneous reinforcement in the instrumental reward and escape situations. The expectancy principle draws its chief support from learning which demands the consideration of derived reinforcement as it is demonstrated in avoidance and secondary reward training. While each principle appears to be coordinated with a particular variety of reinforcement, advocates of each principle have attempted to demonstrate that the principle can also explain learning which depends upon the other types of reinforcement. After a separate characterization of the principles, the claims for each as an exclusive theory of reinforcement will be considered.

The Principle of Substitution

The principle of substitution states that a conditioned stimulus, present at the time that an original stimulus evokes a response, will tend on subsequent presentations to evoke that response. This principle is fundamental in Pavlov's theoretical formulations, and, in one form or another, has been an essential part of most psychological treatments of the phenomena of association. The various statements of the principle of substitution differ principally in the designation of what is substituted. Thus early writers spoke of associations between ideas, or between sensations and impulses. Others have pointed out that associations must be conceived ultimately as relationships between neural processes in the brain. The principle is usually stated in terms of stimuli and responses, however, since these are the events recorded in psychological experimentation. A more precise formulation would state that an activity initiated by a stimulus, occurring at the same time as another activity which results in a response, will tend on subsequent occurrences to evoke that response.

The substitution principle has been applied to the phenomena of conditioning in two ways. The clearest example of this difference is found in the contrast between the theories of Pavlov and of Guthrie. Pavlov states that *substitution will occur only under certain conditions,* and will vary in degree as those conditions approach optimal values. The tendency of a conditioned stimulus to evoke the response with which it has been paired depends upon the time interval separating the two, the intensity of the conditioned and unconditioned stimuli, the number of repetitions of the stimuli, and so forth.

For Guthrie (1935), on the other hand, *substitution occurs always and completely* whenever a stimulus is present at the time that a response is made. Strict simultaneity is necessary, and when association apparently occurs between a stimulus and a response separated in time, the true conditioned stimulus must be identified as a stimulus present at the time of response. The external conditioned stimulus, such as a buzzer, is not necessarily the true conditioner; the true conditioned stimuli may be provided by the sensory consequences of intervening movements which the buzzer evokes. Learning is accomplished in every instance in one trial, and is permanent unless interfered with by new learning. One presentation of the conditioned stimulus on which the response does not occur suffices for unlearning. Stated more generally, this theory declares that the organism in a certain stimulus situation will inevitably do what it did on the last occurrence of that situation. On the face of it, this theory seems to be in contradiction with the common observation that learning is slow and gradual and that responses show variability from one occasion to the next. The stimulus situation, however, must be thought of as including numerous component stimuli or cues, which are never exactly repeated in their entirety. Even if the environmental objects are precisely the same, the organism will view them from a different position or angle. The cues arising from its own body will also be different. Responses will be identical on two successive trials only to the extent that the stimulus situations are identical. The reason that repetition of training trials is effective in increasing the probability of occurrence or the magnitude of a conditioned response is that the response becomes conditioned to the various changing forms of the stimulus situation which appear on successive trials. As more cues are assimilated to the response, adventitious stimuli will interfere less with the behavior, so that the response appears to be better learned.

These two conceptions of the principle of substitution suggest different experimental programs. Pavlov's theory demands the empirical determination of the conditions affecting the process of substitution, and his followers have proceeded to study the influence of time interval, stimulus intensity, generalization, and so forth. Guthrie's theory, on the other hand, does not require any study of such factors, for substitution always occurs completely in one trial. The problem for Guthrie is essentially one of performance, of discovering the laws governing the occurrence of a response, since if the response occurs it is permanently conditioned to all stimulus cues present; if it does not occur it is permanently extinguished. This experimental program would involve the identification of the component cues in the stimulus situation and their separate response tendencies, and the statement of their mutual interrelations (facilitation and inhibition) in determining the overt response.

At the present time, Pavlov's statement of the principle of substitution, while not so comprehensive as Guthrie's, is more susceptible to experimental formulation. The difference depends principally upon the definition, or method of measurement, of the stimulus. Pavlov defines the stimulus in objective terms independently of its effect upon the organism; the stimulus remains the same on successive conditioning trials and its changing relation to the conditioned response is studied. In Guthrie's theory, a change in response from one occasion to another means a change in the stimulus situation. If a dog does not salivate to the bell on the second trial of a conditioning series, it is "because there are uncontrollable differences in the situation on the second presentation" (Guthrie, 1935, p. 100). But it is not possible to designate those stimulus changes; ordinary measurement of the stimulus does not reveal them. The only evidence of their presence is the very circular inference from the failure of the salivation response. Pavlov's more empirical statement of the principle of substitution is directed toward the same objective as Guthrie's but has the advantage that it can be checked and revised at each step of the way.

The substitution principle, in any form, is characterized by the fact that no additional motivational principle is needed to account for learning. Motivation will obviously be a factor in determining the occurrence and magnitude of the original unconditioned response, but the substitution is dependent merely on the fact of response. Motivation may therefore be omitted from central consideration; it is one of a number of circumstances which influence the strength of the original response.

One of the most difficult problems confronting any theory of conditioning is to account for the observed differences between a conditioned response and the unconditioned response on which it is based. The principle of substitution, by itself, does not contain any explanation of these differences; indeed, it demands that the organism should act in the presence of the conditioned stimulus as though it were in the presence of the unconditioned stimulus. Something approximating this occasionally seems to be the case. Pavlov (1934) reports that his dogs, trained to salivate to a light preceding food, were noticed to turn their heads toward the light, and even to lick the light globe. Emotional conditioning, to the extent that it occurs, appears to be an attachment of the emotion aroused by one object to another that happened to be present at the time when the emotion was expressed.

The most common result of classical conditioning, as pointed out previously, is not complete but partial redintegration (Chapter 2, p. 37f.). The conditioned response resembles but does not duplicate exactly the unconditioned response. It may differ in magnitude and in form. Characteristically it is only one component of the original response. In many such instances it is apparent that the situation is also one of instrumental training, and that component responses are strengthened or weakened by heterogeneous or derived reinforcement. The principle of substitution cannot deal directly with responses which show no resemblance to the original response, and in order to account for instances of partial identity, it is necessary to consider that some fractions of the response are more readily conditioned than are others. It is a common observation that there are great differences in the speed of conditioning various responses (e.g., E. L. Walker and Kellogg, 1939).

It has been shown that the principle of substitution is directly applicable to instances of complete redintegration which occur in the classical training situation, and to instances of partial redintegration which can be interpreted as the conditioning of a fraction of the original response. The possible extension of the principle to account for conditioning on the basis of heterogeneous and derived reinforcement will be considered following the discussion of the principles of effect and expectancy.

The Principle of Effect

Studies of heterogeneous reinforcement in the typical instrumental training situation have given rise to a principle of learning which emphasizes the influence of the consequences of an act, that is, the reward or punishment which follows the act. Although some such principle may be found in the writings of earlier psychologists, it was first clearly stated by Thorndike in 1911, who called it the *law of effect:*

Of several responses made to the same situation, those which are accompanied or closely followed by satisfaction to the animal will, other things being equal, be more firmly connected with the situation, so that, when it recurs, they will be more likely to recur; those which are accompanied or closely followed by discomfort to the animal, other things being equal, will have their connections with that situation weakened, so that, when it recurs, they will be less likely to occur. The greater the satisfaction or discomfort, the greater the strengthening or weakening of the bond. (E. L. Thorndike, *Animal Intelligence,* The Macmillan Company, 1911, p. 244.)

The discussions of the principle of effect have been concerned with two basic questions: (1) what kind of "effects" have a reinforcing action and (2) what responses will be reinforced? The former question is essentially the problem of defining the nature of the stimuli which produce heterogeneous reinforcement, and will be considered first.

Definition of Reinforcing Agents. Early statements of the effect principle were couched in the language of satisfaction and annoyance, related historically to the pleasure-pain theories embodied in various hedonisms. At the other extreme, the influence of satisfiers and annoyers on preceding behavior has been given a hypothetical neurological explanation in terms of changes in resistance to conduction along the appropriate nerve paths (Thorndike, 1911; Troland, 1928). Both the affective characteristics of rewarding and punishing agents and the neurological theory have assumed less dominant places in current statements of the effect principle (Thorndike, 1935). Experimental results have shown that acts are reinforced if followed by presentation of food when the animal is hungry, by water when the animal is thirsty, by moderate temperatures when the animal is hot or cold, by a sex object when the animal is in heat, by infant offspring following parturition, by a free situation when the animal has been confined, and by escape from electric shock and other painful or uncomfortable situations. What do these situations have in common? Usually emphasized are either the consciously experienced pleasantness and unpleasantness, or the motivational aspects of the various reinforcements.

The affective character of reinforcing stimuli received clear expression in Thorndike's first statement of the law of effect. In other connections he has spoken of "satisfiers" and "annoyers." A similar conception is implied in Troland's (1928) theory of retroflex action. Carr (1925) has emphasized the sensory aspect of the consequences of an act without specifically stating that they must be affective.

Many writers have attempted to restate the law of effect in such a way as to avoid the philosophical difficulties arising from the inference that affective states of consciousness have an influence on behavior, and to avoid the attribution of consciousness to animals. Thorndike, for example, states: "By a satisfying state of affairs is meant one which the animal does nothing to avoid, often doing such things as attain and preserve it. By a discomforting or annoying state of affairs is meant one which the animal commonly avoids and abandons" (1911, p. 245). Other definitions have emphasized the *goal* character of the reinforcing act. It has been pointed out that the animal in the problem-box or maze is aroused, restless, hypertensed, until the food is reached. After ingestion of food, the animal becomes calm and quiescent. S. Smith and Guthrie (1921) wrote of 'maintaining stimuli' which are removed by the reinforcing act. In this they followed the conceptions of precurrent and consummatory response proposed earlier by Sherrington (1906) and Woodworth (1918). Raup (1925) described the end of goal activity to be the reaching of a state of 'complacency,' similar to that which Cannon (1932) has called 'homeostasis.' T. L. McCulloch (1939c) has proposed that reinforcement may be effective because it causes the disappearance of restless, excited behavior.

Instrumental escape training has been distinguished from instrumental reward training in terms of the particular arrangements of experimental procedure which are customarily employed. Escape and reward, however, are similar in their dynamic action as reinforcement for learning, no matter what specific interpretation of the principle of effect is made. Termination of an electric shock may be considered affectively pleasant or satisfying; it may be considered a consummatory response for the primary drive to avoid pain; or it may be thought of as a return to an equilibrium or state of complacency. Indeed, reward might in some cases be considered an escape from the persisting stimuli which characterize the drive. Muenzinger and Fletcher (1936) have reported an experimental comparison of hunger-food-tension and shock-escape-tension as reinforcement for the learning of a visual discrimination by rats. The effectiveness of each may be interpreted as an escape from tension present in the learning situation; in one case hunger, in the other, pain. Shaffer (1936) has also emphasized tension reduction as the essential characteristic of problem solution.

It is apparent that no definition of effect provides an independent measure of the strength of a reinforcement. The degree of satisfaction, of complacency, or of tension reduction has not been objectively determined. The strength of reinforcement can be given comprehensive definition only in terms of the amount of learning resulting from it. This is, of course, a circular definition, if strength of reinforcement is to be used as a factor determining degree of learning. A partial escape from circularity is achieved by the fact that a stimulus such as food which is found to be reinforcing in one situation will also be reinforcing in other situations, and with other animals.

At the present time it is possible to catalog the reinforcements which are almost universally effective, although it is not possible to formulate a single definition which will include all the examples.

The original formulation of the law of effect stated that responses which are followed by discomfort (i.e., punishment) will tend to be weakened in strength. This statement is obviously not a law of the acquisition of responses, but rather one of the reduction and elimination of responses. As such it is discussed more fully in the following chapter. As Muenzinger and Dove (1937) have pointed out, punishment gives rise to variability of behavior, that is, to a tendency to do something else after failure, while reward leads to uniformity of behavior, or a tendency to repeat the response that was rewarded.

Selection and Elimination by the Principle of Effect. The second question which has been prominently raised in discussions of the principle of effect concerns the relation of the reward to the response which it strengthens. An instrumental training situation is ordinarily designed so that a certain response will be followed by reward and thereby become selected, while other responses which do not lead to reward become eliminated in the course of training. The effective factor in determining the selection of the "correct" response is its proximity in time to the reinforcement. The last response which occurs prior to the reward is the one most strongly reinforced. Experimental results have shown that if the presentation of the reward is delayed for an interval of time, the speed of learning is correspondingly decreased. The relationship between the reward interval and the strength of the conditioned response may be described as the *gradient of reward* (see Chapter 7).

The principle of effect does not require that the behavior sequences strengthened by reward should necessarily be instrumental in securing the reward. The principle contains no implication of purposive behavior or of insight. The responses which are strengthened may be quite incidental to the achievement of the reward, and under some circumstances may be responses occurring after the reward is given (p. 168). All that is necessary is proximity to the reinforcement. The principle of effect becomes a modified law of contiguity, differing from the principle of substitution in its statement of which events are temporally related.

Comparison of the Principles of Effect and Substitution. The principle of effect, like that of substitution, is de-

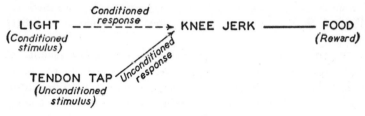

FIGURE 6

COMPARISON OF THE PRINCIPLES OF SUBSTITUTION AND OF EFFECT

According to the substitution principle the conditioned response depends upon the occurrence of the unconditioned knee jerk; according to the effect principle the conditioned leg extension depends upon the food reward. For further discussion, see text.

signed to explain the occurrence and strengthening of the associative connection between a conditioned stimulus (situation) and a certain response which is originally evoked by another stimulus. The difference between the two principles may be made clear by reference to a hypothetical training situation illustrated in Figure 6. A dog, for example, is presented with a conditioned stimulus (light), followed by a stimulus which elicits a knee jerk, which in turn is followed by a reward (food). According to the principle of substitution, the strength of the conditioned response (leg extension to light) depends upon the occurrence and the intensity of the unconditioned knee jerk response. The principle of effect states that the strength of the conditioned response is a function of the occurrence and degree of food reward. Extinction is predicted by the substitution principle when the unconditioned response (based on tendon tap) is omitted in a series of trials; the principle of effect demands that extinction follow the omission of the food reward. A further comparison is possible with reference to the spacing of the stimuli. The time interval between the conditioned stimulus and unconditioned response is crucial for conditioning according to the substitution principle while the interval between the original response and the reward is important according to the effect principle.

Direct comparisons of this sort between the principles of substitution and of effect are not frequently encountered in the experimental literature. In general, the substitution principle is applied in the explanation of the results of classical conditioning, while the effect principle is related to experiments involving instrumental training. Brogden (1939b) has recently studied a situation somewhat similar to the hypothetical example outlined above. Dogs were first trained, by pairing a bell and a shock stimulus, to give a conditioned leg withdrawal response, and then were rewarded with food whenever this response was made. In spite of the omission of the unconditioned shock stimulus on as many as 1000 trials, there was no extinction of the conditioned withdrawal when it was followed by feeding.

The effect principle, like the substitution principle, might conceivably be extended to cover instances of learning other than those from which it is primarily derived. This kind of extension of the term will be considered after the expectancy principle has been discussed.

The Principle of Expectancy

There are many instances of conditioning in which it is impossible to identify the reinforcement in terms of an unconditioned response or of an effect such as described above. Instrumental avoidance training, for example, cannot be accounted for directly by either substitution or effect. If response to shock is considered to be an unconditioned response, substitution would demand that when the shock stimulus is omitted on a series of trials, the conditioned response should become extinguished, whereas it actually is strengthened by the absence of shock. The principle of effect likewise provides no simple explanation, since the shock cannot be considered a reward, and the absence of shock can be rewarding only if some sort of expectation of shock has been established in the subject.

The principle of expectancy has been formulated to account for the strengthening of instrumental responses by derived reinforcement, as exemplified in avoidance and secondary reward training. According to the principle of effect, reinforcement must be affectively pleasant or, stated otherwise, must consummate a primary drive. According to the principle of expectancy, *reinforcement must be such as to confirm an expectancy.* The expectancy itself depends upon previous learning by the subject in the particular situation or in similar situations. An expectancy may be thought of as a secondary or learned motive, differing from a drive in that it is characteristic of an individual and dependent on his prior experience, rather than being unlearned and universal for a species. The experiences of various individuals are so similar in many respects, however, that prediction of behavior on the basis of expectancies may be quite accurate. For example, in all animals the sight of familiar food reinforces instrumental approach or reaching responses.

Tolman's theory of sign-learning is the most systematic formulation of the expectancy principle. According to Tolman (1934), in learning a sequence of acts leading to a goal the subject follows the 'signs' which mark out the 'behavior route' leading to the 'significate,' or goal. The interpretation involves the perceptual or cognitive capacities of the animal. In the presence of the 'signs' the subject 'expects' the goal to appear if it follows the 'behavior route.' In other words, there are intermediaries (intervening variables) between the stimuli and the overt responses. The inference is made that the animal behaves in certain ways consonant with anticipated consequences. If the goal materializes, the expectation is confirmed, and when the situation is repeated similar behavior sequences will again be evoked. If the expected consequences do not materialize, failure will lead to varied behavior on the next trial. Such tentative behavior, entered upon in accordance with expected consequences which are probable but not certain, will be immediately recognized by the reader as familiar in his own experience. Tolman's theory of sign-learning, and Krechevsky's (1932a) doctrine of hypotheses, interpret the behavior of animals in essentially these terms. These theories do not intend anything subjective, however, but they stress the organized relationships of the total behavioral act, in which the goal is significant in relation to the expectations of it, whatever the structural basis of these expectations may be. White (1936), following the lead of several earlier writers, has suggested that fractional anticipatory conditioned responses may provide the objective basis for expectations, reinforcement consisting in goal responses consonant with anticipatory responses.

There are two steps in an explanation of the results of derived reinforcement according to the expectancy principle. The first step, encompassed by Tolman's sign-learning theory, involves a learned sign-significate relationship, so that the situation has a new meaning to the organism based on its prior experience in it. Thus the guinea pigs in the revolving cage of Brogden, Lipman, and Culler (1938) must learn that at the sound of the buzzer the cage is potentially 'dangerous,' i.e., a shock is likely to occur, and that the shock is less likely to occur if they start running when the buzzer sounds. Wolfe's (1936) chimpanzees must know that tokens signify potential food. The second step of explanation requires some manner in which the aroused expectation or signification leads to appropriate conduct. It is assumed by Tolman that if a rat knows the behavior-route to a desired goal, the rat will follow the route. He has been criticized by Guthrie (1935, p. 172) for not coming to grips with the problem of how the rat is led from its expectations to appropriate action. Both the substitution and effect theories refer to strengthened tendencies to respond; what is strengthened according to the expectancy theory is not a tendency to respond, but a tendency to anticipate certain consequences. The theory, stated in this form, does not propose to predict the details of conduct, so that the most varied behavior, if it is consonant with anticipated consequences, may be encompassed by it. A rat expecting punishment at the end of the maze may refuse to enter, may climb over the wall, or may simply crouch in the path and shudder. It shows in its behavior that it anticipates a noxious consequence of running through the maze, but the details of the behavior are not accounted for by the mere acquisition of an expectation. Widely different performances may serve the same purposes, and hence be grouped together in, say, the class of responses going by the name of avoidance behavior. This breadth of interpretation is one of the advantages of the expectancy principle over the principles of substitution and effect, but it is at the same time a source of weakness. All that is learned, according to the expectancy principle, is a new anticipation. The appropriate behavior in relation to the anticipation must have been either inherited or acquired in the earlier history of the organism. Zener (1937) has used the expression 'sign-urge' to refer to his form of the expectancy theory in which he recognizes that signs must be related to specific tension systems in order for the behavior to be explained. An advance will be made in explanation according to the expectancy principle when more detailed analyses are given of the way in which signification leads to conduct.

Generality of the Principles of Reinforcement

Each of the three principles of reinforcement has been discussed with particular reference to the type of training experiment from which it was originally derived. Proponents of each principle, however, claim that it will account for all the phenomena of learning. These claims may now be examined in order to determine the success with which any single principle can encompass the results of conditioning in general.

Principle of Substitution. Although Pavlov's writings imply that substitution is the only principle necessary for the explanation of all varieties of learning, they contain no specific discussion of the problems arising from the consideration of instrumental reward or avoidance training. Other writers, however, have dealt directly with this question. They do not deny that learning takes place in situations involving heterogeneous or derived reinforcement, but believe that such learning can be explained without any new principles beyond that of substitution.

The explanation of instrumental reward training, such as is involved in a problem-box task, requires a statement of why the correct response, and not some other, becomes strengthened so that on subsequent trials it is more readily elicited by the conditioned stimulus. Attempted explanations in terms of secondary principles of frequency, recency, and intensity have met with little success. Guthrie's more recent statement of the principle of substitution permits him to account for such learning without any additional assumptions. The animal, in a problem situation, always tends to do what it did on the last presentation of that situation. Since the correct response is invariably the last response in the situation, it is the one which is learned. Incorrect responses are not permanently learned because the animal remains in the presence of the conditioned stimulus, and as new responses occur, the previous ones are unlearned. Since learning and unlearning require only a single occurrence, it is apparent that the last response made to the conditioned stimulus is the only one which is associated. When next the animal is placed in the situation, it does what it last did; what it last did is always the response just preceding success.

This explanation differs clearly from the principle of effect, according to which the reward is described in terms of affective pleasantness, consummation of drive, or tension reduction. In Guthrie's theory, while the statement of effect remains descriptively appropriate, the important function of the reward is merely to terminate the particular complex of conditioned stimuli. This is usually accomplished by removal of the external environmental stimuli. In the experiments of Guthrie and Horton (1937) in which cats escaped from a problem box to a food reward, the learning appeared to depend very little on the consequences of eating, since the cats often refused the food after successfully operating the mechanism for getting out of the box. While escape may itself have been tension-reducing, the important point for the theory is that leaving the box constituted a terminal act in relation to the stimuli present while the animal was in the box. In situations in which the animal is rewarded in the same environment, there is still a marked change in the total stimulus complex, for the hunger stimuli are presumably terminated by the reward. According to this interpretation, it is the capacity to take the animal out of the situation, to terminate the conditioned stimulus, which makes heterogeneous reinforcement effective in learning.

Guthrie's explanation of instrumental learning has the same advantages and disadvantages as his general theory of substitution. In spite of its consistent logical structure, it does not lend itself readily to precise experimental verification. The action of reward in terminating the stimulus situation cannot be clearly specified in many instances. For example, when a rat eats a pellet of food in the Skinner problem box the stimulus situation is not materially altered. The animal remains in the same box, and the drive stimuli are not eliminated since the animal will continue to eat many more pellets.

In response to criticism of this sort by T. L. McCulloch (1939c), Guthrie (1939) has recently proposed that the act of eating removes the conflicting behavior which is the 'annoyance,' whether or not it removes the internal state which is the 'annoyer.' Hence there is tension reduction in the Skinner experiment as the rat eats a pellet, even though it remains hungry enough to eat many more. The temporary tension reduction is a terminal act removing stimuli, and hence prevents unlearning of responses based on these stimuli. If Guthrie's argument holds, however, as soon as the pellet is consumed and the organism is again in an aroused state it is in a situation favorable for unlearning all that it learned unless it immediately repeats successfully its food-seeking behavior. It is obvious that something has changed when the animal ceases to run or to push levers and begins to eat, but a theory must state more precisely just what the change is which guarantees the learning of the prior response if the theory is to be verified experimentally.

Explanation of the effects of derived reinforcement in terms of the principle of substitution has been undertaken by Hull (1931) and by Guthrie (1935). Both assign major importance to fractional anticipatory conditioned responses as surrogates for expectancy. The complexity of the problem, and the implicit character of many of the relevant events, make this explanation involved and difficult to verify. A more extended discussion of this question will be presented in Chapter 10.

Principle of Effect. Although it was derived from experiments involving heterogeneous reinforcement, the principle of effect might be extended to account for instances of homogeneous and derived reinforcement and thereby give rise to a uniform and comprehensive theory. In order to include the results of classical conditioning under the principle of effect, it would be necessary to demonstrate that the conditioned response is always followed by reward or escape. In the case of Pavlov's experiments, for example, the conditioned salivation is always followed by the presentation of food. In the case of withdrawal from shock, the shock may be considered as a punishment as well as an unconditioned stimulus. Even though the conditioned response does not prevent the shock, the conditioned movements may be interpreted as reactions related to punishment.

The most serious difficulties in explaining classical conditioning by the principle of effect are encountered in experiments in which the unconditioned stimulus does not seem to have any of the characteristics of a reward either intrinsically or in a derivative sense, i.e., it is not satisfying or annoying, it is not tension reducing, and it does not consummate a drive. Close approximation to this is found in the conditioned lid response based on sound stimulation, and in the conditioned pupillary constriction based on light stimulation. The principle of effect also seems inapplicable to cases of 'incidental learning,' in which mere repeated exposure appears to produce learning without reference to any reinforcing state of affairs. A clear example of such incidental learning is furnished by an experiment by Brogden (1939c). A light and a sound were presented together to a dog for a number of trials, after which a conditioned foot retraction was established to the sound stimulus. Tests demonstrated that the light would also evoke the conditioned response, although it would not in other dogs which had not previously received the light-sound training. Similar difficulty is created by the facts of latent learning (Blodgett, 1929). A rat in a maze without food reward does not exhibit error-reduction in successive trials comparable to a rat fed each trial at the end of the maze. So far the effect principle appears to be appropriate. But it may be demonstrated that learning was taking place in the absence of food-reinforcement, by introducing food in the later trials of the series. Now the rats not previously fed in the maze very promptly perform as satisfactorily as the control animals which were fed each trial. The change from the poor non-rewarded performance to the good food-rewarded performance occurs so rapidly as to reflect earlier learning not readily explained in terms of effect.

Derived reinforcement can be subsumed under the principle of effect only by redefining reward to include secondary rewards. A step toward unification of theory is taken, however, if it can be shown that derived reinforcement is based upon learning which involves the effect principle. It may often be demonstrated directly that the situation producing derived reinforcement loses its value unless it is supported, directly or indirectly, by heterogeneous reinforcement. Culler, Finch, Girden, and Brogden (1935), when using the buzzer as a substitute for shock, found it necessary to introduce the shock occasionally as a "reminder." The sight of food loses its secondary reward character if it is not itself reinforced by actual feeding (Grindley, 1929). A sign appears to derive its effectiveness as reinforcement from the degree to which it substitutes for an agent capable of effect reinforcement.

The Principle of Expectancy. To the extent that conditioned responses may be interpreted as readiness or preparatory acts, or as behavior correlated with sets or attitudes anticipatory of reinforcement, they fall under the general concept of expectancy, whether or not reinforcement appears descriptively to be homogeneous, heterogeneous, or derived. In order to extend the expectancy explanation, classical conditioning must be subordinated to goal-behavior. This is similar to the subordination of substitution to effect, except for the interpretation. The acts which are strengthened must be interpreted as cognized behavior-routes leading to the satisfaction of expectancies. Redintegration which is unrelated to goals cannot be explained according to the expectancy principle. To retain the principle of expectancy as an exclusive explanation of learning, simple substitutive or redintegrative learning must be denied.

To the extent that reward reinforcement depends upon a learned anticipation of the reward, the expectancy principle is more appropriate than effect. It has been demonstrated in certain experimental situations that what appears to be law of effect reinforcement may involve the expectancy of a specific goal object. An illustration is provided by Tinklepaugh's (1928) experiments in which a monkey rejected a lettuce-leaf when expecting a banana as reward, although lettuce was acceptable under other circumstances. The animal was working for a reward, but its behavior is better described in terms of expectancy than in terms of effect. That chimpanzees act in accordance with specific reward-expectancy has been demonstrated by Cowles and Nissen (1937).

An essential supplement to the principle of effect is the statement of the gradient of reward; i.e., that a response is strengthened in relation to its proximity to the reward. According to the principle of expectancy, this relationship might be reinterpreted as a gradient of uncertainty. Thus, in a linear maze, animals tend both to anticipate and to overshoot a turn leading to food (Spragg, 1936). This may be explained as lack of certainty with respect to the exact location of the turn. The entrances chosen tend to be near the correct one, with a decreasing number of entrances farther from the correct turn. In the multiple choice word-number experiments of Thorndike (see p. 167f.), when one response is called "Right," the effect may spread to neighboring sequences because of two kinds of uncertainty: an uncertainty as to the exact pair which was rewarded (corresponding to the uncertainty with respect to the correct turn in the maze), and an uncertainty as to why this was rewarded. To play safe, the subject will tend to repeat pairs near the successful one to the extent that such repetition is possible. The gradient of reward would thus be accounted for as a spread of uncertainty. Some doubt, however, is cast on this interpretation by the experiments of Muenzinger and his associates (Muenzinger and Dove, 1937, and Muenzinger, Dove, and Bernstone, 1937). In the first of these, the Thorndike word-number experiment was repeated. To each of 20 words a number from 1 to 10 was assigned by the experimenter. As each word was read to the subject, he was to reply with a number from 1 to 10, and the experimenter announced "Right" or "Wrong" following each reply. In harmony with Thorndike's finding, it was found on repetition that there was a tendency to repeat responses made near to those called "Right," even though these responses had been 'punished' by the previous announcement of "Wrong." In a similar experiment, uncertainty was reduced by teaching in advance those word-number sequences which would be pronounced "Right" by the experimenter. In spite of this prior training there was a spread of reinforcing effect to items just preceding and following the item reinforced by saying "Right." In a second experiment, the spread of reinforcement was determined for rats in an endless maze. Here responses both prior to and following food reward were found to be strengthened. The gradient of reward is therefore a double one, affecting responses beyond the reward as well as those before it. There is no easy way for an expectancy theory to account on an uncertainty principle for the strengthening of behavior *following* eating. It is not plausible that the rat was so confused as to believe that its prior eating depended on its subsequent alley behavior.

The expectancy principle has a distinct advantage over the others in cases in which reinforcement does not fulfill the requirements either for substitution or for effect. If the present limitations of vagueness and lack of quantitative verification are overcome, expectancy may become a very important aid in the interpretation of experimental results in learning.

Present Status of the Problem of Reinforcement

The foregoing arguments have illustrated the attempts to include the results of all three varieties of reinforcement under each of the three explanatory principles. Implicit in the discussion are several distinctions which have not always been recognized in the various attempts to summarize and compare theories appropriate to different experimental situations. The empirical starting point is results achieved within experimental arrangements which throw into focus particular behavioral relationships requiring explanation. We have considered three main groups of experiments: (1) classical conditioning, (2) reward and escape training, and (3) avoidance training and secondary reward training. It is a common error to permit the reference experiment to dramatize a particular process, and then to suppose that the experiment represents a pure case of the process dramatized. Thus the classical conditioning experiment of Pavlov throws into relief the attachment of the conditioned stimulus to the unconditioned response, but it is by no means a pure case of one stimulus substituting for another. Similarly, an experiment involving rewards is not a pure case of learning according to the law of effect. Having chosen certain reference experiments which by the nature of the case could not be pure illustrations of one or another process in isolation, we have inferred particular processes prominent in each of the reference experiments. Through abstracting from the total experiment we have, in a sense, artificially created the pure case. Thus from classical conditioning we have abstracted the process of homogeneous reinforcement, in which behavior is strengthened through being followed by similar behavior; from reward and escape training we have abstracted the process of heterogeneous reinforcement, since the learned behavior and rewarding behavior differ markedly; and from avoidance learning and secondary reward we have abstracted the process of derived reinforcement, since reinforcement is effective in the absence of the stimulus giving rise to the original motivational reinforcement yet is dependent upon this original reinforcement. These abstracted processes are purified aspects of experimental situations, each process suggested by an appropriate reference experiment, but not to be identified with it. Having abstracted these processes from the experiments, we found certain types of explanations closely coordinated with each process. Thus the principle of substitution appears to be an appropriate explanation of homogeneous reinforcement; effect is appropriate to heterogeneous reinforcement; expectancy is appropriate in explanation of derived reinforcement. But those who favor one or another of these explanations do not rest content with it as an explanation of that variety of experiment to which it is most appropriate, but seek to interpret the processes within the other experiments as well. The accompanying table summarizes these attempts. The ef-

forts to achieve a unified explanation of all varieties of reinforcement according to one or another of the explanatory
principles cannot be considered final.

TABLE 2

How Each Principle May Be Proposed as the Exclusive Explanation of
the Learning Process Under Consideration

Type of experiment	Abstracted process	Principle of explanation as applicable to each process		
		SUBSTITUTION	EFFECT	EXPECTANCY
1. Classical conditioning	Homogeneous reinforcement	Substitution principle is directly applicable	Conditioning depends upon drive and heterogeneous reinforcement	Learning occurs only if response is part of a behavior-route to a goal
2. Instrumental reward and escape	Heterogeneous reinforcement	Reward (or escape) terminates conditioned stimulus and the last response made remains conditioned	Effect principle is directly applicable	Reward (or escape) confirms expectancy; what appears to be a spread of effect is a gradient of uncertainty regarding the probability that expected consequences will materialize
3. Instrumental avoidance; secondary reward	Derived reinforcement	Conditioned stimulus evokes fractional anticipatory responses learned by substitution. These are the surrogates of expectancy	Heterogeneous reinforcement is necessary to produce and support derived reinforcement	Expectancy principle is directly applicable

It should be clearly understood that there is no logical necessity for reducing all instances of learning to a single explanatory principle. The alternative theoretical systematization
permits the retention of several principles of learning by
clearly defining the situation to which each is applicable. Most
of the writers who have attempted to deal comprehensively
with the problem of learning have adopted the latter point of
view, speaking of 'types' or 'levels' of learning. In these cases,
however, the scope of application of each principle has not
been given a precise and independent definition. It has been

pointed out above that differences in experimental training procedures do not provide a basis for distinguishing the various types of reinforcement. In the classical conditioning experiment, for example, homogeneous, heterogeneous and derived reinforcement may all be operative. A more useful proposal has been advanced by Skinner (1938). According to this theory, Type S conditioning (corresponding to homogeneous reinforcement) occurs in the case of respondent behavior, while Type R (corresponding to heterogeneous reinforcement) occurs in the case of operant behavior. Unfortunately the distinction between respondent and operant is not always clear. A particular response, such as the eye-blink, may under different circumstances be 'elicited' as a respondent or 'emitted' as an operant, and it becomes difficult to decide to which category a conditioned eye-blink belongs. Skinner (1938, p. 112) has tentatively suggested that Type S conditioning might be limited to the smooth muscle and glandular responses under the control of the autonomic nervous system, while Type R conditioning would apply to skeletal muscle responses under the control of the somatic nervous system. This distinction could be supported only if further analysis demonstrated that the conditioning of responses such as leg flexion, eyelid closing, and the knee jerk did not involve the principle of substitution.

Notes

The various theories of learning discussed in this chapter have developed quite independently of each other, and have only recently been coordinated in such a way as to permit their direct comparison. Conditioning experiments and Pavlovian theory became almost indissoluble through thirty years of close identification. The notion that the conditioned response was simply the original unconditioned response attached to a new stimulus was conceptually so simple, and fitted so nicely the habit of thought inherited from association psychology, that it long remained unquestioned, and even today is often adhered to by those little acquainted with the details of conditioned response experiments.

The Principle of Substitution

The classical and orthodox conditioning theory is derived from the law of contiguity in association psychology. Although Warren's statement that the primary laws of association may be reduced to the single law of contiguity (H. C. Warren, 1921, p. 289) has not been acceptable to all associationists (Robinson, 1932, p. 66), the increasing prominence of contiguity represented a trend within association theory to which simultaneous conditioning was readily assimilated. The change came chiefly in what items were said to be associated. To ideas, various associationists had added sensory processes, complete perceptual acts, affective activities, sets, muscular movements, glandular secretions, inhibitions (Robinson, 1932, p. 27ff.). The emphasis on stimuli and movements represents an attempted objectification and simplification. Guthrie has been taken as representative of other proponents of a substitution theory, important among whom may be mentioned Hollingworth (1928), Holt (1931), Meyer (1934).

The differences between the points of view of Pavlov and Guthrie are brought out in a controversy between them, Pavlov (1932b), Guthrie (1934).

The Principle of Effect

Thorndike's law of effect, announced in his *Animal Intelligence* (1911), has been the source of much controversy. For summaries, see Stephens (1931a), Cason (1932),
Waters (1934), Carr and others (1938). Cason has reviewed the early statements of the principle by Spencer, Bain and Baldwin.

The most extensive experiments giving empirical comparison of substitution and effect are those of Konorski and S. Miller (1928–1937). Unfortunately, few of the details are available in the more familiar languages. Other experiments bearing on the problem are those of Anokhin and Straj (1937), Brogden (1939b), W. T. James (1933, 1934a), Sinkevich (1929).

The Principle of Expectancy

The striving, goal-seeking character of learned behavior, while to some extent recognized in conditioning and trial-and-error theories, has been most emphasized in purposive or hormic theories, such as that of McDougall (1923). Field or equilibrium theories may emphasize the directed character of behavior without subscribing fully to the avowed teleology of McDougall's purposivism (Adams, 1931; Humphrey, 1933; Tolman, 1932). Recognition of the tendency for a learned sequence to progress toward a systematically related end-result was expressed in the theories of confirmation (Hobhouse, 1901), congruency (S. J. Holmes, 1911), and completeness of response (Peterson, 1916). White's (1936) completion theory of reinforcement takes account of the advances in interpretation of conditioning phenomena.

The expectancy principle, involving as it does perception of relationships, cognitive functions, anticipations of consequences, hypotheses, appears to be quite foreign to conditioning theory. Closer scrutiny will show, however, that doctrines of symbolization, set, attitude, expectation, are not uncommon in the literature of conditioning. Pavlov himself is responsible for calling the conditioned stimulus a signal; Gantt, his student and translator, has coordinated Pavlov's signalization with Adolf Meyer's symbolization (Wolff and Gantt, 1935). Liddell, James, and Anderson give an expectancy interpretation of conditioning in sheep when they state that "when warned of an approaching electric shock the 'conditioned' animal seeks to defend itself in the manner *appropriate to the situation*" (1934, p. 54f.). The clearest acceptance of an expectancy interpretation of the Pavlov experiment is by Zener (1937), whose observations were quoted earlier (p. 39). Attitude and expectancy have been found to be of paramount importance in human conditioning (Chapter 11).

Generality of the Principles of Reinforcement

Guthrie's explanation of instrumental reward learning in terms of substitution involves no additional assumptions, since the acquisition of the last act performed in a situation follows as a corollary of his conception of one trial learning. Other writers who reject the principle of effect have used supplementary principles to account for the strengthening of the correct response in rewarded learning. Among these principles are frequency of occurrence and recency

in time (Watson, 1914), and intensity of response (Holt, 1931). The frequency-recency theory of Watson did not survive the many criticisms made of it (e.g., Peterson, 1922; Gengerelli, 1928). Holt's intensity theory is that the correct response is retained because it is prolonged and facilitated by a burst of proprioceptive impulses from muscles involved in the terminal act. Observation of animals does not offer any confirming evidence; the successful response is not necessarily prolonged but is usually quickly interrupted by movements of approach to food and eating.

Thorndike does not insist upon effect as an exclusive principle. He assigns a subordinate rôle to what he calls associative shifting (1935, p. 191), and includes an admixture of expectancy in some of his more recent statements about effect, such as that the effect is a confirmatory reaction or, in some cases, knowledge of results is validating (1935, p. 28). Hull, while distinctly excluding a separate expectancy principle, has implied stimulus-substitution in the form of redintegration particularly in his earlier papers. His fractional anticipatory responses and his pure-stimulus acts, were derived, not in accordance with the principle of effect, but in accordance with a substitution principle. More recently, however, the principle of effect has become for him an exclusive principle (Hull, 1937).

Tolman similarly does not believe expectancy (i.e., sign-learning) to be an exclusive explanation of learning. His point of view is rather that some such theory is necessary to explain certain types of learning (Tolman, 1937). Other kinds of learning may be explained in other ways. In the paper referred to, Tolman lists seven sub-varieties of learning, each of which may have its own laws. Substitute-stimulus learning and trial-and-error learning are included among these. In fairness to Tolman's position, it must be pointed out that the relation of sign learning to the other varieties (substitute-stimulus, trial-and-error and so on) is not a mere additive one.

For him the associationist account cannot be made complete by including a further variety of reinforcement. Tolman believes a radical departure from association theory to be necessary, and objects to the inclusion of his suggestions within a framework of association theory. Hence our inclusion within conditioning of results based on derived reinforcement explained on the basis of expectancy is not a reflection of Tolman's own position, although it owes much to him.

Chapter 5

THE NATURE OF EXTINCTION

REINFORCEMENT has been shown to be the essential condition for the strengthening of a conditioned response. Omission of reinforcement leads to the weakening of a conditioned response, as illustrated in the experimental procedure of extinction. If the conditioned stimulus is repeatedly presented without its usual reinforcement, the conditioned response undergoes a progressive decrement and finally fails to occur. A dog, for example, which has learned to run to the kitchen for food whenever it hears a pan rattled on the floor will gradually cease to respond if it no longer finds food in the pan. In the laboratory, a dog will gradually blink less frequently and less vigorously to a conditioned stimulus which is no longer followed by the customary puff of air to its eye.

This reduction is not a spontaneous decay. Conditioned responses show a very limited tendency to diminish with the passage of time. In the absence of complicating factors there is very little reduction by disuse even over intervals of months. It is apparent, therefore, that the elimination of conditioned responses depends upon some active process. This is called *inhibition,* which may be defined as the reduction in strength of response resulting from positive stimulation of some sort. To call this inhibition explains nothing, but serves to differentiate this kind of reduction from the decrements produced by changes in the conditioned stimulus itself, such as decreased intensity or qualitative alteration, by diminution in strength of drive, by administration of drugs, and so forth. The use of the term inhibition implies that the reduction in strength of response satisfies three conditions: (1) the inhibited response is not permanently destroyed or abolished, but rather is suppressed or prevented from overt expression; (2) the stimulus for the inhibited response is the same stimulus which previously evoked the response with greater strength; and (3) the inhibition depends upon positive stimulation.

Inhibition of conditioned responses results from several different kinds of experimental procedure, such as extinction, discrimination, delay, distraction and so forth (Chapter 2). These various procedures appear to involve two basic processes. The first, *intrinsic inhibition* or *adaptation,* may be defined as the reduction in response resulting from continued elicitation of the response itself. The second, *extrinsic inhibition* or *interference,* may be defined as the reduction resulting from the simultaneous elicitation of another, incompatible response. In many of the situations in which inhibition is observed, either or both types are possible. Before considering such situations, of which extinction is the most prominent example, we will examine the characteristics of the two kinds of inhibition separately.

Adaptation

The essential condition for adaptation is the repeated elicitation of a response. This effect is not limited to conditioned responses but can be observed in any type of reaction.

Adaptation of reflexes is commonly termed *habituation* or *negative adaptation.* It has been studied in many different organisms, ranging from the simplest to the most complex. It has been demonstrated in spinal cats (Sherrington, 1906) and rats (Prosser and Hunter, 1936). The degree of decrement varies widely from one response to another. Startle reflexes are rapidly habituated; flexion reflexes show more decrement than tendon reflexes, while some responses, like the pupillary reflex or the respiratory reflexes, are apparently completely resistant to adaptation.

Adaptation in voluntary responses which are made to instructions is known as *work decrement*. It shows many of the same characteristics as reflex habituation (Robinson, 1934). Adaptation will of course be opposed by any factor tending to strengthen or maintain the response during repetition. Such factors have not been identified for reflexes, but instructions and incentives will prevent decrement in voluntary responses, while reinforcement will overcome adaptation effects in the case of conditioned responses.

The chief characteristics of adaptation can be summarized best from the results of studies which have dealt either with the habituation of reflexes or with the extinction of conditioned responses, in which the factors opposing adaptation are at a minimum. Among these characteristics are the following:

1. *Adaptation is cumulative.* The greater the number of repetitions, the greater the decrement. Although the course of adaptation is progressive, the rate is not constant, and curves plotting strength against repetitions show many minor variations and irregularities. After the overt response has completely disappeared, adaptation may continue "below zero" as shown by the longer time required for spontaneous recovery. This may also be demonstrated directly by using a more sensitive measure of response. By recording very slight incipient movements with a sensitive tambour (Brogden, Lipman and Culler, 1938), or by recording action potentials from the muscles involved (Hilden, 1937), it has been shown that extinction continues after all grossly observable movement has disappeared.

2. *Adaptation is a function of the rate of elicitation of the response.* Although the evidence on this point is far from conclusive, it appears that a faster rate of stimulation results in

more rapid adaptation, whether the responses studied are reflexes, conditioned responses, or voluntary responses.

3. *Adaptation is not permanent.* During an interval of time following adaptation, the inhibited response spontaneously recovers in strength. Recovery begins immediately so that the interpolation of a short rest interval during adaptation will produce some increase in response strength. The rate and extent of recovery vary greatly for different responses. A second adaptation following recovery from the first usually requires fewer repetitions for complete inhibition of the response. This is evidence that spontaneous recovery tends to be incomplete. To the extent that the effects of adaptation are temporary, it may be inferred that the response tendency is suppressed and not destroyed, although the response itself may be reduced to zero magnitude.

4. *Adaptation may be generalized to some degree.* Experimental results on the extinction of conditioned responses show that the adaptation is not restricted to the particular response being elicited, but is reflected in the weakening of other responses as well. This is called secondary extinction by Pavlov, who pointed out that the decrement may in some instances be quite widespread, leading to sleep-like states.

Generalization of adaptation has not been widely studied with reflex habituation. Porter (1938a) noted that adaptation of the galvanic skin reflex to one stimulus resulted in a decrease in the response to another stimulus, from one modality to another, as well as within a modality (Coombs, 1938). However, in adaptation situations with spinal animals (Sherrington, 1906; Prosser and Hunter, 1936), no generalization is observed. A slight change in the point of application of the stimulus to the skin is followed by a response of full strength. This may mean that generalization is not an essential feature of the adaptation process itself, but depends upon the functioning of the higher brain centers.

5. *The stimulus to an adapted response may be inhibitory, rather than neutral.* Although the stimulus no longer elicits its original response, it may yet have an effect on other responses of the organism. Pavlov has demonstrated this clearly by showing that such an inhibitory stimulus, presented together with an ordinarily effective conditioned stimulus, will inhibit the response to the latter (1927). This result is similar to the phenomenon of conditioned inhibition. No data are available to indicate whether or not the same is true of the stimulus for a reflex which has been habituated.

Interference

Adaptation refers to a decrement for which the sufficient condition is the repetition of the same response. Interference, as an explanation of decrement, involves the interaction of two or more responses.

The general principles of the interaction of simultaneous responses have been most carefully worked out in the field of reflex activity. Presentation of two stimuli which individually elicit identical or synergic responses, will result in summation or facilitation, the combined response being larger than that to either of the two separate stimuli, often larger than their sum. If the two reactions are antagonistic, however, interference results. This may take the form of a complete suppression of one response, partial suppression, or alternation of the two responses. Interference will naturally result if the two responses involve the same effector organ. It is not possible to contract the extensors and the flexors of a limb completely at the same time. Ordinarily, the interference does not occur at this peripheral point, but in the neural mechanism which controls the effectors. The stimulus for a flexion reflex in a spinal dog simultaneously inhibits the motor neurons to the extensor muscles of the limb. This is the mechanism of reciprocal innervation which has been so thoroughly studied by Sherrington (1906).

The reciprocal nature of interference is not always as clear in the intact animal or human subject. One activity may inhibit another which does not appear to involve the same responding mechanism. A loud sound, or clenching the fists, may produce no movement of the leg, and yet facilitate the knee jerk. In such instances it is not possible to predict accurately the interaction effect of one activity upon another in the absence of empirical observation. It is generally true, however, that a moderate degree of muscular tension throughout the body has a facilitating effect upon motor and mental performances (G. L. Freeman, 1933), while sudden, novel stimuli have a distracting or inhibiting effect. The degree of inhibition will also be a function of the intensity of the interfering activity (Creed, et al., 1932; Peak, 1936).

Direct evidence on the summation of conditioned responses with reflexes or with other conditioned responses has been obtained in a few studies (Wendt, 1930; Hilgard, 1931; Garvey, 1933). With appropriate time intervals, the behavioral result of presenting together the stimuli for two responses, each of small amplitude, is greater than an algebraic sum of the separate components, agreeing with the findings of reflex physiology.

Interference involving conditioned responses may be seen in several different types of situation. One of the clearest examples is the inhibition of a conditioned response by the concomitant presentation of another stimulus, described by Pavlov as external inhibition. Pavlov has pointed out that the most effective stimuli are strong and unusual ones which evoke marked investigatory reflexes. Repeated presentation of the extra stimulus leads to a progressive loss of the inhibitory effect. External inhibition is temporary, lasting from a few seconds to several minutes or longer depending on the nature

and intensity of the stimulus. Continued inhibition may result from persisting stimuli such as those arising from an irri-
tating injury, distention of the bladder, and sex excitement
(Pavlov, 1927, p. 47).

Interaction effects, whether of summation or interference,

TABLE 3

External Inhibition as a Function of Temporal Interval

Conditioned eyelid responses from 16 human subjects, each tested twice
at each interval. Conditioned stimulus, light; unconditioned stimulus, puff
of air; extraneous stimulus serving to produce external inhibition, vibrator.
Conditioning interval between light and air-puff, 500 msec. (Gorham,
1937.)

	Interval be-tween vibrator and light —msec.	Interval be-tween vibrator and conditioned response * —msec.	Conditioned responses	
			FREQUENCY —PERCENT	AMPLITUDE —MM.
Normal (no vibrator)			98	21
Vibrator precedes light	300	628	71	18
	100	428	55	15
Vibrator follows light	− 50	278	19	7
	− 100	228	23	3

* Based on mean normal latency of 328 msec. for the conditioned response.

are complicated by the temporal relation of the two activities.
The amount of external inhibition, for example, has been
shown to depend on the length of interval by which the inhibitory stimulus precedes the moment of usual occurrence of
the conditioned response. The relevant data are presented in
Table 3 (Gorham, 1937). Within the range of temporal intervals studied, the nearer the presentation of the extra stimulus

(vibrator) approached the conditioned response, the greater the amount of inhibition.

Situations in which there is simultaneous presentation of the stimuli for two different conditioned responses have received almost no experimental study. Sinkevich (1929) trained children by food reinforcement to grasp a rubber bulb with the right hand when a red lamp was lighted, and by shock reinforcement to withdraw the left hand when a green bulb was lighted. When the two stimuli were subsequently presented at the same time, the children reacted in various ways. On some trials grasping alone occurred, on others withdrawal alone, and on still others both grasping and withdrawal. Although the interference situation has not been extensively studied, there are many parallels in the conflict of tendencies established by other than conditioning procedures. Results like those in Sinkevich's experiment have been obtained with well practised voluntary responses (Hovland and R. R. Sears, 1938).

In the situations just described the interference resulted from the presentation together of two stimuli having antagonistic response tendencies. Other examples involve the interference between two responses evoked by the same stimulus. In such cases the incompatible responses cannot be established simultaneously, but must be successive.

To many conditioned stimuli there is already a natural reflex response before conditioning is begun. This response will decrease and disappear as learning proceeds if it is antagonistic to the newly developing conditioned response. If no antagonism exists between the two responses there will be no interference effect. Examples of both results were found in some experiments on conditioned eyelid responses of dogs (Hilgard and D. G. Marquis, 1935). Before training, the conditioned light stimulus evoked a short latency (90 msec.) lid opening of very small magnitude, and a longer latency (200

msec.) partial lid closure. Both responses were bilateral, the
light having been presented to both eyes. During the acquisition of the unilateral conditioned blink reinforced by an air-
puff to one eye, there was no significant decrement in the original opening response, which did not interact because of its
short latency. The partial closure response, however, occurred

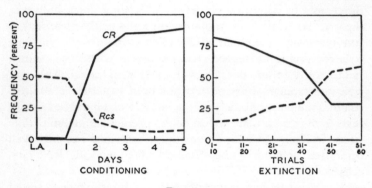

FIGURE 7

ANTAGONISTIC RELATION OF CONDITIONED RESPONSE AND ORIGINAL
BILATERAL PARTIAL LID CLOSURE IN DOGS DURING
CONDITIONING AND EXTINCTION

The bilateral closure (R$_{CS}$), present before conditioning, gave way during
conditioning to a unilateral closure (CR) of similar latency. The decrease in
the bilateral response during conditioning, and increase during extinction, reflect an interference between the two responses (Hilgard and D. G. Marquis,
1935).

at about the same latency as the conditioned response, and
during conditioning was gradually reduced in frequency, to
return during extinction (Figure 7).

A similar illustration of interference was given by Pavlov
(1932b) in his description of the formation of a conditioned
salivary response to the ringing of a bell. The conditioned
stimulus originally evoked typical listening movements; the
dog turned its head and pricked up its ears. The listening

movements gradually disappeared as the dog came to respond to the bell by licking its chops and turning toward the food pan. A more dramatic instance of the same phenomenon was afforded by an experiment, also with dogs, in which an electric shock was employed as a signal for the presentation of food (Eroféeva, 1916). The struggling and yelping elicited by the shock were not compatible with the conditioned responses which were acquired on the basis of food reinforcement, and the original responses gradually diminished until after many training sessions almost no trace of them remained.

If the original response is a previously established conditioned response, interference will result from the formation of a new incompatible response to the same stimulus. This procedure may be termed *counter conditioning;* it is the familiar one of breaking a habit by learning to do something else. The transition from a nocuous to a food conditioned response has been studied by Slutskaya (1928) in young children. The subjects first formed a conditioned avoidance response to the sight of a needle with which they were pricked. In later trials the pricking was always followed immediately by feeding, and in five of the eight children the avoidance response gradually weakened and disappeared, so that finally the sight of the needle occasionally evoked mouth opening and swallowing movements. The drug addict's craving for the hypodermic needle is a familiar parallel.

More detailed study of counter conditioning has been recently undertaken by Kellogg and E. L. Walker (1938a). Dogs were trained to lift the right leg to a conditioned stimulus (buzzer) by shocking the right foot. Then the electrodes for shocking were transferred to the left foot, and conditioning of the left leg response to the same buzzer stimulus was undertaken. The initial effect of the new situation was to intensify the conditioned response of the right leg. In the particular apparatus used the dog was able to lift both legs together by supporting its weight on a wooden stock enclosing its neck, and this double response was common, persisting for as many as 100 trials. Eventually the right leg response disappeared and the dog responded only with the left foot.

An original response is inhibited only as long as the interfering response remains active, and subsequently shows little or no residual impairment. This is clear in the case of external inhibition; a few seconds after the extra stimulus has ceased the conditioned response may be evoked at full strength. The inhibition of an original response to a conditioned stimulus likewise persists only as long as the conditioned response interferes. When the latter is reduced by extinction, the original response reappears (Figure 7). Hull (1934b) has described a corresponding finding in an instance of counter conditioning. Rats were first trained to run down a 20 foot straight alley to receive food. When the alley was lengthened to 40 feet, they showed a tendency to halt at the 20 foot point, but with continued training this tendency disappeared and the animals ran steadily down the entire path. During extinction of the later habit by omission of food reinforcement at the end of the alley, the tendency to halt at the 20 foot point again reappeared. A somewhat comparable finding is reported by Poznanskaya (1934) with children who were trained to give a new conditioned response to the same stimulus after the first conditioned response was extinguished. When the substituted response was extinguished, the earlier conditioned response reappeared. Further evidence for the preservation of the original response would follow from the demonstration of its reappearance when the second response was inhibited by an extra stimulus. Several experimenters have shown that an animal will regress to an earlier habit when strong emotional stimuli are presented (J. A. Hamilton and Krechevsky, 1933; Everall, 1935; N. E. Miller and Stevenson, 1936; Sanders, 1937). The possible relation between this finding and the

Freudian theory of regression has t
eral writers.

The general characteristics of the
interference may be summarized as

1. Interference occurs when two i
evoked at the same time, either by
separate stimuli.

2. The degree of inhibition is a
intensity of the interfering respon
tion of the two responses.

3. Inhibition, which is a suppression of response and not a permanent destruction, persists as long as the interfering activity is present. Recovery from inhibition will not be spontaneous, but will depend upon the removal of the interfering activity by extinction, forgetting, or external inhibition.

The Interpretation of Extinction

The term 'experimental extinction' was used by Pavlov to designate the decrement in a conditioned response during nonreinforced repetition expressly because it did not imply any theory of the mechanism of decrement. Extinction, therefore, properly refers to a procedure rather than to a process. It may involve either (or both) adaptation and interference.

Pavlov's theory of extinction is stated in terms of internal inhibition, which is essentially the same as the mechanism of adaptation described above. Although Pavlov's explanation involved the neural processes of excitation and inhibition, it is possible to ignore the speculative neurological explanation and treat extinction as a change in the relationships between stimuli and responses. The essential theory is that the decrement during extinction is due to a cumulative unresponsiveness resulting from the repeated elicitation of the response itself.

alternative to Pavlov's explanation of extinction, one in terms of interference has been proposed by Guthrie 935) and by Wendt (1936). According to this theory, the decrement in the conditioned response is due to the interference of some new response to the conditioned stimulus which is gradually strengthened during the successive nonreinforced repetitions. Extinction thus becomes the same process as counter conditioning. This theory has the attractive advantage that it explains extinction without the necessity of adding a new principle of adaptation to the two basic principles of reinforcement and interference. In order to weigh the accuracy of the explanation three points demand discussion.

The first point concerns the nature and source of the interfering response. Careful observation often reveals that the subject is not merely withholding the conditioned response, but is instead actively doing something else. During extinction of conditioned feeding responses, infants may show avoidance of the empty nursing bottle by making pushing gestures and by turning the head away (Levikova and Nevymakova, 1929; Denisova and Figurin, 1929; Kantrow, 1937). Monkeys trained to open a drawer on signal to obtain food show during extinction an increase of other activities such as vocalization, biting and pulling the drawer, and racing about the cage (Wendt, 1936). In most extinction experiments, the presence of new antagonistic activity has not been noted, partly, of course, because the experimenter's attention has been directed chiefly to the conditioned response itself. From other experiments (e.g., Zener, 1937), it is clear that new responses during extinction may be original responses to the conditioned stimulus which were inhibited by the conditioning, responses to other features of the total experimental situation, or responses generalized from previous experience with similar non-reinforcing or frustrating situations.

The second point concerns the possibility of successful interference by the new responses. Their presence during extinction is not itself convincing evidence for the interference theory. It may be more plausible to consider them as effects of extinction than as causes. Sleep, for example, may result from generalization of inhibition (Pavlov), or it may be itself a reaction incompatible with conditioning (Wendt). In instances of counter conditioning, the new response is specifically reinforced so that it becomes strong enough to inhibit the original conditioned response. Where such reinforcement is not present, the occurrence of new responses will be possible only after the conditioned response has been weakened sufficiently to permit their appearance. A conditioned response may be weakened without adaptation or interference, as, for example, by a reduction in the intensity of the conditioned stimulus, by fatigue of the conditioned response, by external inhibition, or by attempted elicitation during the refractory period of a previous response (Guthrie, 1935). Some such weakening process must be inferred if antagonistic responses are to reappear, unless a mechanism is suggested for strengthening the interfering responses. The interference interpretation of extinction, if it is not to imply adaptation or other weakening independent of interference, must discover a source for strengthening those responses which are antagonistic to the conditioned response.

This leads to the third point: can the course of extinction, and its other functional characteristics, be accounted for on the basis of an interference theory? Many of the experimental facts fit such a theory very well. The progressive, cumulative course of extinction would be an expression of the degree of learning of the incompatible response, and extinction below zero would be the result of overlearning. Disinhibition would be due to an external inhibition of the competing response. There are, however, three characteristics of extinction which are difficult to reconcile with the interference theory. These are spontaneous recovery, the effect of rate of elicitation, and the effect of drugs.

Spontaneous recovery, according to the interference theory, could occur only to the extent that the competing response is weakened during the interval by forgetting. Experimental data, however, indicate that spontaneous recovery is much more rapid, being measured ordinarily in terms of hours, whereas forgetting is measured in terms of days or months and in many cases is not appreciable over even longer periods. If extinction occurs through interference by a learned response, the spontaneous recovery would be expected to be just as slow as the forgetting of this newly acquired antagonistic response. Extinction by counter conditioning, in which the operation of interference is clear, does fail to show rapid spontaneous recovery, according to the fragmentary evidence now available. Kellogg and Wolf (1939) found that after intervals up to three months there was no recovery of responses inhibited by counter conditioning, and that the new interfering response was correspondingly undiminished. The spontaneous recovery following extinction by punishment for response has not been tested, but subsequent reconditioning was found to require more training than after simple extinction (Brogden, Lipman, and Culler, 1938).

A second line of evidence against the interpretation of extinction as interference from new learning is derived from the study of the effect of rate of elicitation. Massing of trials tends to result in more rapid extinction, but the speed of conditioning is retarded under similar circumstances (see p. 133). If the extinction process were essentially similar to the conditioning process, one would expect a positive correlation between the rates of acquisition and extinction, that is, rapid conditioning corresponding to rapid extinction, slow conditioning corresponding to slow extinction. The numerous correlations reported are, however, predominantly negative. Some of the correlations based on populations large enough to suggest significance are summarized in Table 4.

TABLE 4

REPRESENTATIVE CORRELATIONS BETWEEN RATE OF CONDITIONING AND
RATE OF EXTINCTION

The signs of the correlation coefficients have been arranged so that a negative sign means that rapid or more complete conditioning is associated with slow or less complete extinction.

Subjects, uncon-ditioned stimuli and responses; experimenter	Measures of conditioning and extinction	Number of subjects	Coefficient of correlation
Rats; running to shock; Hunter (1935a)	Trials to 10 successive CR's; trials to 5 successive failures to respond	51	$r = -.36$ $\eta = -.66$
Children; movements associated with eating; Mateer (1918)	Trials for conditioning; trials for extinction	50	$r = .45$
College students; eyelid response to electric shock; Bernstein (1934)	Frequency of CR within 50 reinforcements; number of CR's during extinction	69	$\rho = -.88$
College students; eyelid response to air-puff; A. A. Campbell (1938)	Frequency of CR within 50 reinforcements; frequency within 10 extinction trials	49	$r = -.66$
College students; knee jerk to tap on patellar tendon; A. A. Campbell (1938)	Frequency of CR within 100 reinforcements; frequency within 10 extinction trials	49	$r = -.60$

Further evidence for the functional dissimilarity of extinction and conditioning is derived from the differential effects of certain drugs. Sodium bromide and other drugs of a depressant character retard the rate of conditioning, but accelerate the rate of extinction. Excitants such as caffeine and benzedrine have been found to increase the strength of conditioned responses but to decrease the rate of extinction. It might be inferred that such drug effects are due merely to a change in the general level of reactivity of the organism which would inevitably result in larger conditioned responses and consequently delay extinction. Switzer (1935a) found that this was the result when caffeine was administered to human subjects in an experiment on conditioned galvanic responses. However, this general increase was not sufficient to account for the full extent of the retardation of extinction. When the initial level of responding was equated for both the control and the experimental (caffeine) groups of subjects, there still remained a significantly more rapid rate of extinction in the former. Pavlov, too, was unwilling to accept an explanation in terms of changed level of reactivity. In a dog that had gone into a state of experimental neurosis he administered sodium bromide and observed a reappearance of extinction effects previously impossible. At the same time there was no diminution in the magnitude of the positive conditioned responses.

From the above considerations it becomes evident that a theory of extinction in terms of interference between the conditioned response and newly acquired responses is not sufficient to account for all the experimental facts. Interference will, of course, be a factor in extinction at least to the extent that reinforcement for new incompatible responses is present in the situation. Adaptation appears to be necessary to account for the rapidity of spontaneous recovery, the more rapid extinction with massed repetitions, and the differential effect of certain drugs upon extinction and conditioning. At the same time it is clear that the concept of interference is necessary to account for the differences between simple extinction and counter conditioning. Both processes are found in most instances of extinction.

A theory of extinction must be adequate to account for instances in which the expected decrement does not occur. According to the adaptation theory, extinction must inevitably result from repetition of the conditioned response unless some maintaining influence is strong enough to overcome the effect. Interference will produce extinction whenever a stronger incompatible response is elicited. Several examples of apparent failure of extinction have been reported, although the responsible factor is seldom revealed by the experiments. Many instances can best be understood as the continued operation of reinforcement. This is clearly illustrated in the extinction of responses based on derived reinforcement. A dog which has been trained to lift its foot to escape a shock to the paw may show no extinction when the conditioned stimulus is repeatedly presented without the shock. But in this case, as was pointed out earlier, the shock itself is not the reinforcement; instead the reinforcement is based on absence of expected shock. Continued omission of the shock will therefore not lead to extinction. There is no procedure by which the derived reinforcement can be omitted. Only if the dog should fail to lift his leg sometime for any reason would the absence of the shock weaken the expectancy and lead to extinction. This type of situation may perhaps be typical of habits which persist when no apparent reinforcement follows the act. The fact that "a burnt child shuns the flame" does not require that the child be burned every time he sees the candle; the avoidance response is strengthened rather than weakened whenever the child escapes burning.

When conditioned responses are established with reinforcement presented on only a fraction of the training trials, extinction tends to be slower. This situation has been studied by Skinner (1938), and Humphreys (1939a, 1940c) with concordant results for different conditioned responses in rats and human subjects. These experiments are discussed in more detail in a later chapter (p. 150), and an interpretation is suggested in terms of expectancy. Prior to the beginning of extinction, conditioning by substitution or by effect had been replaced by expectancy of occasional feeding or occasional air-puffs. Since the training procedure maintained this expectancy in spite of occasional omission of the unconditioned stimulus or the reward, the consistent omission during extinction did not produce as rapid a destruction of the expectancy as occurred during extinction in subjects which had received reinforcement on every training trial. A similar explanation is perhaps appropriate for the failure of extinction of conditioned lid responses in monkeys (Hilgard and D. G. Marquis, 1936). This result is puzzling because directly comparable studies in dogs and in human subjects demonstrated typical extinction. The monkeys differed from the other subjects, however, because they closed their eyes completely rather than partially on every occurrence of the conditioned response. The air-puff was therefore received on the eyelid rather than the cornea and presumably was less intense. This would make the conditioning more similar to instrumental avoidance or to the occasional reinforcement training procedure, either of which leads to very slow extinction.

In other examples of the failure of extinction, an expectancy may be established by self-instructions and this takes the place of the original reinforcement which is now omitted. This would be most likely to occur in human subjects. Razran (1935), for example, failed to find consistent extinction of salivary conditioned responses. In a later experiment, he avoided the possibility of subjective attitudes and association sets by misinforming his subjects concerning the experiment (1939l). Under these conditions, extinction was readily demonstrated. Several investigators have reported aberrant results in attempting to extinguish conditioned finger withdrawal in human subjects. It seems that the more completely the response is capable of control by verbal voluntary processes, the greater is the possibility that extinction will fail. A conditioned response reinforced by a purely voluntary act may continue undiminished when the overt reinforcement is discontinued (D. G. Marquis and Porter, 1939). This function of verbal reinforcement has been demonstrated in an experiment by Hudgins (1933) who conditioned pupillary constriction reinforced by a bright light to a series of different conditioned stimuli. Extinction was obtained normally in the response to external stimuli such as a buzzer or hand squeezing, but when the response was finally established to implicit self-spoken commands to "Contract," extinction no longer occurred. A somewhat similar result for vasomotor responses was reported by Menzies (1937).

An apparent paradox in the extinction of voluntary responses is readily resolved if the expectancy principle is accepted. Voluntary responses may be strengthened by derived reinforcement, and hence may not show usual extinction. On the other hand, being under the influence of expectancy, they may under some circumstances show unusually rapid extinction, for counter conditioning may also be reinforced indirectly. Thus Porter (1938d) found in his study of the extinction of conditioned eyelid responses in man that subjects either extinguished very rapidly (in a mean of 6.8 ± 1.0 trials following 75 reinforcements) or they tended to show no extinction at all in several periods of 15 non-reinforced trials. Reports from the subjects make it possible to refer the differences to unlike sets or expectations. Rapid extinction may be a result of a tendency to cease responding which is reinforced verbally, quite as much as failure to extinguish in some cases depends upon continued responding as a precaution against the re-introduction of the unconditioned stimulus.

There are cases of failure of extinction which offer no clear clues to an explanation in terms of continued derived reinforcement. Harlow (1937) found no extinction of conditioned startle response in monkeys to a signal which had been followed by the report of a popgun. Baker (1938) has reported that the conditioned pupillary response to subthreshold stimuli undergoes no decrement with unreinforced repetition. Retention was also perfect over many months, and the only way the response could be eliminated was by counter conditioning. That is, pupillary dilatation was extinguished by following the conditioned stimulus with a bright light, thus establishing conditioned constriction. Confirmation of these results will constitute a strong argument for extinction by interference.

Inhibition in Situations Other than Extinction

Although extinction has been the subject of more experimental study than other situations involving inhibition it is by no means the only procedure within conditioning for the establishment of inhibition. The omission of reinforcement is not the essential condition for inhibition, but merely reveals adaptation and interference in unopposed form. A tendency to adaptation should be found whenever a response is repeatedly elicited, and interference should be found whenever there is a possibility of another antagonistic response being simultaneously evoked. Some of these situations will be described.

Inhibition During Continued Reinforcement. In several experiments it has been found that a decrement in the conditioned response may occur in spite of continued reinforcement, when the successive training trials are presented in rapid succession (e.g., Wendt, 1930; Hilgard, 1933a; Kantrow, 1937). If a rest interval is interpolated in the learning series, spontaneous recovery from the adaptation occurs, and following the interval the conditioned response is stronger than before it. This has been shown for overnight effects in dog, monkey, and man (Hilgard and D. G. Marquis, 1935, 1936; Hilgard and A. A. Campbell, 1936). Adaptation which is not great enough to cause an actual decline in the conditioned response but merely retards the rate of acquisition can be demonstrated by the augmenting influence of a rest period or an extraneous stimulus.

Inhibition by Punishment. If a response is followed by a noxious stimulus it will tend to be weakened in strength and less likely to occur on the next presentation of the situation. This type of procedure has been frequently employed in instrumental training, particularly in discrimination problems, but has not been extensively studied in classical conditioning situations. Brogden, Lipman and Culler (1938) have demonstrated that extinction of conditioned leg retraction in the dog is much more rapid if an electric shock on the chest is given when the dog reacts to the conditioned stimulus and none when it fails to respond.

Although it was part of his original statement of the law of effect, Thorndike (1932a, 1932b) has subsequently questioned the existence of inhibition by punishment. On the basis of extensive experiments with chickens and with human subjects he has concluded that an annoying after-effect has no weakening effect comparable to the strengthening which results from a satisfying after-effect. When responses appear to be weakened by punishment it is only indirectly through strengthening the alternative competing responses. This rather startling conclusion has become the subject of a vigorous controversy. W. Brown (1939) designed an experiment which demonstrated the positive effect of punishment on the choice behavior of rats in a single unit T-maze, and questioned the appropriateness of the experiments which had yielded negative results. Tilton (1939) reviewed the published evidence on the multiple-choice experiments with human subjects, and pointed out that it is not justifiable to measure the effect of "Right" and "Wrong" from a base-line of calculated chance repetition. When allowance was made for the natural tendency to repeat the responses given on the first trial, the results showed that punishment ("Wrong") had a definite weakening effect.

The action of punishment is a subject urgently needing additional research. It is not clear at present whether inhibition by punishment can be accounted for in terms of interference from responses established by the noxious stimulus or whether it represents a different and independent form of inhibition.

Inhibition by Discrimination. In the usual method of contrasts, in which one of a pair of stimuli is reinforced, and the other non-reinforced, the diminution of response to the non-reinforced stimulus is somewhat comparable to extinction, although the processes may differ in detail (Hilgard, R. K. Campbell, and W. N. Sears, 1938). The rate of decrease is complicated by some generalization from the positive stimulus. In some cases the contrast is made more explicit by rewarding response to the positive stimulus and punishing response to the negative stimulus (W. T. James, 1933). While the diminution of response is slower than in ordinary extinction spontaneous recovery also appears to be less, so that discrimination may persist for months close to its original value (Hilgard and Humphreys, 1938b).

Conditioned Inhibition. Multiple stimuli may be used in a discrimination situation, so that a combination of stimuli $S_1 + S_2$ will be rendered negative through non-reinforcement, while S_1 remains positive. In this case, S_2 is called the conditioned inhibitor, and other conditioned responses tend to be diminished in its presence (Pavlov, 1927; Lindberg, 1933). The problems of discrimination are discussed more fully in Chapter 8.

Inhibition of Delay. The period of reduced response during the interval between the beginning of the conditioned stimulus and the appearance of a trace or delayed conditioned response has many characteristics of extinction. There is spontaneous recovery, so that the delay is reduced after lapse of time (Switzer, 1934; Rodnick, 1937a); there may be dis-inhibition by an extraneous stimulus; and other concomitant conditioned responses may be reduced if they are elicited during the delay period (Rodnick, 1937b).

Forgetting. Forgetting differs from the other situations described in that the response is presumed not to be elicited during the interval over which retention is measured, and hence adaptation cannot be the primary interpretation. It is possible, however, that similar conditioned stimuli occur during the retention interval, evoking the conditioned response (or portions of it), so that adaptation cannot be completely ruled out. In view of the accumulating evidence favoring an interpretation of forgetting through retroactive inhibition (Britt, 1936; McGeoch, 1932), it appears that interference may be the more important factor. Competing responses are learned during the retention interval. The dependence of degree of forgetting upon the duration of the interval would thus be really a dependence upon the number and strength of interfering tendencies formed during that time. The resistance of laboratory conditioned responses to forgetting may be due to the highly artificial circumstances of stimulation in the laboratory, so that few competing responses are learned during the interval that the subject is outside that situation.

Disinhibition. When an extraneous stimulus reverses the process of extinction, so that temporarily the conditioned stimulus again evokes its conditioned response at approximately normal magnitude, the effect is known as *disinhibition*. This is the counterpart of external inhibition. In the one case the external stimulus reduces a conditioned response in the course of acquisition, in the other it increases the response in course of extinction. In both cases the effect is temporary, and after lapse of a short time the conditioned response appears at approximately its magnitude prior to the intrusion of the extra stimulus.

Two possibilities of interpretation of disinhibition are suggested by our preceding analysis. As a first possibility, the extra stimulus may have a facilitating influence, and serve to increase the response through summation. This interpretation appears to be applicable to such cases as the disinhibition of adapted reflexes (Humphrey, 1933). As a second possibility, the extra stimulus may interfere through external inhibition with a process which is itself interrupting the conditioning. The apparent paradox that an extraneous stimulus decreases a response in course of acquisition and increases one in course of diminution is in part resolved by considering the extra stimulus as a distraction, temporarily reducing the effect of whatever process is prominent at the time.

Summary

Inhibition is defined as the decrement in response which results from stimulation. Two varieties are distinguished, intrinsic inhibition or adaptation, resulting from the repetition of the response itself, and extrinsic inhibition or interference, resulting from the appearance of antagonistic responses. These processes include more than experimental extinction, and apply to decrements in reflexes and voluntary responses as well as to conditioned responses. Experimental extinction is defined as the diminution of the strength of conditioned responses by the repeated presentation of the conditioned stimulus without reinforcement. It refers to a procedure rather than to a process. Both adaptation and interference are necessary to explain extinction. Adaptation of conditioned responses is comparable to the habituation of reflexes or to the work decrement found in repeated voluntary acts. Evidence for interference comes most clearly from counter conditioning, in which old learning is antagonized by new. Cases in which experimental extinction does not occur with usual rapidity often

arise in situations in which the effects of adaptation and interference are counteracted by derived reinforcement, which
continues although the original unconditioned stimulus, reward, or punishment, is omitted.

There are many other procedures leading to response inhibition, such as discrimination, delay, forgetting. These show
functional similarities, in that adaptation and interference are
important in all. More experimental evidence is needed before
a precise formulation may be made of the relative significance
of adaptation and interference in inhibition.

Notes

Extinction an Active Process

That extinction is an active suppression of response, and not a mere
fading is shown in the long retention
of conditioned responses. A number
of earlier studies are summarized
by Razran (1933a, 1933b). Among
more recent reports may be mentioned the retention of conditioned
motor responses by sheep for 2
years (Liddell, W. T. James, and
O. D. Anderson, 1934); conditioned
eyelid reactions in dogs for 16
months (D. G. Marquis and Hilgard, 1936); conditioned eyelid reactions in man for 20 weeks (Hilgard and A. A. Campbell, 1936)
and for 19 months (Hilgard and
Humphreys, 1938b); conditioned
pupillary responses in man for 2
years (Baker, 1938); conditioned
flexion reflex in the dog for 2½ years
(Wendt, 1937); conditioned salivation in man for 16 weeks (Razran,
1939f); various responses in dogs for
6 months (Kellogg and Wolf, 1939).
The enduring character of condi-

tioned responses, and the temporary
character of extinction, have led
some writers to separate characterizations of 'excitatory' and 'inhibitory' response tendencies, the inhibitory tendencies appearing to be
more labile than the excitatory ones.
An assumption of this sort appears
to be necessary to account for spontaneous recovery following extinction.

It is a mistake, however, to over-
simplify the interpretation of the results of extinction. The facts of rapid extinction and rapid recovery do
not mean that the results of extinction are solely temporary. An illustration of the endurance of consequences of extinction is found in
Keller's results for instrumental responses, in which extinction after an
interval of 45 days showed the deleterious effects of earlier extinction,
in spite of spontaneous recovery
(Skinner, 1938, 94–96). As Skinner
points out, it cannot be concluded
that the animals have 'forgotten the
extinction while remembering the

conditioning.' Another illustration of the endurance of inhibition in a conditioning situation is found in the retention of discrimination. It has been shown that conditioned discriminations may be retained over a year and a half (Hilgard and Humphreys, 1938b). Although the tendency to respond to the positive stimulus survived the interval somewhat better than the tendency to inhibit response to the negative stimulus, the inhibitory tendencies were not lost over this period of time.

Intrinsic and Extrinsic Inhibition in Relation to Pavlov's Concepts

Intrinsic inhibition or adaptation corresponds approximately to the behavioral meaning of Pavlov's internal inhibition, while extrinsic inhibition or interference corresponds in part to his external inhibition. External inhibition, according to Pavlov, referred exclusively to a temporary disruption; extrinsic inhibition, as we are using it, may refer to relatively enduring disruptions due to new habit acquisitions, and hence may explain some of the phenomena which Pavlov would include under internal inhibition.

Adaptation

The habituation or negative adaptation of reflexes is treated incidentally in many studies of reflex action. The parallels with conditioning phenomena are best brought out by Humphrey (1930, 1933), who gives evidence from his own experiments with snails and turtles. The coordi-nation with internal inhibition is made by Oldfield (1937). The relation of reflex habituation to learning is discussed, with experimental evidence, by Dodge (1923), Halstead (1935), Halstead, Yacorzynski, and Fearing (1937), O. H. Mowrer (1934) all of whom are concerned with habituation to rotation. The earlier literature is reviewed in Fearing's history of reflex action (1930).

Examples of 'pure' adaptation are as rare as examples of 'pure' substitution. The wavelike character of curves of extinction (Arakelian, 1939) suggests complications beyond simple cumulative decrement. Skinner (1938) attributes the irregularities to emotional disturbances. Although N. E. Miller and Stevenson (1936) noted the presence of overt agitation during the extinction of an instrumental locomotor response in rats, they were unable to correlate the occurrence of agitation with cycles in the curve of extinction.

Adaptation is superficially similar to fatigue. However, if fatigue is defined as a decrement resulting from the exhaustion of energy supplies or the accumulation of end products of metabolism in the component parts of the responding mechanism, it is evident that adaptation is not fatigue. Disinhibition shows that under favorable circumstances the extinguished response can again be evoked, without waiting for metabolic restoration. Furthermore, a rate of stimulation which is rapid enough to produce adaptation may be too slow to cause fatigue.

When one conditioned response is extinguished, other conditioned responses likewise undergo extinction. This is known as *secondary extinction* (Ellson, 1938; Hill and Calvin, 1939; Youtz, 1939). Generalization of extinction has been studied extensively in so-called irradiation experiments (Anrep, 1923; Bass and Hull, 1934; Hovland, 1937a). These are discussed more fully in Chapter 8.

The generalization of inhibition appeared so prominently in Pavlov's experiments that he identified sleep and hypnosis with it. His theory has not been widely accepted because of lack of direct evidence. The conception has been discussed and extended by Anokhin (1932), Krasnogorsky (1923), Rojansky (1914), M. Levin (1934a, 1934b), S. L. Levin (1934).

Interference

The belief that elimination of a learned act depends on its replacement by a new act has had a long history. The recent setting of it in opposition to Pavlov's explanation of extinction has been shared by several writers, among them Guthrie (1935), Wendt (1936) and Culler (1938b).

The importance of time interval in the interaction of acts at a reflex level has been demonstrated in a variety of experiments on facilitation and inhibition, e.g., Bowditch and S. W. Warren (1890), Yerkes (1905), Wendt (1930), Eccles and Sherrington (1931), Hilgard (1933b), Misbach (1937). The facilitation and inhibition in these studies is of a reflex response, although in some of them the interacting response is

voluntary. Studies in which the modified response is verbal or voluntary include Hofbauer (1897), Allison (1932), Telford (1931), Telford and B. O. Anderson (1932), Telford and N. Thompson (1933).

Counter conditioning is a commonplace in instrumental discrimination situations in which the positive and negative stimuli are presented simultaneously and one response is punished, the other rewarded. The mechanism is exhibited most clearly in situations requiring a reversal of a discrimination (e.g., Bunch, 1939; Buytendijk, 1930; Fritz, 1930; Krechevsky, 1932b; Hull and Spence, 1938). The 'ambiguous conditioning' experiments in which counter conditioning is involved are reported by Kellogg (1939a), Kellogg and E. L. Walker (1938a, 1938b), Kellogg and Wolf (1939).

External inhibition, which provides some evidence for interference, is reported by Gorham (1937), Razran (1939g), Wenger (1936a), Yushchenko (1928). The lack of success reported by A. R. Miller (1934) is accounted for by Lindberg (1936) as a result of failure to fulfill the many conditions necessary for its satisfactory demonstration.

The Interpretation of Extinction

The most thorough review of the facts and theories of extinction is that of Razran (1939j). He summarizes a large number of the behavioral facts of extinction in order to criticize proposed theories, and offers a synthetic hypothesis. Among the chief theories summarized by

Razran are: internal inhibition (Pavlov, 1927); adaptation plus reverse conditioning (Beritov, 1927, 1932); change in attitude or affectivity (Guthrie, 1935; Winsor, 1930a, 1930b); competing behavior systems (Wendt, 1936); change in motivation (Finch and Culler, 1934; Culler, 1938b); muscular relaxation, supplementing specific interference (Wenger, 1937); asynchronization of nervous discharges (Razran, 1930). Razran's present views on the behavioral phenomena of extinction may be summarized in his own words: "(1) 'decrement by repetition' is the most universal factor of extinction, a factor which extinction shares in some way with habituation and adaptation; (2) reverse conditioning—restoration of the original response to the conditioned stimulus—is the general contributing factor of extinction, which distinguishes extinction from habituation and from adaptation; (3) redirected conditioning—conditioning to some action arising in the course of extinction—is a contributing factor that often but not always modifies the extinctive process; (4) changes in affectivity, attitude, muscular tension, motivation, and the like are only modifying organismic states and are not constitutive of the extinctive process *per se.*" (Razran, 1939j, 270–271.)

Apart from matters of emphasis, there is considerable harmony between the views expressed in the text and those of Razran as stated above. The acceptance of both adaptation and interference is a fundamental agreement.

An ingenious explanation of spontaneous recovery consonant with an interference theory has been proposed by N. E. Miller and Miles (1936), and N. E. Miller and Stevenson (1936). The explanation depends on the more rapid forgetting of the less well learned interfering act in competition with the forgetting of the previously acquired conditioned response. The theory demands a rapid forgetting of both conditioned responses, however, which is not in harmony with the relative permanence of conditioning.

While it is true that spontaneous recovery, rate of elicitation, and drug effects tend to differentiate the functional processes of adaptation and interference there is a subordinate aspect of the interference theory which is compatible with certain of these phenomena. One aspect of interference, stressed by Winsor (1930b), and espoused in part by Guthrie (1935), attributes the interference to altered attitudes and emotional states present temporarily as a result of omitted reinforcement. Even relatively short lapses of time may restore equanimity or alter expectancies, and account for the rapid 'forgetting' of the interfering activity required by spontaneous recovery. Attitudes and sets may also be temporarily disrupted by distracting stimuli, so that disinhibition is not excluded. Frustration may be exaggerated in the massed non-reinforcement situation. Hence the very arguments which most strongly support adaptation may also be used to favor a form of interference theory based on expectancy rather than upon the gradual conditioning of incompatible responses. The confident interpretation of any one illustration of extinction can be made only in the light of a detailed analysis of the experimental situation and the particular concomitant activity involved. Theories of attitude and set relative to extinction have not been very thoroughly worked out; they obviously fit in the category of counter conditioning based on derived reinforcement. Symbolic activity as it enters conditioning is treated more fully later (Chapters 10 and 11).

By defining extinction in terms of rate of elicitation and reduction of reflex reserve, Skinner (1938) is able to differentiate between a temporary interruption in responding (an 'emotion' by definition in his system) and an unlearning which reduces the number of responses in the reserve. He has determined, for example, that following a slap upon pressing the lever the rat's responses show 'emotion' rather than extinction by interference or counter conditioning (Skinner, 1938, p. 155). Within his system, therefore, some of the things attributed by us to extinction by interference will not be included within extinction. We agree that any instance of extinction requires careful analysis in order to determine what specific processes are involved, but we are unable to apply Skinner's differentiations to the range of other experiments in which extinction is found. The analysis within his own situation is specific to circumstances of experimentation. Thus, non-reinforcement of a response does not

lead to a standard amount of decrement, but the effect of non-reinforcement varies with arrangements such as those called periodic reconditioning and conditioning at a fixed ratio (Chapter 6, Figures 11–13).

The evidence for spontaneous recovery on which some of the argument in the text rests may be found: for reflexes, in Humphrey (1933), Prosser and Hunter (1936); for conditioning, in Ellson (1939a), Hilgard and D. G. Marquis (1935), Hilgard and A. A. Campbell (1936), Hovland (1937c), Porter (1938d), Razran (1939h), Rodnick (1937a), Switzer (1933). Disinhibition is closely related. Experimental evidence may be found in Hovland (1937c), Hunter (1935c, 1938), Razran (1939g), Rexroad (1937), Reynolds (1936, 1939), Switzer (1933), Wenger (1936a). The failure reported by Skinner (1936) is in part a function of his particular theoretical interpretations.

Evidence on the rate of elicitation in relation to speed of extinction is not conclusive. More rapid adaptation with massing has been shown: for reflexes, by Humphrey (1933), Prosser and Hunter (1936), Hunter (1937); for conditioning, by Calvin (1939), Hilgard and D. G. Marquis (1935), Mikhailoff (1922). This is also true for voluntary responses (Robinson, 1934). Guthrie (1934) has shown that Pavlov's evidence does not support his contention that massing produces more rapid extinction, if reduction is expressed per non-reinforced trial. Porter found no differences between massed and distributed extinction, either in conditioned eyelid reactions with man (1939), or in the extinction of maze-running by rats (1938c).

Specimen studies of the effects of drugs on conditioning and extinction are: alcohol by Andreyev (1934b), Gantt (1935), N. E. Miller and Miles (1936); caffeine by N. E. Miller and Miles (1935), Skinner and Heron (1937), Switzer (1935a, 1935b), Wentink (1938), Wolff and Gantt (1935); benzedrine by C. W. Brown and Searle (1938), Searle and C. W. Brown (1938), Skinner and Heron (1937), Wentink (1938); bromides and other sedatives by Bam (1937), S. L. Levin (1935), Maiorov (1933), Petrova (1934–1937), Wolff and Gantt (1935).

The instances of failure of extinction (or of great difficulty in extinction) are found in: Baker (1938), Baschmurin and Mulberg (1928), Harlow (1937), Harlow and Stagner (1933), Hilgard and D. G. Marquis (1936), Hudgins (1933), Kriazhev (1929a), Menzies (1937), Osipova (1927), Razran (1935).

Chapter 6

STRENGTH OF CONDITIONING

EXPERIMENTATION has reached the stage in which it adds little to report that a given organism can form conditioned responses, or that a given response can be conditioned. The circumstances which modify the course of conditioning, extinction, discrimination, become increasingly important after the demonstration has been made that such modifications occur. If these circumstances could be stated with precision, we would have experimental 'laws' of conditioning. That is, if we could write a formula for the change in rate of conditioning with increasing time interval between conditioned and unconditioned stimuli, or with changes in intensity of stimuli, then we should have laws comparable, say, to Boyle's law in physics which relates the volume of a gas to changes in pressure. There are at present no precise quantitative laws of conditioning. In this chapter the attempt is made to collect specimens of the relationships between independently defined variables which may eventually lead to laws. The serviceability of the conditioning experiment to learning theory depends upon the consistency with which such relationships may be demonstrated experimentally.

Strength of Response and Strength of Conditioning

In order to make a quantitative demonstration of the effect of independent variables upon the strength of conditioning, it is necessary to have measures of this strength. In practice, the determination of the degree of conditioning depends first upon satisfactory measures of strength of response (such as drops of saliva, or extent of movement) and second upon an inference from the measured vigor of response to the strength of conditioning. Not all measures of response are suitable as indexes of strength of conditioning. Thus, for ordinary reflexes, reduction of latency accompanies increased vigor of movement, so that change in latency may serve as one measure of strength of response. In the case of delayed conditioned responses, however, the better established delayed response has a longer latency than the less well-established response. In this case the inference from a given latency change to strength of delayed conditioning must be made opposite to the inference in the case of a simple reflex. In situations in which there is a high correlation between responses during conditioning and the responses during extinction, the latter might be used as a measure of the former (cf. Table 4, Chapter 5). When this correlation is reduced as it is in some experimental situations, resistance to extinction is not a valid measure of strength of conditioning. The same sorts of responses are measured in all these cases, but the inferences to be made from the obtained measurements depend upon an understanding of the total situation. In many cases the performances provide a direct index to the strength of conditioning, and strength of response may be used as a criterion of strength of conditioning, but the exceptions must not be ignored.

Among the measures of strength of response used in inferring strength of conditioning may be mentioned magnitude, latency, percentage frequency, total number of responses, and rate of responding. Magnitude and latency are descriptive of single responses. The other measures are all relative to the opportunities given to respond, i.e., length of time or number of presentations of the conditioned stimulus. Magnitude may be measured in various ways: drops of saliva, millimeters of pupillary constriction, total oscillation of inspiration and expiration, tension exerted by a withdrawal movement, duration of response, and so on. Latency is measured from the onset of the conditioned stimulus to the beginning of response. Percentage frequency, total number, and rate, are obtained by counting the responses which meet the specifications for an acceptable conditioned response in the given experimental situation. Percentage frequency describes the number of responses yielded in relation to the number of times the conditioned stimulus was presented. It is not uncommon during extinction to continue presentations until no more responses occur. It may then be inferred that the total number of responses during extinction bears a relationship to the strength of conditioning before extinction. In the arrangement of Skinner's (1938) experiment, the number of responses in a given time, i.e., rate of responding, is a useful measure, because the animal is free to respond again as soon as the first response is over. Skinner distinguishes between momentary rate and total amount of potential activity, the latter constituting the "reflex reserve."

If all of these measures are possible, which of them really measures strength of conditioning? Such a question is unanswerable in general terms. Practically, any reliable measure may prove to have significance in specific comparisons, and only the use of proper controls and the study of intercorrelations between the measures within a given experiment can determine which measures are most serviceable. Exact values of reported reliability coefficients have little meaning, because such coefficients are relative to the method used in fractionating the data, to the heterogeneity of the population, and so on. With a given population and a given method of computing the reliabilities, relative values are of interest. In reports of split-half reliabilities of conditioned flexion responses in dogs, conditioned eyelid reactions in man, and conditioned knee jerks in man, percentage frequency of response and amplitude have been found to have appreciably higher reliabilities than latency (Kellogg and E. L. Walker, 1938b; A. A. Campbell and Hilgard, 1936; A. A. Campbell, 1938).

TABLE 5

INTERCORRELATIONS OF VARIOUS MEASURES OF CONDITIONED RESPONSES

Values for conditioned flexion responses are means of rank order correlations from several sessions with 3 dogs (Kellogg and E. L. Walker, 1938b). Values for conditioned eyelid reactions in man are product-moment coefficients based on 100 trials with 63 college students (A. A. Campbell and Hilgard, 1936). The coefficients for conditioned knee jerks are product-moment correlations based on 100 trials with 49 college students (A. A. Campbell, 1938).

	Correlation between		
	FREQUENCY AND AMPLITUDE	LATENCY AND AMPLITUDE	LATENCY AND FREQUENCY
Flexion (dog)	+.94	−.22	−.18
Eyelid (man)	+.63	−.15	−.54
Knee jerk (man)	+.63	−.27	−.27

In Table 5 are given raw correlations between percentage frequency, amplitude, and latency of conditioned responses in the three studies cited. The correlation between frequency and amplitude is sufficiently high that it may be assumed that they measure something in common. The correlation between either of these measures and latency is too low to be of significance in prediction.

Once measures from which to infer the strength of conditioning have been selected, it is possible to study the relationship of strength of conditioning to various changes in the experimental situation. From among the welter of relationships which have been studied, three classes of experimental variables have been selected for discussion. These are (1) capacity of the organism, (2) intensity and (3) repetition. A fourth important variable, time interval between stimuli, is discussed in the following chapter.

Capacity of the Organism

The conditioning experiment assumes an organism adapted to the experimental situation, having the necessary sensori-motor equipment and associative capacities to yield conditioned responses in the presence of the chosen stimuli. It may be inquired to what extent these capacities are dependent upon membership in a species, on the one hand, and upon the stage of individual development on the other.

Phylogeny. Within the phylogenetic series, or within mammalia alone, comparisons are extremely difficult to make because of the differences in sensitivity to particular stimuli, differences in response equipment, and variations in motivation. It has been shown, for example, that leg flexion responses cannot be conditioned in the opossum, presumably because such responses are not part of its natural defensive equipment (W. T. James, 1937). Limited comparisons may be made between species whose nervous systems, sensory equipment, and effector mechanisms permit experimentation under circumstances which are highly similar.

Such comparisons have been made by Liddell, W. T. James and O. D. Anderson (1934) on the pig, dog, sheep, goat, and rabbit. Even with animals as similar as these, differences in experimental arrangements are necessary. The sheep, for example, is not a satisfactory subject unless another sheep is tethered in the room with it. In general, it was found in experiments with a tone followed by shock to the foreleg that the pig conditioned most rapidly, requiring only a single reinforced trial, while the dog required 3 to 5 trials, the sheep and goat 7 to 9, and the rabbit 14 to 24. Comparison of conditioned eyelid responses in dog, monkey, and man has been made under similar circumstances of experimentation (Figure 2, p. 32), and the white rat has been added to this series by Hughes and Schlosberg (1938). While many common principles of conditioning are applicable to the four species, the differences do not correspond in any direct manner to their evolutionary levels.

Ontogeny. The earliest reported conditioning is that of the fetus prior to birth. Conditioning has been reported for the chick before emerging from the shell (Gos, 1935). The human fetus has been conditioned *in utero* during the last two gestation months (Spelt, 1938). Conditioned feeding responses have been established by the fifth post-natal day (D. P. Marquis, 1931). Children between the ages of 44 and 117 days have acquired feeding responses in 16 to 72 trials, with no consistent change in the rate of acquisition with age (Kantrow, 1937). Age does appear to make some difference in the ease with which discriminatory reactions may be conditioned (Figurin and Denisova, 1929), but it is not clear whether this is a question of the maturation of sensory functions or of the capacity to learn the motor differentiation. Mateer (1918) found increasing success in conditioning food responses as ages increased from within the first two years to within years 4 and 5. Osipova (1926a), who conditioned finger withdrawal to shock, found conditioning progressively more difficult as ages increased from 7 to 19. The possibility is great that age differences will be found specific to the responses which are conditioned. Changes which take place as language develops will probably affect some varieties of conditioning more than others. With more highly developed symbolic capacities, transfer should be greater and voluntary factors may become more prominent. These are matters urgently requiring more experimentation, although the difficulties in the way of crucial experiments are very great.

Individual Differences. The ease with which a particular organism forms conditioned responses is not a matter solely of membership in a species (phylogenetic differences) or of age (ontogenetic differences). With comparable stimuli, some organisms of the same species and of the same age form responses more readily than others. So striking are these differences in dogs that Pavlov was led to a theory of types of nervous system. The evidence with respect to individual differences is discussed in Chapter 12.

In addition to the more enduring differences, there are a number of temporary states, such as hunger and satiation, health, hormone and drug influences, which affect conditioning as well as other performances of the organism.

Intensity

Intensity of Conditioned Stimulus. The relationship between the intensity of the conditioned stimulus and the strength of conditioning is complicated by the effect upon response strength. Moderate increases in intensity of conditioned stimuli tend to increase the magnitude of conditioned responses. This effect is similar to the dependence of reflex amplitude or of voluntary reaction time upon stimulus intensity. It has been shown for example by Kupalov and Gantt (1927) that the magnitude of the conditioned salivary response in dogs varied with the intensity of the conditioned sound stimulus in the roughly logarithmic relationship characteristic of other responses. The method of constant stimuli used by Newhall and R. R. Sears (1933) in determining visual thresholds by a conditioning procedure showed that response frequency was greater to brighter intensities of lights near the threshold. In these studies, the different intensities of conditioned stimuli were tested after the conditioned response had been well established. They demonstrate that response strength is a function of stimulus intensity, but say nothing about the effect on rate or degree of conditioning.

In order to determine the influence of stimulus intensity on strength of conditioning it is necessary to compare groups of subjects which have been trained with different intensities of conditioned stimulus. This comparison cannot be made simply between the final magnitude of the conditioned responses, but must be made on tests in which the intensity of the conditioned stimulus is equated for the different groups. Only in this way can the effect on response strength be controlled to demonstrate the effect on strength of conditioning. Data fulfilling these conditions are found in three studies by Hovland on generalization (1937b, 1937c, 1937d). He established conditioned galvanic skin responses in two matched groups of human subjects, one with a weak conditioned stimulus (tone, vibrator), the other with a strong conditioned stimulus. After training, both groups were tested with both the weak and the strong stimuli (and in one study also with intermediate intensities). Computation of the original data presented by Hovland demonstrates that there was no reliable superiority of one group over the other. At the present time there is no evidence that strength of conditioning, distinguished from response strength, is a function of the intensity of the conditioned stimulus.

There are undoubtedly limiting intensities for the conditioned stimulus, so that too strong a stimulus may actually reduce the amount of conditioning through interference by the original responses which it evokes. Baker (1938), working with barely perceptible auditory stimuli, found conditioning to be much easier near the threshold than slightly above it. (The sounds described by him as subliminal were actually at or above the threshold, as measured by the more usual psychophysical methods.) Why these barely audible sounds should have been more effective than louder ones is at present obscure, but Baker's results show that the relation of intensity to ease of conditioning is not a simple one. If his results are substantiated, a 'too strong' stimulus may be a stimulus far weaker than usually suggested.

Strength of Reinforcement. The relationship between the strength of conditioning and the strength of reinforcement must be stated differently for each of the varieties of reinforcement.

In conditioning with homogeneous reinforcement, the magnitude of the unconditioned response should be a direct determiner of the strength of the conditioned response which develops. The amplitude of conditioned eyelid reactions of a group of college students correlated + .55 ± .06 with the amplitude of unconditioned reflexes (A. A. Campbell and Hilgard, 1936). Between the amplitude of conditioned responses and knee jerks during conditioning, Schlosberg (1932) found a correlation of + .37 ± .13 and A. A. Campbell (1938) a correlation of + .26 ± .09. These correlations, while barely significant, show that the magnitude of the unconditioned response is one of the factors responsible for the course of conditioning. Anything which affects the unconditioned response will presumably have some effect on conditioning. The most obvious of these factors is the intensity of the unconditioned stimulus. Others, such as motivation and set, through altering sensitivity to the unconditioned stimulus, will affect the size of response. The effective intensity of the stimulus is obviously dependent on the state of the organism.

In conditioning with heterogeneous reinforcement, the effect of any one reward may be expected to bear a relationship to the magnitude of the relevant responses to that reward. Thus a food for which there is appetite should constitute a better reinforcing agent than a food which is disliked or merely tolerated. The strength of reinforcement is related to drive, and to the quantity and quality of reward. These factors are measured in such a variety of ways that any general statement concerning strength of reinforcement is at present impossible. Probably the strength can best be described in some defining situation, other than the conditioning one, so that it may enter the conditioning situation as an independent variable. Too intense a drive may weaken reinforcement, possibly through the introduction of irrelevant and disrupting emotional states.

To measure the intensity of an expectation in a situation involving derived reinforcement is even more difficult. The effectiveness of a secondary reward presumably depends upon two factors: the degree to which it has come to signify reward, and the effectiveness of the original reward. In the avoidance situation the strength of the expectancy may be supposed to depend upon analogous factors: first, the degree to which the conditioned stimulus has come through repetition to signify the impending painful stimulus, and second, the intensity of the painful stimulus itself.

Intensity Relations of Conditioned and Unconditioned Stimuli. It is sometimes assumed that unconditioned responses must be facilitated by the conditioned stimulus in order for conditioning to occur. Some evidence points in this direction, for example, the correlation of $+.60 \pm .10$ which Schlosberg (1932) found between the success of conditioning and the amount by which the conditioned stimulus facilitated the knee jerk to the unconditioned stimulus. This is by no means a necessary relationship for conditioning, however, since it has been shown at the favorable intervals for eyelid conditioning that the conditioned stimulus definitely depresses the responses to the unconditioned stimulus (Hilgard, 1933b).

Razran (1935) has suggested a principle of favorable ratios of excitation. He supposes that there may be a most favorable relationship between the effective intensities of conditioned and unconditioned stimuli for conditioning to proceed. While many observations pointing toward this interpretation are available, the systematic experiments which would be necessary to formulate with precision the intensity interrelationships have not been reported.

Repetition

Practice Curves. Although there is a current tendency among psychologists to subordinate the rôle of repetition or exercise in the formation of habits, all agree that repetition permits other factors to reveal their effects.

Numerous practice curves of conditioning show similar form because of the uniformities that exist among most conditioning experiments. Since conditioned responses are usually not yielded until several reinforcements have occurred, the first portion of the curve is flat, rising from the base as conditioned responses appear. A rising inflection of this kind is known among psychologists as a positively accelerated curve, although it may be described simply as an accelerated one, since there are increasing gains with practice. The phase of increasing gains tapers off as a maximum is approached. This phase, commonly known as negative acceleration, may be described as decelerated, since gains decrease as practice proceeds. Most conditioning curves show double inflection, being at first accelerated, later decelerated. Within the family of curves so described, great differences occur, from the conditioning which is established in a single trial to failure to condition in hundreds of trials. Specimen curves may be found in Figure 5 (p. 59), Figure 7 (p. 112), Figures 10–13 (pp. 149–152), Figure 21 (p. 181), Figure 24 (p. 186), Figure 35 (p. 264). These illustrate the uses made of performance curves in the analysis of the influence of different variables.

Too many consecutive reinforcements may result in a decrease in the magnitude or frequency of conditioned responses. This decremental factor, which Hovland (1936) has termed 'inhibition of reinforcement,' is probably an illustration of adaptation (see p. 124f.), since it is produced by massing of trials, or continuing reinforcement too long, and shows spontaneous recovery during short intervals of time.

The learning curve for instrumental learning depends in part on the degree of environmental simplification achieved by the experimenter. Skinner (1938) finds that a single reinforcement commonly initiates a series of lever-pressings in his rats at their optimal rate. That is, momentary response strength is complete in one trial. Further reinforcements build up a 'reflex reserve,' best described in conventional conditioning terminology as resistance to extinction. S. B. Williams (1938) has demonstrated that such resistance is proportional to the number of reinforcements. Comparisons are difficult when both mechanical arrangements and units of measurement are so unlike that different operations are involved in determining changes in strength of response. Youtz (1938a) has plotted data obtained by Skinner's method in somewhat more conventional units. He finds that the time required for successive 10 responses in the lever situation gradually decreases, in a curve roughly resembling that of Thorndike's time-reduction curves for trial-and-error learning. The curve cannot be carried beyond the first 30 or 40 responses in this manner, because the ingestion of food changes the drive, and the 'learning curve' becomes more nearly a 'satiation curve.'

Under some circumstances, the performance curve for avoidance learning is comparable to those of classical conditioning and of rewarded learning (cf. Figure 5, p. 59). When voluntary factors enter, responses are often at a maximum early, and then tend to drop out (Yacorzynski and Guthrie, 1937; D. G. Marquis and Porter, 1939).

Curves of Extinction. Curves of extinction with repeated non-reinforcement tend to be decelerated, response reduction being more rapid at first, then gradually tapering off as a baseline is approached. Some curves show an initial rise

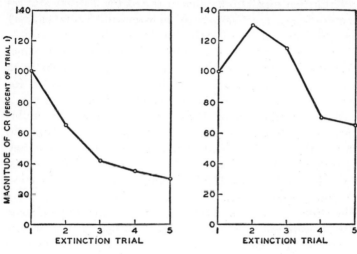

SPECIMEN CURVES OF EXTINCTION

FIGURE 8

Extinction of galvanic skin response immediately following 24 distributed reinforcements. Mean, 20 adult human subjects. (Hovland, 1936.)

FIGURE 9

Extinction of galvanic skin response immediately following 24 massed reinforcements. Mean 20 subjects. Note the initial rise. If reinforcements were fewer or if time elapsed before extinction began, this initial rise was lacking. (Hovland, 1936.)

before the decrease. The sudden change in stimulating conditions occasioned by the omitted reinforcement may be considered to produce a 'disinhibition' following 'inhibition-of-reinforcement.' Adopting this conjecture, Hovland (1936) set up an experiment in such a way that both a decelerated curve and one with the initial rise should have been obtained.

He predicted that the more usual curve would be found with spaced practice, the rising type with massed practice. His results, as shown in Figures 8 and 9, agreed with his predictions.

Extinction may also be demonstrated for instrumental responses which are followed by non-reward. Youtz (1938a) has presented curves of extinction for the Skinner situation. If responses per tenth of extinction time are plotted, extinction time being measured to a criterion of no responses in 20 minutes, a decelerated curve is obtained, similar to that for extinction following conventional conditioning.

The Distribution of Practice. The decremental influences within a series of massed trials disappear with time, so that at the beginning of practice after an interval there may appear concealed or latent conditioning (H. E. Jones, 1930). Spaced practice favors conditioning over massed practice. Pavlov took great care not to crowd practice, particularly when difficult conditioned responses were being formed. Some stimuli were presented never more than once a day. Schlosberg (1934) found it more effective to use 25 rather than 200 paired stimulations per day in conditioning breathing reactions in rats based on a shock to the tail. Humphreys (1940a) has shown that in eyelid conditioning in man the end result after two one-hour periods of conditioning on two days is very nearly the same whether there are 25 trials per period or 50 trials per period. Calvin (1939) has shown conditioned eyelid responses in man, based on shock, to be formed much more readily when trials are spaced at 20 seconds than at shorter intervals. His results are presented graphically in Figure 10.

The effect of spacing on the rate of extinction has been discussed in Chapter 5 (p. 133).

Partial Reinforcement. Not to be confused with the distribution of practice, in which inter-trial intervals are lengthened, is the distribution of reinforcements randomly over a fraction of the trials, so that reinforcement is frequently omitted during the course of training.

In a preliminary experiment, Pavlov (1927, 384–386)

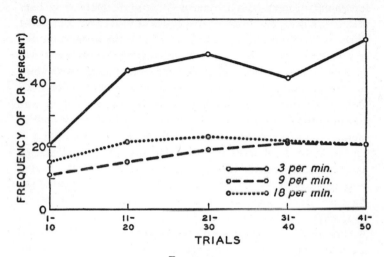

FIGURE 10

EFFECT OF DISTRIBUTION OF PRACTICE ON THE ACQUISITION OF CONDITIONED EYELID RESPONSE

The points represent mean values for conditioned responses from three groups of human subjects, each subject receiving 50 reinforcements at the stated rate. Conditioned stimulus, light; unconditioned stimulus, shock. The interval between the light and shock was constant at 400 msec. for all subjects. After Calvin (1939).

found that conditioned responses developed rapidly if reinforcement was given only every second or third trial, but failed to develop if reinforcement was given only every fourth trial. Similar experiments have been carried out more fully by Brogden (1939a), Cole (1939), Humphreys (1939a, 1939c), and Skinner (1938). Brogden found that with dogs the flexion response to shock was conditioned as readily with reinforcement 40 percent of the time as with reinforcement 100 percent of the time, and there was only slight loss with but 20 percent reinforcement. With food reinforcement, there was a slight decrease in conditioning as the proportion of reinforcement decreased, but even with reinforcement only one-fifth of the time, conditioned responses appeared on four-fifths of the trials. Humphreys found essentially the same thing for conditioned eyelid responses and conditioned galvanic responses in man, conditioning being as satisfactory with reinforcement half of the time as with reinforcement every trial. One of his rather striking findings was that extinction was slower in the group which had received only half the reinforcements. This was true both for conditioned eyelid responses and for conditioned galvanic responses. He has offered evidence for expectancy as a partial interpretation of these results, through a confirmatory experiment (1939b). He has since repeated the experimental findings with the lever-pressing response of rats (1940c).

Skinner has reported a number of results for instrumental learning under an experimental arrangement which he describes as 'periodic reconditioning' (Skinner, 1938, 116–166). In this arrangement, pressing does not deliver the pellet of food regularly, so that most of the trials are not reinforced. However, a single reinforcement occurs periodically, for example, every 3 minutes, or every 9 minutes according to the plan of the experimenter. Under these circumstances, the rate of responding tends to become uniform provided the hunger drive remains relatively constant (Figures 11 and 12). Because of the regularity of responses, it is possible to express the rate of responding as an *extinction ratio,* that is, as the number of non-reinforced responses which occur per reinforcement under periodic reconditioning. For example, under standard conditions of drive, this ratio is approximately 18:1; that

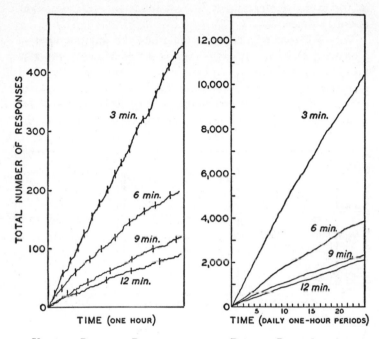

UNIFORM RATES OF RESPONDING UNDER PERIODIC REINFORCEMENT

FIGURE 11

Responses within one session of periodic reinforcement:

The curves are reproduced from the kymographic records of individual rats under each of the four conditions. Reinforcement was given every 3 minutes, 6 minutes, 9 minutes, and 12 minutes, respectively. Note that the more frequent the reinforcement, the more rapid the rate of responding, although each rate is relatively uniform. (Skinner, 1938, p. 121f.)

FIGURE 12

Responses within repeated sessions of periodic reinforcement:

Responses of the same rats whose records are given in Figure 11 are here accumulated for successive daily sessions. The uniformity of rate persists throughout. (Skinner, 1938, p. 120.)

is, for every reinforcement the rat tends to press the lever about 18 times.

Very different results are found when the final member of a counted series of pressings is reinforced. After appropriate preliminary training it is possible to secure a high level of response by reinforcing only the final one of every 192 responses. Between reinforcements, a very rapid series of responses occur (Figure 13). Under these circumstances, the

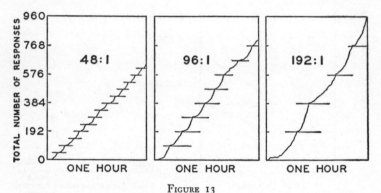

FIGURE 13

ACCELERATED RATE OF RESPONDING BETWEEN REINFORCEMENTS WITH REINFORCEMENT AT A FIXED RATIO

Responses from individual rats reinforced every 48, 96, and 192 responses, as indicated by the horizontal lines. Under these circumstances very high rates of responding develop, the highest rate being found with the lowest frequency of reinforcement. (Skinner, 1938, p. 288.)

less frequent the reinforcement, the higher the rate of responding. Whether classical conditioning could be established by reinforcing only once in 192 trials is extremely doubtful. The difficulty in moving directly from classical conditioning to instrumental conditioning is indicated by some of these striking differences.

Following periodic reinforcement, the decline in rate of response during extinction is much slower than following

ordinary every-trial reinforcement (
This is in full agreement with the r
partial reinforcement. It is impossibl
tative changes, however, because of th
of measurements involved.

Repeated Conditioning and Ex
tinction, reconditioning is very rapid
spontaneous recovery has not interv
perimental conditions will, of course,
relationships, so that ratios of relearning time to original learning must be specific, rather than general. As specimen findings, however, the results of two experiments with dogs may
be cited. Finch and Culler (1935) report for flexion responses
a reconditioning after extinction in from 20 to 25 percent of
the original trials, while Hilgard and D. G. Marquis (1935)
report for eyelid responses relearning in from 20 to 40 percent of the original trials.

Among the factors determining the rate of reconditioning
following extinction are, first, the extent to which extinction
was carried, and, second, the number of prior reconditionings
after extinction. These factors are described in experiments
by Brogden, Lipman, and Culler (1938). As an illustration
of the effects of repeated extinction and reconditioning, one
dog is reported to have required after a first extinction, 18
reinforcements; after a second, 11; after a third, 5; after a
fifth, 1; after a seventh, 2. Because the third and fifth extinctions had included 450 extra non-reinforced trials, the seventh
850 added trials and yet reconditioning was prompt, extinction does not appear to have gone 'below zero' in the repeated extinction-reinforcement series.

Successive extinctions, like successive reconditionings, also
tend to become more rapid until a single non-reinforcement
may suffice (Pavlov, 1927, 54f.). Ellson (1940) carried out
10 successive extinctions, separated by 25 minutes, of the

ssing response in the Skinner apparatus. The average
ber of responses for 12 rats in the successive sessions was
, 16, 6, 6, 5, 3, 2, 1, 1, 0. Shorter intervals between extinctions led to a more rapid disappearance of the response.

Summary

A distinction was drawn between strength of response and
strength of conditioning. Strength of response refers to the
vigor of performance as measured by such criteria as magnitude or frequency. Strength of conditioning is inferred from
strength of response, but is not to be identified with it. This
is obvious, for example, when a conditioned response has been
reduced to zero amplitude. Strength of conditioning may perhaps go 'below zero,' even though strength of response cannot. This would be inferred from tests of spontaneous recovery. A facilitated response may be increased in magnitude
without thereby increasing strength of conditioning. Measurement is always of strength of response; strength of conditioning is always an inference from measured responses.

By appropriate control experiments it is possible to explore
systematically the influence of various experimental variables
on strength of conditioning. The influence of membership in
a species, of age, of intensity of stimuli, of repetition of reinforcement and non-reinforcement, were examined in this chapter. Many consistencies are discovered, but the data are not
yet sufficiently ordered for quantitative laws of conditioning
to be stated.

Notes

Measures of the Strength of Conditioned Responses

For statements of reliability of various measures of both conditioned and unconditioned responses, cf. A. A. Campbell (1938), Humphreys (1940b), Kellogg and E. L. Walker (1938b). Reliabilities can,
of course, be inferred from other

studies in which satisfactory statistical differences have been secured, but they have seldom been reported in the form of reliability coefficients. A correlation of $+.66$ (P.E. $\pm.09$) between the amplitude of conditioned knee jerks within training trials and within test trials (Schlosberg, 1932) is a sort of reliability coefficient.

If individual measures are reliable, low correlations between them may mean that they are measuring different processes. Thus Razran (1935) believes that incidence (i.e., percentage frequency) and magnitude of conditioned responses are variables differently related to physiological and psychological (i.e., attitudinal) factors, incidence being more subject to attitudinal control than magnitude. For intercorrelations of various measures in addition to those described in the text, cf. Razran (1935, p. 64).

Skinner (1938, pp. 15, 27) distinguishes between reflex strength and magnitude of response. Magnitude is a function of intensity of stimulation, so that a strong reflex may exhibit a response of low magnitude if the stimulus is of low intensity. He uses magnitude, therefore, as one measure of what we have called strength of response. Reflex strength, on the other hand, is a momentary function of a certain amount of available activity which Skinner speaks of as the 'reflex reserve.' What we have called strength of conditioning corresponds loosely both to his reflex strength and to his reflex reserve, but the concepts cannot be coordinated strictly. Skinner's concept of the reserve as

a measure of strength of conditioning has been adversely criticized by Ellson (1939b).

Capacity of the Organism

For further details on phylogenetic comparisons, see Razran (1933a); for ontogenetic comparisons, Razran (1933b). A highly speculative theory may be found in Razran (1935). Wenger (1936b) found some difficulty in conditioning very young infants. His results and those of Kantrow (1937) are commented upon by Irwin (1939).

No attempt has been made in the text to treat the details of motivation and drive, and other influences on the state of the nervous system which affect strength of response. Some pertinent references are given here.

Motivation has been thoroughly reviewed by Young (1936). For discussion of hunger and activity, in relation to conditioning, see Babskij and Eidinova (1933), Elliott and Treat (1935), Finch (1936, 1938a), Sackett (1939), Skinner (1938), Zener and McCurdy (1939).

The effect of diet upon conditioned responses has been studied by Arkhangelsky (1929), Crisler (1936), Frolov (1925b), Frolov and Charitonov (1931), Kleitman (1927), Machtinger (1933), Vorobyov (1932), Wolowick (1930), Yushchenko (1927). The relation of conditioning to disease has been discussed by Andreyev (1935), Frolov and Charitonov (1931), Krasnogorski (1931), and Kriazhev (1929b).

Endocrine influences have been

extensively studied, the thyroid by Asimov (1928), Crisler, Booher, Van Liere, and J. C. Hall (1933), Kleitman and Titelbaum (1936), Liddell (1926b), Liddell and Bayne (1927), Liddell and Simpson (1926), Pribytkova (1936), Shastin (1930a, 1930b), Zavadovsky et al. (1928–1932); the parathyroid by Andreyev and Pugsley (1934) and Chechulin (1929); the hypophysis by Kriazhev (1933); the adrenal by Liddell, O. D. Anderson, Kotyuka, and Hartmann (1935) and Yurnan (1929); the gonads by Arkhangelsky (1931a, 1931b, 1935), A. M. Pavlova (1937), Petrova (1936, 1937), Vanderplank (1938).

Conditioned reflexes in relation to sleep have been studied by Kleitman (1930), Mishchenko (1935b, 1936a), and Rojansky (1914); while the effects of hypnosis have been investigated by Fisher (1932), Erickson (1938a, 1938b), S. L. Levin (1934), Lundholm (1928, 1932), Mishchenko (1932, 1935a, 1935b), Nevsky and S. L. Levin (1932), and Scott (1930).

X-ray radiation of the brain has been studied with conditioning techniques by Lyman, Kupalov, and Scholz (1933), and Nemenow (1934). Increased sensitivity of dogs to auditory stimuli following radiation of the head was found by Girden (1935), and Girden and Culler (1933, 1934). Brogden and Culler (1937) showed that the effect was accomplished by a pituitary influence upon blood sugar and a consequent change in the density of the endolymph of the inner ear.

Persisting individual differences

and theories of types are discussed in Chapter 12.

Intensity

Other evidence on effect of intensity may be found in Gantt (1938a), Kupalov, Lyman and Lukov (1931), Mishchenko (1936b), Zevald (1933).

In comparing the relative importance of intensity and time order, Stephens (1934a) found time order to be the more important variable. This need not deny some rôle to intensity, however.

The applicability of a concept of dominance has been proposed by Razran (1930) and Rexroad (1933). A response, in order to be conditioned, must be dominant over other responses. This is not to be confused with the physiological concept of dominance proposed by Ukhtomsky (1926, 1938) and endorsed in relation to conditioning by Bekhterev (1932, p. 256).

Repetition

Numerous performance curves plotting acquisition and extinction are now available. Some specimen conditioning curves are to be found in Brogden, Lipman and Culler (1938), Calvin (1939), Cohen, Hilgard, and Wendt (1933), Finch and Culler (1935), Garvey (1933), Girden, Mettler, Finch and Culler (1936), Hilgard (1931, 1933a), Hilgard and A. A. Campbell (1936, 1937), Hilgard and D. G. Marquis (1935, 1936), Hovland (1937d), D. P. Marquis (1931), D. G. Marquis and Hilgard (1936, 1937),

Hunter (1936b), Kantrow (1937), J. Miller (1939a, 1939b), J. Miller and Cole (1936), Razran (1935), Rodnick (1937a), R. R. Sears (1934), Wendt (1930). Curves for simple instrumental responses may be found in Grindley (1932), Skinner (1932, 1938), Youtz (1938a). Culler's (1928) suggestion that the learning curve is of S-shape was first used in relation to the performance curve of conditioning by Kleitman and Crisler (1927). The double-inflected curve suggests other processes which, by analogy, have sometimes been supposed to underlie conditioning. Thus the curve of autocatalysis is of this sort, and an autocatalytic process has been suggested as the physiological basis for learning. The curve of growth is of this form; therefore growth may underlie conditioning. The integral of the probability curve (the ogive) is also of this form. Hence conditioning may consist in the accumulation of learned elements, the measured result being a complex of subordinate conditionings which behaves in some respects like a normal population of responses. Individual curves depart so widely, however, from a true ogive that the parameters must be worked out with greater care before such theories can be useful.

The typical decelerated curve of extinction is illustrated in Cole (1939), Humphreys (1939a), Kleitman and Crisler (1927), J. Miller and Cole (1936), Switzer (1933). Extinction showing an initial rise may be found in Hilgard and D. G. Marquis (1935), Hovland (1936), Hudgins (1933), Scott (1930), Switzer (1930). The course of extinction of an instrumental response is shown in Hunter (1935d), Youtz (1938a). That there is no one general curve of extinction is emphasized by Brogden and Culler (1935), Finch and Culler (1935), and Hunter (1935a). See also Brogden, Lipman and Culler (1938), Humphreys (1939a), J. Miller and Cole (1936).

Chapter 7

GRADIENTS OF REINFORCEMENT

T HE RATE of conditioning is markedly affected by the temporal relationship of the stimuli and responses involved. In classical conditioning, the important time interval as usually stated is that between conditioned and unconditioned stimuli, as indicated in the summary from Pavlov in Chapter 2 (p. 44f.). In instrumental conditioning several other time relations are involved. In a maze, for example, one may consider the time required to run from a given bifurcation to the food-box as of some importance in the elimination of the blind alley at that choice-point; a delay may be introduced between the time of entering the food-box and the delivering of the food reward. Such intervals are measured between responses, rather than between stimuli, and the variables are defined with differences sufficient to make the empirical laws of one inapplicable to the other, no matter how similar they may be in certain superficial aspects.

When intervals are introduced between events in conditioning experiments, it is commonly found that there is a most favorable interval, with longer or shorter intervals becoming progressively less effective. This gradual decrease in effectiveness of conditioning may be described as a sort of gradient. Since the interval is ordinarily terminated by an unconditioned stimulus, or a reward, or a punishment, it is convenient to refer to the whole class of such gradients as *gradients of reinforcement*. Within this class there are subvarieties, in which the interval is measured between different features of the experimental situation. Among the several gradients of reinforcement may be mentioned (1) the temporal gradient in classical conditioning, which refers to the significance for conditioning of the interval between conditioned and unconditioned stimuli, (2) the temporal gradient in avoidance learning, referring to the interval between the conditioned stimulus and the punishment, (3) the gradient of reward (temporal aspects), referring to the delay between the conditioned instrumental response and the reward, (4) the gradient of reward (non-temporal aspects), referring to the interval between the conditioned response and the reward expressed as distance in space or as remoteness in a series, (5) the temporal gradient within delayed reaction experiments, in which the instrumental response to the conditioned stimulus is prevented for different periods of time, although the reward appears promptly once the response is performed, (6) the goal-gradient, which is a complicated manifestation of the results of repeated trials in which a series of acts have been reinforced by a common goal situation. Only confusion can result from treating these several situations as though they were alike, although there are, of course, analogies between them. Each of the above-mentioned gradients will be considered in the light of present experimental evidence, before any harmonization is attempted.

The Temporal Gradient in Classical Conditioning. The simultaneous conditioned response was considered by Pavlov to be basic to the others, and its formation usually preceded the establishment of other types. The usual procedure for establishing a delayed conditioned response in Pavlov's laboratory, for example, was to condition simultaneously and then to postpone the unconditioned stimulus five seconds each day until the desired delay was reached. Intervals up to five seconds were considered simultaneous by Pavlov, so that it may be inferred that within this interval the differences in ease of conditioning were not very pronounced. It is evident that strict simultaneity is not an essential condition, yet near-simultaneity is more favorable than longer intervals. This suggests some sort of gradient, whereby there

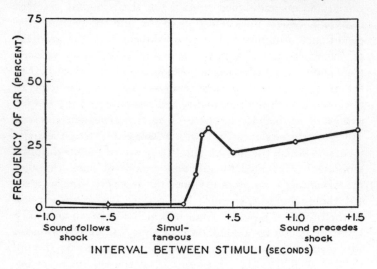

FIGURE 14

TEMPORAL GRADIENT IN CLASSICAL CONDITIONING

The effect of interval between conditioned and unconditioned stimuli in human eyelid conditioning. Conditioned stimulus, click in headphones; unconditioned stimulus, shock to skin surface above infraorbital nerve. (Bernstein, 1934.)

is a gradual transition from favorable to less favorable intervals between stimuli.

Such gradients have been determined for motor conditioned responses by Bernstein (1934) for man, and by Kappauf and Schlosberg (1937) for rats. Some of their results are charted in Figures 14 and 15. The intervals explored are those considered 'almost simultaneous' by Pavlov, and such continuous functions may well be described as temporal gradients.

Bernstein's results show that backward conditioning is slight. The later results from Pavlov's laboratory reversed the earlier denials of the possibility of backward conditioning, but they also showed that backward conditioned responses

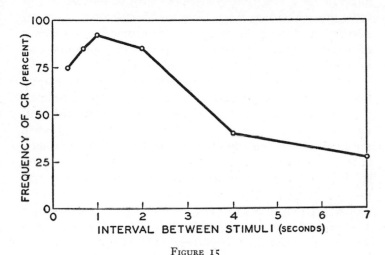

FIGURE 15

TEMPORAL GRADIENT IN CLASSICAL CONDITIONING

The effect of interval between conditioned and unconditioned stimuli in conditioned respiration of the white rat. Conditioned stimulus, buzz; unconditioned stimulus, shock to right foreleg. Frequency of leg flexions was low under all conditions, and respiration proved a more satisfactory index of conditioning. (Kappauf and Schlosberg, 1937.)

can be formed only with difficulty and are evanescent when once formed. Strict physical simultaneity is likewise an unfavorable temporal relationship. Both investigations show that it is desirable for the conditioned stimulus to precede the unconditioned by intervals above 200 msec. There are a number of independent but less complete studies showing the possibility and difficulties of backward conditioning, and the disadvantage of strict simultaneity as compared with intervals at something over one-fifth of a second. The actual range of satisfactory time relations, and the slope of the gradient, probably vary for different responses and for different organisms. It is quite possible, for example, that favorable intervals for a long-latency response such as the galvanic or salivary reaction may differ from the short-latency responses charted in Figures 14 and 15. Unfortunately, systematic studies of temporal gradients within other examples of classical conditioning have not been made.

The most favorable interval appears to be somewhat greater than the latency of the conditioned response, thus permitting the conditioned response to anticipate the unconditioned stimulus. Two facts are important in this connection: (1) when the interval between conditioned and unconditioned stimuli is longer than the minimum latency of the conditioned response, the response temporally anticipates the unconditioned stimulus; (2) intervals too short to permit the anticipatory reaction to appear are unfavorable for conditioning. These empirical findings support the interpretation of the conditioned response as a readiness or preparatory reaction. Whether or not such an interpretation is accepted, the mere fact that the conditioned response tends to precede the unconditioned stimulus may be of very great theoretical significance (Chapters 9 and 10).

In classical conditioning, the interval between stimuli influences latency of response in a systematic way. The minimum latency of conditioned responses in striate muscle appears to be that of voluntary reactions (Hilgard, 1931). These latencies are normally over 100 msec., longer than the latencies of the unconditioned reflexes on which the conditioned responses are based. The latency distributions of conditioned eyelid responses in rat, dog, and monkey, show very similar characteristics, with latencies longer than those of unconditioned reflexes.

While the minimum latency of conditioned responses is determined in part by the sensori-motor systems involved, responses formed with increased intervals between the conditioned and unconditioned stimuli have longer latencies which are determined by other considerations. The latent periods of trace and delayed conditioned responses are roughly proportional to the interval of delay. The latency is ordinarily less than the interval, so that conditioned responses appear an appreciable amount of time before the onset of the unconditioned stimulus. This fact is evident from many of Pavlov's tables (1927, pp. 91–102). With the conditioned stimulus acting alone for 30 seconds, a short delay of 3 seconds is reported; when the conditioned stimulus acts for 120 seconds the longest delay reported is 75 seconds; when acting for 180 seconds, the longest delay is less than 150 seconds. Thus with 3-minute delays conditioned salivation begins at least half a minute before the food is presented.

Latencies of trace and delayed responses have been measured in the studies of Switzer (1933) and of Rodnick (1937a) on galvanic skin responses in man. With intervals of 16 to 20 seconds between the conditioned and unconditioned stimuli the conditioned response increased from an original mean latency of 5 seconds to a final mean latency of 10 seconds, whether or not the delay was established directly or following simultaneous presentations. An interesting observation made by both writers is that the latency of the delayed or trace response tended to decrease overnight to its original lower value, so that in a long series of sessions it had to be reestablished each day. The delay was, however, established more promptly each day, so that the training of the preceding days was not actually lost.

The greater difficulty of establishing trace responses as compared with delayed responses was noted by both Switzer and Rodnick, in agreement with Pavlov.

The Temporal Gradient in Avoidance Learning. H. M. Wolfle (1930, 1932) has reported experiments on the effect of time interval on conditioned finger withdrawal from shock. Subjects were instructed to lift their fingers at the shock, and it was possible to avoid the shock by lifting the fingers in advance of it. Hence the experiment should be classified as avoidance learning, involving voluntary factors. Since time interval between the conditioned stimulus and the shock has meaning only on those trials in which the shock occurs, the gradient described is legitimately considered a temporal gradient similar to that of classical conditioning, although there are, of course, complicating factors. The results of Wolfle's studies are plotted in Figure 16. In common with Bernstein's results for classical conditioning (Figure 14), backward conditioning is slight, intervals near simultaneity are unfavorable, and intervals above 200 msec. are most favorable. That intervals of 1 second or more were found unfavorable by Wolfle may be due to the tendency to restrain voluntary conditioned responses when it is too evident that they are being made (D. G. Marquis and Porter, 1939).

Other illustrations of avoidance reactions in which the interval is measured between a conditioned stimulus and the punishment may be found in the experiments of Carr and A. S. Freeman (1919), Yarborough (1921), and Warner (1932a). In each of these, rats were warned by a buzzer of a closed door or of a shock, and learned to make anticipatory avoidance reactions. Intervals of 1 second and less between the buzzer and the annoyance were found most favorable. Yarborough demonstrated some backward conditioning at 1 second. Warner found some conditioning with forward intervals as long as 20 seconds, but found 30 seconds definitely too long for his rats.

The Gradient of Reward: Temporal Aspects. In simple instrumental learning leading to a reward, the interval to be measured is not that between stimuli, but between the instrumental response and the reward. Furthermore, that which is strengthened is not a response similar to that at the end of the interval (as in classical conditioning), but the instrumental response which is at the beginning of the interval. The

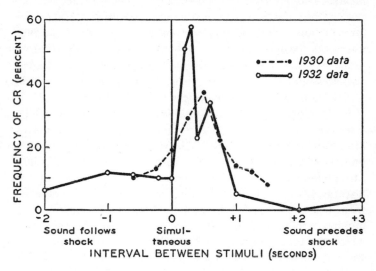

FIGURE 16

TEMPORAL GRADIENT IN AVOIDANCE CONDITIONING

Conditioned finger withdrawals to a sound when the sound was presented at different intervals following and preceding a shock to the middle finger. (H. M. Wolfle, 1930, 1932.)

influence on conditioning of the interval between a response and its reward may be called the gradient of reward, as suggested in Chapter 4 (p. 84).

In some preliminary experiments, Skinner (1938, pp. 72ff.) found delays of 1, 2, 3, and 4 seconds equally efficacious in the lever-pressing situation. The delay was introduced between the pressing of the lever and the delivery of the food. While a temporal gradient appeared to be lacking here, Skinner found such a gradient in other forms of his experiment (139ff.). Following periodic reconditioning (in which reinforcement occurred every 4 or 5 minutes) delays of 2, 4, 6, and 8 seconds were introduced before the periodic reinforcements. The intervals progressively decreased the rate of responding; the rate declined about one-third through the introduction of the 2-second postponement of reward. Skinner interprets the differences as a reduction in the reserve (i.e., as reduced resistance to extinction) rather than as retarded acquisition, and hence distinguishes between his investigation and those of delayed reward, next to be described.

In the more usual instrumental learning situation, in which a sequence of acts leads to a reward, postponing the reward after the terminal act retards learning. There have been a number of experiments on delayed reward, of which Wolfe's (1934) may be taken as representative. He found that the learning by rats of a single T-maze was much slower even with delays as short as 5 seconds. Longer delays, up to 20 minutes, produced progressive decreases in the efficiency with which the task was mastered. A visual discrimination habit was only slightly affected by a 30-second delay, although this as well as longer delays showed deleterious effects. In Wolfe's study, the greater part of the effectiveness of the reward was lost in the first minute.

These studies of delayed reward have in common a rather steep gradient, whereby delays in reinforcement of a few seconds greatly affect the learning. While the evidence is inconclusive, the gradient appears to be somewhat less steep for rewarded learning than for classical conditioning. There is a complication, however, in that the effect situation is always analyzable into a series of acts, which may be discrete stimulus-response sequences or an integrated series of performances leading to a goal. Order of events may in such cases be more important than time interval, and the gradient of reward may be expressed in spatial and sequential terms as well as in temporal ones.

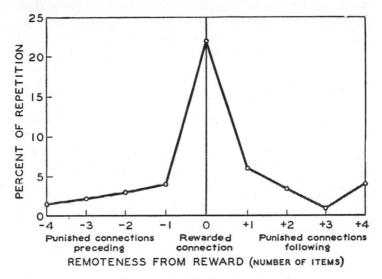

FIGURE 17

THE SPREAD OF EFFECT, A FORM OF THE GRADIENT OF REWARD

The figure summarizes several studies of repetitions of word-number pairs, when most of the pairs are followed by 'punishment' (experimenter says "Wrong"), others by 'reward' (experimenter says "Right"). Each sequence required about 3 seconds, so that the nine steps illustrated represent a range of about 27 seconds. The degree of remoteness is probably a function of the number of steps rather than of the precise intervals of time. After Thorndike (1935, p. 34).

The Gradient of Reward: Non-temporal Aspects.

Thorndike's studies of the spread of effect illustrate non-temporal aspects of the gradient of reward. One of his gradients is reproduced in Figure 17. The subject was given a word and told to say any number from 1 to 6. Following his reply the experimenter said either "Right" or "Wrong." On further repetitions, the effect of the previous announcement of "Right" or "Wrong" resulted in excesses over chance as indicated in the figure. The rewarded connection ("Right") was repeated much beyond chance expectancy; neighboring connections ("Wrong") were repeated, in spite of being 'punished,' because of their proximity to the reward. It is to be noted that the gradient is expressed in terms of steps. The interval between steps was about 3 seconds in the experiments from which Figure 17 was constructed; but the form of the gradient is little affected if the interval is as short as 1.5 seconds between steps. This is not, then, strictly speaking, a temporal gradient. It is a gradient expressed in units of successive stimuli presented to the subject, and may be compared with a similar procedure used with animals by Hunter (1936a).

The bi-directional gradient for maze learning reported by Muenzinger, Dove, and Bernstone (1937) is based upon errors in successive units of an endless maze in which the animals run from goal to goal. Like Thorndike's spread of effect the results are given for successive response units, and it is not clear whether the function is one of (a) the successive order of choices, relatively independent of distance or time interval, (b) spatial separation of choice points, or (c) temporal separation of responses. The results agree with Thorndike's spread of effect, in that responses are strengthened on both sides of the goal; that is, both prior to and following reinforcement.

In view of the lack of definitive experiments, the concept of the gradient of reward may be retained as a general one to describe the strengthening of an act by neighboring reinforcement in proportion to remoteness, however that remoteness is defined. The more detailed statement of the gradient as a function of time, distance, and order of events, awaits further evidence.

The Temporal Gradient within Delayed Reaction Experiments. In order to describe the delayed reaction experiment in terms of conditioning, it is necessary to consider the lifting of the cup which conceals the food, or the opening of the box which contains it, as an instrumental response reinforced by the food reward. The experiment consists in showing the animal the cup or the box as it is being baited, so that there is an immediate tendency to give the conditioned response. This tendency to respond is blocked mechanically by screening the food device or by removing the animal. Thus a delay is introduced between the presentation of the conditioned stimulus and the possibility of responding to it. The longer this delay, the less accurate the choice becomes. This gradient of success with delay is not ordinarily considered a problem within the sphere of conditioning, but it is described at this point as one among many arrangements for interrupting a learned act by introducing a temporal interval before the act may be performed. The delayed reaction experiment is discussed in another context in Chapter 10.

The Goal Gradient. The gradient of running speed for the rat in a straight alley, as reported by Hull (1934b), is a spatial gradient, expressed in units of distance from the goal. If running through the different segments of the path is considered a series of discrete responses, each reinforced by the common reward at the end of the maze, it may be predicted from the gradient of reward that in a given number of repetitions those responses nearer the goal will be more strongly conditioned than those more remote. If running speed corresponds to strength of conditioning, running speed should be faster as the goal is neared. Actually, an integral performance of this sort cannot be completely predicted in terms of the conditioning of responses according to their distance from the goal. One complication which Hull found was a definite retardation in that section just preceding the goal, representing a much more pronounced slowing up than that required to prevent the rat's bumping the end of the alley (cf. Figure 27,

p. 213). It should be noted that the goal gradient as measured in an alley maze may be predicted in part from the gradient of reward, but is not itself a direct measure of an uncomplicated gradient of reward. The spatial gradient for avoidance responses, reported by Bugelski and N. E. Miller (1938), is similarly related to the temporal gradient in avoidance learning. Like Hull's goal gradient, the behavior is measured in an alley situation in which a common punishment affects the behavior along the path in the approach to it.

The temporal gradient reported by J. S. Brown (1939) is related both to the temporal gradient of avoidance and to the goal gradient. The problem was not to find the most favorable interval for the learning of avoidance behavior, but to find to what extent avoidance behavior was manifested at different intervals from a time of usual punishment. Shock stimuli were presented at standard intervals of 12 seconds. The tendency to give avoidance responses was tested by presenting a less intense shock at different times within the 12-second interval. A gradient was shown, more intense reactions being given near the time of usual shock.

These gradients of running speed and of avoidance have in common a single reinforcing state of affairs affecting behavior remote from it in time or space. The gradient as tested is a performance gradient, following learning, and is in some sense the result of learning in accordance with the other gradients. A gradient which refers to the relative efficacy of different intervals between single responses and their rewards may not apply to the strength of individual members of a series with a common reward. Only by studying the goal gradient is it possible to determine whether or not the gradient determined for single responses is also applicable to the case of a series of acts with a single reward. Similar considerations apply with respect to gradients of avoidance.

The Problem of Contiguity

To the extent that the gradients which have been described represent associative strength (i.e., strength of conditioning) as a function of nearness in time and space, they may be considered empirical forms of the law of contiguity (Robinson, 1932, p. 76). It is possible to leave the relationships in this empirical form, or to attempt to account for the gradients in terms of some more fundamental conception of contiguity.

Because of an abhorrence of 'action at a distance' many writers prefer to infer that the events actually associated in conditioning are genuinely simultaneous, that is, contiguous in the sense of being strictly side-by-side or overlapping. When events apparently separated in space or time are associated, these writers look for processes which bridge the gap between the items. The most common form of this conception is that of a stimulus-trace which persists until it is contiguous with the response conditioned. Pavlov endorsed this concept in his notion of the trace conditioned reflex, in which the conditioned stimulus ceased to act before the unconditioned stimulus was presented. Pavlov assumed that some trace of the stimulus persisted in the organism.

A related point of view has been espoused by Guthrie (1933). According to him, the inferred 'true' conditioned stimulus is usually produced by the subject's response to the presented stimulus. This 'true' conditioned stimulus is said by him to be always coincident with the unconditioned response. Since the 'true' conditioned stimulus depends for its arousal upon the presented conditioned stimulus, it follows that the most favorable interval for securing simultaneity of 'true' conditioned stimulus and reinforcing response will be one in which there is a short forward order between the presented conditioned stimulus and the unconditioned stimulus.

According to this interpretation, backward conditioning will be possible only if the unconditioned response persists long enough for it to be coincident with the 'true' conditioned stimulus. Since the arrangement of backward conditioning is unfavorable for such coincidence, it follows that backward conditioning should be relatively unsuccessful. These conjectures have never been directly verified.

Hull (1937) has also been making use of the conception of a stimulus-trace, expressed as a diminishing 'neural reverberation.' His conception of contiguous conditioning is somewhat more complicated than Guthrie's. Like Guthrie, he believes that conditioning takes place only between a stimulus-trace and a response contiguous with it, but, unlike Guthrie, he believes such contiguous conditioning to occur only in the neighborhood of a reinforcing state of affairs. This has two consequences in Hull's theory. A stimulus on the one hand tends to become more strongly associated with responses made immediately, because the stimulus-trace is stronger at first. Its tendency to become associated with responses occurring later in the series is correspondingly less because the trace is weaker. On the other hand, the later responses (particularly goal responses) are nearer to the reinforcing state of affairs, and so even a weaker trace will become more strongly conditioned to them, according to the gradient of reward. Hence it is that stimuli, such as those associated with an alley on the way to food, tend to evoke both the running behavior appropriate to that alley and fractional anticipatory goal responses. At a distance from the goal the running gets conditioned because the stimulus-trace is strong, even though the reinforcement is weak; the goal responses get conditioned to remote stimuli even though the trace is weak because the reinforcement is strong.

Any conjectures regarding the factors underlying the various gradients of reinforcement require empirical verification before they can be accepted as established explanations. Theories of strict simultaneity of associated events tend to ignore the directional character of behavior. Events may be touching and yet be organized in a series in which one event precedes another. The effectiveness of the forward order in conditioning is probably related to a fundamental directional organization of behavior.

Summary

Any conditioning experiment involves a number of events beginning with the conditioned stimulus and ending (for any one trial) with the reinforcement. In terms of effectiveness for conditioning there are more favorable and less favorable intervals between sequential events. Since effectiveness tends to diminish gradually with increasing (or decreasing) interval, the relationship between strength of conditioning and interval may be expressed as an empirical gradient. Depending upon the arrangements of the experiment, and the place in the sequence of events at which the interval is systematically changed, a number of different gradients may be described, such as the temporal gradients within classical conditioning and within avoidance learning, and the gradient of reward within instrumental learning. Since the interval is usually terminated by reinforcement, the gradients have been classed together as gradients of reinforcement.

The goal gradient is closely related to the gradients of reward and of avoidance. It is a result of learning in which the principles underlying the other gradients have been important, but it is not a simple expression of these other gradients. In the first place, the goal gradient always refers to a situation in which a number of serial acts have been reinforced by a common goal situation. In the second place, the acts measured in determining the form of the goal gradient are not discrete conditioned responses, but are parts of a larger behavior pattern in which separate acts are submerged, and in which factors other than the gradient of reinforcement are of significance.

The various gradients may be accepted in their empirically determined forms, or the attempt may be made to account for them on the basis of simultaneous conditioning by inferring some sort of trace or intervening process to span the interval between the events being studied.

Notes

Temporal Gradient in Classical Conditioning

On favorable forward orders of a few tenths of a second, cf. Hilgard (1931), Schlosberg (1928), Wendt (1930). On the unfavorableness of intervals near strict simultaneity, cf. Hilgard and Biel (1937). On backward conditioning, cf. Cason (1935), V. I. Pavlova (1933), Porter (1938b), Pressman (1934), Switzer (1930). Only Switzer reports much success, and it is possible that his results may be a form of sensitization or pseudo-conditioning (Bernstein, 1934; Grether, 1938).

For discussion of minimum latency, cf. Cason (1922b, 1934a), Culler (1938b), Hilgard (1931, 1934), Wendt (1930), H. M. Wolfle (1933). The direction of latency changes in delayed and trace conditioning is discussed by Hull (1929), Pavlov (1927, p. 89), Rodnick (1937a), Steckle (1933), Switzer (1933).

Gradient of Reward

On delayed reward, cf. Clements (1928), E. L. Hamilton (1929),

Roberts (1930), Warden and Haas (1927), Watson (1917), Wolfe (1934), A. B. Wood (1933). Experiments on time discrimination in animals often depend upon the greater efficacy for learning of that segment of the path which involves the least delay, and hence they represent forms of experimentation on the temporal gradient of reward. Among these are experiments by A. C. Anderson (1932), Finan (1939), Sams and Tolman (1925).

The 'spread of effect,' which is Thorndike's statement of the gradient of reward, was announced first in a note in Science (1933a), and elaborated in subsequent publications (1933b, 1935). Because a number of acts are reinforced by a single reward, the 'spread of effect' situation is comparable to the goal gradient (Hull, 1932). The goal gradient principle was not at first coordinated with the law of effect, but the similarity has since been recognized and pointed out by Hull (1935d, 1937), Brandt (1935), Muenzinger, Dove, and Bernstone (1937). It may be noted also that the verbal type of reward in the Thorndike experiment is a secondary or derived reward, so that reinforcement, according to our classification, is of the derived form.

Goal Gradient

The expression 'gradient of reinforcement' was first used by N. E. Miller and Miles (1935) to refer to the fact that acts more remote from reinforcement were strengthened by conditioning less than acts near to reinforcement. They proposed essentially the same distinction which we have adopted between this gradient and the goal gradient which tends to be produced by it, the goal gradient being one of strength of response rather than of strength of conditioning. Deductions based on the goal gradient hypothesis, and their experimental tests, are discussed in Chapter 9.

Contiguity

For general discussions of time interval in association and conditioning see Guthrie (1933), Robinson (1932), Wenrick (1933). Wenrick finds chaos, which Guthrie resolves through the notion of associative mediation, so that according to him all conditioning is actually simultaneous. Robinson, admitting that associative mediation cannot be disproved, believes it more useful to accept the empirical fact that associative strength appears to be a continuous function of time interval, and hence he puts the burden of proof upon those who insist upon absolute simultaneity as basic for association. The empirical gradients may be accepted as valid, whichever position is adopted.

Chapter 8

GENERALIZATION AND DISCRIMINATION

WHEN an organism has learned to give a conditioned response to a particular stimulus it can be shown that other similar stimuli will also elicit the response even though these other stimuli have not been used in the conditioning experiment. The partial equivalence of different stimuli in evoking a conditioned response is known as *sensory generalization*. There is also a degree of equivalence among responses which may be called *response generalization,* so that a stimulus which has come through training to elicit a particular response may, under some circumstances, elicit a different response without special training. It is evident that generalization is important in the adaptive economy of the organism because environmental situations never recur in nature without changes. If situations had to be repeated in identical form in order that previous experience might be effective, learned adjustments would be of little service. On the other hand, generalization must in many cases be restricted to a narrow range of stimuli and responses, as the organism learns in its natural environment to react selectively to certain stimuli or aspects of stimuli and not to others. Selective reaction is the opposite of generalization: it involves discrimination of stimuli and corresponding differentiation of response.

The basic facts of stimulus equivalence and of response equivalence are not limited in application to conditioned responses, but are true of reflexes and of complex voluntary responses. Every response is elicitable, not just by one stimulus, but by a class of similar stimuli. Correspondingly, every stimulus elicits, not just one response, but one of a class of responses. In the case of unlearned reflexes, the degree of generalization is determined by the inherited structural organization of the nervous system. With learned responses, however, the degree of generalization is modifiable through experience. The study of generalization and discrimination in conditioned responses offers the possibility of determining the fundamental principles of such modification in simple, experimentally controlled situations.

Sensory Generalization

Generalization to Stimuli Differing in Quality and Intensity. The experiments of Hovland on the generalization of a conditioned galvanic skin response to tones differing in pitch or in loudness serve as convenient illustrations of generalization along dimensions within a sensory modality.

For the generalization of pitch (1937a), four tones were selected by psychophysical methods to be separated in pitch by 25 just noticeable differences (j.n.d.'s). The frequencies chosen were 153, 468, 1000, 1937 cycles. The tones, having been equated for loudness, now represented a scale of approximately equal units on a dimension of pitch similarity, as judged by the verbal reports of the subjects. One group of subjects was conditioned to the lowest tone, and then tested on the others to determine the magnitude of the generalized responses. A second group was conditioned to the highest tone, and tested with the three lower tones. Permutational orders of presentation made possible the pooling of the results of all subjects into a single curve representing the generalization of tones separated in pitch by 25, 50, and 75 j.n.d.'s. The curve, reproduced in Figure 18, shows that the degree of generalization decreases progressively with greater differences in pitch, producing, when plotted, a concave (decelerated) gradient. Humphreys (1939c) has extended Hovland's observations by measuring the generalization to tones differing by only 5 and 15 j.n.d.'s. Since the greatest decrease in the gradient of gen-

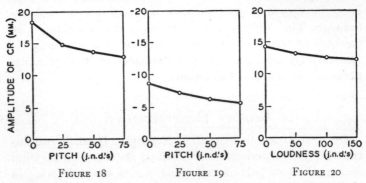

FIGURE 18   FIGURE 19   FIGURE 20

FIGURE 18. GENERALIZATION OF PITCH: CONDITIONING. The abscissa is in units of 25 j.n.d.'s. The actual frequencies involved were 153, 468, 1000, and 1967 cycles, equated for loudness. Half of the 20 subjects were conditioned to 153, half to 1967 cycles, and tested at all four frequencies. (Hovland, 1937a.)

FIGURE 19. GENERALIZATION OF PITCH: EXTINCTION. All frequencies were reinforced, so that the conditioned responses to all were similar in amplitude. Only the extreme frequencies were extinguished, and the others tested. The ordinate represents the amount by which the response as tested was less than the conditioned response at the end of training. Modified from Hovland (1937a).

FIGURE 20. GENERALIZATION OF LOUDNESS: CONDITIONING. The abscissa is in units of 50 j.n.d.'s. All tones were 1000 cycles, at 40, 60, 74, and 86 decibels above threshold. Half of the 32 subjects were conditioned at 40 db., half at 86 db., then tested at all four intensities. (Hovland, 1937b.)

eralization occurred at the first interval, it may be concluded that the gradient is concave, even for stimuli differing only slightly from the conditioned stimulus.

The generalization of extinction was studied by Hovland in other subjects after conditioned responses were established equally to the four frequencies. Responses of half the subjects were then extinguished by presenting the highest tone without reinforcement, the other half by presenting the lowest tone. Generalization of extinction was determined by the amount of reduction of response to the other frequencies. The curve of generalization of extinction was found to be similar to that of the generalization of conditioning, as shown in Figure 19. The important features of both curves are (1) a large amount of generalization even with gross differences in frequency, and (2) a concave (decelerated) gradient in the magnitude of generalized responses with increasing difference in pitch from the stimulus conditioned.

A similar experiment was performed for the generalization and extinction of responses based on the intensity of tones (Hovland, 1937b). Four tones of 1000 cycles were selected, spaced at intensities corresponding to 50 j.n.d.'s in loudness. The curve of generalization, while similar to that for pitch, is much flatter; that is, generalization is greater for intensity than for frequency (Figure 20).

Generalization to Spatially Separated Stimuli. Another form of generalization is that in which the stimuli remain qualitatively alike, but are presented at different places on the skin, so that the sensory effects differ in location. This is the arrangement used in the classical studies of 'irradiation' in Pavlov's laboratory (Pavlov, 1927, p. 152ff.). The sensory consequences of the stimulation of neighboring points are presumably more similar than the consequences of stimulating remote points. Anrep (1923), using the method of conditioned inhibition, found a spatial gradient of generalization for the dog similar to that found by Hovland, provided points on the dog's skin were tested immediately after stimulation with the inhibitory combination. Spatial gradients of generalization of both conditioning and extinction were reported in man by Bass and Hull (1934), using the conditioned galvanic skin response based on electric shock reinforcement. Vibro-tactual stimulators were placed one on the back near the shoulder, one on the left side of the small of the back, one on the left thigh, and one on the left calf. When a conditioned response

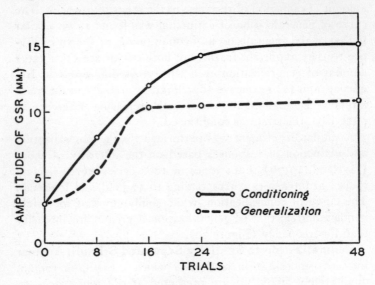

FIGURE 21

STRENGTH OF GENERALIZED RESPONSES DURING THE COURSE OF CONDITIONING

The solid line represents the amplitude of the galvanic skin response to the conditioned stimulus at successive stages of conditioning. The broken line represents the amplitude of the same response to the generalized stimulus. (From Hovland, 1937d.)

was established to stimulation of the point on the shoulder (or on the calf), the response generalized to the other stimulators, progressively less as distance increased. They reported the gradient of conditioning to be convex, that of extinction to be concave.

The concave gradients found by Hovland and by Humphreys may be accepted as of more general significance, since their stimuli were arranged in a single dimension of equated distances. E. J. Gibson (1939) has reported a gradient of similar form for voluntary responses. The precise form of the

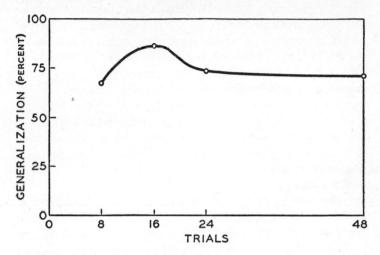

FIGURE 22

RELATIVE AMOUNT OF GENERALIZATION DURING THE COURSE OF CONDITIONING

The data of Figure 21 have been replotted to show the percent of generalization at successive stages of conditioning. Each point on the curve represents the ratio of the strength of generalized responses to the strength of conditioned responses.

gradient may depend on other facts in the testing situation than those considered above. Its relation to degree of conditioning and of extinction has not been measured although changes may be expected with practice, as indicated in the next section. Anrep (1923) has reported that the form of gradient depends on the time interval elapsing between the training stimulus and the stimulus which tests the generalization, but these results have been questioned by Loucks (1933).

Generalization as a Function of the Strength of Con-

ditioning. As reinforcement is repeated, generalization increases gradually to a maximum, and then begins to decrease (Beritov, 1924, p. 123). Another of Hovland's experiments (1937d) presents quantitative data on this point. In Figure 21 are given corresponding curves of the amplitude of reinforced and of generalized responses at different stages of practice. It is evident that as reinforcement continues, both responses increase, but at different rates. The curve for the generalized response flattens earlier. The relationship between the two responses is shown in Figure 22. Here the generalized response is expressed as a percentage of the reinforced conditioned response. While the absolute amount of generalization increases throughout the period of practice studied, the relative amount of generalization reaches a maximum and then declines slightly.

Great caution is required before the results from isolated situations can be applied to other experimental arrangements that introduce complications which have not been tested empirically. This is shown in some findings of Razran (1939e) regarding the effects of repeated reinforcement on generalization. He conditioned salivary responses of human subjects, using lights as conditioned stimuli. When single lights were used, other lights of different color showed generalization similar to that reported by Hovland. There was an initial rise in the per cent of generalization, followed by a decrease, as shown in the solid curve of Figure 23. However, when patterns of lights were used as conditioned stimuli, Razran found that the amount of generalization increased progressively with practice, as shown in the broken curve of Figure 23.

The Extinction of Responses Elicited Through Sensory Generalization. Some interest centers in the ease with which generalized responses can be extinguished, for this bears upon the rapidity with which a discrimination can be established. Hovland (1937c) has reported data on this problem.

After 16 presentations of a vibrator followed by a shock, when the generalization should be at its maximum, the conditioned galvanic response was tested both by the stimulus used in

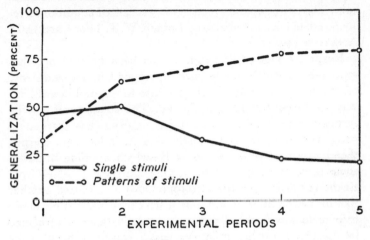

FIGURE 23

GENERALIZATION WITH SINGLE STIMULI AND WITH PATTERNS OF STIMULI

Generalization of salivary conditioned responses in 16 human subjects. The reinforced conditioned stimuli were flashings of red and green lights; the tested stimuli blue and yellow lights. Lights were presented either singly, or in geometrical patterns, with the differences as indicated. Percent generalization is derived by dividing the mean salivation to the equivalent stimulus by the mean salivation to the reinforced stimulus. (Plotted from the data of Razran, 1939e, Table 1.)

training, and by one differing in intensity. Half of the subjects were trained with each stimulus, to control the effect of the difference in strength of stimuli. The conditioned responses to the reinforced stimulus were found to extinguish more slowly than the generalized conditioned responses to the other stimulus. After four extinction trials, the conditioned response remained at 89 percent of its original magnitude, while the generalized response had fallen to 60 percent of its original magnitude. The more rapid extinction of the generalized response was followed by greater spontaneous recovery, so that 24 hours after extinction the difference between generalized and conditioned responses was no longer statistically significant. The more rapid extinction of generalized conditioned responses had been noted also by Liddell, W. T. James, and O. D. Anderson (1934).

Response Generalization. It has been pointed out that an organism which has learned to respond in a certain way to stimulus A, has thereby learned also to respond in a similar way to an equivalent stimulus A'. The counterpart on the response side is as follows: if an organism has learned to react with response B to a stimulus A, it has also learned thereby to react with a response B', which is unlike B, but in some respects equivalent to it. One illustration comes from Bekhterev (1932, p. 216) who found that a dog lifted another foot to the conditioned stimulus when the one which normally responded was fastened down. Another instance is furnished by Lashley's (1924) monkey, which solved a problem of manipulation with the other hand after the hand which had always been employed previously was paralyzed due to a brain operation. Further observations of the kind suggested by Bekhterev have been reported by Kellogg (1939b). Following buzzer-shock conditioning in which the shock was applied only to the right hind foot of a dog, it was found that each of the four legs occasionally responded to the buzzer. Responses in the more remote legs were less frequent than those in the shocked leg, the relative frequencies of conditioned responses being in the order right hind leg (the one shocked), left hind leg, right foreleg, left foreleg. This represents a crude generalization of response with remoteness from reinforcement, corresponding somewhat to the sensory gradients previously described. Since most of the instances of response generalization which have been studied in relation to conditioning involve a transfer of training based on previous learning, their consideration is postponed to Chapter 10.

Discrimination

Every conditioned response involves discrimination to some degree. A response to a particular sound is not evoked by all sounds, and sometimes not by the same sound presented in different positions (Girden, 1938). The experimental problems of discrimination arise, however, when there has been a prior generalization, so that stimuli are responded to as equivalent, and subsequently it is desired to secure a discrimination between them. To the extent that generalization is incomplete, there is already a partial differentiation of response, but it is often desired to increase this in order that the limits of discrimination may be tested.

Discrimination in Classical Conditioning. Although repeated reinforcement reduces generalization, it never results in very fine differentiation. In order to produce finer discrimination the generalized responses are extinguished by non-reinforcement, while reinforcement of the conditioned response continues. This is known as the *method of contrasts,* and has been used widely by Pavlov and by other students of sensory processes.

Specimen curves showing the course of conditioned discrimination in man are reproduced in Figure 24. In the experiment illustrated, the negative stimulus was introduced only after conditioned responses to the positive stimulus were well established. The discrimination plotted was between two adjacent illuminated apertures, easily distinguished by the subjects, so that threshold capacity was not involved.

Discrimination in Instrumental Conditioning. The classical discrimination experiment of Pavlov is carried out by presenting the positive and the negative stimuli successively rather than simultaneously. The same procedure may be used equally well with instrumental responses. When the positive stimulus is presented, the proper response is re-

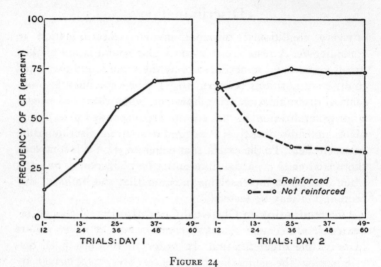

FIGURE 24

COURSE OF DISCRIMINATION BY THE METHOD OF CONTRASTS

The curves represent mean values of the conditioned eyelid responses of 10 human subjects. The positive stimulus was the illumination of one aperture, followed by an air-puff to the cornea. The conditioned response to the positive stimulus was established on the first day. The negative stimulus, introduced in random alternation with the positive stimulus on the second day, consisted in the illumination of an adjacent aperture. The negative stimulus was never reinforced. When the negative stimulus was introduced there was at first generalization, then selective extinction. (From Hilgard, R. K. Campbell, and W. N. Sears, 1938.)

warded; when the negative stimulus is presented, no reinforcement is given, and in some cases, punishment may be administered if the response occurs. Experiments of essentially this kind have been carried out by Elder (1934, 1935) and by Wendt (1934). Elder taught chimpanzees to react to a telegraph key following a ready signal, provided a tone was heard. The animals learned to refrain from response after the ready signal when the tone was absent. Wendt's method was similar. Monkeys learned to open a drawer which contained food following the positive auditory stimulus. The drawer was locked following the negative (i.e., absent) stimulus, and the animal learned to withhold reaction.

Skinner (1933, 1938) has reported two types of discrimination experiment using the lever-pressing situation. In the first, similar to the experiments just described, lever-pressing is rewarded in the presence of a differential cue, such as a light, and non-rewarded when this cue is absent. In the second type of experiment, a differential characteristic of lever-pressing is rewarded, i.e., only responses above a certain force will secure food. Skinner makes the distinction between the rat's discriminating among environmental stimuli, and differentiating among its own responses. It can, of course, be taught either type of discrimination, as choice-reaction experiments illustrate.

Choice-Reaction Discrimination. Discrimination learning is commonly studied in experimental situations in which the positive and the negative stimuli are presented simultaneously, but in differing spatial relationship. For example if the positive stimulus is on the right side, the animal is rewarded when it makes the proper response such as proceeding to the right side. If the animal makes the wrong response, that is, goes to the left, no reward is given, and punishment may be administered. On succeeding trials, the positive stimulus is presented in random order on the right or left side until the animal has learned always to proceed to the side corresponding to the positive stimulus. Many different kinds of reaction have been used in this type of discrimination learning. The subject may be trained to pull a string on the left or right which will bring food if correct (Klüver, 1933), to open one of two possible boxes to secure food (Spence, 1934), to jump through an opening (Lashley, 1930b), to push open a door (Munn, 1931), and so forth.

There are three important differences between the choice-reaction and the Pavlovian procedures for studying discrimination learning. (1) The two stimuli are presented simultaneously rather than separately on successive trials. The relational characteristics of the stimuli are presumably more apparent when the stimuli are present together. (2) The choice is between two reactions rather than between reaction and restraint. Each of the reactions may have a double determination, being an approach to one of the stimuli and a reaction away from the other. (3) The subject makes a choice on every trial, since reinforcement or punishment is given only after the reaction has occurred. In the Pavlovian procedure, reinforcement by the unconditioned stimulus is presented after each occurrence of the positive stimulus regardless of the reaction made.

These differences will be very important in the empirical problems of the speed or limit of any particular discrimination, and must be considered in the formulation of a general explanation of discrimination.

Mechanism of Discrimination Learning. The simplest explanation of the process of formation of a differential response to two stimuli is in terms of the reinforcement of one conditioned response and the extinction of another response which was previously learned or which was generalized from the reinforcement. These two modifications cannot proceed independently, however, for each will have an effect upon the other. Strengthening of the response to the positive stimulus will automatically strengthen the response to the negative stimulus through generalization. Similarly, weakening of the response to the negative stimulus by extinction will simultaneously tend to weaken the positive response through generalization of extinction. It is apparent that if generalization were complete, as would occur if the two stimuli were identical, no progress in discrimination would take place. To the extent that the two stimuli are dissimilar, however, the primary effect of reinforcement or extinction will be greater than the generalized effect, and after a sufficient number of repetitions, the discrimination will be perfect. The number of necessary repetitions will increase as the degree of generalization increases. This is illustrated in the familiar fact that it is more difficult to establish a discrimination than a simple conditioned response, and that the difficulty of a discrimination is a function of the similarity of the two stimuli employed.

The first of several careful attempts to treat the discrimination experiment quantitatively in terms of conditioning principles was undertaken by Spence (1936). On the familiar conditioning assumptions that reinforcement results in a cumulative increase in reaction tendencies and non-reinforcement in a cumulative decrease, Spence was able to deduce several of the most prominent characteristics of discrimination learning.

The first of these deductions concerns the behavior of the animal during the early trials of discrimination training. Krechevsky (1932b) carried out a series of investigations with the white rat in which he showed that the reactions of the animal during the pre-solution period were not a chance affair but consisted of systematic modes of response such as position and alternation habits. He termed these systematic pre-solution responses 'hypotheses', and interpreted them as attempted solutions of the problem by the rat. Spence (1936) set up a hypothetical situation in which he was able to derive such non-random behavior from the assumption of cumulative strengthening and weakening of the tendencies to the two stimuli. Krechevsky's conception implies that the training during the pre-solution period has no influence in determining the ultimate correct solution except to eliminate incorrect hypotheses. Spence's theory, on the other hand, demands that each reinforced or non-reinforced trial contribute to the strength of the response tendency. A critical experiment would be one determining the effect of reversal of the positive and negative stimulus values during the pre-solution training. T. L. McCulloch and Pratt (1934) found that such a reversal significantly retarded the learning of the correct solution, while Krechevsky (1938) found that there was no effect. Further experimental data are necessary to resolve this discrepancy.

Another feature of discrimination learning is the frequent occurrence, at least in the higher animals, of sudden solutions following periods of apparently chance response. This phenomenon has been emphasized by those who propose explanations in terms of 'insight' or 'reorganization of the sensory field.' Spence (1938), however, found that analysis of the learning curves of chimpanzees indicated that sudden learning, like gradual, was closely correlated with the relative strengths of the tendencies to respond to the two stimuli as determined by the number of previous reinforcements and non-reinforcements. Sudden solutions were more likely to occur in animals which were fast learners as compared with slow learners, since the increment in strength of conditioning resulting from each reinforcement was inferred to be greater.

A third problem which has been prominent in discussions of discrimination learning is concerned with the question of response to relative as contrasted with absolute properties of the stimuli. It is a typical finding that an animal which has been trained to select the brighter of two lights will select the dimmer one if it is presented together with a still dimmer light. Gestalt arguments against association theories have frequently cited transposition experiments, in which stimuli are equivalent by virtue of relationships of pattern, brightness, or other 'transposable' properties. By adding some plausible assumptions with respect to the quantitative aspects of generalization of conditioned responses to stimuli varying in a single dimension, Spence (1937b) has deduced types of discrimination which are usually considered to be based on the relational character of the stimuli. The nature of Spence's

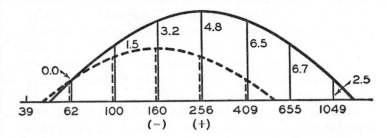

FIGURE 25

SPENCE'S THEORETICAL REPRESENTATION OF DISCRIMINATION

Areas of the visual stimuli used in the experiment are represented along the baseline. During the training, response to 256 is rewarded, response to 160, extinguished. As a result of reinforcing 256 the generalization represented by the solid lines results. That is, tendencies to react positively are generalized to the neighboring stimuli in proportion to the heights of the solid lines above each stimulus size. The non-reinforcement of 160 leads to a generalization of inhibition represented by the broken lines, extending also to stimuli on either side of 160. The resulting reaction tendencies, obtained by subtracting the negative from the positive, are indicated by the figures above each stimulus size. (Spence, 1937b.)

The use of the diagram to explain the results of transposition experiments is described in the text.

analysis is illustrated by Figure 25, which is reproduced from his paper. As indicated in the caption to the figure, the gradients of conditioning and of extinction are set up by training with stimulus 256 as positive (reinforced) and stimulus 160 as negative (non-reinforced). Suppose now that a test of transposition is made with the pair of stimuli 409 and 256. From the diagram it is evident that the strength of the tendency to react to 409 (6.5) is greater than the tendency to react to 256 (4.8). Hence 409 will be reacted to, in spite of the fact that 256 was the positive stimulus during training. For this pair of stimuli, results conform to reaction to 'relatively larger' although no assumption is made that the organism detects such a relationship. Suppose, however, the pair 655 and 1049 are presented. Now the strengths are 6.7 for 655 and 2.5 for 1049. Here the reaction will be to the smaller of the two stimuli, contrary to the prediction based on reaction to relations. The crucial test supporting Spence's theory lies in the failures of transposition when tests are made with stimuli remote from those used in training. Such failures have indeed been found in experiments by Gulliksen (1932), Klüver (1933), and Spence (1937a).

More recently, Hull (1939b) has presented a discussion of stimulus equivalence which represents an elaboration and refinement of the type of argument used by Spence. He has adopted a concave gradient of generalization instead of the convex one illustrated in Figure 25, and has expressed the consequences of the interaction of positive and negative tendencies of the two gradients in precise mathematical form. Another mathematical theory of discrimination learning has been elaborated by Gulliksen and D. L. Wolfle (1938a, 1938b). The theories of Spence, Hull, and Gulliksen and Wolfle in spite of differences in detail have in common the assumptions (1) that every reinforcement leads to an increment in the tendency to repeat the behavior in the presence of the stimuli preceding reinforcement, (2) that every non-reinforcement leads to a decrease in the tendency to react again to the stimuli which preceded non-reinforcement, (3) that the tendencies are generalized to other stimuli along dimensions defined psychophysically, (4) that these reaction tendencies, both increases and decreases, interact algebraically, (5) that discriminatory reactions are based on the resolution of the competing tendencies in favor of reaction to that stimulus which has the greater excess of positive reaction tendencies conditioned to it.

This formulation of the problem of discrimination does not represent a final theory in any sense. Whatever revisions are made in the future, the papers discussed above represent important advances in clarifying assumptions, delineating implications, framing propositions for experimental testing, and providing a common mathematical structure for diverse phenomena. Limitations are suggested at the present time by the observed difference in degree of generalization when patterns of stimuli are involved (Figure 23), and by the results of experiments on partial reinforcement (Chapter 6). The influence of partial reinforcement in the discrimination situation has been studied experimentally by Brunswik (1939). Rats running a simple T-maze, with but a single choice-point, were fed occasionally on the right, occasionally on the left. Brunswik found that choices came to be made either to the right or left roughly in proportion to the number of trials on which reinforcement had been received on one side or the other (Table 6). This behavior, which Brunswik interprets as

TABLE 6

CHOICE RESPONSES OF RAT IN RELATION TO PROBABILITY OF FOOD
REINFORCEMENT (BRUNSWIK, 1939)

Groups n = 48 each	Percent of reward for each type of choice		Difference in percentages of reward	Ratio of percentages of reward	Frequency of choice B in last 8 trials	
	CHOICE A	CHOICE B	(A–B)	(A/B)	MEAN AND S. D.ₘ	CR WITH CHANCE
(1)	100	0	100	Inf.	$0.56 \pm .21$	16.7
(2)	50	0	50	Inf.	$1.25 \pm .30$	9.2
(3)	75	25	50	3:1	$1.62 \pm .37$	6.5
(4)	100	50	50	2:1	$2.21 \pm .44$	4.0
(5)	67	33	33	2:1	$3.75 \pm .46$	0.5

reaction in accordance with the probability of reward (hence in terms of the animal's hypotheses), would be interpreted by Spence in accordance with a calculus of reinforcement and extinction. That is, in Spence's analysis each reward on the right would strengthen the tendency to turn right, each absence of reward would weaken the tendency. The probability theory of Brunswik is a sign-learning explanation of the influence of past experience on present performance, and as such is an important alternative to a conception of simple summation of reinforcement and extinction.

A simple probability theory arrives at predictions very similar to those based on reinforcement and extinction, since every strengthening by reinforcement is at the same time an increase in the probability that the stimulus will be reinforced again if reacted to. It has been shown by Humphreys (1939a, 1939b), however, that a simple probability theory does not suffice, since expectancies are complicated by patterns of past successes and failures as well as by the total number of experiences of reward and non-reward. He shows conclusively for human subjects that a single non-reinforcement following a pattern of uniform reinforcement leads to the expectation of uniform non-reinforcement, while following a pattern of random reinforcement and non-reinforcement the expectation of uniform non-reinforcement requires several non-reinforced trials. His interpretation permits him to account for the more gradual extinction found in both human subjects and rats following random alternation of reinforcement and non-reinforcement. The corrections which Humphreys suggests apply both to probability theories and to theories based on the summation of reinforcement and extinction. In its present form the probability theory espoused by Brunswik (1939) makes more allowance for these corrections than the reinforcement-extinction proposals of Spence (1936) and of Hull (1939b).

Threshold Measurement. Several different procedures for the establishment of conditioned discrimination have been described above. To these must be added the usual psychophysical methods employing instructed verbal response with human adult subjects. The chief interest in the comparison of the various methods lies in the measurement of thresholds. Many problems require the determination of absolute and of differential thresholds in animals where verbal response is not possible.

In man, thresholds obtained by conditioning methods may be compared with those obtained by the more usual psychophysical judgments. Newhall and R. R. Sears (1933) compared absolute visual thresholds obtained simultaneously by verbal report and by conditioned finger withdrawal. Using the method of constant stimuli they found that the thresholds by the two techniques were similar. Neet (1936) compared several conditioning methods. He found that conditioned eyelid reactions yielded auditory thresholds similar to those obtained by verbal report; manual response and conditioned respiratory responses yielded slightly higher thresholds. A threshold is therefore relative to the method chosen for measuring it. That conditioning may occur to subliminal stimuli is not necessarily contradictory to the reports that the thresholds by conditioning and other methods are equivalent, for by definition of the limen in the method of constant stimuli, a certain number of correct responses must be given to 'subliminal' stimuli.

In animals, thresholds obtained by classical conditioning methods may be compared with those obtained by other methods, such as the discrimination box of Yerkes and Watson (1911), or the electrical responses of the cochlea (Stevens, H. Davis and Lurie, 1935). Conditioning methods appear to be somewhat more sensitive than the original locomotor form of the discrimination box. This was suggested by Anrep's

(1920) greater success with tonal discrimination in dogs than Johnson's (1913). Subsequently, discrimination procedures involving instrumental response have been greatly improved by arrangements for presenting the reinforcement immediately following the animal's reaction, without the long delay inherent in the Yerkes-Watson apparatus. This change is illustrated in Lashley's (1930b) method, in which the stimuli to be discriminated are mounted on doors against which the animal must jump across an intervening space. If it jumps to the negative stimulus it finds the door locked, and falls into a net. If the positive stimulus is selected, the door gives way under the force of the jump, and the animal finds food on the platform behind the door. The immediate reinforcement provided by this procedure results in more rapid discrimination learning and in more precise threshold values.

The value of conditioning and closely related procedures in the conventional problems of sense-physiology may be illustrated by some of the recent advances in audition and vision. Localization of tonal frequencies in the cochlea, substantiating certain aspects of the Helmholtz resonance theory of pitch, has recently been found by several methods. The electrical methods agree with the results of conditioning experiments (Culler, Willmann, and Mettler, 1937). The duality of the visual process in the rabbit, represented by a shift of the bright visibility curve by approximately 30 $m\mu$ toward the red end of the spectrum from that of dim visibility has been demonstrated by R. H. Brown (1936a, 1937) by means of conditioned respiration. Using the method of contrasts, he also established a differential response to two hues of equal visibility (R. H. Brown, 1936b). This is the first convincing demonstration of color vision in mammals below the primates.

Discrimination as a threshold method depends upon experimental arrangements such that the animal reacts differentially to the minimum stimulus difference which it can perceive.

Successful differential response secured under proper experimental conditions guarantees that the animal can discriminate the relevant differences; unsuccessful discrimination does not, however, mean that the differences involved are beyond the perceptual capacities of the organism, for with some other experimental arrangement the differentiation might be found. Failure of discrimination may be due, for example, to insufficient training. Instances in which an entire year of training has been found necessary are reported (Liddell, W. T. James, and O. D. Anderson, 1934). In other cases, the animal may become upset and refuse to cooperate at all in the experimental procedure. Failure to demonstrate capacity in performance may mean that relationships within the situation, other than the perceptual ones, are too difficult for the animal. The history of animal experimentation contains many instances in which modified methods have resulted in modified thresholds. In man, conditioned discrimination has been shown to depend on factors other than the capacity to discriminate between the stimuli, factors such as time interval between stimulus and reinforcement, knowledge of stimulus relationships, and instructions with respect to response.

Similarity and Difference as Experimental Problems

Generalization and differentiation are the processes within conditioning which throw light on perception, and perception historically has been one of the important fields of psychology. Some of the theoretical problems arising out of the equivalence of stimuli are particularly important, because interpretations of perceptual organization have been the bulwark of the Gestalt attack on the types of learning theory among which conditioning theories are included. To the extent that a perceptual whole is more than the sum of its parts in other relationships, it may also be more than the sum of its parts in conditioning experiments. As a method for detecting equivalences, conditioning may be expected to disclose results similar to those obtained by other methods.

Patterns of Simultaneous Stimuli. When a combination of stimuli has been regularly reinforced, the component stimuli are not equally effective in eliciting responses when presented alone. Pavlov (1927, 141ff.) reports that one member of the compound stimulus may elicit responses of full strength, while others remain ineffective, especially if parts of the compound are presented to different senses. Razran (1938d and later) has performed a number of studies in configural conditioning. One of his methods tested salivary conditioning to the component lights of a pattern which the human subjects had watched while eating. In order to avoid the disturbing effect of voluntary attitudes, the experiment was represented to the subject as concerned with the effect of eye-fatigue on digestion. The results show a tendency for a gradual shift of effectiveness from one component part of the whole to another. In general, that part which was at first effective was relatively simple (a strong Gestalt), while the effective part after many reinforcements was more complex (a weaker Gestalt). This is consonant with the restriction of generalization with practice, for the more complex part actually represented the particular pattern more specifically than the simpler parts at first responded to. Since the organization of patterns appeared to shift with practice, Razran interpreted his results as contradicting the static laws of pattern organization implied in some of the Gestalt writings.

Tonal patterning has been studied by Kleshchov (1932a–1936). He found, for example, that after conditioning to a musical fifth, generalization was greater to other pairs of tones when their ratio was that of a fifth rather than a third. This represents a form of equivalence included in von Ehrenfels's definition of a Gestalt-quality. Related observations have been reported by Razran (1938d).

The component stimuli of a combination may be differentiated from the whole without loss of effectiveness by the whole. It is possible to condition an animal to make one response to a pattern of stimuli and another, qualitatively different, response to the individual components (Beritov, 1932). The reference experiment for this type of differentiation employs the procedure known as conditioned inhibition (see p. 126). A given stimulus is invariably reinforced when it is presented alone. When a second conditioned stimulus is presented along with it, the combination is not reinforced. It is evident that conditioned inhibition is simply one arrangement for discrimination by the method of contrast. The contrast in the stimuli is produced by addition of a stimulus rather than by a change in some dimension of the original positive stimulus. An instance of conditioned inhibition in eyelid responses of human subjects has been reported by Shipley (1934b). A buzz provided the positive conditioned stimulus, followed by a striker to the cheek which produced a lid response. A flash of light served as the conditioned inhibitor; when both light and sound were present together, reinforcement was omitted. The buzzer alone did not lose its capacity to evoke a response, although responses to it were reduced when it was presented in combination with the light. It is, of course, possible to reverse the usual practice of conditioned inhibition, and have the combination positive, the individual components both negative. The important thing is that one pattern of stimuli may be differentiated from another, and the parts do not serve in the whole as they serve alone.

Patterns of Successive Stimuli. The difference between the positive and the negative stimulus may be one of arrangement, rather than one of addition or subtraction. Thus geometrical figures alike except for their orientation, or sequences of stimuli similar in component parts but dissimilar in order, may be discriminated. In some early experiments from Pavlov's laboratory four tones of vibration frequencies of 290, 325, 370, and 413 d. v. were employed in different permutations, only the order 1-2-3-4 being reinforced. There are 24 permutations, such as 4-3-2-1, 2-1-3-4. According to Pavlov (1927, p. 146) all of the sequences were absolutely discriminated from the one sequence which was reinforced. This was a pattern of ascending pitch. Differential response to it illustrates a patterning or organization of perceptual response, as emphasized prominently by Gestalt psychology. Humphrey (1928b) showed how patterning in an arpeggio or melody could conceal a particular tone to which finger withdrawal had been conditioned.

Generalization and the Definition of Similarity. In the experimental treatment of similarity it is possible to select stimuli arranged according to a logical or conventional dimension of difference, and then to discover the amount of generalization which occurs to stimuli along this dimension. The end result is a refining of the scale of similarity along this dimension for the organism under consideration. Confusion arises only if it is asserted that the organism is responding *to* similarity in the stimuli, rather than that it is responding to the stimuli *as* similar. The former statement requires a definition of similarity independent of the organism under question, the latter makes no such demand.

Response *to* similarity in the stimuli is based on the conception that stimuli are physically similar. The limitations of a physical definition of similarity are apparent in the study of the generalization of conditioned responses to tones of different pitch. Humphreys (1939c) established a conditioned galvanic response to a tone of 1967 cycles and tested the magnitude of the generalized response to other tones. The response to a tone of 984 cycles, which is an octave of the reinforced tone, was reliably greater than that to a tone of 1000 cycles, which is more similar to the reinforced tone in terms of physical frequency.

There are a number of types of equivalence between stimuli (and the responses which they evoke) which cause the stimuli to be reacted to *as* similar, so that conditioned responses formed to one of the stimuli will be generalized to the other. Among these may be mentioned: partial identity (whereby stimulus A + B is similar to A + C); sensory similarity (so that two colors are more alike than a color and a tone); formal similarity (for example, two patterns of ascending pitch); affective similarity (equivalence mediated by emotionally flavored processes, as in the 'dark-brown-taste' or 'blue Monday'); and mediated similarity (as in the equivalence of words of different sounds, but of common meanings). Of these relationships, only the first (partial identity) may be conceived of as physical similarity. The second (sensory similarity) may be mediated by relatively primitive physiological processes, as represented in the classical experiments on generalization within a sensory modality. The others all depend upon relatively complex processes, many of which require previous learning in order that the stimuli involved may be responded to as similar.

Learned mediation in conditioning experiments may be illustrated by an experiment in which physical equivalence is clearly out of the question. Children 7 and 8 years old, taught to give conditioned grasping responses to sound or to light, gave the responses when the words "sound" or "light" were spoken by the experimenter, or were presented as printed words on cards (Smolenskaya, 1934). It is evident that the similarity between a word and that for which it stands is a similarity of reference which has been learned in the earlier experience of the child. Such similarity has to be acquired.

Lundholm (1928, 1932) showed that it was possible to utilize hallucinated stimuli in hypnosis as a basis for conditioning and extinction. Responses produced in the presence of hallucinated lights were given as conditioned responses to genuine lights. In his experiments the verbal suggestions of the experimenter aroused processes which substituted for sensory stimulation.

Mediation depends upon intermediate responses of some sort. This interpretation is supported by the fact that long-trace conditioned responses tend to be generalized widely. According to Pavlov, they exhibit "a permanent and universal generalization, involving all the analyzers" (1927, p. 113). Accepting the interpretation of trace responses as conditioned to the subject's own responses (p. 171, Chapter 7) generalization of these trace responses may be understood in terms of the similarity of the postural adjustments made to a variety of stimuli.

Summary

When a conditioned response has been developed by repeated reinforcement of one stimulus, another similar stimulus may elicit the (qualitatively) same conditioned response without reinforcement. If stimuli are scaled along a single psychophysical dimension (such as pitch or loudness of tones), the degree of generalization may be expressed as a gradient, generalization decreasing as the stimuli become less similar. With repeated reinforcement, generalization becomes at first more widespread, and then somewhat more restricted, provided generalization is expressed as a ratio of the generalized response to the conditioned response. In terms of absolute magnitude, the conditioned response generalized to neighboring stimuli tends to increase in size as reinforcement of the original conditioned stimulus continues. Generalization may be reduced by the method of contrasts, in which one of a pair of stimuli is always reinforced, the other not reinforced. Discrimination then results, provided the stimuli are sufficiently different. The method may be used for studying the discriminatory abilities of animals, both in respect to differentiation along a single dimension, and in respect to the patterning of stimuli either in simultaneous patterns or in serial patterns. When compound stimuli are reinforced, the effectiveness of separate components for eliciting the conditioned response must be tested empirically. The effectiveness varies both with the nature of the component stimuli and with the stage of training, so that a simple redintegrative principle is not sufficient to account for the data.

Generalization makes possible an empirical approach to the problem of similarity. Among the types of similarity which have been discussed briefly are partial identity, sensory similarity, formal similarity, affective similarity, and mediated similarity.

Notes

Gradients of Generalization

The form of the gradient of generalization is important in the attempts to derive phenomena of discrimination from generalization. There is no reason to believe that one form of the gradient will be found universal. For discussions of the problem cf. Hull (1939b), Razran (1938c), and Spence (1939). Loucks's (1933, 1937b) criticisms of the irradiation studies are directed against temporal aspects of generalization, not against the spatial aspects.

Choice-Reaction Discrimination

Choice-reaction discrimination cannot be accounted for completely through reinforcement and extinction of the alternative responses, because there are many other complications in the arrangements, such as the introduction of delays, punishments and rewards before choice, at the moment of choice, and after incorrect choices (Muenzinger and associates, 1935–1937). Shock at the moment of choice may delay learning through general disorientation with respect to the stimuli, leading to position habits (Muenzinger and A. Wood, 1935; Fairlie, 1937), just as delay prior to choice may improve learning through making the animal more attentive to the stimuli to be discriminated (Muenzinger and Fletcher, 1936; Honzik and Tolman, 1938). The theoretical alternatives to conditioning explanations of behavior at a choice-point are presented by Tolman (1938a).

Mechanism of Discrimination Learning

The treatment of discrimination learning proposed by Spence (1936) initiated a controversy which carries on earlier disputes between exponents of association theories and the competing theories of Gestalt and sign-learning. This continues at the time of writing.

Krechevsky's studies of presolution hypotheses are presented in a series of papers (1932a, 1932b, 1933a, 1933b). Only a detailed analysis can factor out the relative significance of systematic solution (e.g., with 'insight,' 'hypotheses') and solution determined as an algebraic consequence of reinforcements and non-reinforcements. Papers bearing directly on this aspect of the problem of discrimination are: Haire (1939a, 1939b), Hull (1939b), Humphreys (1939a, 1939c, 1940c), Krechevsky (1937, 1938), T. L. McCulloch (1939a, 1939b), Spence (1936, 1938). The interpretation of sudden solution in terms of insight has been proposed by many writers, of whom Köhler (1925) and F. T. Perkins and Wheeler (1930) may

be taken as representative. The problems of relative and absolute discrimination (i.e., transposition) have received treatment recently by Gulliksen and D. L. Wolfle (1938a, 1938b), Hull (1939b), Jackson and Dominguez (1939), Jackson, Stonex, Lane and Dominguez (1938), F. N. Jones (1939a, 1939b), Korotkin (1938), Lashley (1938), Maier (1939a), Razran (1938c, 1939e), Spence (1937b, 1939), Tolman (1939). The theory proposed by Brunswik (1939) goes beyond the others in embracing many additional facts of perception, such as those reported by Fieandt (1938), who relates perceptual learning to the problem of sensory conditioning.

Two mathematical treatments of discrimination are concerned with other problems—Householder (1939) with a neural mechanism, Hilgard (1938) with the relative influence of set and voluntary factors in conditioned discrimination in man.

Threshold Measurement

Classical conditioning has been widely used as a method for determining sensory abilities in animals and infants. The early studies on dogs from Pavlov's laboratory were reviewed by Yerkes and Morgulis (1909); later studies were summarized by Razran and Warden (1929). Razran has also reviewed the work on animals other than dogs (1933a) and on children (1933b). Many inaccessible studies are reported by Beritov (1927).

The most extensive recent work has been on audition. As illustrative of studies reporting measurements by conditioning and closely related techniques are: Ades, Mettler, and Culler (1937); Andreyev (1934a); Anrep (1920); Britt (1935); Brogden and Culler (1937); Brogden, Girden, Mettler, and Culler (1936); Bull (1928); Culler (1936); Culler, Finch and Girden (1935); Culler, Finch, Girden, and Brogden (1935); Culler, Willmann, and Mettler (1937); H. Davis, Derbyshire, Kemp, Lurie, and Upton (1935); Dworkin (1934b, 1935a, 1935b); Dworkin, Seymour, and Sutherland (1934); Elder (1934, 1935); Engelmann (1928); Girden (1935, 1938, 1939); Henry (1938); Herington and Gundlach (1933); Horton (1933, 1934, 1935); Kasatkin and Levikova (1935); Kemp (1936); Kleshchov (1932a–1936); Muenzinger and Gentry (1931); Neet (1936); Ten Cate (1934a, 1934b); Thuma (1932); Upton (1929); Wendt (1934); Wever (1930).

Examples of studies dealing with visual sensitivity are those of Bogoslovski (1937, 1938), R. H. Brown (1936a, 1936b, 1937), Bull (1928, 1930, 1935), Frolov (1924, 1925a), Kennedy and K. U. Smith (1935), D. G. Marquis (1934), Newhall and R. R. Sears (1933), K. U. Smith (1934, 1935), Spence (1934), Ten Cate (1934a).

Olfactory and trigeminal responses have been studied by W. F. Allen (1937, 1938), temperature sensitivity by Bull (1936), static and kinetic reactions by Oppenheimer and Spiegel (1937), vibratory sense by Sutherland and Dworkin (1932).

Studies of conditioning to subliminal stimuli have been carried out by Cason and Katcher (1933), Newhall and R. R. Sears (1933), Silverman and Baker (1935), Neet (1936), Baker (1938).

Studies of sensory processes concerned primarily with the neural mechanisms involved are reported in Chapter 13.

A precaution always to be kept in mind in studies of capacity is that the indicator chosen by the experimenter may not be a sensitive one from which to infer the organism's potential discriminations by other methods. Discriminatory conditioning, for example, does not always occur, even when the to-be-discriminated stimuli are well above perceptual thresholds as measured in other ways (Cole, 1939; Hilgard, A. A. Campbell, and W. N. Sears, 1937; Hilgard, R. K. Campbell, and W. N. Sears, 1938).

Similarity and Difference as Experimental Problems

Discriminatory reactions have taken on new importance in psychological theory with the increasing recognition of the operational nature of the concepts used in laboratory investigations. Thus Boring (1933, p. 234) says: "Consciousness is *discriminative*, and discrimination is the symptom of consciousness."

Hull (1939b) considers stimulus equivalence to be dependent on three fairly distinct mechanisms: (1) partial physical identity, (2) primary or physiological generalization (irradiation), and (3) secondary generalization. Under secondary generalization he would include the mediated varieties of similarity discussed in the text.

Studies of the transfer effect of learning to respond to one stimulus on the acquisition of the same response to a second stimulus presented together with the first have been carried out by Winslow (1938, 1939) and Winslow, Kantor and Warden (1938). Successive combinations of this type required fewer trials than the preceding ones. The relation of this type of training to higher order

conditioning, as studied by Finch and Culler (1934), was pointed out by the authors.

The Russian studies on generalization and discrimination of patterns of simultaneous and successive stimuli have been little accessible to English readers. They have recently been made available through a comprehensive review by Razran (1939a). The most extensive program has been carried out in Beritov's laboratory, with locomotor situations using dogs and rabbits.

Chapter 9

SERIAL LEARNING

THE BASIC principles and experimental laws of conditioning which have been outlined in the last five chapters were derived from relatively simple and uncomplicated experiments which had been designed expressly to demonstrate such principles as clearly as possible. One of the chief interests in conditioning among psychologists today, however, lies in the systematic relation of conditioning to general problems of learning. What light does the study of conditioning throw on the learning of complex skills such as typewriting, card sorting, and maze running, or the solution of complex problems involving reasoning and insight? This question has been discussed and answered in various ways, as indicated in Chapter 1. The most carefully conceived and elaborated theory of learning based primarily on principles discovered in conditioning experiments is that of Hull. He rejects as superficial and misleading the simple conceptions of conditioning as a single law of association by contiguity, a building-block unit of which habits are composed, or an analogue of all learning situations. Conditioning is, rather, a source of behavioral principles which can be utilized as postulates for the deduction of statements about more complex learning.

The postulates of any theoretical system, whatever their sources, are considered logically as pure assumptions. The theorems or hypotheses which are derived by deduction from the postulates are subjected to experimental test, and the postulates are retained in the theory so long as the deductions check with fact. With this freedom in the choice of postulates, the theorist about learning will naturally be guided to select those relationships which appear most plausible and comprehensive. Most of the postulates in Hull's system are essentially the same as the experimental laws of conditioning described in the previous chapters. For his purposes, they become assumptions; they are accepted as stated and the problem becomes that of understanding some of the more complicated phenomena of learning in terms of them.

Although Hull's theoretical formulations represent an attempt to comprehend complex learning situations in terms of conditioning principles, there is no implication that habits are merely compounds of conditioned response units. He has expressly stated this position as follows:

> In order to correct a frequent misunderstanding, due presumably to the wide dissemination of the views of J. B. Watson, the writer wishes to make it quite clear that neither here nor in any previous publications has he assumed that the more complex forms of behavior are synthesized from reflexes which play the rôle of building blocks. This may or may not be true. His working hypothesis is, rather, that the *principles of action* discovered in conditioned reaction experiments are also operative in the higher behavioral processes. The compound adjective in the expression, 'conditioned-reflex principles,' accordingly refers to the locus of *discovery* of the principles rather than to their locus of *operation*. (Hull, 1935c, p. 227n.)

It is not necessary, according to Hull, to analyze complex behavior into its component conditioned responses. It is only necessary to base hypotheses regarding more complicated learning on conditioning principles, and to test these hypotheses by experiment. If success is achieved, common relationships may be inferred within conditioning and other learning. These relationships may themselves be in need of explanation, but it is evident that even before they are explained a genuine scientific advance will be achieved if data superficially very unlike are harmonized around a few common principles of action.

The extension of conditioning principles has been most carefully worked out in two rather limited fields of learning. In this chapter an account of serial learning will be presented, and in the following chapter, problem solving behavior will be considered.

Characteristics of Serial Learning

In many experiments the learned activity is more than a single response such as an eyelid closure or a finger withdrawal. This is particularly true of instrumental training in which the reward is secured only after a series of responses have been carried out. A trained dog will respond to the command "Fetch it" by running out into the field, picking up a stick, returning, and laying the stick at the trainer's feet. Even the simplest instrumental responses involve a series of movements. The rat in the Skinner apparatus secures food by taking successive steps to approach the region of the lever, lifting its forelegs from the floor, pressing downward on the lever, lowering its body to the food cup, lowering its head, and opening its mouth. In a single straight alley, the locomotion of the rat from one end to the other to secure food may be considered a serial response by analyzing the speed of running separately for the successive segments of the total path.

When an instrumental act is considered as a single response, the principles of conditioning may be directly applied. For example, the maze reaction, considered as a unit, will be more rapidly acquired if the reward is large and the animal is hungry; it will be more slowly learned if the reward is delayed. Gradual disappearance of the reaction will follow trials on which the reward is omitted, and spontaneous recovery from this extinction will occur during an interval of no training. There are many facts about maze learning, however, which cannot be encompassed by this direct application of conditioning principles to the reaction as a unit. There is no possibility of explaining why the rat takes a shorter rather than a longer route through the maze, why some blind alleys are eliminated sooner than others, why mazes of different pattern vary in difficulty. The answers to such questions can be obtained only if the total maze reaction is analyzed in terms of its component part reactions. An adequate account of the serial organization of the habit as a whole calls for a consideration of the stimuli evoking the successive responses, the reinforcement of the separate responses, and the condensation or short-circuiting of serial acts.

Stimuli for Serial Reactions. The stimuli which evoke the successive responses in a serial act must occur in a fixed and unvarying sequence. There are two possible ways in which this order is guaranteed. The first requires the presentation of a series of environmental stimuli, to each of which a response is made. The serial nature of the response thus depends upon the regularity of the external stimuli. If a rat has been trained in a discrimination problem always to go to a lighted doorway in preference to a dark one, its route through a multiple discrimination apparatus, which presents 10 such choices in succession, will be determined by the visual stimuli. After many trials in this situation, with the lights unchanged, the rat may take the same route even when no visual cues are present. The stimuli for the successive responses are now presumably internal. Each act itself provides proprioceptive stimuli for initiating the one next in the series. This second way of securing a fixed order of stimuli is customarily called *chained conditioning*. Pavlov and subsequent writers have placed emphasis on the interpretation of both instincts and habits as chained responses. Holt (1931) has pointed out the importance of chaining in such circular reflexes as the grasp of the new-born infant. Stimulation of the palm of the hand evokes grasping, and the closing of the fist prolongs and increases the stimulation of the palm, thereby increasing the strength of the grasp. Another illustration of chained reflexes is provided in the act of swallowing, in which each component movement propels the food farther along the alimentary tract and thus provides the stimulus for the next successive movement.

Learned serial habits presumably involve chained responses similar to reflex chains, except that the connections between

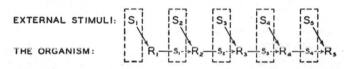

EXTERNAL STIMULI: S_1 S_2 S_3 S_4 S_5

THE ORGANISM: R_1—s_1→R_2—s_2→R_3—s_3→R_4—s_4→R_5

FIGURE 26

THE INTEGRATION OF SERIAL LEARNING

The reactions R_1, R_2, R_3, R_4, R_5 to the external stimuli S_1, S_2, S_3, S_4, S_5 become integrated as a series by the proprioceptive stimuli s_1, s_2, s_3, s_4 from the muscles used in the reactions. Original responses are represented by solid arrows, learned responses by broken ones. After Hull (1930a).

the stimuli and the responses are conditioned. In view of the importance of this mechanism it is strange that so few experimental demonstrations of the chaining of conditioned responses have been made. It is evident from several studies that reaction-produced stimuli may function as conditioned stimuli for other responses, and it is therefore altogether plausible that chaining operates in serial learning. An analysis of the process in conditioning terms by Hull (1930a) is presented in Figure 26. S_1, S_2, etc., represent the successive external stimuli provided by the environment, each evoking in the organism a separate response, R_1, R_2, etc. The sequence of responses is entirely dependent on the serial order of the external stimuli. But each response produces a characteristic proprioceptive stimulus complex such as s_1, s_2. By the principle of substitution, the internal stimulus s_1, which in repetitions of the total situation always occurs at the same time that S_2 evokes R_2, will come to evoke that response in the absence of the external stimulus. The dotted arrows in the diagram represent the newly acquired conditioned responses. As a result, if the sequence of external stimuli is interrupted after S_1 occurs, the serial responses may nevertheless be called forth.

In most situations the integration of a behavior series depends both upon the chaining mechanism and upon the sequences of stimuli in the environment. Thus the restricted pathways of a maze confront the organism with a systematic sequence of external stimuli, if it but runs through the maze. Similarly, a revolving memory drum will expose new items to the learner if he but waits and watches. Whatever integration he may achieve because of the conditioning of reaction-produced internal stimuli, the learned serial behavior often requires the support of the orderly series of environmental events. An individual who has learned to follow a finger-maze correctly may not be able to draw its pattern on paper without the support of the stimulus cues furnished by the maze itself.

Reinforcement of Serial Reactions. The component responses of a serial reaction are usually not separately and independently reinforced. Reward is not given following each segment of a maze, but only at the termination of the sequence. The important consequences of this fact have been pointed out by Hull in his goal gradient hypothesis:

The mechanism . . . depended upon as an explanatory and integrating principle is that the goal reaction gets conditioned the most strongly to the stimuli preceding it, and the other reactions of the behavior sequence get conditioned to their stimuli progressively weaker as they are more remote (in time or space) from the goal reaction. (Hull, 1932, pp. 25–26.)

This principle, as suggested in Chapter 7 (p. 169), may be considered an extension to the serial learning situation of the

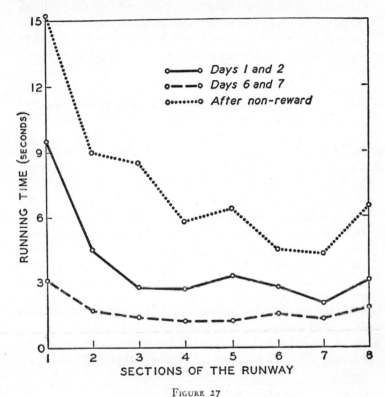

FIGURE 27

LOCOMOTION GRADIENT OF RAT IN 40-FOOT RUNWAY

Composite graphs from 14 animals showing the time consumed in traversing each of the eight 5-foot sections at the two extremes of training and a subsequent restoration of the gradient following non-reward (i.e., absence of food at the end of the alley). Although the gradient has virtually disappeared by the end of training, non-reward restores it in its earlier form. (Hull, 1934b, p. 404.)

gradient of reward. Let Figure 26 represent the five successive segments of a straight single-alley maze which a rat traverses to secure food reward at the end. The final act R_5 will become conditioned to the stimulus complex $S_5 + s_4$ more strongly than any of the previous acts become conditioned to their stimuli because it is closer to the terminal reinforcement. Responses 4, 3, 2, and 1 will be progressively less strong. As applied to running speed, Hull's experimental test of this principle is illustrated in Figure 27.

Condensation of Serial Reactions. It is a common observation that some of the component responses in a serial reaction tend to drop out during continued practice. This short-circuiting tendency will result in more efficient performance when the eliminated components are 'errors' or unnecessary movements. The typist gains speed by eliminating the visual locating of the proper keys; the child learns to count without touching his fingers. In other instances the short-circuiting tendency results in less efficient performance, as when a person steps on the starter in his automobile before he has turned on the ignition, or begins to run before he has securely caught the football thrown to him. But no matter what the outcome, the tendency toward condensation of serial reactions is a familiar one.

An explanation of the mechanism of condensation in terms of conditioning principles has been offered by Hull (1930a). He points out that in addition to the successive external and internal stimuli controlling a serial reaction, there is a persisting stimulus which remains fairly constant while the succeeding responses occur. This is represented by the symbol S_D in Figure 28. It may be thought of concretely as a continuous green light, or the sight of the memory drum in which the separate items are presented, or the stimuli arising from continuous knitting of the brows, or (more typically, in animal experimentation) the stimuli arising from a continuous drive condition such as hunger. From Figure 28 it is apparent that S_D will be conditioned to each of the responses, but according to the goal gradient principle, will be most strongly conditioned to R_5, somewhat less to R_4, and so on. If at any time during learning the tendency of S_D to evoke R_5 should be stronger, for example, than the tendencies of S_2, s_1 and S_D together to evoke R_2, the final response will occur and seg-

EXTERNAL STIMULI:

THE ORGANISM:

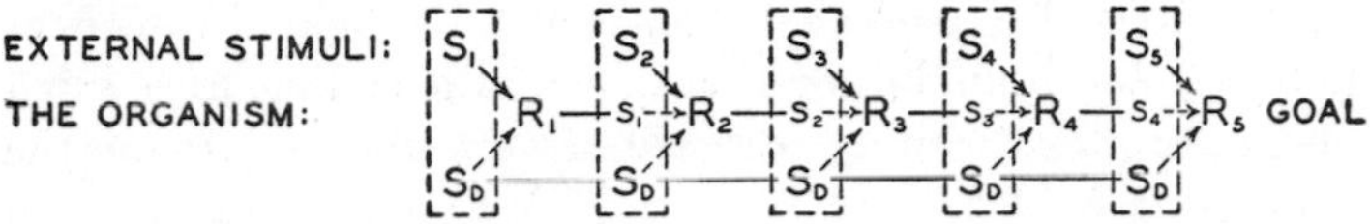

FIGURE 28

THE INTEGRATIVE FUNCTION OF AN ENDURING STIMULUS

To the stimuli and responses of Figure 26 have been added the enduring stimulus S_D, conditioned to each of the responses in the series, as shown by the broken arrows (Hull, 1930a, 1931). All of the conditioning is influenced by the reinforcement based on the goal situation at the end.

ments R_2, R_3, and R_4 will be short-circuited. The premature intrusion of a response is frequently designated as an *anticipatory response*. The anticipatory characteristic of simple conditioned responses has been pointed out before (p. 162). The mechanism may be similar to that described here, for the conditioned stimulus (or some consequence of it) persists from its onset until the reinforcement occurs. Complete short-circuiting such as that just described is not adaptive if the anticipatory response interrupts progress to the goal. There are some anticipatory reactions, however, which are not in conflict with progress toward the goal. Among these, for example, are chewing movements and salivation preparatory to eating at the end of the maze. Such *fractional anticipatory goal reactions* become very important in the later extensions of Hull's theory.

Following this brief survey of the characteristics of serial reactions, we will turn to a consideration of the two most extensively studied examples of serial learning—the maze, and rote verbal learning.

Maze Learning

The value of the maze for the analytical study of serial learning lies in the ready identification of the component units of the series. The pathway down which the animal runs contains a number of bifurcations, one path ending as a blind alley, the other leading forward toward the reward at the end. At each such point the animal makes a choice-reaction discrimination. The stimulus basis of the discrimination is a complex one, comprising external as well as proprioceptive stimuli. The chief problem in the study of maze learning is concerned with the explanation of successful choice-point reactions. With reward inevitably following either correct or incorrect choices, how do the blind alleys ever become eliminated?

Although other writers have discussed the maze in relation to conditioning, the most thorough attempt to account for the details of maze learning in terms of conditioning principles is that of Hull (1932, 1934a). The goal-gradient principle is made one basis of blind alley elimination. Although either a correct or an incorrect response will be reinforced by the reward at the end, the incorrect response receives less reinforcement because it is more remote from the goal (Figure 29). The path which represents a shorter distance to the goal will come to be chosen in preference to one which represents a greater distance.

The rapidity of learning the correct response at any choice-point depends upon the difference between the strengths of reinforcement of the two alternative responses. If the difference is small many repetitions will be necessary before the

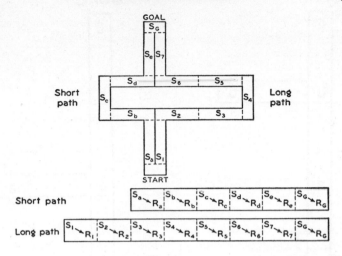

FIGURE 29

EXPLANATION OF THE PREFERENCE FOR THE SHORTER OF ALTERNATIVE PATHS
ACCORDING TO HULL'S GOAL GRADIENT HYPOTHESIS

In the upper diagram a maze is shown in which the short path consists of 5 units of length from start to goal, the long path, of 7 units. The stimuli associated with each unit are simplified as a series S_a to S_G and S_1 to S_G for the two paths. The goal gradient hypothesis assumes that sequences of stimuli and responses as represented in the lower portion of the figure will be strengthened in proportion to their distance from the goal. If, then, there have been equal runs by way of the two paths in the past, when the animal is now confronted with the two stimuli S_a and S_1, the choice will be made on the basis of the tendency of S_a to evoke R_a as compared with the tendency of S_1 to evoke R_1. It is evident that the sequence S_a–R_a will be the more strongly conditioned because it lies nearer the goal. Therefore the short path will be entered. Stimulus components furnished by the drive and the movements of the organism have been omitted for purposes of simplicity in exposition. They have been included by Hull (1932).

error response is completely eliminated. If the difference is large, learning will be more rapid. Experimental results (Yoshioka, 1929) demonstrate that it is the relative rather than the absolute difference between the two reinforcement strengths which determines the speed of learning. From this it follows that long blind alleys will tend to be eliminated more

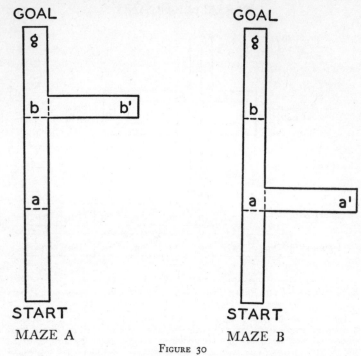

FIGURE 30

EXPLANATION OF THE MORE RAPID ELIMINATION OF BLINDS NEAR THE GOAL
ACCORDING TO HULL'S GOAL GRADIENT HYPOTHESIS

By determining the difficulty of eliminating blind *bb'* in Maze A and blind *aa'* in Maze B, a comparison may be secured between a blind near the goal and one more remote. It is assumed that the choice-point behavior is determined by the relative lengths of paths with a blind compared with the length without the blind. Thus, at choice-point *b* of Maze A, the tendency to take the true path as compared with the blind may be expressed as the ratio of their lengths:

For choice-point *b*, Maze A:

$$\frac{\text{(Path with blind)}}{\text{(Path without blind)}} = \frac{bb' + b'b + bg}{bg} = \frac{3}{1} = 3.0$$

Similarly, for choice-point *a*, Maze B:

$$\frac{\text{(Path with blind)}}{\text{(Path without blind)}} = \frac{aa' + a'a + ab + bg}{ab + bg} = \frac{4}{2} = 2.0$$

Since the relative difference of true path and path with blind is greater in Maze A than in Maze B, blind *bb'* will be more readily eliminated than blind *aa'*. This is what the deduction set out to prove. It is not assumed that this is the only principle applicable, or that the comparison could be made experimentally in mazes as simple as those diagrammed.

readily than short ones, since a long blind results in a greater relative lengthening of the path than a short one. For similar reasons, a blind alley near the goal should be eliminated more readily than one near the entrance. The argument is illustrated in Figure 30. There are sufficient confirmations of these predictions in certain types of mazes to have excited a great deal of interest in Hull's analysis. It is evident that predictions of this kind go beyond the mere assertion that maze-behavior is conditioned. A single analogy from conditioning would not suffice to make the predictions.

Experimental tests of the goal gradient principle in maze situations have given somewhat ambiguous results, because, whether or not the goal gradient principle is correct, many other factors are also present. Three of these additional factors are quite important. Centrifugal swing (Schneirla, 1929; Ballachey and Buel, 1934a) is a matter of the inertia of running, which tends to favor either continuing in a straight path, or running off at a tangent after a turn. This is a matter of performance, rather than of learning, and determines behavior in the very first run through the maze, before there has been any chance for learning to occur. This factor of the general inertia of running is not as effective in linear mazes, which are therefore preferable for use in testing principles such as the goal gradient. A second factor significant in maze learning is the tendency to anticipate later turns, particularly the final turn leading to the goal. A third factor is the tendency of the animal to orient in the general direction of the food-box. In a linear maze with food on the right of the center, more errors are made in alleys on the right than in alleys on the left. This may be a turning habit based on the anticipation of the last unit of the maze instead of an orientation to the food-box (F. N. Jones and Taylor, 1938). Figure 31 illustrates a linear maze used by Spence and Shipley (1934), in which food orientation, goal gradient, and anticipation may all be effec-

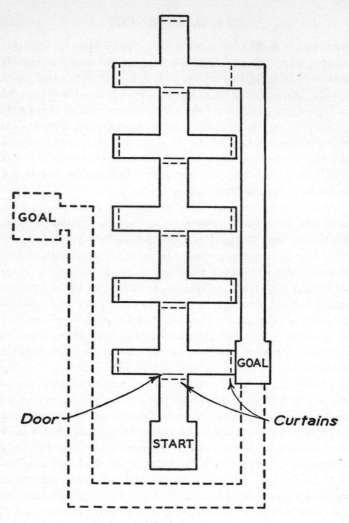

FIGURE 31

MAZE USED BY SPENCE AND SHIPLEY (1934) IN TESTING PRINCIPLES OF
RELATIVE DIFFICULTY OF BLINDS

The dotted path shows a modification of the maze introduced by F. N. Jones
and Taylor (1938) placing the food-box on the left. In their experiment
entrances were also more frequent in the right-hand blinds, showing that
anticipation of the right turn is more important in this maze than orientation
in the direction of the food-box.

tive. Indications within the data suggest that at different stages of the learning different factors are important. Thus within the first five trials it was found that the errors became increasingly more frequent in the goal-pointing rather than in the non-goal-pointing blinds. The order of elimination of blinds was according to the goal gradient, most errors being made in blinds remote from the goal. Nearer to mastery, however, the order was reversed, more errors being made in the blind just prior to the goal-turn. This suggests the prominence at this stage of the anticipatory tendency.

Alleys pointing away from the goal are believed by Hull to be eliminated largely on the basis of the competing alternative tendencies which are more strongly reinforced according to the goal gradient, while the major factor in the elimination of blinds pointing toward the goal is believed to be inhibitory in nature, based on the extinction of the tendency to enter goal-pointing alleys (Hull, 1934a). If maze behavior is in accordance with these principles, important deductions follow with regard to the different effects of spontaneous recovery, of spaced and massed practice, and of the injection of drugs on behavior in the two types of alleys. By combining the goal gradient hypothesis with other conditioning principles such as extinction, external inhibition, disinhibition, generalization, and spontaneous recovery, Hull has proposed a number of specific deductions. The growing literature on maze behavior contains many studies related to these deductions. The data indicate that his account, with all its detail, does not cover all the complexities of maze behavior. Nevertheless, the papers are models of the possibility of deducing phenomena which are not directly analogous to conditioning experiments.

Serial Verbal Learning

Rote memorization of a list of words or nonsense syllables is a serial task that has been the subject of extensive study. In the customary training procedure, the successive items are exposed singly by a memory drum apparatus with an interval of 2 or 3 seconds between items. The first item serves as the stimulus for the response of pronouncing the second; the appearance of the second item indicates to the subject that his response was right or wrong, and in turn serves as the stimulus for pronouncing the third item. The serial character of the task is guaranteed at first by the fixed order of item presentation, and after mastery, each response by the subject evokes the next in order without any stimulus cues from the environment. The reinforcement for the acquisition of new associations in this situation is of a complex derived type involving prompting and knowledge of results. It is important to note that reinforcement occurs after each item in the series and not just at the end of the series. In this respect serial verbal learning differs from animal maze learning, and the goal gradient hypothesis would not be expected to apply.

While relationships between memorization and conditioning had been suggested earlier, Lepley (1932) made the first attempt to apply conditioning principles deductively to the phenomena of rote learning. He argued that each item in the series serves as the cue or conditioned stimulus for eliciting later syllables as conditioned responses. The tendency to respond with the immediately following item may be thought of as a simultaneous conditioned response, while the tendencies to respond with items farther along in the list (remote associations) may be considered as trace conditioned responses. The characteristic anticipatory tendency of trace responses results in the erroneous intrusion of items from later portions of the series. The suppression of these anticipatory intrusions is said to be an inhibitory process with properties which resemble internal inhibition. From this analysis, Lepley deduced several of the characteristics of rote learning, most important of which is the decelerated form of the curve of retention. Initial forgetting is rapid because the remote tendencies which were inhibited recover rapidly and appear in the retention tests as erroneous responses. Since these remote tendencies are not as firmly fixed as the direct simultaneous tendencies, the curve flattens out as time passes, and residual memory persists for a long time.

Hull (1935a) expanded the Lepley hypothesis on the as-

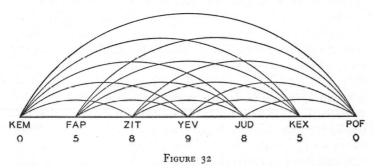

KEM	FAP	ZIT	YEV	JUD	KEX	POF
0	5	8	9	8	5	0

FIGURE 32

AN EXPLANATION IN TERMS OF INHIBITION OF DELAY FOR THE DIFFICULTY
IN MEMORIZATION AT THE MIDDLE OF A SERIES OF NONSENSE-SYLLABLES

The figure, which is taken from Hull (1935a), shows remote associations in the forward direction by curved lines. Backward associations are neglected for purposes of simplicity. The amount by which intervening items are interfered with ('inhibited') may be determined by counting the number of lines spanning each item. The numbers are presented below each syllable. It is evident that the ends of the list will be favored in memorization, while items toward the middle will be progressively more difficult to learn.

sumption that, when remote associations are formed, intervening items are inhibited in accordance with the principle of inhibition of delay. He accounts in this manner for the fact that the middle items of the list are harder to memorize than the items at either end. How an analogy to the inhibition of delay may be used to account for the relative difficulty of items within a memorized series is illustrated in Figure 32. Every associative tendency which is shown to span an item is assumed to depress that item. By counting the number of such connections passing over an item, the amount by which it is inhibited may be determined.

The deductions which followed from Hull's analysis led to several strikingly satisfactory confirmations. Many of the deductions were known to conform to facts already established about memory, for example, that there is greater difficulty at the middle than at either end of the series memorized, and that spaced practice is advantageous over massed practice. In addition, several novel phenomena were predicted and later confirmed in the laboratory. Among them was the theorem that the middle of the list should be recalled more satisfactorily after the lapse of a short time, yielding an initial rise in the curve of retention. This follows from the assumption that inhibitory tendencies disappear more rapidly with time than excitatory ones. The predicted phenomena were demonstrated conclusively by Ward (1937), who also confirmed some predictions with respect to the latent time of the responses to different items in the series. Hovland (1939) has shown that in paired associates learning in which serial character is destroyed by presenting pairs in altered random order on successive trials, the inhibitory tendencies within the series are less than those in serial anticipation learning so that there is found neither the initial rise in the curve of retention nor the advantage of spaced practice. One of Hull's deductions, having to do with the effects of caffeine, was not completely confirmed (Hull, 1935b). The extent of agreement between predictions and findings has been remarkably satisfactory, and an occasional failure serves to indicate the direction which modification of the theory must take. In a more recent publication, Hull and his collaborators (Hull, Hovland, Ross, M. Hall, D. T. Perkins, and F. B. Fitch, 1940), have presented a closely argued extension of the theory. More than 50 theorems are stated, and the proofs of their derivation are given in mathematical as well as in verbal form.

Because of the success achieved in the deductive account of serial verbal learning, there may be a tendency to overlook some of the difficulties in the analogies which have been used. The basic analogy in Hull's (1935a) theory is that of the inhibition of delay. It is known experimentally that trace conditioned responses are very slowly established. The greater difficulty in the middle of the list, however, is found after the first time through the list, and is in fact more pronounced early than late in memorization (Robinson and M. A. Brown, 1926). This is quite unlike the establishment of a delay. In the second place, the tendency of delayed responses to occur prior to the reinforcement is very great. It is more likely that the inhibition observed in serial verbal learning represents an interference between the correct tendency and the tendency to respond with the remote association as a simultaneous response, rather than a true inhibition of delay. For example, when free association is permitted to the separate items of a memorized list presented in random order following memorization, the latencies of remote associations do not correspond at all to the actual time intervals between the items in the memorization (McGeoch, 1936). In the third place, the effect of a time interval after conditioning, which results in rapid recovery from inhibition, leads not only to a disappearance of the inhibition of delay, but to an exaggeration of the tendency to give trace responses at shorter latencies (Rodnick, 1937a). This recurrence of anticipatory intrusions was part of the original Lepley (1932) hypothesis and accounted for rapid forgetting. Recovery from inhibition cannot be used to account both for reminiscence through reduced inhibition (Hull, 1935a) and for forgetting through increased interference (Lepley, 1932) without careful quantitative investigation of what is actually occurring. Some important alternatives to Hull's analysis have been suggested by E. J. Gibson (1938) and by Hovland (1940) based on principles of generalization and interference. These are unfortunately not yet available in complete enough form for exposition. Their very existence, however, indicates that Hull's analysis must not be accepted as final, for alternative sets of postulates may be found to account equally well for the facts which Hull explains.

It is to be noted that the logic of the deductive approach to serial learning does not require the adoption of conditioning as a starting point. Associative strength may be defined empirically by the responses in free association experiments such as those of McGeoch (1936) or Raskin and Cook (1937), just as Spence (1936) in his deduction of discriminatory learning, defined his units of reinforcement by responses within a simple discrimination. The point at which analogies with conditioning are most strained is in the identification of the unitary responses which are said to be reinforced or extinguished. This difficulty is circumvented by accepting empirical findings at the point where the analogy with conditioning is the hardest to apply.

Notes

Chained Conditioning

Emphasis on kinesthetic stimuli as the basis of integration of the maze habit is probably due largely to Watson (1907). This emphasis was extended to other forms of learning by S. Smith and Guthrie (1921), who have continued to lay stress on proprioceptive stimuli as integrators of movement, Guthrie (1935), S. Smith (1935), S. Smith and E. E. Fitch (1935), Carter (1936).

Evidence showing that reaction-produced stimuli may be used as conditioners is found in Hudgins (1933), Menzies (1937), Skinner (1938). While many other writers have shown the participation in conditioning of concomitant responses (Beck, 1939; J. Miller and Cole, 1936; Schlosberg, 1932), chaining of conditioned responses has never been demonstrated unequivocally. Hull (1934c) interpreted the Miller and Konorski experiment as a type of chaining, since a tone which had accompanied passive lifting of the leg prior to feeding later caused both leg-lifting and salivation. The behavior, however, lacks any definite serial character, whereby the stimuli resulting from one conditioned response act as the instigators of a second act. Other chains of acts (Skinner, 1934) secure their serial character through environmental supports, and hence are not clear cases. Shipley's experiment (1933, 1935) is a type which requires more study. One interpretation of transfer in his experiment, as pointed out in Chapter 10 (p. 230), is the mediation of a second response by the evocation of a first. This, if acceptable, represents genuine chaining.

Maze Learning

That the sensory control of the maze habit may be independent of kinesthesis has been shown by Lashley and Ball (1929) and by Honzik (1936). A review of the many factors leading to maze errors and to their elimination may be found in Buel (1935).

The more important maze studies directly or indirectly influenced by the attempt to apply or to criticize the deductive use of conditioning principles include: A. C. Anderson (1933), Ballachey and Buel (1934a, 1934b), Bruce (1937, 1938), Buel (1934, 1938, 1939), Buel and Ballachey (1934, 1935), Dennis (1935), Dennis and Sollenberger (1934), Drew (1939), Gilhousen (1938), Honzik and Tolman (1936), Hull (1934a, 1934b), Hull and Spence (1938), Hunter (1935b, 1936b), F.

N. Jones and Taylor (1938), Leeper (1935), Liddell (1934), Lumley (1932), N. E. Miller (1935), N. E. Miller and Miles (1935, 1936), N. E. Miller and Stevenson (1936), C. T. Morgan and Fields (1938), Reynolds (1936, 1939), F. L. Ruch (1934), Snygg (1936), Spence (1932), Spence and Shipley (1934), Spragg (1933, 1934, 1936), Tolman (1933), Zieve (1937).

Serial Verbal Learning

No attempt will be made to cite references to the voluminous literature on serial verbal learning. Reviews and summaries may be found in Hunter (1934), McGeoch (1934). A classified bibliography is given in McGeoch (1933).

Lepley's (1932) hypothesis regarding the applicability of conditioning to memorization was proposed originally in a seminar which Hull conducted. Among the studies relating conditioning specifically to memorization and retention may be listed E. J. Gibson (1938), Hovland (1938a, 1938b, 1938c, 1939, 1940), Hull (1935a, 1935b, 1937), Hull, Hovland, Ross, M. Hall, D. T. Perkins, and F. B. Fitch (1940), Lepley (1932, 1934, 1936), Patten (1938), Peak and Deese (1937), R. R. Sears (1936), Shipley (1939), Ward (1937), Witmer (1935).

Chapter 10

PROBLEM SOLVING

THERE are many laboratory situations in which the interest of the experimenter is centered on the success achieved by a subject on the first trial in a novel situation, or on a successful performance which appears suddenly after repeated failure, and is thereafter sustained. Experiments in which behavior of this sort typically occurs are commonly called problem-solving experiments, and are designed to study the 'higher mental processes.'

Conditioning is primarily concerned with those instances of behavior modification which depend upon repeated trials. The effect of reinforcement can be tested only by a subsequent presentation of the same stimulus situation. Conditioning principles, therefore, appear not to be applicable to instances of insightful learning, since the term insight implies a kind of learning in which a conspicuous readjustment occurs in a single trial. The implied novelty or discontinuity with the previous history of the organism seems to contradict association or conditioning principles. Thus Guthrie has stated: "In so far then as insight means the ability to meet a new and unique situation with an adequate response it must remain in the category of luck" (1935, p. 195). A conditioning theory of problem solving obviously requires continuity of some sort with the past learning of the organism, but in order to use the concept of insight it is not necessary to assume that the discontinuity with the past is complete. No believer in insight would deny that the insightful solution of a mathematical problem requires a knowledge of the symbols, conventions,

228

and operations characteristic of a particular branch of mathematics. Novelty enters as the events are structured in new relationships. The important thing to be stressed in insightful solution is that the possession of sufficient past experience to provide the materials essential to solution does not of itself guarantee the solution. One organism, given the same past experience and habit acquisitions as another, may not be able to solve a problem which the other can solve. Therefore a conditioning account of insightful learning must explain both how the raw materials relevant to the solution are learned, and how they are assembled in the way appropriate to the problem at hand. Such an account cannot be made easily in conditioning terms, but there is no *a priori* reason to believe it impossible.

Mediated Stimulus and Response Equivalence

The clearest examples of problem solution are found in experiments which rule out the possible influence of repeated reinforcement of the correct response; that is, when solution is demanded on the first trial in a novel situation. A conditioning explanation must relate the correct solution in some way to the subject's prior experience with the elements of the problem situation. Although the most hopeful suggestion for explanation through the concepts of classical conditioning is the phenomenon of generalization, simple sensory generalization alone is not adequate to account for the degree of novelty which exists in most problem situations. Many examples of insightful behavior can be redescribed as the appropriate combination of two or more previously learned experiences. The combination involves the mechanism of mediated stimulus equivalence (mediated generalization, cf. p. 201).

An example of learned stimulus equivalence has been described by Brogden (1939c). A light and a bell were presented together to a dog for 200 trials, after which the dog was trained to retract its foreleg to the bell followed by shock. On a subsequent test it was found that the dog responded with leg retraction to the first presentation of the light. This is not simple conditioning, because the light had never been followed by shock; it is not higher-order conditioning, because the light and bell were not combined after the bell had become a conditioned stimulus; it is not simple sensory generalization, for dogs without the previous light-bell trials did not respond to the light after training with the bell. An explanation in conditioning terms involves the inference that some reaction (not necessarily an observable or overt one) which is originally made to the bell becomes conditioned to the light in the light-bell trials. This hypothetical *intermediate reaction* may be considered the mechanism of the learned equivalence of bell and light in eliciting leg withdrawal. Brogden's experiment gives no clue to the nature of the reaction. In the situation as described, the intermediate reaction serves no instrumental function in securing a reward or avoiding a punishment; it is comparable to what has been termed in other connections a perceptual response, an idea, a symbolic process, or a pure stimulus act.

The possible rôle of intermediate reactions in learned stimulus equivalence is more clearly demonstrated in a recent experiment by Lumsdaine (1939) in which an overt reaction was studied. Following a procedure employed earlier by Shipley (1933, 1935), Lumsdaine established conditioned eyelid responses in human subjects by presenting a light reinforced by the blow of a mechanical striker on the cheek near the eye. A finger withdrawing movement was subsequently conditioned by combining the striker with a shock to the finger. After this course of training, it was found that the light evoked finger reactions in a large proportion of the subjects, although it had never been followed by shock. The records reproduced in Figure 33 illustrate the sequence of events in

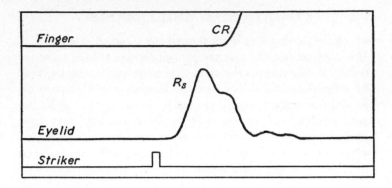

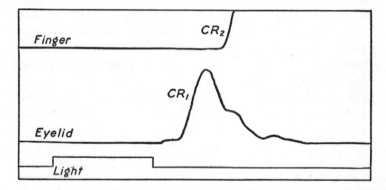

FIGURE 33

THE LID REFLEX AS AN INTERMEDIATE RESPONSE IN THE LEARNED
EQUIVALENCE BETWEEN A LIGHT AND A STRIKER AS STIMULI FOR
CONDITIONED FINGER RETRACTION

The upper record shows a conditioned finger retraction (CR) after the striker has been repeatedly followed by shock. The eyelid reflex to the striker (R_s) is present incidentally, but stimuli produced by it may have become conditioned stimuli for finger movement. Conditioned eyelid responses had previously been conditioned by reinforcing a light with the striker. In the lower record is shown the result of presenting the light after the finger conditioning has intervened. The light elicits the conditioned lid response (CR_1) in accordance with the prior training, but perhaps because of stimuli related to the lid response, conditioned finger retraction (CR_2) is also evoked. (Traced from unpublished photographic records, courtesy of A. A. Lumsdaine.)

which the lid response is considered the intermediate reaction. If it may be inferred that the proprioceptive stimuli from the reflex lid response to the striker became conditioned stimuli for finger withdrawal, any stimulus leading to lid closure might produce a tendency to finger withdrawal. Since the lid reaction had been conditioned to the light, the light may have evoked finger withdrawal by way of the stimuli from the lid movement. The situation is not, of course, quite as simple as this, and just any blink would not, after this training, cause finger movements. When other supporting stimuli are present (i.e., the familiar apparatus, the finger on the electrode, etc.) the proprioceptive stimuli from the lid may be sufficient to set off the response. Here the lid reflex to the striker was a definite, vigorous response. In the experiment of Brogden mentioned above, it may be assumed that something equivalent to this lid reflex occurred in response to the buzzer even though it was not observed experimentally.

It can be seriously doubted that all learned stimulus equivalence is mediated by proprioceptive stimuli arising from intermediate reactions, as would be implied by a thoroughgoing motor theory of thinking and of consciousness. In Lumsdaine's experiment (as in a related study by J. Miller and Cole, 1936), the finger response did not always wait for the eyelid response but in a few instances coincided with it or preceded it. This suggests the possibility that the eyelid response may not be an essential step in the sequence, but merely an overt indicator of a central 'set' which is common to both the light and the striker stimuli. Loucks (1931) has presented the most critical evidence on this point. He trained rats in a delayed temporal alternation problem which required a choice reaction on the basis of some sort of internal cue. Successful performance was not destroyed when the rats were given a general anesthetic during the five minute period of delay before choice. Under such conditions it is not possible to assume that the reaction was based on the proprioceptive stimuli arising from some intermediate response such as a maintained posture. More direct study of the mechanism of learned stimulus equivalence in animals has not yet yielded conclusive results (Loucks, 1939).

Sign-learning Experiments. In an attempt to show the inadequacy of a conditioning theory of learning, Tolman (1933) performed an experiment which he designed expressly to test the relative applicability of his sign-learning ('sign-Gestalt') theory and conditioning. One group of rats were shocked in the food-box at the end of a locomotor problem. This produced retardation (i.e., avoidance learning) to be expected from conditioning theories. Another group of rats were shocked in the food-box, having been placed there without the usual run through the path. The question is whether the rats will respond appropriately at the beginning of the maze on the next trial. Conditioning theory, according to Tolman, would predict no influence, since the maze running response was itself not punished. Sign theory would predict retardation, since the food-box would be signified as 'bad.' The rats behaved as Tolman thought they should according to conditioning theory; that is, their behavior was not affected by the separate punishment in the food-box.

N. E. Miller (1935) objected both to Tolman's analysis and to his experiment. He predicted that, according to conditioning theory, rats should evidence anticipatory avoidance behavior, even though they were shocked in the food-box without having run to it. He then set up an experiment in which he felt a better test could be made. At the end of a straight alley one group of rats found a reward device which consisted of a box which made the rats cramp their bodies to the right in order to secure food. Another group of rats found a device which required them to twist their bodies to the left in order to secure water. Food and water-deprivation were used as appropriate conditions of motivation. Presumably the devices were sufficiently different so that fractional anticipatory reactions to them would differ, whether these reactions depended upon the difference between anticipated food and water or upon the differences between right and left body positions. Half of the group trained to water and half of the group trained to food were now shocked outside the maze, but while utilizing the reward device. When they were next placed in the alleys, their running speeds were markedly reduced. When, however, the rats composing the other half of each group were shocked in the device not used in the maze, their running was much less affected. A third group, shocked under quite different circumstances, showed no effects whatever upon their performance.

These results are interpreted by Miller as demonstrating a learned equivalence between the reward device and the alley itself. The common element in the two situations is the fractional anticipatory goal reaction (r_g) which occurs, after training with food reinforcement, at the beginning of the alley as well as at the termination (p. 215, Chapter 9). The r_g plays the rôle of the intermediate reaction, comparable to the eyelid response in Figure 33. When the animal is placed in the reward device for shocking, the r_g is elicited as usual, and the internal stimuli arising from it become conditioned to the avoidance responses which were evoked by the shock. When the animal is subsequently placed at the start of the alley, r_g also occurs, producing the stimuli to which the avoidance responses have just been conditioned. These responses interfere with forward locomotion, so that it is prevented or slowed. Comparison of Miller's results with Tolman's suggests that the distinctiveness of the goal reaction, and consequently of the fractional anticipatory goal reactions, is an important factor in determining the degree of equivalence of shock after running, and shock in the goal device not following running.

Delayed Reaction Experiments. In the direct method now commonly used in the study of delayed reaction, an animal is shown two containers, such as inverted cups. Food is placed under one cup while the animal is watching. Now a screen is interposed, or the animal is taken away for a short interval of time. When the screen is lifted, or the animal returned, a choice between the two cups is permitted. Successful response consists in choosing correctly in a series of trials above chance expectancy. An analysis of delayed reaction performance along the lines of the experiments discussed above would indicate that there is a learned equivalence between the cup on the test presentation, and the food stimulus. Past training has established an approach response to the sight of food and hence also to the anticipatory reaction (r_g) aroused by the sight of food. When one cup is presented together with the food stimulus, the overt approach is prevented, but the r_g becomes conditioned to the cup stimulus. On the subsequent test when the food is hidden, the cup stimulus evokes the r_g which produces stimuli evoking approach movements.

According to this interpretation of delayed reaction successful performance should be determined by three factors in addition to the inherent capacity of the subject: the strength of conditioning of r_g to the sign stimulus (cup), the strength of conditioning of approach movements to r_g, and the degree of difference (i.e., the discriminability) of the two r_g's evoking left or right approach movements. Although the interest in delayed reaction experiments has been directed predominantly toward comparison of the intelligence of various species (or of individual animals after cerebral damage) some data bearing on the factors listed above are available. The strength of conditioning of r_g to the sign stimulus is a function of the preliminary presentation. It should be noted that in the typical procedure the cup and the food are shown together for only one trial. No systematic study has been made of variations in frequency of repetition of the preliminary presentation. On the other hand the strength of conditioning of approach movements to r_g is a function of training which took place before the experiment proper. Since the direct method utilizes a habit of approaching visible food, a habit that has been practised throughout the subject's life, the conditioning has been found to be stronger than in the case of the indirect method in which training is given experimentally to establish an approach response to a stimulus such as a light. The third factor—the difference between the alternative r_g's—is of course not open to direct observation. They should differ in proportion to the difference in the final goal reaction of the left and right approach responses. It has been found that performance is better on the basis of spatial cues than on non-spatial cues (Nissen, Riesen and Nowlis, 1938), and that it is improved by increasing the spatial separation of the two food containers. These points require much further analysis before a conditioning interpretation of delayed reaction becomes plausible.

There is no explanation in the above analysis of the operation of the limiting factor of delay interval. The commonly observed finding that delayed reaction becomes progressively less successful as the interval is lengthened from a few seconds to a few minutes probably depends upon an entirely different mechanism. Short delays are presumably bridged by the same process that is involved in short trace conditioned responses and short delayed rewards; namely, by whatever constitutes the stimulus trace. The maintenance of a posture, or the continuation of the reverberating effects of some other muscular or neural activity, may be postulated as the mechanism of the shortest delays. Longer delays probably depend upon types of learned mediation which are not direct functions of the duration of the interval.

Reasoning Experiments. Maier (1929) has conducted a

series of experiments on reasoning in rats. After being taught the necessary segments of behavior for problem solution, the rats were placed in a situation in which the learned habits could not function directly, for the old segments of the task appeared in new relationships. If the animals could behave in accordance with the new relationships they would exhibit reasoning. This they appeared to be capable of doing. Hull (1935c), accepting the facts as demonstrated by Maier, has given a deduction conforming to his other analyses of learned behavior. The most important rôle is played by the fractional anticipatory responses.

Hull proposes to account for the behavior that would occur in a conventionalized form of the Maier situation, as shown in Figure 34. There are first four sequences of acts separately learned, as follows:

(1) Hungry; R to X, rewarded with food at X.
(2) Hungry; U to X, rewarded with food at X.
(3) Thirsty; R to U, rewarded with water at U.
(4) Thirsty; R to H, rewarded with water at H.

The problem which now tests the rat's capacity for reasoning is introduced. The rat, when hungry, is placed at R. Since it has been trained to run from R to X for food, it sets out in the direction of X. But a barrier has been interposed at B (Figure 34), so that this sequence is blocked. The choice of two paths now confronts the rat. Its tendencies to take them were previously equated, but then under circumstances in which it had been deprived of water. Now, not thirsty, but deprived of food, the question is whether the rat will choose the path R to U to X and reach food, rather than the path R to H.

An anthropomorphic explanation would be as follows. The rat perceives and remembers the spatial relationships involved. It has learned two approaches to food, starting from R and starting from U. Therefore, it reasons, if there is some way of getting to U, it can get to the food at X. But it has gone to U from R before, so it does so now. The reasoning in most reduced form is as follows: "The only alternative way of get-

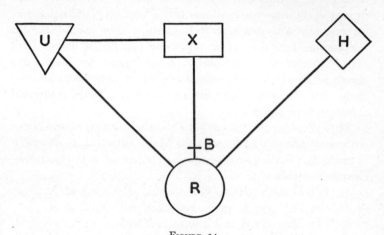

FIGURE 34

A 'REASONING' EXPERIMENT

Diagrammatic representation of a conventionalized form of Maier's 'reasoning' experiment with rats, as used by Hull in attempting to deduce the behavior from conditioning principles. The runways are similar, but the platforms, R, U, X, and H are made as different as possible in form and in surface texture, so that they may be readily discriminated by the rat. (Hull, 1935c.)

ting to X is via U; since I know how to get to U, I can get to X."

It is Hull's problem to find a substitute for this 'reasoned' solution. His answer to the problem involves substituting inferred reactions for the understanding of relationships. The choice for the rat instead of lying between paths symbolized by ideas is between paths as represented by competing reaction tendencies. There are two paths to choose between, so that all that is necessary is to find an anticipatory reaction which throws the balance in favor of the path R to U as against the path R to H.

The broad outlines of Hull's analysis may be indicated without recounting the details. Anticipatory tendencies are presumed to be aroused at the starting point R for each of the locomotor responses made on the several paths, as a result of the previous runs through each of the paths. It is assumed that these locomotor tendencies are equal, so that if based on them alone the choice of one path or another would be at chance frequency. Another set of anticipatory tendencies are conditioned to the drive stimulus. These are not alike for all paths, because in the earlier training the hunger drive functioned for paths R to X and U to X, the thirst drive for paths R to U and R to H. The anticipatory tendencies based on internal drives are conditioned appropriately to these different paths. The problem faced by Hull is to sum up the competing anticipatory tendencies when a hungry animal is at R, and the usual preferred path R to X is blocked. The anticipatory locomotor tendencies are equal for the alternative paths R to U and R to H. Neither path has anticipatory goal reactions conditioned to the hunger drive, since training on both paths was with the thirst drive. Entrances into one or the other path would therefore be by chance, if some added tendency were not discovered favoring one over the other. This added tendency is one anticipatory reaction conditioned to the food drive that is common to path R to U, and not to path R to H. This is a tendency r_U, based on the response to U when the animal, previously hungry, had learned to run from U to X. Since there is also an anticipatory tendency r_U based on reaction to U when running from R to U while thirsty, these two r_U's turn the balance, and the rat chooses path R to U instead of R to H. Once at U, the old habit of running from U to X when hungry is free to become active, and the problem is solved.

When the difficulties of exposition are circumvented, it is

evident that the choice of pathway R-U-X depends entirely on the locomotion tendency evoked by the proprioceptive consequences of the anticipatory reaction r_U. This tendency is greater than the competing reaction evoked by r_H while the animal is at the starting point because the animal is hungry. It is the movement equivalent of the animal's recollection that another way to get to food is by way of U, thus supplementing the tendency the animal already has to go to U.

The question will immediately be raised whether the concept of reacting differentially to fractional anticipatory goal reactions is not as difficult to assimilate into a theory of behavior as discriminating between perceptual representations. Can a starting point, such as U, on the way to food, be recognized as equivalent to a goal point, the same geographical U, when that place has been used as the terminal point for a thirst-quenching sequence? Hull's answer is, briefly, "Yes, because the anticipatory reaction r_U will be common to both situations." At the present time this is a matter of conjecture, not of demonstration. It is merely attributing to the animal the capacity for equating in terms of its responses place U approached from one direction with one purpose and the same place when left in another direction for another purpose. The simultaneous presence of all of the anticipatory reactions is itself particularly difficult to account for on the basis of proprioceptive discrimination, although Hull (and Maier) attempted to make this easier by providing great differences in texture at R, U, X, and H.

Since the proprioceptive consequences of fractional anticipatory reactions have been made by Hull the basis for solution both in this situation, and in others involving goal attraction and purpose, it is important to examine the data bearing upon the organism's capacity to discriminate between its own internal stimuli in situations comparable to those in which behavior is being deduced.

Hull recognized the importance of furnishing such evidence, and he demonstrated experimentally (Hull, 1933) that rats can be taught to turn one way when hungry, another way when thirsty, in an otherwise comparable external environment. While the task was more difficult for the rats than naturalistic observations might have led one to expect, the demonstration was made satisfactorily. Leeper (1935) by modifying the experimental arrangements slightly, was able to secure the differentiation much more promptly. N. E. Miller's (1935) experiment, reported above, is also pertinent. It is clear that anticipatory responses do occur, and that an animal can differentiate between them.

Habit-Family Hierarchy. An hypothesis to explain response equivalence in terms of conditioning has been presented by Hull (1934a) in his concept of the *habit-family hierarchy*. A family of habits is defined as a group of two or more response sequences, all of which may be initiated by a particular stimulus and terminated by a particular reaction. The individual habit sequences are still alternative in the sense that only a single member of the family can be active at once. At the same time they are equivalent in that all are alike in bringing about substantially the same final goal reaction. A simple example of a habit-family is found in the many alternative spatial paths that an animal can take from one point on an unobstructed floor to another point at which food is placed. Hull has stated his hypothesis as follows:

When an organism for any reason succeeds in solving a problem by a sequence of acts which is substantially that of one member of a habit-family, the other members of the family, particularly those occupying a more favored position in the hierarchy, will automatically become active in the new situation without any specific practice whatever. This transfer may be thought of as being mediated mainly through the anticipatory reaction (r_g) which is common to all members of the habit-family hierarchy and which therefore as a stimulus is conditioned to evoke the initial reactions of each member. (Hull, 1934a, p. 147.)

According to this principle, after discovering food by a circuitous route in a free field, the animal would on the next trial tend to adopt a direct path. The habit-family hierarchy principle is thus a substitute for such field principles as least action. The tendency to take the direct path may account for multiple-path behavior of the rat in the maze (Dashiell, 1930), for goal-orientation in the maze (to the extent that it exists), and for the adoption of the shortest alternative pathway to the goal when the direct path is blocked.

Circumventing a Barrier. Lewin (1933, 1935) has proposed a number of problems which arise particularly in the behavior of young children, when a goal-object is sought by the child, but a barrier makes a direct approach impossible. The behavior of the child is accounted for by Lewin in terms of valences and forces. For example, if the goal-object is at the center of a circular barrier, the child tends to circle around the barrier. This behavior permits locomotion without increasing the distance from the goal. If, however, the child is in the center and the desired object outside, the field properties of the situation are such that running around the inside of the circle does not occur. Instead there is oscillation in a small arc at the side near the goal. The situation becomes more complicated when positive and negative valences appear together, as when a desired toy floats on water which the child fears to approach. These situations are, of course, much freer in their possibilities than a maze in which the paths are fixed, and conditioning explanations appear to be proportionately the more difficult.

Hull (1938) has analyzed the behavior which Lewin describes by applying the principles of the goal-gradient and the habit-family hierarchy. He begins with a few basic assumptions such as that the goal-gradient hypothesis is applicable to visible goal-objects, and that the child possesses a habit-family hierarchy based on its earlier experiences. The most important experience assumed is that the larger the angle made by the beginning of the pathway with the straight line to the object, the longer the path to the object. From these assumptions many consequences flow. For example, too large a lure may increase the difficulty of a problem. This is known to be true from Köhler's (1925) studies. Similarly, too strong a drive may make solution more difficult. This has also been demonstrated in certain problem situations (e.g., Yerkes, 1934). Naïve subjects, through the misleading action of the angular hierarchy, will under certain circumstances choose the longer of two paths. Certain of Lewin's precise findings, such as the circling of the barrier, are also deduced. The goal-gradient hypothesis and the principle of the habit-family hierarchy, originally used in relation to maze behavior, have been found by Hull to be widely applicable to other behavioral situations, particularly those in which single-trial learning occurs through acquired response equivalence.

Insightful Behavior in Typical Conditioning Experiments. Instances of learned sensory and motor equivalence producing a novel response on the first presentation of a new situation have been recorded in connection with conditioning experiments. For example, it has been found true of human subjects who were trained to withdraw the right hand to a buzzer, that if the left hand was placed on the stimulating electrodes it was withdrawn the first time the buzzer was sounded (J. J. Gibson, Jack, and Raffel, 1932). This "solution" evidently depended upon the equivalence of the original and the altered stimulus situations in evoking withdrawal response, and the equivalence of right hand and left hand responses. Similar examples of spontaneous transfer of conditioning effects have been reported in studies of the knee jerk (J. J. Gibson and Hudson, 1935), and of leg retraction in dogs (Kellogg and E. L. Walker, 1938a). Wickens (1938, 1939b) found that if the position of the hand in relation to the stimulating electrodes was reversed, the conditioned response changed spontaneously from extension to flexion. In these cases the equivalence is obviously learned, but data on the history of the component reactions is lacking. In the adult human subject the intermediate reaction is undoubtedly often a verbal one.

Intermediate Reactions and Derived Reinforcement

The theoretical possibilities discussed in the previous sections show that the assumption of intermediate reactions may be used to account for several forms of problem-solving which appear, before analysis, to demand ideation or foresight. This suggests the desirability of reexamining the principle of expectancy, which has been used to explain learning based on secondary reward and on the avoidance of punishment. It may be possible to reduce the explanation of derived reinforcement to the principles of substitution and effect.

When instrumental responses are reinforced by a secondary reward such as a token, there is no satisfaction of any primary physiological drive. The token, by reason of its repeated association with a primary reward, has acquired an effectiveness in reinforcing behavior in new learning situations. This effectiveness has been termed derived reinforcement. It may safely be assumed that the token elicits fractional anticipatory goal reactions, but it is difficult to state how such r_g's would have any reinforcing effect upon instrumental responses leading to the token. White (1936) has suggested that reinforcement may best be described in terms of a 'completion hypothesis.' In any learning situation the organism possesses a certain need or want, which can be restated as the presence of anticipatory reactions relevant to the goal. The completion of the anticipatory reactions (by the goal response itself) tends to reinforce recent and concomitant stimulus-response connections. Thus, if the organism had learned to want the token, i.e., had anticipatory token reactions, the securing of the token would complete the sequence and be a reinforcing agent. By this conception, however, if the organism had come to expect shock in a certain situation, the occurrence of the shock would be reinforcing. Actually, of course, the opposite effect may result. At the present time, no satisfactory explanation of the operation of secondary reward in conditioning terms has been put forward.

Can an explanation in terms of r_g's be applied to avoidance learning? An affirmative answer is intimated by the experiment of N. E. Miller (1935) previously reported, in which avoidance behavior was explained in terms of the anticipation of reinforcement involving punishment. That the avoidance responses are aroused increasingly as the punishment is approached may be inferred from the gradient of avoidance reported by Bugelski and N. E. Miller (1938). This gradient can best be interpreted as the result of heightened anticipatory avoidance reactions as the noxious stimulus, e.g., shock, is neared. This heightening is what would be expected from the conditioning of r_g's more strongly to stimuli close to the shock. If it be recalled that instrumental escape learning is a form of rewarded learning ('safety' being rewarding), a possible explanation of avoidance learning on the basis of heterogeneous reinforcement may be obtained. It need only be supposed that as the animal initiates a series of acts which have led to shock, the conditioned stimuli will arouse r_g's which are anticipatory of the reaction to shock itself. These anticipatory reactions will conflict with the completion of the series of acts, and produce a state of heightened tension. This heightened tension is relieved by the avoidance behavior, as, for example, by running in the other direction. Since the animal succeeds in reducing tension, the situation has become dynamically that of escape learning, and the responses prior to the escape are strengthened by heterogeneous reinforcement. Just as rapid forward running is furthered by food at the end of the maze, so rapid running in the reverse direction is strengthened by the relief of the tensions aroused by the r_g's. The strengthened responses are those which conflict with the approach to the shock point. Hence in later trials, although the shock is not received, the avoidance behavior continues to be reinforced, because escape inevitably reduces the conflict produced by approach to the shock point. The derived reinforcement is therefore based on the escape from tension, rather than on the punishment. A similar explanation has been proposed by Mowrer (1939) who identifies the anticipatory r_g's with fear or anxiety. Any act which operates to reduce the anxiety will thereby be reinforced. In the case of both analyses, however, there is no explanation of the commonly observed fact that the anticipatory responses (anxiety) seldom demonstrate any diminution through extinction, in spite of the fact that the painful stimulus constituting their reinforcement is not received by the organism.

It must not be supposed that these conjectures represent solutions of the problems of derived reinforcement. They are offered as suggestions pointing toward the form which solutions in terms of conditioning may take. It has not yet been demonstrated that conditioning theories are able to give completely satisfactory explanations of the processes involved.

Problem Solving Capacity

The attempts to reduce derived reinforcement to heterogeneous or homogeneous reinforcement may or may not succeed; certainly the contemporary accounts are not yet final. The fact that experiments clearly demonstrate the reality of learning based on secondary rewards and other kinds of derived reinforcement does not prevent controversy over interpretations. The token or sub-goal serves in some sense as a signal upon which the organism's 'expectations' are based. There are those who believe that the ability to form expectations based on signs may be deduced from the principles appropriate to homogeneous and heterogeneous reinforcement. There are others who believe that the capacity for expectation is one of the fundamental capacities of the organism, not to be explained away by reducing it to something else. The whole question is but one form of the familiar nature-nurture problem, cropping out in a new context. Consider, for example, the controversy between Tolman (1937, 1938b) and Guthrie (1937). Associationism, which Guthrie endorses, assumes a minimum of native endowment. Gestalt psychology, however, with which Tolman has some affiliations, is prepared to accept a maximum of potentiality grounded in the nature of the organism, and maturing through the normal processes of growth (e.g., Koffka, 1924). In a reply to Guthrie, Tolman points out that Guthrie best explains all stupid behavior while he himself best explains all intelligent behavior. In a sense it is Guthrie's task, as representative of association and conditioning, to explain how intelligent behavior is derived from stupid behavior, while it is Tolman's task to show that behavior is occasionally stupid only because circumstances have made the use of intelligence impossible. The argument is not over the relative amounts of stupidity and intelligence in actual performances (there is enough of each to keep the theorist occupied); the argument is over what is to be attributed to the natural endowment of the organism and what is to be attributed to experience. Even though an organism is stupid at birth, its acquisitions are not solely a matter of experience, although it may know nothing but what it has learned. There remains the problem why one organism profits by experience and another does not. Similarly, just because an organism can face a new problem intelligently, one need not deny that past experience plays a rôle in his solution of the problem.

No matter how complete our knowledge of the history of specific abilities may become, at some point we shall always be forced back to certain primitive inherent capacities. At the lowest level these include such obvious capacities as depend on the possession of sense-organs; at the highest level they may include the possession of capacity for problem-solving. Meaningful discussions of the problems will demand the fullest possible history of specific abilities.

What are the fundamental capacities which different writers posit? Tolman (1932) finds it convenient to accept problem-solving capacities (e.g., means-end capacities) as among the givens. Both Guthrie and Hull, on the other side, admitting mature problem-solving *abilities,* do not accept problem-solving *capacity* as given. Both seek in anticipatory conditioned responses a means of deriving problem-solving behavior. According to Hull (1938) the fundamental capacities which make possible the intelligent solution of problems are two: the capacity to react in proximity to a goal according to the goal gradient, and the capacity to form habit-family hierarchies. Both depend on the more fundamental capacities for the establishment of fractional anticipatory reactions, and for differential reaction on the basis of several concurrent anticipations. Thus one animal might be able to solve a problem which another could not solve, although both had sufficient past experience available in the form of conditioned anticipatory responses. The more intelligent one might be able to discriminate better between its anticipations than the more stupid one.

Appraisal of Conditioning as an Explanation of Learning

The present chapter and the previous one have been devoted to discussion of attempts to relate conditioning principles to the problems of laboratory learning. The exposition has been intermingled with criticism, so that now a review may be desirable in order to furnish a basis for estimating conditioning as an explanation of learning.

When we undertake to relate the specific facts found in conditioning experiments to the quantitatively stated conclusions from other learning experiments the difficulties turn out to be very great. It is necessary to assume, first of all, that instrumental acts may be conditioned by a reinforcing sequence of behavior to which they lead; at the same time we must also assume more conventional conditioning in the form of redintegrative substitution. Then we encounter derived reinforcement involving the expectancy principle, which adds a foreign and unfamiliar note. Without these supplementations, conditioning would remain an artificial experimental result, inapplicable to the large proportion of learning situations outside of the conditioning laboratory. With these modifications, the way is opened for the systematization of a large proportion of learning experiments in terms of conditioning. Further assumptions with regard to the rôle of anticipatory responses, the gradient of reinforcement, the habit-family hierarchy, are needed in order to move from conditioning facts to the data of complex learning experiments. The most thorough attempts to follow the necessary steps have been made by Hull and his associates, much of whose work has been summarized in this and the preceding chapter. Their success has been sufficient to make it imperative upon all students of learning theory to give careful consideration to their proposals. Admittedly the limitations are great enough, however, that greater service will be done by proposing constructive alternatives than by confining arguments to specific proposals as they now stand in the literature.

Two problems connected with the explanatory use of conditioning principles should be distinguished. The first problem is whether it is possible to systematize theory so as to include all that is known about learning. The answer lies in the further elaboration of the kinds of deductions set forth in these chapters, until they include many more facts of learning. A good learning theory must not be contradicted by any of the known facts of learning, and it must have in it something relevant to each of the facts. It is obviously too early to decide how finally satisfactory such an extension of conditioning principles will become.

The second problem is a more practical one. Can recommendations regarding training, with respect to the use of rewards, punishments, intrinsic motives, the most economical methods of learning, and the like, be derived from systematic theory? Since the answers to practical questions of learning usually involve specific information as to capacities, motivations and the prior habits of the subject, no matter how true abstract principles may be, they can be serviceable only within rather narrow limits. Thus a theory of maturation can never predict the actual vocabulary of third-grade school children in Kalamazoo, yet their actual vocabulary may be important if one is to make use of the maturational principle; e.g., in the selection of reading material.

The emphasis on deduction in the extension of conditioning principles, while important for systematic theory, is to a certain extent misleading. It must not be forgotten that prediction and control in psychology, as in other sciences, will be deductive only to a limited extent. Atomic numbers and tensor equations have not made superfluous the tables of empirical constants found in chemists' and physicists' handbooks.

Therefore, while we seek relationships of the highest degree of generality, we must continue to study relationships of greater specificity. Laboratory data will never be superseded entirely by general principles. Even if systematization should be completed to the psychologist's satisfaction, empirical relationships would continue to have an important status.

It follows that the direct application of conditioning principles to practical problems involves the study of learning in specific practical situations. That is, experiments must be done with hunting-dogs and school children if pertinent advice is to be given specifically for the training of dogs or the teaching of children.

When everyday situations are examined carefully, it is soon discovered that they involve features which are very little represented in the literature of conditioning. Much practical learning goes on in a social context, involving imitation, suggestion, emulation, rivalry. These cannot be studied conveniently in the conditioned response situation, although the problem has been reflected in isolated experiments. It has been mentioned that it is necessary to keep a 'social sheep' in the room with the experimental animal. Here social factors are part of the undifferentiated background, and do not enter the data. W. T. James (1936, 1939) has reported that in experiments in which dogs were conditioned simultaneously, the social pattern of dominance and submission affected their conditioning as they stood in adjacent stands. The evidence drawn from learning outside of conditioning experiments, however, is so much richer than that within conditioning, that it would be foolhardy at present to attempt to regulate social behavior on the principles of conditioning.

Many practical situations involve the organization of a number of acts into a smooth-running skill, as in the operation of a typewriter. Within the conditioning experiment there is no opportunity to study the detailed composition of such skills, so that errors can be diagnosed and corrected. Such studies have to be made in the context of the skill itself.

The learner often profits by guidance in the form of diagrams and explanations in developing new modes of behavior. How to improve such aids to learning, and how to profit from them in the most efficient manner cannot be learned from conditioning.

Illustrations like these serve to show the futility of expecting conditioning principles (or other systematic principles of learning) to take the place in practical situations of analyses made within whatever concrete situation is under consideration. In order to give advice with respect to practical learning on the basis of conditioning we must be willing to use loose analogy, and to run the risk of extending conditioning principles to situations so remote from those in which they have been derived that their validity is questionable. The great detail required by Hull to give a trustworthy account of such relatively stereotyped behavior as maze running should give pause to anyone who attempts at the present time to offer advice with regard to the formation and breaking of habits on the basis of known facts of conditioning.

Notes

Although insightful behavior is most conveniently studied in situations requiring successful solution on the first trial, it is not limited to such situations. A subject may make repeated errors or random choices in the usual discrimination or trial and error situation, and then suddenly 'discover' the solution and react correctly thereafter. Because the same overt response has been previously made (by chance) and rewarded, it is difficult to separate the influence of reinforcement from the possibility of insight. Krechevsky's emphasis on hypotheses in discrimination learning (p. 189) represents an explanation in terms of insight to the extent that the hypotheses arise from sources outside the particular discrimination training. Other writers have pointed out that the behavior of animals in the trial and error situation yields evidence of more intelligent behavior than is implied in the simple process of stamping in correct responses and stamping out wrong ones (e.g.,

Adams, 1929). In a series of papers, Hull has derived many of the adaptive characteristics of trial and error behavior in terms of conditioning principles (1930b, 1937, 1939c).

Mediated Stimulus and Response Equivalence

The importance given to fractional anticipatory responses (r_g's) in conditioning interpretations of problem-solving behavior cannot be over-emphasized. They are the surrogates for ideas in such conditioning interpretations as those offered by Guthrie and Hull. In most of the deductions they are inferred, rather than observed. More experimental confirmations, in which the inferred intermediaries are observed and measured, are needed.

A type of indirect evidence for anticipatory goal responses as integrators of activity is furnished by those experiments in which a foretaste of the reward facilitates learning. According to a simple law of effect interpretation, such a foretaste might interfere with learning through reducing the drive. On the other hand, by arousing r_g's more vigorously, the behavior supported by r_g's is furthered. That such pre-rewards aid learning is shown by Hull (1933), Bruce (1937, 1938), C. T. Morgan and Fields (1938).

Field Theories and Conditioning Theories

Hull's proposal of the habit-family hierarchy as an alternative to certain aspects of field theory is a definite attempt to meet the criticisms of conditioning theory as too analytical and too unresponsive to the present structure of the field (e.g., in relation to barriers and possible alternative routes). The contrast between Hull's approach and that of field theory may be illustrated by the alternative explanations of the rat's choice of the shorter of two paths through a maze. According to Hull, this choice depends on prior conditioning, so that the entrance to the shorter path arouses more vigorous anticipatory responses than the entrance to the longer path, and the competition between the anticipatory responses determines the choice (cf. Figure 29, p. 217). According to the field principle of 'least action,' on the other hand, so long as the rat can discriminate between the longer and shorter paths, the choice is determined by the fundamental principle of animal nature which leads the rat to take the path requiring least energy expenditure in reaching its goal (Adams, 1931; Gengerelli, 1928; Helson, 1927; Tolman, 1932; Wheeler, 1929). Unfortunately, the principle of least action has not been based sufficiently on observations in which actual energy relationships are investigated (Crutchfield, 1939). The same situation exists with respect to other so-called field principles. It is not entirely clear just at what points the field theories are in conflict with conditioning theories of the type proposed by Hull, and at what points the two approaches, except for differences in exposition, are in essential agreement. It may be noted, for example, that in applying the goal-gradient hypothesis to the situation in which the subject perceives a goal-object at a distance beyond a barrier, Hull implies much of what Lewin means by valence and force in relation to distance (Hull, 1938; Lewin, 1933, 1935). In this connection, Hull's own comments are pertinent (personal communication):

"As I see it, the moment one expresses in any very general manner the various potentialities of behavior as dependent upon the simultaneous status of one or more variables, he has the substance of what is currently called field theory. My habit-family hypothesis is presumably a field principle in this sense. It is probable that my equation expressing the goal gradient hypothesis (gradient of reinforcement) and even the one expressing the generalization gradient (gradient of irradiation of Pavlov) might also qualify as bits of field theory. On the other hand, some might object to this usage on the ground that equations of this nature are not peculiar to gravitational or electromagnetic fields but are almost universal in natural science theory. Moreover the variables and the constants, together with their interrelationships, which have so far appeared in equations expressing behavior theories, seem to differ radically from those which appear in the equations of physical field theories. The notable lack of such equations in current Gestalt field formulations, while paradoxical, is probably symptomatic. For such reasons I prefer to be rather sparing in my use of the expression 'field theory'; if one has the substance, the use of the term is scientifically unimportant however valuable it may be for purposes of propaganda. But if one means by field theory what I have indicated, I am all for it and I see no inherent disagreement on this point between stimulus-response theory and Gestalt theory."

Conditioning and Learning

Guthrie (1935, 1938) discusses learning rather informally in terms of conditioning and chooses many of his illustrations from everyday life. Hence there is some practicality in his suggestions for ordinary habit formation, but such suggestions are not necessarily grounded in the details of laboratory conditioning.

Hull's program of explanation is much more formal, and now increasingly mathematical. It represents a particular type of scientific logic, and has been subjected to analysis in this respect, e.g., Adams (1937), Kattsoff (1939), J. G. Miller (1939), Woodger (1938). The last two of these are attempts to formalize Hull's system in accordance with modern symbolic logic.

Chapter 11

VOLUNTARY ACTION

THE RELATIONSHIP between the conditioned response and voluntary activity has been the source of much argument and confusion. The earliest studies of conditioning in human subjects raised the question whether the results indicated anything more than conscious, deliberate response on the part of the subject. Later studies have pointed out the importance of voluntary attitudes in determining the course of conditioning. On the other hand, Pavlov always considered the conditioned response essentially reflex in nature, and therefore to be understood without recourse to traditional concepts of volition and consciousness. In his sense conditioning would be basic to the explanation of voluntary behavior, and some investigators have attempted to demonstrate this relationship in experimental detail.

Degrees of Voluntary Control

The term 'voluntary' has never been rigorously defined. If it is taken to mean activity under the control of the will, this leaves the mystery of the will to be explained. Neural definitions, which identify volition with control by 'higher' brain centers, are unsatisfactory because these centers are now known to be involved in types of automatic behavior which do not conform at all to the generally accepted meaning of voluntary. In common language, 'voluntary' refers to acts which are preceded by an idea or intention, acts of which

255

the individual foresees the consequences. They are acts over which the individual has the greatest degree of control; they are not compelled inevitably by a particular environmental situation. The knee jerk, for example, is classified as involuntary because it depends so largely upon a blow to the patellar tendon. On the other hand, the extension of the arm to reach an object on the table is considered voluntary because the movement is quite independent of the particular external stimulus, and can be initiated or completely prevented by suitable instructions. Both movements may be the inevitable result of the total situation and the experience of the individual, but the determinants cannot be described in the same way.

Mere freedom from determination by specified external stimuli does not suffice to characterize volition, for certain types of self-initiated activity are not sufficiently under control to be classified as voluntary. In a delirium, for example, responses may be quite unpredictable from the external situation. They are self-initiated by the individual, but they are beyond that individual's control. Certain types of self-initiated activity possessing little coherence or evident purposiveness, are spoken of as *spontaneous movements,* as in the random squirming and thrashing about of the newborn infant. The nature of the control which is called *volition* has eluded direct description. Introspective studies have discovered feelings of effort, kinesthetic sensations, determining tendencies, and so on, as correlates of voluntary activity, but such studies have not satisfactorily exposed the nature of the control.

If voluntary behavior is defined in terms of factors which are subject to experimental control or measurement, it must be defined at present by exclusion; that is, as that form of activity which is least dependent upon specific measurable stimuli for its initiation and characteristics. In the laboratory voluntary behavior may be identified as actions which are evoked, without repetitive training, by instructions given to the subject. Instructions to press a key when a light is flashed are, of course, stimuli, but they are not related to the response in the same way as the stimulus from which latency is measured. The instructions initiate preparatory actions which predispose to a certain response in the presence of an external stimulus which then serves as the signal (or trigger) to release that response.

Voluntary Action Compared with Reflex Action. If the characteristics of voluntary activity, as recorded in the laboratory, are measured carefully in comparison with reflex activity, it is found that there is no sharp line delimiting one from the other. Peak (1933a, 1933b) has demonstrated this clearly in a study of the relation between the voluntary wink and the reflex wink. She classified the possible differences between them into the following three groups: (1) *Descriptive features of the response.* Although in general the voluntary wink has a longer latency, a greater amplitude, and a longer duration, there is considerable overlapping in the distributions of the measures of the two responses. When the sampling of responses is increased, the distribution of any single characteristic tends to become continuous. (2) *Determinants of the response.* The voluntary wink is elicited following instructions to the subject which are not necessary for the reflex wink. On the other hand, the reflex wink is elicited by a loud sound which is not essential for the voluntary wink. But even this difference does not offer a clear-cut classification. The reflex will be modified in latency and amplitude if the subject is instructed to relax or to press a key when he hears the sound. And the voluntary wink will be influenced by the nature of the stimulus serving as a signal for the wink, decreasing in latency, for example, as the stimulus is increased in intensity. The stimulus and the instructions each influence both reflex and voluntary winks, and the distinction is one of degree only. (3) *Functional relations between the de-terminants and the response*. Although the same determinants are effective for both reflex and voluntary responses, it is found that they influence the responses in a different way or to a different degree. For example, the duration of the open-ing phase of the wink is definitely modifiable by instructions in the case of voluntary but not of reflex winks. Again, the latency of the voluntary wink is markedly increased by in-structions to relax whereas the latency of the reflex wink is only slightly altered by the same instructions.

Although the evidence indicates that no sharp distinction between the descriptive characteristics of reflex and voluntary action can be made, it is desirable to retain these concepts to designate the two extremes of a distribution of responses which differ in the nature and amount of their relationship to certain determinants. Reflex may be used to designate re-sponses whose determinants are most completely described in terms of experimental stimuli, while voluntary may be used to refer to responses which are relatively independent of the specific nature of the stimulus, but are easily modifiable un-der the influence of instructions or intentions.

This criterion becomes very difficult to apply to the be-havior of animals and of infants without language. The dif-ferentiation of reflex and voluntary action is customarily made in such cases by analogy with similar behavior in human adults.

Automatic or Habitual Acts. It is necessary to point out a further class of activities which are commonly called auto-matic or habitual. After hundreds of repetitions of the situa-tion in which an individual has unlocked his house door by turning the key to the right, the movement may become highly automatic and stereotyped. Automaticity is not, of course, a necessary consequence of extensive practice. When automaticity is achieved the stimulus situation seems to evoke the response with complete regularity, for if the lock is changed so that the key must be turned to the left, the original response shows a strong tendency to persist. Such an automatic habit, then, is an involuntary action in the sense that it is determined by the stimulus situation in a regular, unvarying manner. But it was originally a voluntary response, so that it is distinguished from a reflex on the basis of its history.

It is evident that the criterion of voluntary control is not a distinction between learned and unlearned. An act may be learned, and yet be involuntary. Thus William James called trained reaction-time activity "reflex pure and simple" (1890, I, p. 90). Involuntary automatic habits, based on activities once voluntary, may again be brought under voluntary control. Hence a particular kind of performance may shift back and forth in the lifetime of the individual from relatively involuntary to relatively voluntary behavior, depending upon the extent to which it is under control.

Degree of Voluntary Control of Conditioned Responses

Where does the conditioned response fall on such a scale of involuntary-voluntary response? There is no categorical answer to this question. Conditioned responses may fall at any point along the involuntary-voluntary scale, depending upon the particular experimental situation in which they are established. The criterion of location on this scale must be the same as for any other variety of response: the extent to which instructions, sets, and attitudes affect the incidence, magnitude, and qualitative characteristics of the response.

Experimental studies of the voluntary control of conditioned responses can therefore be carried out best with human subjects who are responsive to instructions and who can give reports on their attitudes. The question has been raised particularly with reference to the classical type of conditioning, involving substitution. In instrumental or avoidance training, with mature human subjects at least, the original response is itself voluntary, and the learning consists merely in discriminating the appropriate situation in which to perform the response. In this class would fall the bulb-pressing response used extensively by Ivanov-Smolensky with children, the reaction-time experiment, color naming, and so forth.

The immediate problem at issue in the study of voluntary influences in conditioning is this: Do the principles of conditioning, derived from experiments on relatively involuntary responses in animals, suffice to account for the modifications resulting from analogous training in human subjects? If not, what further variables must be considered, and what are the laws of their operation? Incidental results from many experiments and a few more recent systematic investigations indicate that conditioned responses established by the classical training procedure in human subjects range from completely involuntary to completely voluntary. Some typical examples of the different degrees of voluntary control will be discussed.

Involuntary Conditioned Responses. While involuntary conditioned responses are likely to appear when the unconditioned response is itself involuntary, it does not follow that the conditioned response will fall at the same point on the voluntary-involuntary scale as the unconditioned response on which it is based. It has been repeatedly demonstrated that the nature of the conditioned response is not completely determined by the unconditioned response. If the unconditioned stimulus has the characteristics of a reward or punishment, the subject may give an instrumental response which is already in his repertory of voluntary behavior. If this complication can be avoided by the use of a neutral unconditioned stimulus, if the unconditioned response is quite independent of verbal control, and if the conditioned response occurs without the subject's awareness, it appears justifiable to speak of the conditioned response as involuntary. One of the best examples fulfilling these conditions in adult human subjects is the conditioned pupillary response, since the unconditioned stimulus (illumination change) is not highly toned emotionally, and the subject is not aware of the response. Responses in very young infants, in primitive organisms, and in decorticate and spinal animals, are other examples of involuntary conditioned responses. Whatever influence voluntary factors may have in mature adults, at the other extreme there are conditioning phenomena independent of voluntary processes.

Semi-Voluntary Conditioned Responses. Most of the experimental work on conditioning in human subjects has resulted in conditioned responses which fall into the broad category of semi-voluntary responses. Examples are conditioned salivation, knee jerk, galvanic skin response, and lid reflex, all of which are based on quite automatic unconditioned reactions. The conditioned responses are not voluntary because they cannot be perfectly duplicated in response to instructions, nor can they be completely prevented. Yet they are not involuntary because in all cases they are definitely modifiable by the effects of instructions or of voluntary attitudes and sets.

It has been found that the conditioned salivary response in human subjects is erratic and not predictable from the particular properties of the stimuli and amount of training. Razran (1935) found that although nearly all of his subjects showed some signs of conditioning, it was often sporadic and variable (cf. L. F. Jones, 1939). Thus one subject might give consistently large secretions, another almost none, and a third actually give a decrease in the flow of saliva in response to the conditioned stimulus. The same subject might react differently when in the presence of a group than when alone, and results might be quite different on successive days. On the assumption that the nature of the conditioned response which a subject yielded was to be attributed to his attitude, Razran attempted to control the attitude experimentally by specific instructions. When subjects were directed to form associations between the conditioned and unconditioned stimuli the responses were greater and more stable than when instructions not to form certain associations were given. On the other hand, when the establishment of such determining attitudes was prevented by forcing the subjects to concentrate on the task of learning a manual maze while the conditioning stimuli were presented, the resulting conditioned response showed a regular progressive acquisition and stable reliable magnitude (Razran, 1936a). In later studies, by misleading the subjects with respect to the purpose of the experiment, Razran (1939l) has been able to secure relatively involuntary salivary conditioning which much more nearly follows the rules to be expected from Pavlov.

The conditioned eyelid response, reinforced by the lid reflex to sound or to cutaneous stimulation such as shock or air-puff, is a representative example of the conditioned response in human subjects. Under suitable conditions its development and extinction follow the regular and progressive course typical of the Pavlovian reference experiment. Voluntary influences, however, are not without effect. For example, if the subjects are directed to make a voluntary hand movement whenever the conditioned stimulus is presented, the conditioned lid response is more rapidly and stably formed (J. Miller and Cole, 1936). Extinction resulting from the omission of the unconditioned stimulus is slower when the manual response is still called for. As soon as the subject is told to cease making the manual response, extinction becomes very rapid.

TABLE 7

EFFECT OF SUPPLEMENTARY INSTRUCTIONS ON FREQUENCY OF
CONDITIONED RESPONSES

Conditioned stimulus, light; unconditioned stimulus, air-puff to one eye; interval 400 msec. The groups are arranged in order of increasing success of conditioning. Modified from J. Miller (1939b).

Group	Instructions	Percent of trials on which conditioned responses appeared
(1) Inhibitory	"Be sure that you do not wink or start to wink before you have felt the puff" (n = 20)	26
(2) Voluntary antagonism	"Open your eyes each time the air-puff strikes your eye" (n = 20)	28
(3) Noncommittal	Only minimum instructions necessary for photographic recording (n = 25)	38
(4) Informed	Told that light would be followed by air-puff (n = 20)	44
(5) Voluntary supplementation	"Wink voluntarily to the air-puff" (n = 20)	55 [*]
(6) Facilitatory	"In case you feel your eyes closing or starting to close, do nothing to prevent it" (n = 20)	71

[*] Subjects fell into two groups, as described in text.

The effect of various types of instructions on the rate of acquisition and extinction of the conditioned lid response has been studied systematically by J. Miller (1939b). Some of his results under different instructions are summarized in Table 7. Efforts to inhibit response (Groups 1 and 2) reduce the frequency very little below the control groups uninstructed with respect to response (Groups 3 and 4). This suggests that the subjects in groups 3 and 4 had adopted an inhibitory set without specific instructions. Instructions not to prevent responses (Group 6) resulted in a greatly increased frequency of response, and in slow extinction (Figure 35). The form of the responses showed clearly that they were not voluntary reactions. The results confirm the conjecture that conditioned eyelid responses normally develop against opposed inhibitory sets (Hilgard, 1938). The subjects instructed to wink voluntarily to the air-puff (Group 5) apparently adopted one of

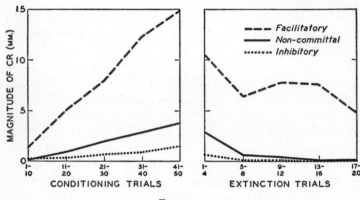

FIGURE 35

EFFECT OF INSTRUCTIONS ON COURSE OF ACQUISITION AND EXTINCTION OF CONDITIONED EYELID RESPONSES REINFORCED BY A PUFF OF AIR

The three groups received different instructions, as reported in Table 7. The groups represented in the figures are (1) inhibitory, (3) non-committal, (6) facilitatory. The plotted values represent the mean magnitude of response, absence of response being included as zero value. After J. Miller (1939b).

two sets. Thirteen of the subjects attempting to wink to the puff, irrespective of the light, reacted promptly to the puff at a latency of simple reaction time (157 msec.). The other 7 subjects evidently were concerned to discriminate between the light and the air-puff. The discrimination set was shown objectively by the longer reaction time of the voluntary winks to the puff (198 msec.). Conditioned responses were given on only 18 percent of the trials, while the 13 subjects who did not adopt a discrimination set gave conditioned responses on

75 percent of the trials. It is evident that the nature of the instructions can determine the degree of conditioning, even though the response is not completely under voluntary control. Furthermore, uninstructed subjects cannot be assumed to be free of any determining attitudes. Apparently many of them were trying to prevent the appearance of any response to the light.

The degree to which specific instructions can influence the conditioned eyelid response has been further studied in the discrimination experiment. The course of discrimination under the usual circumstances of a conditioning experiment was described in Chapter 8, Figure 24. In a study of the effect of instructions all subjects were conditioned on the first day to the positive stimulus, all trials being reinforced. On the following two days, during which the negative stimulus was introduced without reinforcement, the groups differed in the instructions given. The resulting characteristics of responses to the positive stimulus are summarized in Table 8.

TABLE 8

Effect of Instructions on Characteristics of Conditioned Eyelid Responses to Positive Stimulus Within a Discrimination Experiment
(After Hilgard and Humphreys, 1938a, p. 301)

Groups in order of amount of voluntary supplementation of response	Characteristics of responses to positive stimulus Mean, 10 subjects in each group		
	FREQUENCY —PERCENT	AMPLITUDE —MM.	LATENCY —MSEC.
Instructed to refrain from responding to either stimulus	55	13	448
Instructed to refrain from responding to positive stimulus but instructed to respond to the negative stimulus	71	16	404
Without instructions with respect to response	74	19	401
Instructed to respond to positive stimulus, not to negative stimulus	90	35	319

Responses are found to show increasing frequency, increasing amplitude, and decreasing latency when they are arranged in order from voluntary restraint through no instructions to voluntary facilitation. This is evidence that instructions make possible some control over the process. On the other hand, voluntary restraint does not succeed in overcoming the positive conditioning tendencies. It cannot be asserted that the responses are completely voluntary, any more than that they are completely automatic. The sharpest break is found, in fact, between the responses which are most completely voluntary (i.e., those under instructions to respond) and the others which represent the more usual conditioned responses. Corresponding results were found for responses to the negative stimulus. Except under direct instructions to respond, the negative stimulus always elicited responses at lower frequency and with smaller amplitude than the positive stimulus, but the same trends were found. Conditioned responses persisted in spite of voluntary effort to restrain them, and they increased when voluntary restraint was reduced as well as when there was added voluntary effort to respond.

A report by Cole (1939) supplements the investigations reported above. He found that verbal instructions greatly influenced the acquisition and extinction of conditioned eyelid responses, but he also discovered a limiting case in which verbal knowledge was ineffective. In a series in which reinforcement and non-reinforcement alternated, the subjects could report the order being followed, but their eyelid responses did not follow this order.

A conditioned response based on an involuntary unconditioned response, and itself relatively involuntary, may exhibit a certain amount of indirect susceptibility to verbal control. The conditioned galvanic skin response, for example, is a reaction of which the subject is quite unaware, and over which there is no direct voluntary control. Instructions to make or to withhold the response are ineffective. Since the response is a correlate of expectancy of pain, however, indirect instructions will cause its modification. If an untrained subject is told that he will be given a strong shock 2 seconds after a light is flashed, there will be a strong 'conditioned' galvanic skin response on the first presentation of the light (Cook and Harris, 1937; Mowrer, 1938). This is an indirect control; the subject already has a naturally acquired galvanic conditioned response to the expectation of shock, and this response may be 'reinforced' through instructions. If, instead of giving this information verbally, the light and shock are presented together for a series of trials, the conditioned galvanic skin response becomes gradually stronger, and seems to be following the typical course of conditioning. It is possible that the mechanism is similar in both cases, since expectation of shock is built up gradually in the course of the repeated double stimulus presentations.

Just because a response is influenced by knowledge of the expected stimulus we cannot infer that it is completely voluntary. In the eyelid experiments it has been shown that subjects who were told that the negative stimulus would be given without reinforcement discriminated more promptly than those subjects for whom the negative stimulus was introduced without prior information regarding it (Hilgard, R. K. Campbell, and W. N. Sears, 1938). This more rapid discrimination, correlated with expectancy, did not result in 'voluntary' discriminatory responses, however, such as were made when the subject was told to react to the positive stimulus and to refrain from responding to the negative stimulus (Hilgard and Humphreys, 1938a). There is a gradation in degree of control, which permits a distinction to be made between semivoluntary and voluntary responses.

Voluntary Conditioned Responses. Several studies have been made of the responses occurring when the classical conditioning procedure is carried out with a voluntary act as the unconditioned response. In this situation the 'conditioned' response is essentially the same as a false reaction in the usual reaction time experiment, the conditioned stimulus taking the place of a ready signal. If we accept this analogy, certain conditioning principles such as generalization, extinction, recovery, and disinhibition are found to be applicable (Hunter, 1938; Rexroad, 1936, 1937). Some of these modifications suggest that the responses have become relatively automatic with practice, and are to that extent semi-voluntary rather than voluntary.

Direct comparison of conditioned responses based on voluntary reinforcement has been carried out on the eyelid response (D. G. Marquis and Porter, 1939). If a stimulus (light) is repeatedly followed by a weak sound stimulus to which subjects have been instructed to wink, conditioned winking to the light may be established. Significant differences are found between this response and one established by pairing the light with an air-puff stimulus which elicits involuntary reflex winking. Conditioned voluntary responses are brisk, complete lid closures whenever they occur; conditioned involuntary responses are small and show recruitment. Curves of acquisition and extinction of conditioned voluntary responses do not show the gradual and progressive changes characteristic of conditioned involuntary responses.

Under typical experimental conditions favorable for establishing conditioned involuntary winking, it was almost impossible to secure any conditioned voluntary responses. Analysis indicated that the adoption of a discrimination set by the subjects, evidenced by the long reaction time to the sound stimulus, was the effective factor preventing responses to the light. Reduction of the intensity of the light, elimination from the instructions of any mention of the light, and elimination from the experimental procedure of any isolated presentations of the light abolished the discrimination set, shortened the reaction time, and greatly increased the incidence of conditioned voluntary responses. When the same changes in procedure were carried out with reflex reinforcement, however, the effect was just the opposite; i.e., the frequency of conditioned responses decreased. These results indicate that different functional relationships hold for conditioned responses based on voluntary reinforcement as compared with reflex reinforcement.

Similar characteristics have been found for conditioned finger responses established with a voluntary instructed reaction as the unconditioned response (Yacorzynski and Guthrie, 1937; Wickens, 1939a). In general, such conditioned responses tend to be identical with the voluntary response. There is no gradual progressive increase in amplitude during training; the response occurs in all-or-none fashion. The course of acquisition and extinction in terms of frequency is not progressive. The response is established in the first few trials and subsequently may increase or decrease or remain constant depending upon factors other than repetition. Extinction usually occurs abruptly in one or two trials. Under instructions, subjects can perform or prevent the response to the extent that any equally automatized voluntary response can be controlled.

It is likely that the numerous investigations of conditioned finger withdrawal with shock reinforcement have actually been dealing with a conditioned voluntary response. This is particularly clear in those cases in which instructions to withdraw have been used (e.g., H. M. Wolfle, 1932), but it may be true even in those cases in which no instructions were given. The finger withdrawal to shock is not a reflex in the sense of the flexion reflex; it is just as voluntary and just as involuntary as rising from a chair after sitting on a tack. The latency of the response is of the order of voluntary responses rather than of the extremely short flexion reflex, and some subjects have been found to misunderstand the demands of the experiment so completely as to leave their fingers on the electrodes throughout the shock.

Conditioned responses established on the basis of withdrawal to shock show many of the typical characteristics of conditioned voluntary rather than conditioned involuntary responses. With human subjects it has usually been found impossible to secure the gradual, progressive learning curves that have been supposed to be typical of conditioning. Instead, the conditioned response appears as an all-or-none reaction, with no progressive change in magnitude as the result of training. It may occur on the first few trials and very often decreases in frequency with further training. It is not identical, however, with the withdrawal response based on an instructed unconditioned response, as Wickens (1939a) has recently shown. Shock reinforcement results in more rapid and stable conditioning, and the conditioned response has a different form, a greater resistance to extinction, and less susceptibility to inhibitory instructions. It is apparent that no categorical distinction can be drawn between voluntary and involuntary responses. Under different experimental circumstances, conditioned responses differ in degree rather than in type. But a useful distinction may be drawn among the factors determining the nature and strength of conditioning. The conditioning principles outlined in earlier chapters may be distinguished from a class of factors which are roughly grouped as voluntary.

The Effect of Voluntary Factors on Conditioning. With human subjects, the results of any conditioning experiment will tend to be complicated by the influence of voluntary factors. Since the laws of conditioning do not extend to such factors, the discovery and formulation of conditioning prin-

ciples depend upon the devising of experimental situations in
which voluntary influences are impossible or are eliminated.
Three types of procedure have been adopted in the attempt
to eliminate as variables all factors except the stimulus-response relationships embraced in the laws of conditioning.
In the first place, subjects can be selected which do not have
the capacity for appropriate voluntary reactions. For this reason, animals and young infants have been found to be 'good'
subjects. Second, a response may be selected for study over
which the subject has a minimum of voluntary control. Pupillary responses, salivation, and other autonomic reactions fit
this category best. Third, although the subject is capable of
a degree of voluntary control over the conditioned response,
the experimental conditions may be so arranged that this control is not exercised. Most experiments with human subjects
have attempted to realize this situation, although with varying
success. For example, the subject may be given no knowledge
concerning the purpose of the experiment, or of the stimulus
sequences to be employed. Subjects may be selected who have
not had previous experience with conditioning. The subject
may be instructed to take a passive attitude, and not to try
to control any responses he may make. Since any normal person is bound to take some attitude toward the rather unusual
experimental conditions with which he is confronted, some
experimenters have sought to distract the subject so that he
would not notice the relevant features of the situation. The
stimuli may be made to appear weak and incidental (D. G.
Marquis and Porter, 1939); the subject may be given some
material to read (Thorndike, 1932a); he may be given another irrelevant task to perform and misinformed about the
true purpose of the experiment (Razran, 1939l). The last
method has been found particularly effective. Scott (1930)
discovered that conditioning may be more effective in hypno-

tized than in normal subjects, possibly because of attentional changes involved.

When voluntary factors do enter the conditioning situation, their effect is to establish response tendencies which interact and summate with the tendencies strengthened by the conditioning procedure. While the relationships are quite complex, as the data in Tables 7 and 8 reveal, the discontinuities are not great. The sharpest change is introduced when there is deliberate supplementation of response with the effort to react voluntarily to one or another of the stimuli. Information about the stimuli and efforts at restraint produce less striking changes. Voluntary restraint may produce only slight changes because such restraint already characterizes the usual conditioning situation. Thus J. Miller (1939b) found that an inhibitory attitude assumed by uninstructed subjects in the eyelid conditioning experiment was apparent not only in the reduction of the frequency of conditioned responses, but also in a tendency to open the eyelids. This was shown by a cutting off of the duration of both conditioned and unconditioned lid closings, and by a greater frequency of small lid opening movements. The correlation between frequency of lid openings and frequency of conditioned responses in 25 subjects was $\rho = -.84$.

The interrelationship between voluntary factors and problem-solving behavior as discussed in the preceding chapter is apparent. The integration of acts by proprioceptive consequences appears in theories of voluntary control as well as in theories of problem solution. In human adults, the language mechanism adds so richly to self-initiated behavior that both problem-solving and voluntary action in man often appear qualitatively different from the behavior of sub-human animals, but the distinctions may be quantitative rather than qualitative.

Acquisition of Voluntary Control

Pavlov believed that a complete account of the conditioned responses of an individual would also be an account of his voluntary behavior. He made no specific attempt to show experimentally how voluntary control is developed, but he maintained that every action is inevitably determined by the complex of external and internal stimuli according to the individual's previous experience. The conclusion is not self-evident, however, for as we have seen in the examples discussed earlier in this chapter, most conditioned responses, unless established by reinforcement with an already existing voluntary response, differ significantly from voluntary behavior.

An experimental investigation of conditioning as an explanation of the acquisition of voluntary control has been reported by Hudgins (1933). Constriction of the pupil of the eye, a response over which an individual has no voluntary control, was reflexly elicited by strong illumination. The problem was to condition this response to some self-excited stimulus such as subvocal verbalization, so that the response could be aroused whenever the individual wished. The first step was to condition the pupillary constriction to a bell stimulus which was presented simultaneously with a bright light. After 125 to 225 trials a conditioned constriction was regularly evoked by the bell. Then the subject was instructed to squeeze a dynamometer with his hand when the experimenter gave the command "Contract." This hand movement closed electrical circuits which presented the bell and light stimuli. After further training, it was found that the pupil constricted when the subject contracted his hand, even when the bell was omitted. The hand response was eliminated after about 200 more trials, leaving only the verbal command as a conditioned stimulus. Finally, the subject was required to repeat the verbal command vocally, then by whispering, and finally sub-vocally. In several individuals it was thus possible to establish an ability to constrict the pupil to self-initiated sub-vocal verbalization of the word "Contract." The same procedure was effective in training the subjects to dilate the pupil to the word "Relax." The particular commands used had no significance aside from the training procedures, because a subject could be trained to constrict the pupil to the word "Relax," or to respond to nonsense words such as "sig" and "tok."

Although attempts to repeat Hudgins' experiment have not met with complete success, the theoretical possibilities which it suggests are extremely valuable and should be investigated further with responses of other types. Some of the phenomena have been confirmed with vasomotor responses (Menzies, 1937; Skinner, 1938, p. 114). Such experiments do not, however, offer a complete solution to the problem of voluntary control. They demonstrate that an involuntary response can be conditioned to a stimulus already under voluntary control, but they do not answer the question of what initiates the subvocal verbalization which evokes the pupillary or vasomotor response.

In discussing the possibility of 'voluntary' control over autonomic activities, Skinner (1938, p. 112 ff.) points out four possible mechanisms by which such control may be learned. (1) The first consists in producing the autonomic response by exteroceptive stimulation. Thus, if a hungry man were given food whenever his blood pressure rose, he might resort to sticking a pin into his arm to produce that effect. This would not ordinarily be called voluntary control of blood pressure, but the blood pressure rises as a result of self-initiated stimuli. (2) The second case is similar to the preceding, with proprioceptive stimuli substituted for exteroceptive ones. The hungry man might run up and down the stairs a few times to increase his blood pressure in order to be fed. (3) The third case consists in the production of the autonomic response by an exteroceptive stimulus which has been conditioned to it. Thus a state of excitement may be aroused by reading a book deliberately chosen to be exciting. The book contains material to which autonomic responses have been conditioned, and hence choosing the book is one form of self-stimulation to produce the emotional state. (4) The fourth case substitutes proprioceptive conditioned stimuli. For example, the subvocal recitation of poetry may produce the proprioceptive stimuli which have been conditioned to produce an emotional state which includes autonomic responses. Skinner points out that Hudgins' experiment is concerned with the last two of these categories.

No simple experimental demonstration of the acquisition of voluntary control seems possible, for the relevant events are buried deep in the complexities of the nervous system and by their very nature are not expressed completely in terms of external stimulus and overt response—the data with which the psychologist deals. A theory of voluntary behavior can do no more than indicate the manner in which the principles of learning, isolated in uncomplicated experiments, are also illustrated in the acquisition of voluntary control.

An individual possesses a repertory of responses before there has been any opportunity for learning. These responses are not all of the same nature. Some, customarily called reflex, are evoked only by certain definite stimuli. Others, called spontaneous or operant, are capable of being evoked by a wide range and variety of influences including external and internal stimuli and some sort of central process which seems relatively independent of afferent stimuli.

The acquisition of voluntary control implies two changes in the mechanism of responding. Spontaneous movements become more adaptive and purposeful, and both they and reflex movements become elicitable by self-initiated processes as in

Hudgins' experiment. Random responses, through trial-and-error learning, come to be evoked in appropriate situations. Since a response must occur before there is any opportunity for learned modification, and since every occurrence of a response is necessarily the occasion for some sort of learning, it follows naturally that the spontaneous responses, occurring under the greatest variety of conditions, will be most subject to learning. Arm movements, for example, will be conditioned to thousands of different stimulus situations, and the precise discriminations that will be formed are so complex as to defy any attempt at genetic description. Movements which have certain features in common, such as reaching movements, will be organized in relation to each other as 'concepts,' and relatively novel situations will evoke reaching on their first presentation because of this conceptualization. As the child acquires language, the word 'reach' is repeatedly associated with the arousal of these movements, and eventually he can respond to commands given by another person or to self-initiated instructions. Such behavior is voluntary by any definition that can be proposed.

Experiments dealing with the refinement of spontaneous movements under instructions, and with the acquisition of voluntary control over originally reflex responses, contribute fundamentally to the understanding of mature behavior as we find it. Even the practical problems of developing 'will-power' may be treated more wisely as we advance toward this understanding. At the same time, it must be recognized that far more progress must be made before it will cease to be arrogant of the experimenter to suppose that he has solved the age-old problem of volition. To discover that self-instructions may serve as conditioned stimuli for all manner of behavior (including that which is peculiarly reflex) does not yet account for the origin and organization of self-instructions. It is the self-commands which can be made relatively independent of present environment stimuli—often in the presence of great obstacles, and in line with remote goals and purposes—which constitute the essential problem in volition. To date no conditioning experiment has dealt with the problem as so defined.

Notes

Degrees of Voluntary Control

Skinner points out the correspondence in some respects between operant behavior as he defines it and what has traditionally been called voluntary behavior (1938, p. 112).

It has been contended by some writers that conditioned responses should be classified as voluntary because their minimum latency corresponds to that of voluntary responses, even when the reinforcement is by an involuntary act. This does not follow, however, because latency may be a correlate of the neural complexity of the task, and neural complexity is not itself the criterion of voluntariness. The longer latency of conditioned responses as compared with reflexes and the corresponding neural complexity do suggest, however, the possibility of greater variability and greater control, thus making most conditioned responses fall into the category of semi-voluntary activities.

The designation of most conditioned responses as semi-voluntary arises out of their susceptibility to influence by verbal instructions or concomitant voluntary activity. Among the papers dealing with voluntary or attitudinal modification of conditioning may be mentioned Cason (1934b), Cole (1939), Cook and R. E. Harris (1937), G. L. Freeman (1930), Grant (1939a), Hamel (1919), Hilgard (1938), Hilgard, R. K. Campbell and W. N. Sears (1938), Hilgard and Humphreys (1938a), Hudgins (1933, 1935), Hunter and Hudgins (1934), Menzies (1937), J. Miller (1939b), J. Miller and Cole (1936), Montpellier and Colle (1939), Porter (1938d), Razran (1934, 1935, 1936a, 1939k), Schilder (1929), Schlosberg (1932), Steckle (1936), Steckle and Renshaw (1934), Wendt (1930).

Some of the earlier studies of the conditioning of voluntary responses have been summarized briefly by Razran (1936b). Among the papers dealing with conditioning on the basis of voluntary unconditioned activity are: Cohen, Hilgard, and Wendt (1933), Cowan and Foulke (1934), Eaton (1937), Gantt (1938c), J. J. Gibson (1936), E. J. Gibson (1939), Hunter (1938), Kline and Kohler (1935), D. G. Marquis and Porter (1939), Peak and Deese (1937), Razran (1933b, pp. 71–73 for Russian work on children). Rexroad (1936, 1937), Stephens (1934–1937), Wickens (1939a), Yacorzynski and Guthrie (1937).

Acquisition of Voluntary Control

The experiments which were unsuccessful in the attempt to repeat Hudgins' (1933) study on the development of the voluntary control of the pupil are those of Steckle and Renshaw (1934) and Steckle (1936). See also Hudgins' reply (1935). The pupillary response has been successfully conditioned in animals and man by Baker (1938), Cason (1922a), Kotliarevsky (1935), Ten Cate (1934b), Harlow and Stagner (1933), Metzner and Baker (1939) and there appears little reason to doubt that results similar to Hudgins' may be reproduced.

The mechanism by which conditioned responses to self-initiated stimuli are established is not entirely clear. The various possibilities suggested by Skinner are important. He and Delabarre found, for example, that one of his subjects was producing vasomotor changes by involuntarily controlling his breathing. Here the semi-voluntary act of breathing was conditioned to verbal stimuli, and served as the intermediary for vaso-constriction. Corresponding intermediaries may be found for the pupillary response, since the pupil is activated normally not only by changes in the amount of light falling on the retina but by emotional changes and by changes in accommodation and convergence. The latter changes are under some measure of voluntary control before the experiment begins. Vasomotor responses are similarly aroused by respiratory, emotional and postural reactions which are capable of voluntary control. For other experiments dealing with the verbal conditioning of vasomotor responses, cf. Kotliarevsky (1936), Menzies (1937).

The acquisition of voluntary control over involuntary processes was experimentally studied by Bair (1901) before conditioned responses were discovered. He taught subjects to move their ears, a movement which was not under voluntary control before the experiment began, and which was also not a 'spontaneous' or 'operant' response. Two methods were used. One consisted in a course of training involving facial gyrations which included ear movements. Gradually excessive movements were reduced, and only ear movements remained. This is an interesting illustration of what is sometimes spoken of as the differentiating of a specific response out of earlier mass action. The second method consisted of stimulating the motor nerve while the subject was making the effort to move his ears, thus giving him the 'feel' of the movement. This resulted in more prompt learning. In a sense, this might be thought of as conditioned, since a movement was occurring while the conditioned stimuli (self-aroused) were present.

Chapter 12

PERSONALITY

A NEW field of application for conditioning procedures and theories was opened through some experimental observations made by Shenger-Krestovnikova in Pavlov's laboratory in 1914 (Pavlov, 1927, p. 291ff.). A dog was trained to salivate when a luminous circle was projected on a screen. After the conditioned response was well established, a discrimination was obtained between the circle and an ellipse with a ratio between the semi-axes of 2:1. The discrimination was acquired comparatively quickly. The shape of the ellipse was then approximated by stages to that of the circle, and the discrimination training continued. Finally an ellipse with a ratio of the semi-axes of 9:8 was reached. At this point the discrimination not only did not improve, but in three weeks of training it became worse.

At the same time the whole behavior of the animal underwent an abrupt change. The hitherto quiet dog began to squeal in its stand, kept wriggling about, tore off with its teeth the apparatus for mechanical stimulation of the skin, and bit through the tubes connecting the animal's room with the observer, a behavior which never happened before. On being taken into the experimental room the dog now barked violently, which was also contrary to its usual custom; in short it presented all the symptoms of a condition of acute neurosis. (Pavlov, *Conditioned Reflexes,* Oxford University Press, 1927, p. 291.)

This discovery of experimental neurosis led not only into the field of psychopathology, but also drew attention to individual differences. Not all dogs reacted alike when discrimina-

279

tions became difficult. The problems of individual differences, of emotions, of psychopathology, and of mental hygiene, now have a substantial place in the literature of conditioning.

Experimental Neuroses

The functional disturbances which made his dogs unsuitable for experimentation were labelled experimental neuroses by Pavlov by analogy with human neuroses. The neurotic person, compared with the usual normal individual, overacts to some stimuli and remains apathetic in the presence of others, and to this extent the phenomena of human neuroses parallel those of the dog. On the other hand, superficial similarity in symptoms does not permit the underlying dynamics to be identified as similar, until more precise comparisons are made. It is preferable, for the present, to think of the experimental neurosis simply as a set of symptoms of disturbance appearing in conditioning experiments under certain circumstances, and to postpone judgment about the relationship of such symptoms to those of human neuroses.

Experimental Neurosis in the Dog. According to Pavlov, experimental neuroses develop only in animals of extreme types, either the extremely inhibitable or the extremely excitable. There are three circumstances under which the neuroses are said to arise: the application of a strong conditioned stimulus, when the animal is accustomed to a weak one (overstrained excitatory processes); protracted inhibition, as in excessive delays (overstrained inhibitory processes); and clash of excitation and inhibition, as in a too difficult discrimination. Results similar to those reported from Pavlov's laboratory have been obtained in Gantt's laboratory at Johns Hopkins (Gantt, 1936). The following observations made in his laboratory are described from an account by Loucks (personal communication).

Behavioral disturbances were studied in a pitch discrimination experiment. When the pitches of the tones to be discriminated were brought too close together, symptoms of restlessness and disorganization developed. All the dogs showed occasional periods of excitement in which the signals would cause them to bark, back away from the food chute, and even reject food if the experimenter tried to feed them by hand. Of three dogs studied for several years, only one developed a lasting excitement, so that it was unsuitable for further experimentation. This dog was seen by Dr. Andreyev, an associate of Pavlov's, who regarded it as a clearcut instance of experimental neurosis. It was 'neurotic,' however, only in the experimental situation. It behaved normally in its living quarters, and had a good appetite. The events leading up to experimentation, such as entering the laboratory or fastening the salivary disks, brought on the state of excitement so that further training was impossible. The only evidence of abnormality outside of the experimental situation was shown if the pure tones used in the training were sounded while the animal was eating outside the experimental room. The tones would cause it to drop the food, whimper, and even back up or run to a corner of the room.

Experimental Neurosis in the Sheep. Liddell and his coworkers at Cornell have studied conditioned responses in sheep for a number of years. Neuroses have been observed since 1926. Upsets were developed in the sheep by several methods. One was the overcrowding of metronome-shock combinations, with a 5 second interval of delay between the metronome and the administration of shock. Another was attempted differentiation of closely similar rates of the beating metronome. Others included training with too long a delay, and the regular alternations of signals for shock and no-shock when separated by equal rest periods.

A neurotic sheep may be 'diagnosed' by a number of common symptoms which distinguish it from a normal animal. Among these, Liddell (1938) lists the following: (1) The sheep resists being led from the barn to the laboratory. (2) When placed in the Pavlov frame with loops under its legs and with electrodes fastened to the left foreleg it cannot stand quietly, but exhibits a stereotyped form of hyperirritability in which persistent tic-like movements and sometimes tremor of the left foreleg are accompanied by sudden starts and irregular respiration. (3) Negative conditioned stimuli, actually signals indicating no shock, elicit vigorous leg flexion. (4) The capacity to delay the conditioned response has vanished. (5) Administration of drugs produces abnormal effects. Subcutaneous injection of epinephrine decreases the vigor and number of leg movements which occur at the signal in anticipation of the shock, while at the same time the movements of the reaction limb during the rest period are increased. Cortin has the reverse effect. (6) At the conditioned signal, the pulse rate is increased promptly and strikingly, persisting many minutes after the shock. This is quite unlike the reaction of the normal sheep.

The neurotic behavior is evidenced also outside the laboratory. The indicators used outside the laboratory were pedometer records of activity, 24-hour records of activity obtained by placing the animal on a large suspended platform, records of pulse, taken by a remote stethoscope, and records of respiration. Each of these indicated an upset, excited state. Pulse and respiration were much more irregular than normal; the diurnal variations in activity and rest were very atypical. Normal animals have long periods of rest during the night; the neurotic animals showed the same restlessness at night as during the day. Vacations from the laboratory temporarily restored the normal rhythm of rest and of activity, but the deviations returned as soon as the animals were again working in the laboratory.

Of five cases which have been observed (there is no statement of the proportion of sheep which these represent) all have continued in the neurotic state for five years or more. One animal, which developed a neurosis at the age of 4.5 years, died nine years later, at 13.5 years, having remained in its disturbed state to the end. Two others were observed for six years in the disturbed state. While the animals might appear normal after a long rest, resumption of the conditioning tests always precipitated the characteristic abnormalities of overreaction within a few days.

The neurosis in these animals showed a remarkably uniform course of development. A premonitory non-reactive or inhibitory phase of several days' or weeks' duration was followed by the abnormalities of activity, respiration, and pulse, as described.

Experimental Neurosis in the Pig. The following account of a pig trained by G. F. Sutherland, is reported by Liddell (1938). Shortly after weaning the pig was taught to run on a leash. Resentment was overcome gradually until the animal could be led around the pasture and finally into the experimental enclosure. At each stage of environmental restriction the pig was likely to exhibit tantrum behavior before it became tractable. It was taught to nose up the lid of a box to secure pieces of apple, and finally to stand quietly in a harness before this box for experimental purposes. A spring electrode was attached to its foreleg. Strong shock caused it to flex its foreleg, but 200 combinations with a tone did not result in conditioned flexion. Instead of struggling or squealing when shocked, the pig would lift the lid of the food-box. In other words, whatever happened in the experimental room was taken as a sign of food.

The situation was gradually made more complicated. The pig was fed and shocked on alternate days, feeding and shocking being preceded by discriminable tones. The pig was noticeably upset on shock days, but quiet on feeding days. Between tests the pig spent much time opening the lid of the box. This is interpreted as a tension-reducing mechanism, similar to the sheep's nibbling of the dry leaves in a maze when there is no other substitute activity. So far the animal could not be considered neurotic.

In order to reduce the frequency of the approaches to the food-box between signals, the pig was now shocked if it raised the lid before the apple was delivered. Finally the delivery of the apple was withheld until the pig raised the lid. It was therefore necessary for it to 'make a decision' to open the box, to risk shock on its nose if it was wrong, to receive the apple if the choice was correct. The conflict was now too strong, and the pig developed a neurosis. It delayed response for a long time, occasionally as long as an hour. During this time its eyes would be closed, its snout resting on the screen of the enclosure. For many minutes it would maintain a rigid posture with occasional trembling and growling. During the period of immobility a piece of apple could be balanced upon the pig's snout without the animal attempting to remove it. Opening of the food-box, when it occurred, was impulsive. At the time of Liddell's report the pig refused on the food day to open the box at all or to eat the pieces of apple as they fell, even when the lid of the box was propped open.

Outside the laboratory the pig's behavior was also changed. It had formerly been friendly and docile at all times. Now it kept away from the other pigs, frequently fighting with them and occasionally attacking the attendant when he entered the pig pen.

Experimental Neurosis in the Rat. Until quite recently, attempts to produce experimental neuroses in the rat have been rather unsuccessful. Rats would keep working under quite adverse circumstances, and although occasionally refusing to run in the maze, or taking excessive amounts of 'time out' in order to wash an already thoroughly washed face, they were seldom rendered unusable as experimental animals.

Successful development of experimental neurosis has been reported by Cook (1939b). From among a group of six rats, three developed disorders of behavior in a situation described as follows:

> The rats were strapped to a stand so that the only sizeable limb movement possible was a flexion of the right foreleg. Under certain conditions such a flexion was rewarded with a food pellet; under other conditions it was punished with an electric shock. Observations indicated that the animals experienced two principal stresses: the first, when they were required to delay the food-bringing flexion until they received a bright-light stimulus; the second, when they were required to make a very difficult discrimination between a bright-light stimulus which permitted a food-bringing flexion and a dim-light stimulus which prohibited such a flexion on pain of shock. Because, under such conditions, the organism was receiving simultaneously stimuli to the excitation and inhibition of the same response, the stresses experienced have been characterized as comprising a "clash" between the neural activity of initiating a response and the neural activity of inhibiting the same response. (Cook, 1939b, pp. 307–308.)

Cook points out that restraint of activity is an essential feature of the experimental situation leading to abnormal behavior. In three other conflict problems which permitted more freedom in bodily activity no disturbance was produced.

A distinction between nervous, agitated behavior, often observed in difficult discrimination or conflict situations, and a definitely abnormal breakdown has been drawn by Maier (1939b), who would restrict the use of the term 'experimental neurosis' to the latter. Maier trained rats in a discrimination problem with the Lashley jumping apparatus. When the rats developed resistance to jumping toward the stimuli, they were forced to react by shocking them or by directing a stream of compressed air against them. In certain cases a striking pattern of abnormal behavior was induced. During the initial active phase the animal ran violently and exhibited convulsions and tics. In the succeeding passive phase the animal was apparently in a coma and could be molded into almost any posture. It is very significant to note, as Maier points out, that this 'seizure' occurred only when the compressed air was employed to force jumping. In control observations it was found that the sound of the escaping air itself would produce the seizure in some cases in the absence of any conflict situation. Similar seizures have been induced in mice by the sound of jangling keys (Dice, 1935), and in rats by the sound of escaping air (C. T. Morgan and J. D. Morgan, 1939) or of an electric bell (Humphrey and Marcuse, 1939). The rôle of the conflict situation in the induction of the seizure is not entirely clear at present. Maier found that seizures were more frequent when the rats were facing the discrimination problem, but the number of animals was too small to permit a definite conclusion.

Experimental Neurosis in Man. Social considerations make the deliberate development of experimental neuroses in human subjects out of the question, but it is possible to produce minor upsets in laboratory situations which are somewhat comparable to the animal experiments. The best summary in English of cases studied by Pavlov's methods is that of Krasnogorski (1925), who described a number of experiments by other workers in his laboratory.

A child of 6 years had a motor conditioned response to a metronome beating 144 times per minute. This was successfully discriminated from 92 beats and from 108 beats. Minor symptoms developed as the negative stimulus was increased in rate to approach the positive one. When the discrimination had to be made between 144 and 120 beats per minute the child was described as "taciturn," "refuses to go to the laboratory," "walks and mounts the apparatus slowly." The discrimination was now made more difficult by increasing the rate of the negative stimulus to 132 beats per minute. Positive and negative stimuli were alternated. The discrimination broke down completely, and responses were given to both stimuli. The child was now described as "rude, fights, disobedient, excited, yawns, closes eyes, falls asleep."

Other reports are concerned with the behavior of pathological children. An experimental neurosis was developed in a cretin by attempting too fine a differentiation between neighboring points on the skin. A rowdy 6-year-old post-encephalitic boy was conditioned to a metronome which was reinforced by food. A tactile stimulus combined with the metronome provided a negative combination which was not followed by food. Ordinarily the repetition of negative stimuli leads to drowsiness or experimental sleep, but in this case the child became very excited, cried, and breathed irregularly.

Luria's (1932) work shows that the conflicts which are aroused in free association experiments may also be revealed in disorganization of movements. While his work is not concerned with conditioning, strictly speaking, it suggests that personality disturbances may well be reflected in the kinds of measurements studied within conditioning experiments.

Theories of Neurosis

Theories of neurosis have been related to conditioning in two ways. Certain theories arose directly from the observations on experimental neurosis. Pavlov's and Liddell's theories are of this variety. Other theories of clinical origin have been correlated later with the facts of conditioning. Chief among these are a number of attempts to relate the theories of psychoanalysis to the work of Pavlov. These two varieties of theories merit separate discussion.

Theories of Neurosis Arising out of the Experimental Work on Animals. Pavlov's theory of neurosis rests on his conception of the fundamental antithesis between excitation and inhibition in the cortex. The processes of inhibition and excitation are said to interact both spatially and temporally to result in a variety of states ranging from extreme excitation to extreme inhibition somewhat as follows: extreme irritability, when an inhibitory process becomes very difficult or impossible; normal waking state, representing an equilibrium between the processes of excitation and of inhibition; a state of equalization, when all stimuli, independent of their intensities, act exactly equally; the paradoxical phase when only weak stimuli act and when strong stimuli have either no action at all or a barely noticeable effect; the ultra-paradoxical phase, during which only the previously elaborated inhibitory agents have a positive effect; finally, complete inhibition which Pavlov identifies with sleep. It is the isolation and fixation of the transitory intermediate states which Pavlov believes to mark the pathological condition. He summarizes all pathological instances as follows:

. . . it is a difficult collision, an unusual confronting of the two opposing processes of excitation and inhibition (be it in time or intensity relations or even in both together), which leads to a more or less permanent destruction of the normal balance existing between these two processes. (Pavlov, 1928, p. 361.)

Whether or not one is willing to follow Pavlov's doctrine of excitation and inhibition (see Chapter 13), it is evident that the experimental neuroses which he observed depended upon a state involving conflicting tendencies. Liddell has attempted to describe this conflict without reference to its neurological locus. He believes that the training to stand quietly in the harness is the behavioral side of the learned inhibition. When the discharge of excitation through the channel of positive conditioned responses becomes too difficult, the dammed up excitement interferes with the practiced quiescence, and neurotic behavior results. In a situation permitting free locomotion (such as the maze) neurotic behavior does not arise because alternative methods of discharging the pent-up excitement are available. Pavlov noted that the recovery of animals was aided by freeing them from the experimental stand. The following illustration from the Cornell laboratory supports this interpretation. An animal which had developed a neurosis under the restraint of the conditioning situation was subsequently tested in a situation free from restraint (personal communication from Dr. Richard Parmenter). The sheep was placed in a pen five feet square on the floor of the experimental room, where it was free to move about. In this situation the objective signs of the neurosis disappeared; for example, the tic movements of the foreleg were not present. "The animal appeared curious rather than alarmed at the sound of the buzzer, and his actions were those of avoidance and not panic. He received the shock calmly, lifting his leg rather slowly and the hard kick previously noted was absent." This change, however, was in no sense a "cure," for on the following day the animal, when tested in the original restraining situation, manifested the neurosis in all its former severity.

The facts of experimental neurosis are unquestionably of great importance, and more detailed experimentation is urgently needed. On the other hand, the symptoms shown by animals and human patients are not identical, and the conflict situations which are revealed in the psychiatric interview are not readily reduced to Pavlov's formula. In his later years, Pavlov identified the results on animals with some of those clinically observed in man. Clinical observations of the effects of frustration and conflict in human subjects show behavior somewhat similar to that observed in the experiments, notably hypertension, disorganization of response, and, occasionally, somnolence. The motivational organization within conditioning experiments, however, is not sufficiently complex to include the more important conflicts which involve personal-social motives in a complicated culture. To include these conflicts and the symptoms which are related to them requires processes of analogy and deduction not yet justified by conditioning facts.

At the present time the significance of the study of experimental neuroses lies chiefly in the procedure which has been developed for creating behavior disturbances experimentally in animals. In general, the method involves the conflict of opposing action tendencies. The tendencies need not necessarily be established by laboratory conditioning procedures; they may have been acquired in the course of natural learning or they may be highly practiced voluntary reactions. The particular advantage of conditioning for the study of conflict is that the strength of the tendencies can be controlled and measured in terms of the experimental reinforcement. The laboratory study of conflict and resulting disturbances has shown the possibility of such work; further investigation must deal with the nature of the disturbance, the conditions under which it appears, and the possibilities of therapy and reeducation.

Attempts to Correlate Conditioning with Psychoanalytic Doctrines. Among a number of attempts to harmonize Freud and Pavlov, a paper by French (1933) may serve to illustrate the more serious efforts to estimate the possibilities and limitations of a coordination between psychoanalysis and conditioning. The problem of positive association causes French no trouble, for the analogy between the establishment of an affective association and the development of a conditioned response is readily acceptable. Symptom formation may be based upon generalization and induction. The studies of conditioned emotion make the parallel a plausible one between conditioning and the relatively unintelligible associations which patients form under stress. The more difficult problem, and the one crucial to an acceptance of a parallelism between Freud and Pavlov, is to relate conditioned inhibition to Freudian repression. There is a possible parallel between the two types of inhibition (external and internal) and two kinds of repression, that caused by an extraneous motive such as fear (corresponding to external inhibition), and that caused by a failure of gratification (corresponding to internal inhibition). The difficult problem is to account for ego-manifestations, as in wishes, sublimation, and so on. According to French, the problem can best be envisaged in terms of discrimination. Sublimation involves a discrimination between that which is socially acceptable and that which is not. This discrimination may become more difficult if there is an increase in drive. It is known experimentally that increases in drive may make problem-solution more difficult (Chapter 10). In psychoanalytical experience this is illustrated, for example, by the difficulty encountered in normal heterosexual adjustments at puberty. Adjustment to reality may be thought of as a matter of conditioning and discrimination. French is aware that most of his analogies with conditioning involve situations more similar to Thorndike's reward and punishment learning than to Pavlov's reinforcement. They are illustrations of Freud's pleasure principle rather than of his repetition principle, and it is the latter which corresponds more closely to Pavlov.

R. R. Sears (1936) has subsequently presented an account of repression in conditioning terms which differs from that of French because he does not assume a parallel between any single Freudian principle and a Pavlovian principle, but attempts to analyze the mechanism of repression into its component stimulus-response sequences. The phenomena of repression may be illustrated by the order of events in Morton Prince's well-known bell-tower case (Prince, 1921, p. 389ff.). A young woman was praying in a hospital room for the successful outcome of an operation being performed on her mother in the room below. Outside the window she looked upon a church-spire in which a bell was tolling. In her distressed condition she was greatly annoyed by the bells, particularly because they symbolized death. Her mother died. She later developed a phobia of bell-towers which made her avoid the streets on which churches were located. She had forgotten the source of the fear, but the story was later recovered through automatic writing. The primary repression arose because of the great significance of the mother's death in the daughter's emotional life. It had become intolerable for the daughter to dwell upon the circumstances of death. The secondary repression, symptomatized both by amnesia for related events, and, in this case, by the phobia of bell-towers, protected the girl from stimuli which might arouse the primary memories.

Sears' account of repression follows a procedure similar to that used by Hull in deducing other forms of behavior from conditioning. The main point is that any stimuli associated with repressive sequences tend, by conditioning, to evoke avoidance behavior. Hence recall is interrupted by avoidance, and the patient appears amnesic for the events which the cues would normally reinstate. A partial experimental confirmation of his theory was reported by R. R. Sears (1937). This explanation of amnesia has much in common with the suggestions made in Chapter 10 (pp. 245f.) with regard to avoidance behavior. If it be assumed that tensions are aroused in the presence of cues which lead *almost* to the arousal of the repressed painful experience (i.e., cues which arouse r_g's), then the diversion of the behavior sequence to neutral acts will be tension-relieving. Thus the avoidance behavior is strengthened through tension-reduction without a recurrence of the original unpleasant memories.

Guthrie's (1938) theory of neurotic symptoms is based largely on the proposition that neurotic behavior never gets extinguished because the neurotic individual avoids the stimuli in the presence of which extinction might take place. Thus fear of high places can never be overcome if the person with that fear always avoids high places. The avoidance sequence which in Sears' theory is given a positive explanation, is in Guthrie's given a negative explanation in terms of non-extinction.

At the present stage of experimentation and theory, it is probably unwise to expect a comprehensive coordination between the rich data of psychoanalysis and the restricted data of conditioning. Partial harmonization or coordination, such as that attempted by Sears, is probably more fruitful than more ambitious attempts to account for the whole range of clinical findings.

Conditioned Emotions

The story of Albert and the rat as reported by Watson and Rayner (1920) is a classic in conditioning literature. A rat was shown to the child at the same time that a loud sound was produced by striking a steel bar. The sound caused the child to cry. After a few repetitions, the child cried at the sight of the rat. This fear was generalized to other furry objects, such as to his mother's fur neckpiece. This single case study has remained the prototype of discussions of the development of emotions, although later experimenters have been unsuccessful in duplicating it. English (1929) reported three cases of attempted emotional conditioning; Bregman (1934) reported fifteen. Their lack of success indicates that the process is not as simple as the story of Albert suggests.

While the Watsonian account of emotional conditioning has been convenient for pedagogical purposes, its contemporary importance is lessened by two developments since the case report on Albert and the rat. In the first place, the difficulties in securing clean-cut repetitions of the experiment have called attention to other factors in the social situation which are at least as important as contiguous stimuli in producing the affective transference to novel objects. In the second place, a greater interest in maturation now directs attention to other ways than conditioning by which a few primitive emotions might become differentiated as a child grows older.

The limitations of direct analogy from the conditioning experiment to the acquisition of emotional responses are evident enough if one thinks of commonplace situations in which such learning occurs. A child is playing in a room with its mother. The mother spies a mouse and utters a frightened shriek. According to the pattern of the Albert experiment, the child, being frightened by loud noises, is frightened by the mouse, which is present while the noise occurs. If the simple association principle is to be applied, and the noise is the source of the fear, why does the child not fear the mother, who is more intimately associated with the shriek than the mouse? As a matter of fact, the child runs to the mother for protection. In order to be applicable, the conditioning explanation has to be supplemented by allowing for a number of additional facts. The mother has prestige, and the object of the mother's fear is the object of the child's fear. But this is not according to the conditioning prototype. It does not follow because fears are learned that simple conditioning is a sufficient explanation. The forms of emotion which are socially important, such as anxieties, feelings of guilt, loyalties, are developed in a social context with which conditioning has never adequately dealt. What service conditioning could render by emphasizing the learned nature of emotions has already been given. The next stage requires a much more detailed treatment of the socialization of the emotional life.

The possibility that emotions are modified by growth as well as through specific experienced associations has been examined by a number of investigators. H. E. and M. C. Jones (1928) studied the fear responses of children and adults to a harmless snake. Children up to the age of two showed no fear of the snake; definite avoidance responses emerged gradually, and were most pronounced in adults. The interpretation is not that adults had been more often frightened by snakes, but that their general perceptual and intellectual development contributed to their fear in a situation involving potential danger. Goodenough (1932) described a somewhat dramatic instance of the possibility of maturational factors in emotional expression. A ten-year-old girl who was totally blind and deaf from birth showed emotions by facial expressions and gestures similar to those of seeing and hearing children, although she obviously had not learned them through observational experience. The increasing specificity and sequential differentiation of emotional patterns with age, similar to other developmental items, is reported by Bridges (1932).

The chief service of conditioning to the mental hygiene of emotions has been its emphasis upon the acquired character of many affective manifestations. It was perhaps wholesome for a time to overemphasize the learned nature of fears and attitudes, many of which had earlier been thought to be instinctive. It is equally important now, however, to correct earlier exaggerations in the light of accumulated knowledge. It is not sufficient to attribute to conditioning all specific emotional attachments which have been acquired in the lifetime of the individual. Because hysterical and other neurotic symptoms represent bizarre and unreasonable learning, apparently often as a result of chance association, conditioning analogies appear to be appropriate. However, until the precise forms of phobias, compulsions, and other symptoms have been compared and coordinated with the data derived from conditioned response experiments, analogies must be resorted to very cautiously.

Closely related to the conditioning of major emotions is the conditioning of preferences and attitudes of approval and disapproval. Several suggestions along these lines have been made recently by Razran (1938a, 1938b), who found that preferences for modern music could be increased by playing the music while the subjects were eating a free meal. Similarly, preferences for names or faces (photographs) could be modified. The results are not yet available in complete enough form to be valued as more than interesting suggestions.

Psychotherapy

Conditioned response techniques have been used successfully for many years in both the diagnosis and the treatment of psychoneurotic conditions.

The detection of sensory function in simulated and hysterical anesthesia is a natural application of conditioning techniques, because sensory thresholds are measured without dependence on the verbal report of the subject. Bekhterev early reported his success with hysterical deafness (1912), and his procedure was confirmed later by Myasishchev (1929). R. R. Sears and Cohen (1933) studied a case of hysterical anesthesia, analgesia, and astereognosis by conditioning methods. They found that when conditioned responses were established to stimulation of supposedly anesthetic areas the anesthesia disappeared. Cohen, Hilgard, and Wendt (1933) were able to demonstrate visual sensitivity in a patient with hysterical blindness, but the symptoms did not disappear as a result of conditioning. Various methods for detecting functional disorders are available, and there is at present no convincing evidence that conditioning works where other methods fail.

In addition to diagnosis, conditioning may be used in therapy. The following case, previously unreported, is described in some detail to illustrate the kind of clinical application which is feasible.

Miss H., an unmarried school-teacher of 32, had been in a motor car accident six years before coming for treatment. During these six years her left arm had been entirely useless to her, being totally paralyzed and anesthetic. Neurological examination showed the anesthesia to be of the glove type, with a line of demarcation at the shoulder. The symptoms were thus shown to be functional. The arm and hand showed considerable atrophy from disuse. Attempts by a psychiatrist to give the patient insight into the functional nature of the abnormality met with great resistance, although the fact that the patient had returned to the hospital voluntarily in the hope of a cure was considered a hopeful sign. The psychiatrist arranged to have the patient treated by conditioning methods in the psychological laboratory which adjoined the psychiatric unit.

A finger-withdrawal experiment was arranged. Two electrodes were used, one for each hand. The first series of experiments consisted in presenting a shock to the anesthetic hand as the conditioned stimulus, a shock to the normal hand as the unconditioned stimulus. This was designed to give evidence of sensitivity in the anesthetic hand, since a shock to it served as the signal for withdrawal of the normal hand. While little conditioning occurred, the desired effect was produced, and sensitivity gradually returned in the anesthetic hand and arm. Experiments were repeated daily, and the improvement was gradual. After recovery of sensitivity, the conditioning procedure was reversed for purposes of developing voluntary control. The normal hand was given a light shock which served as the conditioned stimulus. For the unconditioned stimulus, the paralyzed hand was given a more severe shock, to which it was now fully sensitive. Presently movement began to occur in the paralyzed hand at the signal given to the normal hand. This was the beginning of control, and voluntary movement was gradually restored. At this stage, the patient was given physiotherapy to strengthen the muscles which had been so long unused. The symptoms had not returned two years later, nor were any additional symptoms reported.

This case illustrates both the feasibility of conditioning procedures in the treatment of psychoneurotic symptoms, and the difficulty of interpretation. The experimental situation was one that permitted recovery without loss of face on the part of the patient. She believed the machine to be making the cure; in fact, the patient was so pleased with the contrivance that she wished to purchase it for home use! While the conditioning procedure was the effective means for bringing the symptoms to an end, other dynamic factors in the situation were probably of great importance.

A word of precaution with respect to the use of conditioning as a means of psychotherapy is probably in order. To use a method like that in the case above except under supervision by someone experienced in psychotherapy would be to run the risk of merely treating symptoms. Conditioning, like suggestion, may occasionally be useful, but its use is to be regulated in relation to all the factors in the case history as they bear upon the present symptoms.

Conditioning offers some possibilities as an alternative to suggestive therapy in cases of drug addiction and alcoholism. Remarkable success with alcoholics has been reported by Kantorovich (1929). Twenty alcoholics were treated by a conditioning procedure, while 10 others were treated by medication and hypnosis. The method used in conditioned therapy was the presentation of exposure cards with the words 'vodka,' 'alcohol,' 'drunk,' followed by severe shocks. Also included were bottles of liquor, the odor of alcohol, the injection of alcohol, each followed by shock. Interspersed were other words like 'health,' 'work,' 'sober,' and stimuli such as the odor of oil of cloves and the injection of physiological salt solution. These were not followed by shocks. Follow-up was reported on 17 of those treated by conditioning. Of these, 14 refrained from drinking for from one to several months after treatment, while 3 were drunk within a few days. Of the control group, only 3 refrained from drinking for from 2 to 6 weeks, while 7 of the 10 got drunk within a few days. Without more information about the cases, the results can be accepted only as interesting illustrations of the way in which a modified conditioning procedure might be tried out.

Individual Differences

Anyone considering personality problems is confronted with evidence that individual differences exist between organisms of the same age and species. Pavlov noted that some dogs appeared to be more excitable than others, and, contrariwise, some appeared to be more inhibitable. He lent the weight of his authority to a classification of dogs according to types on the basis of their reactions in his experiments. The types were not considered to be rigidly distinct, but as points on a continuous scale, many dogs representing intermediate types. The differences between dogs were coordinated by Pavlov with the ancient classification of temperaments attributed to Hippocrates. The extremely excitable dog was classified as choleric, the extremely inhibitable as melancholic. The central groups included the sanguine and the phlegmatic, with tendencies toward excitation and inhibition, respectively. The scaling is essentially one based on inhibition at one end and excitation at the other.

Just what Pavlov meant by the temperamental differences between his dogs is best brought out through descriptive summaries selected from his books. The following statements agree closely with sentences from the books, but they have been assembled from different places and rearranged in order to gain continuity.

The *excitable type* of dog (choleric) develops positive conditioned responses with ease. The responses reach their maximum quickly, and persistently remain at this strength. They remain steady in spite of attempted extinction. Inhibitory conditioned responses develop, if at all, with great difficulty. If inhibitory and excitatory stimuli follow too closely together, the conflict results in a neurotic condition in which only excitatory processes are retained, while inhibitory ones disappear almost completely. The condition is likened by Pavlov to neurasthenia. Bromides and calcium salts are useful in therapy.

The *central type* of dog represents a normal balance of excitation and inhibition. There are two sub-types, one leaning toward excitation (the lively type), and the other toward inhibition (the stolid type).

The *lively type* (sanguine) is vivacious, alert, demonstrative. Varying stimuli are continually necessary. This type normally seeks such stimuli and is capable in their presence of expressing great energy. With monotonous stimuli, however, it quickly and easily falls into a state of drowsiness and sleep. It is necessary to develop a variety of conditioned responses concurrently, both excitatory and inhibitory, in order to keep an animal of this type alert in the experimental situation. If handled in this way, it is a satisfactory experimental animal.

The *stolid type* (phlegmatic) is normally quiet, peculiarly indifferent to external happenings, but always on the alert. It does not enter into either friendly or antagonistic relations with anybody, even its master. Both positive and negative conditioned responses are extremely precise. It never shows drowsiness in the stand. Pavlov once aroused a dog of this kind by making extraordinary sounds with a toy trumpet while wearing a frightening animal mask. The dog then lost its usual restraint, barked determinedly, and attempted to attack him.

The *inhibitable type* (melancholic) is timid or cowardly. It moves cautiously, with tail tucked in, and legs half bent. At the beginning conditioned responses are exceedingly difficult to form, but when the difficulties are overcome, the dog acts like a perfect machine. Inhibitory conditioned responses are very stable; positive ones easily vanish in the presence of unusual stimuli. Under strain, the excitatory processes are weakened, and the experimental neurosis takes a form likened by Pavlov to hysteria. No cure, other than a rest of five or six months, was found.

Pavlov, in attempting to choose excitable dogs, would at first pick them by their characteristic behavior outside the experiment. When chosen in this manner, a dog selected as most excitable was often found to go to sleep in the stand. His classification would therefore be changed from 'choleric' to 'sanguine.' No description of naturalistic behavior is available by which to differentiate the type of excitable dog which goes to sleep in the stand from the type of excitable dog which never shows signs of inhibition. Razran (1935) in experiments with human subjects could not predict from one situation to another what 'type' his subject would belong to, and he made no effort to relate his types to other personality characteristics.

W. T. James (1934b) found that he could differentiate excitable and inhibitable dogs on the basis of their responses in a discrimination experiment. Excitable dogs showed immediate generalization and did not develop stable discriminations. The more inhibitable dogs did not respond at all to the negative stimulus. There appears to be some relationship to morphological form. The characteristic dog of the passive type is the basset hound, of the excitable type, the German shepherd and saluki (W. T. James, 1938). Breeding experiments are now under way at the Cornell Anatomy Station, Lake Mohegan, N. Y., to determine with greater specificity the relationship between bodily form and behavior.

Loucks (personal communication) has described some of

the relationships between behavior under the natural living conditions and in experimental neurosis. He does not believe that the naturalistic behavior and the laboratory behavior are very highly correlated. For example, a dog showing highly 'neurotic' symptoms in the laboratory (whining, refusal to eat, etc.) may act outside the laboratory in much the same

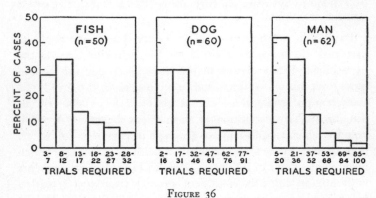

FIGURE 36

SPECIMEN DISTRIBUTIONS OF EASE OF CONDITIONING

The data for fish are from Stetter (1929), those for dog from Pavlov's laboratory. Both of these distributions are taken from Razran (1935). The data for man are from A. A. Campbell and Hilgard (1936). The criteria of conditioning are not alike in all the experiments, so that phylogenetic comparisons are unwarranted.

way that it has always acted. Under other circumstances, there may be convincing carry-overs. Thus Drabovitch and Weger (1937) found one dog which went into an inhibitable state, described as a state of rest, which lasted for a month.

Pavlov's failure to present statistical evidence for the relative frequency of types is in part corrected by Razran's summary of the rate at which conditioned responses were first formed in 60 dogs from Pavlov's laboratory. The distribution is reproduced in Figure 36 together with results for other organisms. It is evident that most dogs condition readily, with only a few resistant to conditioning. If readiness of conditioning is taken as a mark of excitation, the excitable types are apparently more prevalent than the inhibitable ones. There is no evidence whatever of multimodality. Other distributions of conditioning, both in animals and man, while differing in skewness, ordinarily agree in having a single mode.

Distributions based on ease of differentiation have not been presented. James' work, cited above, suggests that these might be more significant for temperament than distributions based on rate of simple conditioning.

Pavlov's dimension of excitation-inhibition is, of course, not the only possible dimension by which dogs can be classified. W. T. James (1936, 1939) has made an interesting use of a dominance-submission dimension in classifying the responses of some of his dogs. Conditioning in a social situation is greatly influenced by the temperamental characteristics of a dog in relation to a second animal, toward which it may react under everyday conditions as dominant or as submissive. During the first stages of such a study it is natural to classify animals into groups as predominantly submissive or predominantly aggressive, but these 'types' must presently give way to a scale on which all dogs can be classified. Only after the dominant-submissive dimension of behavior has been coordinated with a sufficiently large variety of other behavior can such a trait be said to have much significance. This is a program left for the future.

Whenever efforts have been made to secure intercorrelations of measures between two conditioning situations or between aspects of conditioning situations and other personality measurements, such as intelligence test scores, suggestibility measures, personality inventories, the results have invariably yielded low or insignificant correlations. There is no type or trait theory of conditionability which is yet satisfactorily established.

Clinical Types

Extreme forms of derangement in human beings have often served as a point of departure for personality study. Pavlov in his later years became very much interested in them, and one writer has even been so bold as to designate him "the psychiatrist of the future" (Liddell, 1936b).

Starting from his conceptions of types of nervous systems, and of the neuroses resulting when the extreme types are subjected to strain, Pavlov arrived at an interpretation of both neuroses and psychoses. Neurasthenia he thought is the result of serious conflict in which excitation prevails. Its extreme form is the manic-depressive psychosis. It may be recalled that some dogs become extremely excitable (manic), while some excitable dogs go to sleep in the harness (depressed). Hysteria, on the other hand, is a neurosis resulting from conflict in which inhibition prevails. The tendency for the normal unification of cortical activity to break down in hysteria led him to compare it with schizophrenia, which he interprets as an exaggerated instance of such cortical disintegration. Among Pavlov's last papers were some attempted interpretations of obsessional neuroses and paranoia. These he explained as perseverative phenomena based on a pathological inertness of cortical cells.

A number of investigators have studied the conditioned behavior of psychopathic individuals. Inconsistencies in the findings make it difficult to give any general summary of their results. Excitable subjects have been reported to condition readily, and manic-depressive patients appear to be somewhat more readily conditioned than schizophrenics. This presumably is in gross agreement with Pavlov. Schizophrenics, however, have been found to equal or exceed the normal in certain experiments with the galvanic response (Shipley, 1934a), although in a knee jerk experiment they were less reactive than either the normal subjects or the manic-depressives, and gave more negative responses (i.e., kicking backwards) (Pfaffmann and Schlosberg, 1936). This might be interpreted also as supporting Pavlov's contention that schizophrenics represent an extreme form of the inhibitable type. These agreements become unimportant, however, as soon as it is recognized that the conditioned responses give simply a rather poor instance of the well-known clinical picture of excitement in the manics and of the negativism that marks schizophrenia. The more crucial evidence, that the nervous systems were of these types prior to the onset of the symptoms, cannot be secured from such experiments.

Appraisal of Conditioning in Relation to Personality

Interest in the study of personality centers both in persisting individual differences and in the ways in which personality changes. The process of conditioning is fundamentally a process of change, and hence it is relevant to explanations of emotional attachments, and, in certain instances, to explanations of symptom formation and elimination. The usefulness of conditioning in relation to personality will be enhanced to the extent that it actually provides a satisfactory system of learning. Up to now the value of conditioning as a method for revealing persisting idiosyncrasies has been exploited because of Pavlov's theory of types and his demonstration of experimental neurosis.

The evidence for experimental neurosis is dependable, although the relation of these experimental upsets to neurotic behavior in man is not clear. The presence of conflict in the genesis of experimental neuroses suggests a relationship to the Freudian theory of neurosis, although there is little similarity in the designation of the conflicting tendencies. The generalization from experimental findings to theories of hysteria, neurasthenia, schizophrenia, and manic-depressive psychosis, is obviously premature. To have discovered that experimental neuroses may be produced under standard conditions, and studied under laboratory controls, is an important contribution which may have great significance in the future. Outstanding limitations of the conditioning technique for personality study result from the use of but one animal at a time, with motivations essentially physiological, whereas human personality is preeminently social, and its conflicts are predominantly between the needs of a person and the demands of his culture.

Notes

Experimental Neuroses

Although experimental neuroses were not discovered in Pavlov's laboratory until 1914, Bekhterev saw certain clinical possibilities for conditioning almost as soon as he began working with it (1908, 1909). A prize for the detection of simulated deafness by a conditioning method was awarded to Bekhterev in 1912 (Bekhterev, 1932, p. 204). In America early interest in the relation of conditioning to mental disease and to mental hygiene is represented by Watson (1916b) and Burnham (1917).

The following references present data bearing on experimental neurosis: in the dog, Babkin (1938), Drabovitch and Weger (1937), Dworkin (1939), Gantt (1936, 1938b), Pavlov (1932a, 1935), Petrova (1934a, 1937b); in sheep, O. D. Anderson and Liddell (1935), Liddell (1936a, 1938), Liddell and Bayne (1927), Liddell, W. T. James and O. D. Anderson (1934), Liddell, Sutherland, Parmenter, and Bayne (1936); in the pig, Curtis (1938), Liddell (1938); in the rat, Cook (1939b), Humphrey and Marcuse (1939), Maier (1939b), C. T. Morgan and J. D. Morgan (1939); in birds, Bayandurov (1932); in cats, Dworkin (1939), Dimmick, Ludlow, and Whiteman (1939); in man, Gantt (1936), Hamburger (1933), Ivanov-Smolensky (1927a, 1927b), Krasnogorsky (1925, 1931, 1933b),

Liddell (1936a, 1936b), Razran (1933b). The methods for producing experimental neurosis have been reviewed by Cook (1939a).

Among the more important attempts to relate psychoanalytic theory to conditioning may be mentioned Drabovitch (1935), French (1933), Hardcastle (1935), Hull (1939a), Humphrey (1920, 1921), Ischlondsky (1930), Kubie (1934), O. H. Mowrer (1939, 1940), Schilder (1929, 1935, 1937), R. R. Sears (1936).

Conditioned Emotions

A comprehensive account of the experiments on emotional conditioning is given by M. C. Jones (1933). The more important experiments on the learning and unlearning of emotions by techniques related to conditioning are those of Bregman (1934), English (1929), Gauger (1929), F. B. Holmes (1936), H. E. Jones (1931), M. C. Jones (1924a, 1924b), Moss (1924), Watson and Rayner (1920).

Changes in preferences by conditioning are discussed by Khozak (1934), Kovsharova (1934).

Psychotherapy

The uses of conditioning in psychotherapy are discussed by Bekhterev (1912, 1923a, 1923c, 1932), Delmas (1930), Burnham (1917, 1921), Cohen, Hilgard, and Wendt (1933), Drabovitch (1931), Gantt (1938c), Golla (1921), Guthrie (1938), Harrington (1938), Liddell (1936b), Marinesco and Kreindler (1935), Myasishchev (1929), Pann-

horst (1932), Schaeffer (1936), R. R. Sears and Cohen (1933), Shaffer (1936), Tinel (1930).

The unpublished case reported in the text was studied by Hilgard in collaboration with Dr. Stanley B. Lindley.

Gesell's (1938) review of the conditioned reflex in relation to the psychiatry of infancy lists 57 references. The most important previous review is that of Seham (1932). Among the more significant accounts are those by Gemelli (1937), Hamburger (1914, 1933), Ivanov-Smolensky (1927c), Karger (1923), Krasnogorski (1925, 1930, 1931, 1935), Peiper (1934).

Some of the considerations of special symptoms are the following: alcoholism, Ichok (1934), Kantorovich (1929); allergy, Morhardt (1930); anorexia, Rouquier and Michel (1934); enuresis, Krasnogorski (1933a), J. J. B. Morgan and Witmer (1939), O. H. Mowrer and W. M. Mowrer (1938); anxiety, H. Harris (1934); hysteria, Gackell (1928), Marinesco (1937), Marinesco and Kreindler (1935), R. R. Sears and Cohen (1933), Tinel (1930); morphine addiction, Rubenstein (1931); narcolepsy, M. Levin (1934b); psychogenic depression, Ivanov-Smolensky (1928); sexual aberrations, Bekhterev (1923a), Kostyleff (1927), Max (1935), Meignant (1935); stuttering, Moore (1938).

Individual Differences

The descriptions of Pavlov's types are summarized chiefly from Pavlov, 1927, 285–300; 1928, 360–390.

The classification is by somewhat arbitrary criteria, and the classificatory scheme underwent a few changes during the last years of Pavlov's life. Frolov (1937) states that three dimensions are needed for classifying a dog; strength-weakness (referring to ability to tolerate strong conditioned stimuli); lability-inertia (degree of stereotypy); balance-unbalance (predominance of excitation or inhibition). The four main types described in the text persist, however. Their order of frequency, from most common to least common, is said to be melancholic, sanguine, choleric, phlegmatic.

Individual differences in conditioning have been coordinated to type theories by Belialev and Lukina (1930), Cowan and Foulke (1934), Frolov and Charitonov (1931), W. T. James (1934b, 1938), Marinesco and Kreindler (1935), Marinesco, Kreindler, and Coppelman (1935), McDougall (1929), Osipova (1926b), Pen (1933), Razran (1935, 1939m), Rosenthal (1932), Timmer (1931), Petrova (1934–1937).

Differences independent of type theories were studied by A. A. Campbell (1938, 1939), A. A. Campbell and Hilgard (1936), Darrow and Heath (1932), Mateer (1918), Osipova (1927), Razran (1933a, 1933b), Schlosberg (1932). Correlations of these differences with intelligence have been reported by A. A. Campbell and Hilgard (1936), Mateer (1918), Osipova (1927), Schlosberg (1932); with suggestibility by Berreman and Hilgard (1936), Schlosberg (1932); with personality measures by Darrow and Heath (1932), Marinesco, Kreindler and Coppelman (1935), Schlosberg (1932); with morphological form by W. T. James (1934b, 1938), Timmer (1931).

Clinical Types

Pavlov's papers dealing with clinical types include: neuroses in general (1932a), hysteria (1933), obsessional neurosis and paranoia (1934), neurotic and psychotic symptoms (1935). His theory of schizophrenia is reported by Kasatkin (1932). Pavlov during the last years of his life spent much time in the wards of mental hospitals making observations on which to ground his theories.

Data on the conditioning of clinical patients have been reported on epileptics by Franklin (1928), Lukina and Matusova (1929), Martino (1933); on manic-depressive psychotic patients, Ivanov-Smolensky (1925), Pfaffmann and Schlosberg (1936); on progressive paralysis, Kantorovich and Lukina (1926), Rabinowich (1932); on schizophrenia, Bender and Schilder (1930), Guk (1934), Landkof (1938), Mirolyubov and Ugol (1933), Pfaffmann and Schlosberg (1936), Shipley (1934a); on senile psychosis, Tatarenko (1934).

Chapter 13

NEUROPHYSIOLOGICAL MECHANISM OF CONDITIONING

P AVLOV's study of conditioning was almost entirely directed toward understanding the functioning of the central nervous system. His theories were expressed in the terminology of neural physiology, and he considered the investigation of conditioned responses as the true physiology of the cerebral hemispheres. The extension of Pavlov's work in America has consisted largely of attempts to formulate a theory of learning in behavioral terms, but many special studies bear on the relation between neural function and conditioning.

Pavlov's Theory of Cortical Function

The fundamental conceptions in Pavlov's physiological theory are those of excitation and inhibition, conceived as states or processes with their locus in the cerebral cortex. The theory holds that as a result of afferent stimulation an excitatory process is initiated at a definite point in the cortex from which it gradually spreads over the entire sensory area or "analyser," diminishing in intensity with distance from the primary point. This phase of irradiation is followed by a recession or "concentration" of the process to the point of its initiation. The duration of the irradiation and concentration varies in different experiments from a few seconds to twenty minutes. On the assumption that the receptive surface of the body is geometrically projected upon the cortex, the progress of irradiation and concentration can be charted by their effect upon conditioned responses elicited from adjoining points of the receptive surface. In this respect inhibition shows the same characteristics as excitation.

As the cortical process subsides at any point, it is succeeded in many cases by the opposite process. Pavlov has called this after-effect "induction." Negative induction refers to the intensification of inhibition under the influence of preceding excitation; positive induction is the intensification of excitation following inhibition. The combination of induction with irradiation and concentration gives the completed picture of cortical function. Excitation, aroused at a particular point, spreads over the cortical analyser in wave-like form, the crest of the wave representing the excitatory process at its maximum. During the next phase there is a reversal leading to a concentration of the excitation at the starting point, and a heightened inhibition at surrounding points. The phase of concentration is said by Pavlov to endure some five times as long as the phase of irradiation.

The mechanism of the formation of a simple conditioned response is explained by Pavlov as follows. The excitation initiated by a neutral stimulus at point A irradiates over the cortex, and will be concentrated at any other focus of excitation such as that aroused by an unconditioned stimulus. After a number of repetitions of the two stimuli, the excitation aroused by the neutral stimulus is drawn to the locus of the unconditioned stimulus in sufficient intensity to elicit the conditioned response. The direction of the drainage of excitation is from the weaker to the stronger or more dominant focus of excitation. The phenomenon of generalization follows from the fact that excitation at a point B aroused by a stimulus similar to the conditioned stimulus will likewise irradiate widely and be drawn into the excitable focus of the unconditioned response, either directly or by way of point A. Continued training channels the pathway between point A and the response point, and the gradual lowering of the excitability of the cortex outside this pathway accounts for the progressive decrease in generalization. If point B is extinguished by presenting its stimulus without reinforcement, the process at that point is changed from excitation to inhibition, which also irradiates over the surrounding region of the cortex. The extent of irradiation from any point will be a function of the limitations imposed by induction from other positive and negative points in the cortex. In an animal which has been subject to numerous conditioning series, the cortex can be considered as a functional mosaic of points of excitation and of inhibition representing various conditioned responses, whose interaction is governed by the principles of irradiation, concentration, and induction.

Other forms of behavior are interpreted by Pavlov according to the same principles. Sleep is considered the result of extreme irradiation of the inhibitory process over the entire cortex and into the lower brain regions. Hypnosis is a form of partial sleep, or less extensive irradiation of inhibition. Neurosis is regarded as a functional pathology of the cortex in which, as a result of an unusually acute clashing of the excitatory and inhibitory processes, or of the influence of strong and extraordinary stimuli, there is an exaggerated predominance in the animal of either excitation or inhibition, analogous respectively to the hysteria or neurasthenia observed in human patients.

In spite of its tempting simplicity and scope, Pavlov's conception of cortical physiology has not met with any wide degree of acceptance. Four primary objections may be raised to it.

1. Concepts of cortical physiology should be based upon more direct measures of cortical function. Pavlov's inhibition and excitation are purely inferential concepts derived from

measures of overt movements or of amount of saliva secreted. Likewise irradiation, concentration, and induction are derived solely from the behavioral observations of generalization, discrimination, and after-effect. The concept of drainage is merely a figure of speech without any accepted neurophysiological basis. Inferential concepts are of course necessary in the systematization of the experimental data, but little is gained by asserting that such concepts denote cortical processes unless specific verification can be obtained through more direct observation of the cortex.

2. The temporal characteristic of irradiation, one of the most fundamental points in Pavlov's systematization, does not rest upon adequate experimental verification. A careful analysis by Loucks of the original data of the experiments on irradiation indicates that there is no "significant evidence for a sluggish spreading of an inhibitory disturbance from one restricted region to surrounding areas" (1933, p. 44). The general validity of any simple statement of irradiation for all regions of the cortex must be seriously doubted in view of recent findings by Dusser de Barenne and W. S. McCulloch (1938). Using electrical recording of neural activity induced by application of strychnine to a point on the cortex, they have shown that within certain areas (visual cortex and Brodmann's area 5 of the somato-sensory cortex) there is almost no spread of activity to surrounding cortex, while in other areas there is irradiation to widely distant regions. This irradiation, moreover, is not uniform in all directions. Stimulation of a point in one area activates a second area, whereas the second area may not activate the first. A given point may augment the spontaneous activity of one area and depress that of a second.

3. The spatial character of Pavlov's conception of cortical irradiation limits its general application. The assumption of

a geometric projection of the skin surface onto the cortex is particularly relevant in accounting for the generalization of a conditioned response from one cutaneous point to a neighboring point. This explanation is not applicable to generalization among stimuli differing in intensity or quality which are applied to the same cutaneous point. In these cases the distance of cortical irradiation cannot determine the degree of generalization. The difficulty becomes clear in considering generalization in the intensity dimension, where the neural excitation may be mediated by identical fibers but at different frequency. All discrimination may perhaps depend on some sort of dynamic separation of areas of excitation, as suggested in the Gestalt concept of isomorphism (Köhler, 1929), but this remains to be empirically demonstrated. Even the theory of isomorphism does not imply simple areal representation as proposed by Pavlov.

4. Pavlov's physiological conceptions are explicitly based upon the premise that conditioning is exclusively a cortical function. Recent experimentation which will be summarized later demonstrates, however, that conditioning is possible at a subcortical level. Although the importance of the cortex in learning by higher mammals is unquestionable, any theory that neglects the functioning of lower levels of the nervous system must be inadequate. The two-dimensional character of Pavlov's irradiation concept does not easily permit extension of the theory to embrace the integrated functioning of cortical and sub-cortical centers.

Anatomical Localization of Conditioning

Experimental investigation of the neurophysiological mechanism of conditioning has not been directed toward the examination of Pavlov's theories, but instead has been almost entirely limited to the problem of the locus within the central nervous system of the modification responsible for conditioning.

Pavlov believed that conditioning was impossible in the absence of the cerebral cortex. Subsequent work, however, has forced a modification of this view. His judgment was based upon the failure of Zeliony (1929) in 1912 to establish conditioned responses in dogs after surgical removal of the cerebral hemispheres. Later, Poltyrev and Zeliony (1930) were able to establish motor conditioned responses to visual and auditory stimuli in three decorticate dogs, and Lebedinskaia and Rosenthal (1935) were successful in establishing a conditioned salivary response to a metronome. In all of the animals the operations left a small remnant of cortex at the base of the brain, and so great was the influence of Pavlov's opinion that in both studies the conditioning was attributed to the residual cortical tissue. Clear evidence of subcortical conditioning, however, has been presented by Ten Cate (1934c), who established a conditioned response to a bell in a totally decorticate cat, and by Culler and Mettler (1934), Girden, Mettler, Finch, and Culler (1936), Poltyrev (1936), Zeliony and Kadykov (1938), who trained decorticate dogs in conditioned responses to optic, cutaneous, and auditory stimuli based on unconditioned electric shock to the foreleg. Incidental observation of learned responses have been reported in other studies of decorticate cats and dogs (Rothmann, 1923; Schaltenbrand and Cobb, 1931; Dusser de Barenne, 1919; Bard, 1934).

The possibilities of subcortical conditioning can perhaps be better evaluated from experiments which involve partial removal of the cerebral cortex. Pavlov's students and many subsequent investigators have shown that bilateral removal of a cortical sensory area does not prevent the establishment of conditioned responses to stimuli of that sense modality. Pavlov believed that such conditioning was mediated vicariously by the remaining cortical tissue. Two lines of evidence render this interpretation highly improbable: (1) Conditioning has been demonstrated after complete removal of the cerebral hemispheres. Similarly, destruction of the sensory areas which removes the only direct anatomical pathway by which impulses from the sense organ reach the remaining cortex, does not prevent conditioning. (2) Conditioned responses established prior to cortical operation can be retained after operation without any further training (D. G. Marquis and Hilgard, 1936). Direct test of the vicariation hypothesis has been made by Lashley (1922) using an instrumental response to brightness in rats, and by Ten Cate (1938) using conditioned leg retraction to light in dogs. The learned response, which survived bilateral removal of the occipital lobes, was found to be unaffected by removal of any portion of the remaining cortex. The only satisfactory interpretation of these studies is that conditioning does not necessarily depend upon cortical functioning. When the cortical projection area which normally participates in the response is lacking, the function is not taken over vicariously by other cortical areas, but is presumably mediated by subcortical association centers, together with remaining non-specific cortex which may have participated in the learning of the original act.

The cortical motor center for the unconditioned response has likewise been found not to be essential for the formation of conditioned responses. Conditioned salivation is possible after removal of the area controlling salivation; conditioned blinking is unimpaired by removal of the motor eye area. The results obtained in attempts to establish conditioned leg withdrawal responses in dogs after destruction of the cortical sensorimotor region are still a subject of controversy.

The idea of an association center in the cortex—a region involved in all learned responses irrespective of stimulus modality—was common in the speculation of early workers. The frontal lobes, having no other demonstrable function, have often been assigned an association function. Experimental investigation, however, has revealed no impairment in conditioned responses or simple instrumental discriminations following removal of the frontal lobes in dogs (Pavlov, 1927; Bekhterev, 1923b; D. G. Marquis and Hilgard, 1936; Ten Cate, 1938) or in monkeys (Franz, 1907; Jacobsen, 1936).

The possibilities of conditioning at the subcortical level are definitely limited, at least in the dog and higher mammals. After complete decortication, conditioned responses can be obtained only with intense stimuli and after long periods of training. Moreover, only the simplest forms of discrimination have ever been demonstrated. Culler and Mettler (1934) used a training method which permitted the dog to escape the shock to the paw by a prompt withdrawal response following the conditioned stimulus. In normal dogs the first few conditioned responses involved widespread activity such as struggling and yelping and resembled the unconditioned response to shock. With further training the response became restricted to a precise adaptive leg flexion. The decorticate dog showed only the former type of conditioned response. The possibility that decortication prevents the establishment of instrumental avoidance responses while still permitting conditioning by substitution deserves further investigation.

After removal of the sensory areas the possibilities for conditioning are greater than after complete removal of the cortex. Quantitative study of the characteristics of conditioned lid closure to light in dogs and monkeys demonstrated that removal of the visual cortex produced almost no change (D. G. Marquis and Hilgard, 1936, 1937). The rate of acquisition and extinction of the response did not differ in the operated animals from the normal. The form of the response was unaltered, although its latency was slightly increased. Simple instrumental discrimination of light intensity was also unimpaired, and the differential threshold was only very slightly raised (D. G. Marquis, 1934; Klüver, 1936; K. U. Smith, 1937). Discrimination of visual shape, size, color, and position, however, seems to be impossible. The difference between the residual visual ability of decorticate animals and of animals with only the visual cortex removed cannot be explained on the basis of present evidence. It seems likely that the greater deficiency of the former is due to the impairment of non-visual functions involved in the performance of the particular conditioned response.

The part played by the cortex in learning can only be adequately understood in the light of the evolution of the nervous system. In submammalian vertebrates there is no true neocortex, and learning is mediated by striatal, thalamic, and tectal centers of the brain stem. Within the mammalian series, as the cortex becomes relatively larger and more highly differentiated, certain functions originally localized within lower centers of the brain are mediated by the cerebral hemispheres. This *functional encephalization* has been recognized by anatomists and physiologists as the underlying principle of the evolutionary development of the central nervous system. Conditioned responses may be expected to show a greater dependence upon the integrity of the cortex in the dog as compared with the rabbit, and less in the dog than in the monkey and man. Although the available evidence is far from complete, much of it is in line with this view (D. G. Marquis, 1934, 1935; Harlow, 1936).

Functional Components of the Conditioning Mechanism

The neurological mechanism of the association formed in a substitutive conditioned response may be considered in terms of the components of the afferent-efferent system which are susceptible to separate experimental study. The basic problem is to determine the locus of the association by which the conditioned stimulus is able to evoke the unconditioned response or some fraction of it. This association could logically be formed at any point at which the conditioned and unconditioned pathways converge. Without specifying the neurological level, which might be cortical, subcortical, or peripheral, we can list the possible loci of the association as lying in (1) the pathway activated by the conditioned stimulus, (2) the pathway activated by the unconditioned stimulus, (3) the motor pathway of the response to the unconditioned stimulus, or (4) an association pathway lying outside any of the three named above. These components and their possible interrelations are represented diagrammatically in Figure 37. This diagram does not denote anatomical regions or neurons, but merely represents the functional components which must necessarily be considered in any analysis of the mechanism of conditioning. Before such an analysis can be carried out in neuroanatomical detail it must be pushed farther on a behavioral level.

Pavlov's conception of the mechanism of conditioning implies that the association is formed at M, where the excitation irradiating from CS is concentrated. Razran (1930) points out that the locus of modification must lie in the unconditioned rather than in the conditioned pathway because of the greater generalization which occurs among conditioned responses involving the same response than among those having the same stimulus but different responses. Beritov (1924) believes that the foci of the conditioned stimulus, the unconditioned stimulus, and the unconditioned response all have an increased excitability. The modifications in US play the most important part in the early stages of conditioning, while direct association of CS and M occurs in the well-established conditioned response. The evidence bearing on the rôle of each of the components in the process of conditioning will be presented below.

The Pathway of the Conditioned Stimulus. Complete interruption of the afferent pathway of the conditioned stimulus will necessarily prevent the formation or performance

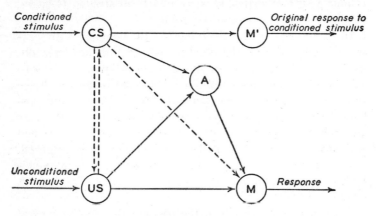

FIGURE 37

SCHEMATIC DIAGRAM OF THE POSSIBLE RELATIONS AMONG THE COMPONENTS
INVOLVED IN SUBSTITUTION CONDITIONING

There are four possible points at which the convergence of the pathways would logically permit the formation of the association implied in conditioning: *CS*—the pathway activated by the conditioned stimulus, *US*—the pathway activated by the unconditioned stimulus, *M*—the motor pathway of the response to the unconditioned stimulus, *A*—a hypothetical association pathway outside the three named above.

of the conditioned response. Sense organ stimulation, however, is not necessary, and may be replaced by electrical stimulation at any point on the sensory pathway. For this purpose Loucks (1934) has developed a method for stimulation of the nervous system in intact unanesthetized animals. A paraffin covered coil of wire is embedded under the skin of the animal and insulated wires are led from it to the particular point to be stimulated. No wires penetrate the skin, and the animal remains in normal health for unlimited periods of time. The buried coil can then be activated by induction from a primary coil external to the animal. With this method successful conditioning has been produced by substituting electrical stimulation of the spinal cord, cerebellum, (Gantt, 1937) or cortical sensory area (area striata) (Loucks, 1938b) for the conditioned stimulus.

Incidental evidence concerning the functioning of the central representation of the conditioned stimulus has been obtained from observation of hysterical and hypnotic sensory changes. A conditioned stimulus is rendered ineffective if the subject is hysterically anesthetic (Bekhterev, 1912), but prolonged training may break down the anesthesia (R. R. Sears and Cohen, 1933). Under hypnotic anesthesia the conditioned stimulus is likewise ineffective (Lundholm, 1928; Erickson, 1938b). Lundholm (1928) has shown in addition that a hallucinatory sensation can serve as a conditioned stimulus (cf. pp. 201f.).

A direct demonstration of the participation of the cortical sensory area in the conditioning modification has been reported by Martino and Fulchignoni (1938). They used strychnine, which when applied locally to a neural center causes an abnormal overactivity of the nerve cells. A dog was trained to give a conditioned blink response of the left eyelid to red light, and of the right eyelid to violet light. (The effective difference in the two stimuli was probably one of intensity since dogs are color blind.) When strychnine was applied to the visual center in the right occipital lobe, red light would provoke clonus of the left eyelid, followed by generalized epileptoid seizures first appearing in that muscle. Violet light had no effect. If the strychnine was applied to the left occipital lobe, violet light produced the same results in the right eyelid, while red light was ineffective. Presumably, the conditioning of the left eyelid to red light had "opened" a pathway from the right occipital visual center to the motor center in the right hemisphere controlling the eyelid on the left.

The Pathway of the Unconditioned Stimulus. The sense organ and afferent pathway of the unconditioned stimulus are not essential in the establishment of the conditioned response as long as excitation reaches some central point and evokes an unconditioned response. Successful conditioning has been produced by substituting for the unconditioned stimulus electrical excitation of lumbar posterior roots or dorsal columns of the spinal cord (Loucks and Gantt, 1938), and of the lateral cerebellar lobe (Brogden and Gantt, 1937). In stimulating the spinal cord a moderate strength which evoked leg movement was not adequate for conditioning; stronger stimulation, however, was effective. The difference is attributed by the authors to the excitation of pain fibers in the latter case.

An early experiment by Lang and Olmsted (1923) raised the question whether or not the sensory pathway of the unconditioned stimulus must be intact for the performance of an established conditioned response. In their experiment a conditioned leg withdrawal to a buzzer accompanied by a shock to the leg was established in dogs. Hemisection of the spinal cord on the side opposite the trained leg, interrupting the ascending pathway of pain fibers, abolished the foot withdrawal response to the buzzer although the respiratory response remained. More recently Martino (1939) has reported that the conditioned blink response in dogs is abolished by anesthetization of the skin around the eye—the receptive field of the unconditioned response. He concluded that a constant stream of neural impulses from the unconditioned receptor must be present to summate with the excitation from the conditioned stimulus in evoking the conditioned response. Other investigators (Raeva and Rappoport, 1934; Yushchenko, Rolle, and Pupko, 1934; Settlage and Harlow,

1936), however, have failed to find any disruption of the conditioned response resulting from interruption of the pathway of the unconditioned stimulus. The divergent results remain unexplained. Harlow (1937) has shown that a conditioned response is not abolished by functional inactivation of the unconditioned pathway through habituation, indicating that the central as well as the peripheral pathway of the unconditioned response need not be active during the performance of a conditioned response.

The Unconditioned Response. Conditioning does not occur if the unconditioned response is directly elicited by stimulation of the motor pathway, but only if the excitation is initiated reflexly; i.e., by way of the central nervous system. If a conditioned stimulus is repeatedly followed by electrical stimulation of a motor nerve evoking muscular movement, conditioning is unsuccessful (Tracy, 1927; Hilgard and M. K. Allen, 1938), although some modification of behavior will occur in human subjects through voluntary facilitation of reactions secondarily aroused by the twitch (Yacorzynski and Guthrie, 1937). Loucks (1935) has shown that if an unconditioned leg response is evoked by stimulation of the motor cortex in dogs (with the buried coil technique), no conditioning results in hundreds of trials. The nervous system is not impaired in any way by the procedure, for instrumental responses are readily formed by giving the dog food after the leg movement.

Similarly, if the unconditioned response is produced by drugs which act directly on the response mechanism, no conditioning is possible. The injection of pilocarpine causes an increased secretion of saliva, but no amount of pairing with a neutral stimulus will lead to conditioned salivation (Kleitman, 1927; Finch, 1938b). On the other hand, conditioned salivation is readily established by the injection of morphine (Kleitman and Crisler, 1927). The difference lies in the fact that morphine acts upon neural centers to excite the nerves to the salivary glands, whereas pilocarpine acts peripherally upon the gland cells themselves. For the same reason failure is encountered in the attempt to establish conditioned hyperglycemia by injection of epinephrine (Gantt, Katzenelbogen, and Loucks, 1937; Loucks, 1937a), and conditioned gastric secretion by injection of histamine (Katzenelbogen, Loucks, and Gantt, 1939). These responses are aroused by peripheral action of the drugs. Other responses, such as fear, which are aroused at the same time through reflex pathways by the injection procedure, are susceptible to conditioning.

Further evidence on the rôle of the response pathway is derived from studies in which the unconditioned response is prevented from occurring during conditioning. This prevention must be accomplished by some means which does not impair the other components of the conditioning mechanism or the results are not conclusive. Crisler (1930) was able to establish conditioned salivation in dogs based on the unconditioned response to morphine even though the actual salivary secretion was prevented throughout the training period by paralyzing the glands with an injection of atropine. Similar results were obtained by Finch (1938c), using salivation to acid in the mouth as the unconditioned response. Light and Gantt (1936) paralyzed the right hind leg in four dogs by crushing the ventral motor roots, and trained the dogs by repeated combination of an auditory signal with a shock to the paralyzed leg. A generalized conditioned response developed which involved defensive reactions of other parts of the body but no movement of the paralyzed leg. Training was discontinued while the crushed nerves regenerated. After function was restored in the paralyzed limb, the conditioned stimulus was found to evoke leg withdrawal—the appropriate and specific conditioned movement, but one which had never been evoked during training. The interpretation of these results is not clear because of the fact that the conditioned stimulus elicited a general conditioned response at all stages of the training, and the specific paralyzed response then usually occurred in the tests as a portion of a larger avoidance pattern. In one dog, however, the movement occurred in an isolated way without other defense movements.

Complete motor paralysis was secured by Harlow and Stagner (1933) by using curare. Training in which a buzzer was associated with an electric shock failed to produce a conditioned motor response in animals tested after they had recovered from the curare paralysis. It might be objected that the drug depressed brain functions, but pupillary dilatation to the shock, which was not paralyzed by the drug, showed conditioning. Girden and Culler (1937) found that even in complete curare paralysis a small twitch of skeletal muscles can be reflexly evoked, and that this response can be conditioned. They suggest that curare depresses cortical functions which are necessary for adaptive motor conditioning, and that the conditioning of the pupillary response and of the muscle twitch represent subcortical conditioning. Until the possible central effects of curare are better understood these experiments do not permit unequivocal interpretation (Culler, Coakley, Shurrager, and Ades, 1939; Harlow and Settlage, 1939).

An Association Pathway. The available evidence, although not conclusive, indicates that the locus of the conditioning association lies outside the regular pathways of the conditioned stimulus, the unconditioned stimulus, and the unconditioned response. The obvious alternative is the assumption of an association pathway, as represented by A in Figure 37. This does not, of course, imply the existence of an "association center" in the brain. Anatomical evidence reviewed earlier rules out the possibility of a single region in which associations are formed, but does not conflict with the conception of an association pathway which is different for each combination of stimuli involved in the conditioning.

The assumption of an association pathway fits the data concerning the changes in excitability of the component responses. If the association were at CS it should be reflected in a greater excitability of the original response to the conditioned stimulus. This response, however, usually shows a progressive decrement during conditioning (see Figure 7, p. 112). If the association were at US or at M an increased excitability of the response to the unconditioned stimulus would be expected, while the typical result is a decrement in this response also. If an independent association pathway is postulated, the strength of the conditioned response can vary independently of the strength of the original responses to the conditioned and unconditioned stimuli.

Studies of the effect of anesthetics and drugs indicate that conditioned responses are much more affected than are the original reflex responses to the conditioned and unconditioned stimuli, implying that the central pathways are not identical. Settlage (1936) has undertaken conditioning in cats which were given a dose of amytal sufficient to prevent the appearance of any conditioned responses but which did not depress the original unconditioned response to shock on the leg. Subsequent tests after recovery from the drug showed that a conditioned response had been successfully formed although it never appeared during the training.

Cortical association pathways might be found to lie within the primary sensory areas, in surrounding areas, or at a distance. Direct evidence of location in areas bordering on the primary area, but outside it, appears to have been obtained in an experiment by Culler, of which only a preliminary abstract has been published (1938a). Dogs were trained to withdraw the leg in response to a tone stimulus presented in combination with a shock to the paw. The response was observed as a contraction in the exposed semi-tendinosus muscle of the leg. The cerebral hemispheres were then exposed by removing the overlying bone under suitable anesthesia. Exploratory electrical stimulation of the cortex contralateral to the trained leg revealed a small spot, not over 2 mm. square, located in the anterior ectosylvian gyrus, from which the conditioned leg response could be elicited. This spot was not in the primary auditory area nor was it in the somesthetic sensory area; it was not the motor point for leg flexion, which was 20 to 25 mm. distant near the cruciate sulcus. Dogs tested prior to any conditioning showed no evidence of response to stimulation of the spot, and the response could be evoked only so long as the muscle responded to the conditioned tone stimulus. When the conditioned response was extinguished by unreinforced repetitions of the tone, the response to electrical stimulation of the spot also disappeared. When the response to tone was reconditioned, the response to the spot could again be evoked. These observations indicate that the site of the association pathway may be very discretely localized, and open a vast field of study of the neural mechanism of conditioning.

The Nature of Synaptic Modification

The preceding discussion has been concerned with the gross localization of the events involved in conditioning, and the nature of the actual neural modifications may now be considered. The problem is to understand how a stimulus which originally does not elicit a certain response, comes by virtue of the reinforcement procedure to evoke that response. Stated more generally, the essential alteration is a relatively permanent decrease in the threshold for evoking the response by the conditioned stimulus. This alteration occurs in the brain centers. Since conduction of the nerve impulse along a fiber is believed to be "all-or-none" throughout its length, the changes in threshold must be localized at the point of excitation; namely, at the synaptic junctions between neurons. Although the knowledge of synaptic transmission has been tremendously advanced in recent years, the experimental studies have been concerned exclusively with the immediate effects of stimulation. The excitatory process which gives rise to a propagated impulse has a very brief duration (0.2 msec.) (Lorente de Nó, 1938a). It is followed by alterations in threshold, associated with negative and positive afterpotentials, which may endure for 40 to 100 msec. (Eccles, 1935). Theories of the more permanent modifications responsible for learning are necessarily speculative, and are based on extensions of current conceptions of neural excitation. Many of the earlier speculations have been invalidated by subsequent experimental data. Some of the more plausible theories will be briefly summarized here.

Anatomical Growth of Axons and Dendrites. Kappers (1917) has proposed that relatively permanent new connections between neurons are established by the growth of neural processes under the influence of bioelectric potentials resulting from stimulation. If two cells are simultaneously excited, the resulting ionization is assumed to direct the growth of axons toward the cathode region, and of dendrites toward the anode, such that a new synaptic connection is established. This theory, which arose out of an attempt to account for changes in position of tracts and nuclei in phylogenetic development, has been used intensively by Holt (1931) who makes it the basis for a complete theory of learning. No direct experimental evidence exists either to support or to disprove the theory. It is not necessary to postulate that anatomical growth is essential for the establishment of new neural connections. Histological study demonstrates a very rich branching and interlacing of neurons in the central nervous system, and physiological observations of the spreading of response after administration of strychnine indicate that there is a potential anatomical connection between any afferent and any efferent neuron.

Changes in the Physico-Chemical Properties of the Nerve Cell. Excitation of a neuron is believed to be a process of breaking down (depolarizing) the membrane at the point of the synaptic connection. Among the changes suggested as necessary for learning are changes in one or the other of these properties: a concentration of some substance within the cell, a reorientation of the molecules of the membrane, changes in the collodial dispersion within the cell, changes in surface tension, changes in the interior-exterior potential gradient. There is no dependable knowledge relating these processes to learning.

The primary problem of the neurophysiology of learning, however, is to specify the conditions of this change, whatever it may be. This may be stated in its simplest form by reference to Figure 38: starting with an anatomical but not a functional connection between fibers CS and a, how does simultaneous stimulation of fibers CS and $UncS$ alter the threshold of a so that subsequent stimulation of CS alone will activate a and thus R_{UncS}? Watson (1914) and others have made the unqualified assumption that repeated activation of any pathway increases its excitability. Repetitive activity, however, is the typical condition for adaptation, which presumably depends upon the *decreased* excitability of a synapse. Pavlov does not present any specific solution of this problem, but speaks of drainage or irradiation of "neural energy," without considering the properties of nerve excitation and conduction. Translated into the terms of Figure 38, his conception would assume that simultaneous excitation of fiber a by two axons somehow produces a long-lasting decrease in threshold. More explicit mechanisms have been suggested by Cason (1925b) and by Washburne (1935) in terms of ionic interchange, by Johnson (1927) in terms of a tuning of membrane film-frequencies, and by Marinesco and Kreindler (1935) in terms of equalization of chronaxie. The essential basis of all such theories is the simultaneous activation of a neuron from two sources. Recent experimental work (Lorente de Nó, 1938b)

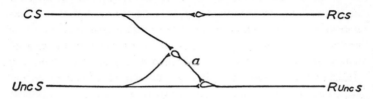

FIGURE 38

SCHEMATIC ARRANGEMENT OF NEURONS TO ACCOUNT FOR CONDITIONING BY ALTERATION OF SYNAPTIC THRESHOLD

Impulses in neuron $UncS$, set up by the unconditioned stimulus, evoke a response in the neuron R_{UncS}, which participates in the unconditioned response. Impulses in CS excite neuron R_{CS} (the original response to the conditioned stimulus) but are not effective at first in exciting a. If CS and $UncS$ (and therefore a) are simultaneously activated, there occurs an increase in the excitability of a such that CS alone is eventually able to excite it.

This diagram differs from conventional ones only by the addition of the fiber a. If the collateral of CS ended directly on R_{UncS}, the threshold change in the latter neuron would necessarily be accompanied by an increased excitability of the reflex response to the unconditioned stimulus. The present diagram permits the threshold of the conditioned response to vary independently of the original responses.

has demonstrated that spatial summation of at least two simultaneous impulses is necessary to excite a neuron under any conditions. No explanation has yet been proposed why such excitation produces a permanent threshold change in some cases and not in others.

Continued Activity in Closed Neural Chains. Recent observations indicate that the path of neural impulses from sensory to motor nerves is not a single "straight-through" pathway (Lorente de Nó, 1938c). Histological and experimental data indicate that the internuncial neurons are arranged in two types of chains: multiple chains, in which several collaterals of a single fiber, after traversing one or more synapses, converge upon a motor neuron, and closed chains, in which a collateral excites a circle composed of several neurons. In the latter case the chain of neurons may maintain its activity indefinitely in the absence of peripheral afferent impulses. This arrangement suggests another possible mechanism of learning which would not necessarily involve any permanent alteration in the physico-chemical properties of the neurons. Closed chains, set into activity by the training procedure and continuing in the absence of any external excitation, would summate with otherwise inadequate afferent impulses to produce the conditioned response (Figure 39). Rashevsky (1938) has presented a mathematical analysis of a scheme which is based on a combination of the two postulates of altered neuron properties and activity of closed chains. From this he is able to derive the effect of stimulus strength, the time (or trials) necessary for conditioning, and the influence of the interval between trials.

If learning (according to the closed chain theory) is assumed to depend on continuing activity in closed chains when once excited, it might be supposed that anesthetics, interfering with states of excitation, should produce forgetting. A possible objection to the theory may be based on the fact that anesthetics do not produce forgetting. It is known, for example, that cortical action potentials are greatly modified under deep anesthesia (Derbyshire, Rempel, Forbes, and Lambert, 1936), yet anesthetics do not result in loss of previous learning.

Influence of Bioelectric Fields. The theories outlined above all assume that the modification in threshold of a neuron is a function of impulses traversing the synapse. Any alternative would involve some sort of "action at a distance."

Neural activity is accompanied by changes in electrical potential, and activity in large numbers of contiguous neurons will establish relatively great potential differences which might alter the threshold of unactivated neurons lying within the

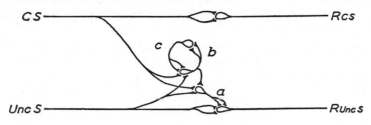

FIGURE 39

SCHEMATIC ARRANGEMENT OF NEURONS TO ACCOUNT FOR CONDITIONING BY CLOSED CHAINS

The assumption is made that activation of a nerve cell occurs only when the cell receives excitation from two axon endings simultaneously. The symbols are the same as in Figure 38. Impulses in CS are ineffective with respect to neurons a and b. If impulses in $UncS$ and CS arrive simultaneously, however, they summate to excite b. This sets the closed chain b–c in continuous activity, and impulses in CS now summate with collaterals from fibers in the chain to activate a and $R_{Unc}s$. Simultaneous excitation of b will occur by chance if CS and $UncS$ are stimulated together repeatedly. The chances of simultaneity are increased if the frequency of impulses in CS and $UncS$ is greater; i.e., if the intensity of the stimuli is greater. While the speed of conditioning in any single neuron unit is thus largely a matter of chance according to this scheme, the sum of the changes in many such units would result in a gradual increase in the number of $R_{Unc}s$ fibers activated.

This scheme is not elaborated here to account for extinction, or other phenomena of conditioning. Inhibitory effects might be introduced by the addition of specific inhibitory collaterals, or by consideration of temporal relations resulting in refractory period decrement.

electrical field. Such a conception is implied in certain Gestalt theories (Köhler, 1929; Lashley, 1930a; Gengerelli, 1934; Washburne, 1935), but its application has never been worked out in detail.

The above theories all attempt to account for classical conditioning, and nothing except pure substitution is encompassed by any of them. Neurological theories of the mechanism of the principle of effect may first reduce effect to substitution (Holt, 1931), or may attempt to formulate the action of effect directly in neural terms. Troland's (1928) retroflex theory is the most complete presentation of the latter position. Learning of the trial-and-error variety is analyzed first into the increase or decrease in conductance of the neural pathways involved in specific responses. Troland speaks of punishments as nociceptive stimuli, and rewards as beneceptive stimuli. His neural theory is that "the stimulation of nociceptive afferent channels reduces the conductances the paths of cortical conduction which are operative at the moment, or have been operative over a limited prior interval; and that, on the other hand, the excitation of beneceptive channels will cause a corresponding increase in conductances" (1928, p. 205). He recognizes that the changes in conductance must be relatively permanent and must be cumulative over successive trials, and suggests several possible mechanisms for such changes. There might be inhibitory and facilitatory nerve fibers from the affective centers of the thalamus to all the association points of the cortex, or there might be a general diffuse discharge from the thalamus which would be inhibitory at a high frequency and facilitating at a low frequency. Or the thalamus might act to control the liberation of two different kinds of hormones which would circulate in the blood stream and facilitate or inhibit concurrent cortical activity. These suggestions are not supported by any direct evidence at the present time. One objection to the general scheme is that it renders impossible the simultaneous strengthening of one response and weakening of another.

Actual instances of learning are of course much more complicated than the discussion of neural theories would imply. Any stimulus-response unit involves a large number of neurons on both the afferent and efferent sides. For the sake of simplicity, the mechanism of threshold change has been discussed in a single neuron unit. From the all-or-none law of excitation, it will be seen that activation by the conditioned stimulus will occur suddenly in any single neuron, although a number of repetitions of the stimuli may be required before the critical point is reached. The conditioned response will appear as overt activity only when a sufficient number of the neuron units are activated by the conditioned stimulus. It is a reasonable assumption that these various units will require different amounts of training (Hoagland, 1930), the result of which would be a gradual curve of acquisition such as is ordinarily obtained. The activity of single motor units in the conditioned flexion response of the rat has been recorded by Hunter (1937) from concentric needle electrodes placed in the gastrocnemius muscle. Conditioning was apparent as an increase in the number of active units, and an increase in frequency and decrease in latency of any single unit. Extinction presented the opposite picture: a decrease in the number of active units, and a decrease in frequency and increase in latency of any single unit.

Opposition has frequently been raised to any explanation of learning in terms of specific synapses whose traversibility is altered by the training procedure. It has been pointed out that a learned response may be evoked by stimulation of afferent conduction paths which were not active during the process of learning. Moreover, the adequate stimulus for a learned response is not necessarily one which stimulates certain particular afferent neurons. The facts of relative discrimination, transposition, perceptual constancy, and so forth, indicate that the stimulus can be better designated as a ratio of intensities distributed in time or space. These considerations place definite limitations upon the form of a neural theory, but do not preclude the possibility that modification takes place in specific pathways. Equivalent stimuli which activate different absolute groups of afferent neurons presumably have some central conduction pathway in common, and the learning modification would occur in that part of the pathway which is common to both stimuli. No alternative to the theory of modification of synaptic resistance has ever been stated in a form specific enough to permit critical evaluation.

Inhibition. It should be made clear again that the validity of the concept of inhibition as applied to behavioral observations in no way rests on any particular theory of the neural mechanism of inhibition. In the past fifty years new physiological explanations of inhibition have replaced the old with regularity. None of these changes has affected the psychological concept in other than an analogical manner. Current neural theories are perhaps in greater flux than ever before, and it is beyond the province of this discussion to attempt to evaluate them.

In the discussion of the nature of extinction the statement was made that repetition of any response leads to adaptation unless some other influence such as reinforcement counteracts the effect. This has been repeatedly observed in studies of reflex conduction in the spinal cord, and more recently has been carefully studied in the cortex (Dusser de Barenne and W. S. McCulloch, 1937, 1939). After repetitive electrical stimulation of a point on the motor cortex of a monkey, there is a period of reduced excitability which is most pronounced after several seconds, and which may be distinguished from reciprocal inhibition, fatigue, and refractory phase. The degree of reduced excitability is a function of the voltage, wave-shape, frequency, and duration of the electrical stimulation. The effect is never absolute and may be overcome by an increase in strength of the second stimulus or by the summation of two stimuli.

Summary

Pavlov's theory of cortical activity is expressed in terms of excitation and inhibition which interact through irradiation, concentration, and induction. There are definite limitations to the validity of Pavlov's conceptions of neural function in conditioning.

The earlier insistence that the cortex was essential for conditioning has now given way before satisfactory evidence that conditioning may be mediated by subcortical structures. This has in turn made unnecessary the postulation of vicarious functioning to account for learning in the absence of given cortical areas. The cortex remains important in normal conditioning, and, according to the principle of functional encephalization, its importance increases throughout the phylogenetic series to man.

Experimental demarcation of the anatomical locus of conditioning suggests that the essential modification is central. Peripheral structures can be largely dispensed with in the formation of conditioned responses. Moreover, the association appears to lie outside the regular pathways of the conditioned stimulus, the unconditioned stimulus, and the unconditioned response. The remaining possibility is an association pathway, but only fragmentary direct evidence for it now exists. This does not imply a general association area.

Speculations regarding the nature of synaptic modification include anatomical growth of axons and dendrites, changes in the physico-chemical properties of the nerve cell, continued activity in closed neural chains, and the influence of bioelectric fields. Evidence is lacking for any of the proposed explanations, and at best the speculations serve only to account for stimulus-substitution which has been shown to be but one of several forms which conditioning takes.

Eventual explanation of conditioning in neurological terms depends upon the convergence of two experimental trends. In the first place, the psychologist must furnish a more precise statement of the fundamental factors in response modification, defining, for example, the effect of reinforcement for the simplest cases. With the behavioral facts in better order, the task of explanation faced by the neurophysiologist will be clearer. In the second place, neurophysiological study of long-lasting modifications in synaptic function will accumulate the necessary data for a verifiable explanation of these simplest instances of learning.

Notes

In the present status of knowledge, neural theory is not basic to conditioning theory. The known facts of neural function cannot be utilized to predict or to limit the results of behavioral studies. None of the several principles and facts presented in earlier chapters can be deduced from present direct knowledge of the nervous system. Even the basic law that a response varies in magnitude with intensity of stimulus would be equally true if the nerves were copper wires or pneumatic tubes. The facts of speed of conduction and synaptic delay cannot predict the latency of a conditioned response, for we have no idea what length of nerve or how many synapses are involved. New findings may reduce the temporal summation interval of a synapse from 40 msec. to 0.2 msec. without altering the principle of temporal summation of stimuli. The demonstration of adaptation of synapses yields no clue to the prediction that the eyelid reflex will adapt more rapidly to light than to an air-puff. Many of the so-called neural facts, such as reflex inhibition, which seem most relevant to conditioning are in reality behavioral laws stated as relations between afferent and efferent nerve activity without direct observation of any intermediate neural events (Skinner, 1931). This point of view of course does not preclude the possibility that on the basis of future work neurological prediction of behavioral facts may be achieved.

Pavlov's Theory of Cortical Functioning

Pavlov's theory of cortical functioning is presented in his two books (1927, 1928). Critical discussions and supplementations of his conceptions are presented by Beritov (1924, 1927), Borovski (1929), Razran (1930), Denny-Brown (1932), and Bekhterev (1932).

Anatomical Localization of Conditioning

The utilization of training procedures in the study of the localization of cerebral functions was undertaken at approximately the same time by Pavlov, Bekhterev, and Franz. Reference will be made here only to the work on mammals. Learned responses to auditory stimuli after removal of the temporal lobes have been demonstrated in dogs by Krijanovsky and Babkin in Pavlov's laboratory (Pavlov, 1927, p. 332–334), Kalischer (1909), Swift (1912), although Rothmann (1908) and Sutherland and Dworkin (1932) reported negative results; in rats by Wiley (1932), Pennington (1937). Conditioned responses to olfactory stimuli have been demonstrated in dogs after removal of the pyriform lobes by Zavadsky (1910), after removal of the anterior half of the cortex by Saturnov and by Kouraev (Pavlov, 1927, p. 371), after transection of both fornices by W. F. Allen (1938), and in rats after destruction of large portions of the cerebrum by Swann (1935). Successful training in optic responses after removal of the area striata has been reported in rats by many researchers following work by Lashley (1929), in cats by Kennedy (1939), Ten Cate (1934a, 1939), and K. U. Smith (1937), in dogs by Koudrin (Pavlov, 1927, pp. 331, 343), Kalischer (1909), D. G. Marquis (1934), D. G. Marquis and Hilgard (1936), and in monkeys by Rosenzweig (1935), Klüver (1936), and D. G. Marquis and Hilgard (1937). Proprioceptive and cutaneous conditioned responses aft-er removal of portions of the sensorimotor cortex have been studied in rats by D. E. Smith (1939), in cats by Storey (1937), in dogs by several of Pavlov's students (Pavlov, 1927), and in primates by T. C. Ruch and Fulton (1935), T. C. Ruch, Fulton, and German (1938), and Harlow and Settlage (1936).

The effect of destruction of the cortical motor center for the unconditioned response has been studied by several investigators. Pavlov (1928, p. 97–98) reported that conditioned salivation was unaffected by bilateral removal of the cortical salivary center. Bilateral removal of the motor center for blinking (pre-cruciate cortex) in dogs did not affect the formation of conditioned eyelid responses (D. G. Marquis and Hilgard, 1936). Surgical extirpation of the motor cortex in monkeys has been shown by Lashley (1924) and Jacobsen (1934) to result in no loss of learned motor performances involving the hands. Asratian (1935), Ten Cate (1938) and Rosenthal (1938) found that conditioned leg withdrawal was not abolished by removal of the motor cortex bilaterally in dogs, but Bekhterev (1923b) and W. F. Allen (1938) reported a severe impairment, corresponding to that observed after complete decortication by Culler and Mettler (1934). This problem needs further research. The effect of removal of one entire hemisphere in dogs has been studied by Blagoveshchenskaya (1929), Rosenthal (1937), Rosenzweig (1935), Poltyrev and Alexejev (1936).

The possibility of establishing conditioned responses in the isolated spinal cord has been demonstrated recently by the experiments of Culler (1937), and Shurrager and Culler (1938) on flexion responses in spinal dogs. A pressure stimulus at the tip of the tail was followed repeatedly by a shock to the paw of one hind leg. No conditioned response involving movement of the limb developed, but when the semitendinosus muscle was exposed and directly observed, a small twitch of one end of the muscle was apparent. Extinction and spontaneous recovery of this response could be obtained. Further experimental study is necessary before the relation of these results to conditioning in general becomes clear.

Functional Components of the Conditioning Mechanism

The only thorough and comprehensive treatment of this phase of the subject is by Beritov (1924, 1927). No attempt has been made here to repeat his theory in detail, but rather to summarize the experimental studies which have appeared subsequently.

Non-neural conditioning, in which the agent producing the unconditioned response acts through the blood stream without intervention of the central nervous system, is implied in studies of conditioned vegetative changes such as leucocytosis, antibody formation, agglutination, diuresis, and pancreatic secretion. These studies have been summarized by Hull (1934c), Loucks (1937a), Metalnikov (1934), Razran (1933a); and Razran (1937) gives a full list of references. Their interpretation

is not clear at present. In several instances the results have been questioned because of inadequate experimental controls, and in other instances the possibility has not been excluded that the agent producing the unconditioned response actually stimulates neural centers to produce the reaction reflexly.

Although the essential modification in conditioning is central, it is still possible that such changes are reflected in peripheral function. Drabovitch and coworkers have demonstrated changes in the chronaxie of the muscles of the limb coincident with the elicitation of a delayed conditioned leg withdrawal response in dogs. The series of experiments published during the past four years are summarized in a recent article (Drabovitch, 1937). During the interval following the onset of the conditioned stimulus (a prolonged tone), the chronaxie of both flexors and extensors of the leg increases to a value which may be double the resting value. During the conditioned reaction, the chronaxie decreases. These changes are paralleled in the chronaxie of the cortical motor point for flexion of the limb, so that an approximate isochronism of the motor pathway exists. The interpretation of the chronaxie measure (H. Davis and Forbes, 1936) is not clear enough to justify further speculation concerning a mechanism of conditioning.

The Nature of Synaptic Modification

Reviews of the recent advances in the knowledge of synaptic transmission may be found in Fulton (1938), Lorente de Nó (1938a, 1938b, 1938c), and Gasser (1937). A symposium on the synapse by a number of leading neurophysiologists appeared in the September, 1939, issue of the *Journal of Neurophysiology*. (Vol. 2, No. 5.) References to the earlier, speculative theories of the synaptic modification in learning may be obtained from Lashley's review (1934).

Mathematical derivation of the possibilities of neuron circuits has been presented in full detail in a recent book by Rashevsky (1938). Extensions and elaborations have subsequently been published by Householder (1938a, 1938b) and Landahl (1938a, 1938b).

The requirements and present alternatives for a theory of central inhibition have been reviewed by Fulton (1938). The rapidly growing evidence that the properties of the synapse do not differ qualitatively from those of peripheral nerve lends special weight to theories expressed in terms of the positive after-potential of internuncial neurons (Gasser, 1937), or of the temporal relations of impulses summating at a synapse (Lorente de Nó, 1938c).

Glossary

Prominent in the glossary are terms specific to conditioning, including translations of Pavlov's terms, which are designated by his name. The index may serve in locating the usage of words and expressions not included in the glossary.

adaptation. The decrement in a response which is a consequence of its repeated elicitation. (Syn. **intrinsic inhibition;** cf. **internal inhibition;** contr. w. **extrinsic inhibition, interference**)

association. The establishment of functional relations between psychological activities and states in the course of individual experience. A broader term which includes conditioning. (Cf. **conditioning**)

associative shifting (Thorndike). Considered by Thorndike to be the more general case of which the conditioned response is a special case. If a situation S_1 originally evokes R_x, i.e., $S_1 \rightarrow R_x$, then S_2 may be made to evoke R_x by additions until $S_1 + S_2 \rightarrow R_x$ and later subtractions until $S_2 \rightarrow R_x$. (Contr. w. **trial-and-error learning**)

automatic act. An involuntary act occasioned by the stimulus, distinguished from a reflex in that it has been acquired in the course of individual experience. (Cf. **reflex**)

avoidance training. A training procedure in which the learned movement circumvents or prevents the appearance of a noxious stimulus. (Distg. fr. **instrumental escape training**)

backward conditioning. The experimental arrangement in which the conditioned stimulus is presented after the cessation of the unconditioned stimulus.

choice-reaction discrimination, see **discrimination**

classical conditioning experiment. An experiment after the prototype of Pavlov, which consists in the repeated presentation of the conditioned and unconditioned stimuli in a controlled relationship so that there occur alterations in reaction tendencies with respect to the conditioned stimulus which would not arise except for its relationship to the unconditioned stimulus and response. Distinguished from instrumental reward and escape training and from avoidance training in that the conditioned response neither delivers nor prevents the appearance of the unconditioned stimulus. (Cf. **avoidance training; instrumental reward training; instrumental escape training; secondary reward training**)

complete substitution, see **redintegration**

concentration (Pavlov). 1. The focussing of the hypothetical nervous processes of excitation and inhibition within restricted cortical areas. (Contr. w. **irradiation**) 2. Behaviorally, restricted generalization. (Cf. **generalization**)

conditioned inhibition (Pavlov). A variety of internal inhibition defined by the experimental arrangements under which it is obtained. The negative, non-reinforced, combination to be differentiated from the positive conditioned stimulus consists of the positive stimulus plus an added stimulus known as the conditioned inhibitor.

conditioned response. A response which appears or is modified as a consequence of the occurrence of a conditioned stimulus in proximity to reinforcement. (Syn. **conditioned reflex** or **conditional reflex** [Pavlov]; **association-reflex** [Bekhterev]; **individual reflex** [Beritov])

conditioned stimulus (Pavlov). The experimental stimulus to which a new or modified response

becomes related through the process of conditioning. (Syn. **conditional stimulus, inadequate stimulus, substitute stimulus**)

conditioning. The process of training which results in the formation of conditioned responses. (Cf. **association**)

counter conditioning. Extinction under circumstances in which the response decrement is hastened by the reinforcement of a response which displaces the original conditioned response. (Distg. fr. **adaptation**; cf. **interference**)

delayed conditioning (Pavlov). The conditioned stimulus begins from 5 seconds to several minutes before the unconditioned, and continues until reinforcement occurs. (Distg. fr. **trace conditioning;** not to be confused with **delayed reaction experiment** [Hunter])

derived reinforcement. The strengthening of a conditioned response by reinforcement with a stimulus which depends for its reinforcing value on prior association with a reward or punishment. (Contr. w. **homogeneous reinforcement; heterogeneous reinforcement;** cf. **avoidance training, secondary reward training**)

differential inhibition (Pavlov). A form of internal inhibition arising in respect to the negative stimulus when stimuli are discriminated by the method of contrasts. (Cf. **discrimination**)

discrimination. The inferred basis for differential responses to unlike stimuli. Discrimination is always measured by differential responses, but absence of a specified differential response is not necessarily an indication of lack of discriminatory capacity. The **method of contrasts** refers to an arrangement for studying discrimination in which one of a pair of stimuli (the positive stimulus) is invariably reinforced, the other (the negative stimulus) invariably non-reinforced. Discrimination is inferred from the greater strength of conditioning to the positive than to the negative stimulus following this procedure. **Choice-reaction discrimination** refers to the method in which a particular response is demanded to one of a pair of stimuli, a different response to the other member of the pair, correct responses to either stimulus being rewarded.

disinhibition (Pavlov). A temporary increase in the strength of an extinguished conditioned response as the result of an extraneous stimulus. While called by Pavlov an "inhibition of inhibition," the term may be used in a strictly behavioral sense. (Contr. w. **external inhibition**)

dominance (Ukhtomsky). A physiological description of the interaction of certain reflexes, whereby following repeated stimulation, the dominant one is evoked by stimuli appropriate to other reflexes, while at the same time the normal responses to these stimuli are inhibited. (Sometimes used incorrectly

as a synonym for prepotency [Sherrington])

effect principle. The principle that the tendency to repeat an act depends on its proximity to a reinforcing state of affairs. While the principle is particularly appropriate in the explanation of instrumental reward and escape learning, in which reinforcement is a consequence of the conditioned response, the principle does not demand that the learned act be instrumental to reinforcement. (Cf. **goal-gradient** [Hull]; distg. fr. **expectancy principle; substitution principle**)

excitation (Pavlov). One of two hypothetical nervous processes in the cortex, interacting with inhibition, its opposite. (Cf. **inhibition**)

expectancy principle. The principle which interprets the animal's learned behavior as consonant with anticipated (expected) events or consequences. (Syn. **sign learning** [Tolman]; distg. fr. **effect principle, substitution principle**)

experimental extinction, see **extinction**

experimental neurosis (Pavlov). A disturbed state appearing in some animals as a result of conditioning procedures, such as too difficult discriminations, or prolonged periods of delay. The animal is unsuitable for experimentation, but may or may not appear to be disturbed when outside the experimental situation.

external inhibition (Pavlov). A temporary reduction in the strength of a conditioned response as a result of the occurrence of an extraneous stimulus. (Contr. w. **disinhibition**)

extinction (Pavlov). The specific procedure of presenting the conditioned stimulus unaccompanied by the usual reinforcement; also the decrement in a conditioned response which results from that procedure.

extinctive inhibition (Pavlov). The variety of internal inhibition which appears with non-reinforcement of a conditioned response. (Cf. **extinction**)

extrinsic inhibition, see **interference**

facilitation. A temporary non-learned increase in strength of response as a result of the occurrence of a second stimulus or response. (Distg. fr. **reinforcement**)

forgetting. Decrement in a response when elicited after an interval during which it has not been elicited. Forgetting differs from extinction and other forms of adaptation through repetition. (Cf. **adaptation; extinction; retroactive inhibition**)

fractional component conditioned response. That result within classical conditioning in which the conditioned response,

while not fully duplicating the unconditioned response, is best described as resembling it or some of its components. (Syn. **fractional anticipatory goal response** [Hull]; cf. **preparatory response; redintegrative response**)

generalization (Pavlov). The behavioral fact that a conditioned response formed to one stimulus may also be elicited by other stimuli which have not been used in the course of conditioning. If one stimulus is like another except for a difference in a single dimension (e.g., pitch or loudness of tones as determined by psychophysical experiments) the degree of generalization will vary inversely with the distance of the stimuli from each other along this dimension. The function expressing this relationship is called the **gradient of generalization of conditioning.** Its form varies with circumstances of experimentation. There is a corresponding **gradient of generalization of extinction** resulting when each of several similar stimuli evokes a conditioned response, and the response to one of them is extinguished. Stimuli otherwise unlike may participate in generalization through the equivalence of the responses which they evoke. Such generalization is known as **mediated generalization.** (Cf. **irradiation; response generalization; spatial generalization**)

goal gradient. (1) An earlier and somewhat specialized statement

of the gradient of reward (Hull).
(2) A performance gradient in which
parts of a serial act are reinforced
by a common goal situation, acts
being more vigorous the nearer they
lie to the reinforcing state of affairs.
The goal-gradient so defined is explained in part by the gradient of
reward, but is a gradient of strength
of response rather than of strength
of conditioning and is modified by
factors other than proximity of individual responses to the reinforcement. (Cf. **gradients of reinforcements; spread of effect**)

gradient of generalization,
see **generalization**

gradients of reinforcement.
The class of functions describing the
effect of proximity of reinforcement
on strength of conditioning. Among
these is the **temporal gradient
within classical conditioning,**
referring to the influence of interval
between conditioned and unconditioned stimuli. A short forward order of a few tenths of a second is
usually found most advantageous.
Also included is the **temporal gradient within avoidance learning,** which refers to the influence
of the interval between the conditioned stimulus and the punishment.
The **gradient of reward** has both
temporal and non-temporal aspects.
A conditioned response is strengthened by the reward type of reinforcement in inverse proportion to the
time elapsing between the response
and the reinforcement, strengthening being less as the reward is delayed. This is the temporal aspect of
the gradient of reward. A similar

gradient is found for non-temporal
aspects of the separation of response
and reward, when proximity is defined in terms of distance or in terms
of number of responses removed. The
**temporal gradient in delayed
reaction experiments** is not
strictly a gradient of reinforcement,
since the delay is introduced between the presentation of a discriminatory conditioned stimulus and the
opportunity to respond to it. (Cf.
**goal-gradient; spread of ef-
fect**)

habit-family hierarchy (Hull).
A number of habitual alternative
behavior sequences having in common the initial stimulus situation
and the final reinforcing state of affairs, the alternative sequences having a preferential order which constitutes them a hierarchy.

**heterogeneous reinforce-
ment.** The strengthening of a conditioned response through reinforcement which depends on a response
which does not resemble the conditioned response. This is characteristic of reward and escape learning,
but not limited to it. (Contr. w.
**homogeneous reinforcement;
derived reinforcement**)

**higher-order conditioned re-
sponse** (Pavlov). A conditioned
response based on reinforcement by
another conditioned stimulus and
response. A first-order response is
reinforced by an unconditioned stimulus, a second-order response (or
secondary response) by a first-order
conditioned stimulus, and so on.

homogeneous reinforcement. The strengthening of a conditioned response by reinforcing with an unconditioned stimulus which evokes activity similar to the conditioned response. Required according to the substitution principle. (Contr. w. **heterogeneous reinforcement; derived reinforcement**)

inhibition. 1. (Pavlov). One of the two hypothetical cortical processes, interacting with excitation, its opposite. 2. Behaviorally, any decrease in the strength of a response which is occasioned by positive stimulation, either of the response itself (as in extinction) or of some other response (as in external inhibition). (Cf. **conditioned inhibition, differential inhibition, external inhibition, extinctive inhibition, extrinsic inhibition, inhibition of delay, inhibition of reinforcement, internal inhibition, intrinsic inhibition**)

inhibition of delay (Pavlov). That form of internal inhibition manifested during the latent period of a delayed conditioned response. That the interval of delay is inhibitory is evidenced by (1) the ease with which disinhibition may be demonstrated, and (2) secondary inhibition of weak conditioned responses if the attempt is made to elicit them during the period of delay.

inhibition of reinforcement (Hovland). The diminution of a conditioned response which may occur within reinforcement trials if such trials are repeated at short intervals. The phenomenon is like adaptation, in that it is temporary, and may be recovered from by rest.

instrumental escape training. That form of training in which the strengthened act terminates a noxious stimulus to which the organism has been reacting. (Distg. fr. **avoidance training**)

instrumental reward training. That form of learning in which the strengthened act (usually manipulation or locomotion) produces an unconditioned stimulus capable of satisfying a drive. (Cf. **avoidance training; instrumental escape training; secondary reward training; trial-and-error learning**)

interference. The decrement in a response which is a consequence of the elicitation of another incompatible response. (Syn. **extrinsic inhibition;** cf. **adaptation, extinction**)

internal inhibition (Pavlov). That form of inhibition which depends upon stimulation by a conditioned stimulus. (Contr. w. **external inhibition**)

intrinsic inhibition, see **adaptation**

involuntary response. A response which, regardless of its earlier history, is now largely determined by the experimental stimulus and is relatively slightly affected by instructions or substitutes for instructions. (Cf. **voluntary response; semi-voluntary response**)

irradiation (Pavlov). 1. The wave-like spread of excitation and inhibition through the cortex, the inferred physiological basis for generalization. (Contr. w. **concentration**) 2. Behaviorally, used chiefly in reference to spatial generalization. (Cf. **generalization; spatial generalization**)

learning. Change in the strength of an act through training procedures (whether in the laboratory or the natural environment) as distinguished from changes in the strength of the act by factors not attributable to training.

mediated generalization, see **generalization**

mosaic of functions (Pavlov). A conception of localization of functions in the cortex. For Pavlov, the mosaic is determined in part anatomically (the analyzers), in part functionally, as a result of the integration of conditioned excitation and inhibition.

negative adaptation, see **adaptation**

negative conditioned stimulus. A conditioned stimulus which, through repeated presentation, either alone or in combination, without being followed by reinforcement, tends to be followed by reduced or inhibited conditioned responses.

negative induction (Pavlov). The intensification of inhibition under the influence of preceding excitation. (Contr. w. **positive induction**)

operant (Skinner). An act which first appears as a random movement. The operant commonly becomes related to a discriminated stimulus, which then sets the occasion for the operant behavior, but, strictly speaking, does not elicit it. (Cf. **random movement**; contr. w. **respondent**)

paradoxical phase (Pavlov). A state of the cortical processes lying between that of equalization and complete inhibition in which only weak conditioned stimuli lead to responses and strong stimuli either elicit no responses at all or have a barely noticeable effect. (Cf. **phase of equalization; ultra-paradoxical phase**)

partial reinforcement. A modification of simple conditioning in which the reinforcement occurs on only a fraction of the trials. Under some circumstances random alternation of reinforcement and non-reinforcement leads to a normal acquisition rate, and at the same time increases resistance to extinction. Two special forms of partial reinforcement within instrumental training lead to unlike consequences. **Periodic reconditioning** (Skinner) refers to the reinforcing of instrumental acts according to a time schedule, such as reinforcement every 3 minutes. Under such circumstances, the longer the interval between reinforcements, the less the rate of responding. **Reinforcement at a fixed ratio** (Skinner) refers to the reinforcing of instrumental acts according to a schedule determined by the number of responses, such as reinforcement every fifth response. Under these circumstances, the higher the ratio (i.e., the fewer the reinforcements) the greater the rate of responding.

periodic reconditioning, see **partial reinforcement**

phase of equalization (Pavlov). A state of the cortical processes lying between that of normal waking and sleeping in which all conditioned stimuli, independent of their intensities, are equally effective. (Cf. **paradoxical phase; ultra-paradoxical phase**)

positive induction (Pavlov). The intensification of excitation under the influence of preceding inhibition. (Contr. w. **negative induction**)

preparatory response. A form of conditioned response within classical conditioning, often unlike the unconditioned response, which may be appropriately characterized as a response in readiness for the appearance of the unconditioned stimulus (Cf. **fractional component response; redintegrative response**)

primary punishment. A stimulus capable of reinforcing avoidance

behavior because of defensive responses which it evokes, rather than because of prior association with other noxious stimuli. (Cf. **primary reward**)

primary reward. A stimulus deriving its reinforcing value from the fact that it satisfies an organic need, rather than from the fact of prior association with other need-satisfying stimuli. (Cf. **secondary reward**)

pseudo-conditioning (Grether). The strengthening of a response to a previously neutral stimulus through the repeated elicitation of the response by another stimulus, without paired* presentation of the two stimuli. (Cf. **dominance; sensitization**)

pseudo-reflex (Skinner). A relation between a stimulus and a response which superficially resembles a reflex by Skinner's definition, but depends upon or involves other terms than those expressed in the relation. The clearest example is the discriminated operant. (Cf. **operant**)

pure-stimulus act (Hull). An act which serves no biological function other than to provide stimuli which aid in the integration of the organism's behavior.

random movement. An act for which no stimulus determinant can be specified. The random character disappears as soon as the act becomes correlated with an observable stimulus. (Syn. **spontaneous movement;** cf. **operant**)

recency principle (Guthrie). A principle explanatory of associative learning which states that an organism when next confronted with a stimulating situation closely resembling an earlier one tends to react as it last did in such a situation.

To be distinguished from that form of the 'law of recency' which states that associative strength is a function of the time elapsed since the association was established. Guthrie's principle is that of recency in order of occurrence, not of recency in time.

reconditioning. The reestablishment of a conditioned response by reinforcement after it has been diminished by extinction or forgetting.

redintegration. The arousal of a response by a fraction of the stimuli whose combination originally aroused it. (Cf. **substitution principle**)

redintegrative response. That form of conditioned response in classical conditioning which is essentially a replica of the unconditioned response. (Cf. **fractional component response; preparatory response**)

reflex. 1. Preferably, a stimulus-determined act which can occur without specific training of the organism. 2. Any of the motor activities of the body, whether simple or complex, to the extent that they may be considered as determined (Pavlov). Hence, **exploratory reflex, freedom reflex, social reflex,** etc. 3. The analytical unit of behavior for describing the observed relation between a stimulus and a response, when the correlation between stimulus and response is lawful (Skinner).

reflex reserve (Skinner). The total number of times a conditioned response will occur without further reinforcement, granted that the environmental conditions are adequate for its repetition. Hence, one measure from which to infer strength of conditioning. (Cf. **strength of conditioning**)

reinforcement (Pavlov). 1. The experimental arrangement of presenting the conditioned stimulus accompanied by the unconditioned stimulus, or, more generally, the arrangement of following the conditioned stimulus and response by reward or punishment, or some substitute for these. 2. The process which increases the strength of conditioning as a consequence of these arrangements. (Distg. fr. **facilitation;** cf. **derived reinforcement, heterogeneous reinforcement, homogeneous reinforcement, partial reinforcement**)

respondent (Skinner). That form of response which is elicited by a stimulus, and hence to be distinguished from an operant. (Cf. **operant**)

response. A stimulus-occasioned act. A general term for acts correlated with stimuli, whether the correlation is untrained or the result of training. (Cf. **reflex**)

response generalization. The behavioral fact that following the conditioning of one response, other responses may be elicited by the same conditioned stimulus although there has been no specific training to establish a relationship between this stimulus and these responses. (Syn. **equivalence of responses; transfer;** distg. fr. **sensory generalization**)

response tendency. A tendency to respond which is inferred from other responses. The tendency may be expressed in units of behavior if it is inferred from measured behavior.

retroactive inhibition. A principle coming chiefly from experiments on verbal memorization and retention which accounts for forgetting as the result of disruption or interference by new learning interpolated between memorization and recall. (Cf. **forgetting**)

secondary conditioned response (Pavlov), see **higher-order conditioned response**

secondary extinction (Pavlov). The extinction of other conditioned responses which results when any one conditioned response undergoes extinction. (Syn. **generalized extinction;** cf. **generalization**)

secondary reward. A stimulus which derives its reinforcing value from prior conditioning in which it has been associated with a primary reward. (Cf. **derived reinforcement; sub-goal; token**)

secondary reward training. That arrangement of an instrumental reward experiment in which the reinforcement is by way of a secondary reward. (Cf. **instrumental reward training**)

semi-voluntary response. A response which lies midway on the continuum between involuntary and voluntary responses in that it is determined both by the experimental stimulus and by instructions. Many conditioned responses are of this nature.

sensitization (Wendt). The increase in the strength of a reflex originally evoked by a conditioned stimulus through its conjunction with an unconditioned stimulus and response. Differs from conventional conditioning in that the response which is strengthened is appropriate to the conditioned stimulus, not to the unconditioned stimulus. (Syn. **alpha conditioning** [Hull]; cf. **pseudo-conditioning** [Grether])

sensory generalization, see **generalization**

set. A selective predisposition to respond to a stimulus in a prescribed manner which is established by instructions or by some substitute for instructions. (Cf. **expectancy**)

sign learning (Tolman). The formation of an expectation that a first stimulus-object is going to be followed by a second stimulus-object, as testified by behavior preparatory to the second stimulus-object. (Syn. **sign-Gestalt learning**)

simultaneous conditioning.
1. Preferably, the procedure of conditioning in which the onset of conditioned and unconditioned stimuli is coincident. This is ordinarily an unfavorable relationship for conditioning. 2. The procedure in which the conditioned stimulus is presented from a fraction of a second to 5 seconds before the unconditioned stimulus, and continues until reinforcement occurs (Pavlov).

spatial generalization. That form of sensory generalization in which the gradient of generalization of conditioning or of extinction is expressed as a function of the distance between stimuli, usually on the body surface. (Cf. **generalization; irradiation**)

spontaneous movement, see **random movement**

spontaneous recovery (Pavlov). The return in strength of a conditioned response, whether partial or complete, brought about by lapse of time following its diminution by extinction.

spread of effect (Thorndike). Rewarding a particular act (connection) leads not only to the strengthening of this act but to the strengthening of neighboring acts both preceding and following the rewarded act, the influence diminishing as the acts are more remote from the rewarded one. (Cf. **effect principle; gradient of reward**)

stimulus. An external or internal object or event which occasions an alteration in the behavior of the organism.

strength of conditioning. The extent to which a conditioned stimulus tends to evoke a given conditioned response, as inferred from the strength of response to the conditioned stimulus. Strength of response is not, however, a direct measure of strength of conditioning, for in inferring strength of conditioning due regard must be paid to prior and subsequent responses. Thus, of two responses equal in magnitude, one may represent an inhibited response, another may be facilitated, and strength of conditioning may differ accordingly. Similarly, responses unequal in magnitude may represent equal strengths of conditioning, if the conditioned stimuli differ in intensity. (Syn. **associative strength;** distg. fr. **strength of response**)

strength of response. Any descriptive characteristic of single responses (such as latency or amplitude) or of groups of responses (such as percentage frequency or rate) which may be expressed quantitatively and hence enter as data with respect to magnitude or vigor of response. Which measures of strength of response are most serviceable must be determined empirically. (Distg. fr. **strength of conditioning**)

sub-goal. A stimulus regularly reacted to in the series of events leading up to the goal, so that this stimulus derives reinforcing value from its association with the goal.

(Cf. **derived reinforcement; secondary reward; token**)

substitution principle. The principle explanatory of conditioning which states that a conditioned stimulus acting at the time of an unconditioned response tends on its recurrence to evoke that response, and hence may be said to substitute for the unconditioned stimulus. (Cf. **effect principle; expectancy principle**)

temporal conditioned response. When an unconditioned stimulus is presented at regular intervals, a conditioned response may appear at or near the usual time of appearance of the unconditioned stimulus, even if the unconditioned stimulus is omitted. Such response is known as a temporal conditioned response.

temporal gradient in avoidance training, see **gradients of reinforcement**

temporal gradient in classical conditioning, see **gradients of reinforcement**

temporal gradient in delayed reaction experiments, see **gradients of reinforcement**

token. A secondary reward characterized by the fact that it must be manipulated in a prescribed manner in order to produce the primary reward. (Cf. **secondary reward**)

trace conditioning (Pavlov). The conditioned stimulus is permitted to act and then is removed before the onset of the unconditioned stimulus. Trace conditioned responses are more difficult to establish than delayed conditioned responses. In **short-trace conditioning** the conditioned stimulus is terminated a few seconds before the unconditioned stimulus is presented; in **long-trace conditioning** the conditioned stimulus is terminated a minute or more before the unconditioned stimulus begins to act. (Distg. fr. **delayed conditioning**)

trial-and-error learning (Thorndike). The mode of learning in which the learner tries various movements in its repertory, apparently in a somewhat random manner and without explicit recognition of the connection between the movement and the resolution of the problem situation. Tentative movements which succeed are more frequently repeated in subsequent trials, and those which fail gradually disappear. (Syn. **selecting and connecting** [Thorndike]; contr. w. **associative shifting** [Thorndike])

types of nervous system (Pavlov). A classification of individual differences in conditioning, on the basis of the relative susceptibility to excitation and inhibition. The final types, with their correspondence to the ancient Greek classifications of temperaments, are as follows: (1) **excitable type** (choleric), (2) **central type,** with two sub-types, **lively type** (sanguine), and **stolid type** (phlegmatic), (3) **inhibitable type** (melancholic).

ultra-paradoxical phase (Pavlov). A transitory state of the cortical processes sometimes occurring before complete inhibition, in which only inhibitory agents have a positive effect. (Cf. **phase of equalization; paradoxical phase**)

unconditioned stimulus (Pavlov). That experimental stimulus in a classical conditioning experiment which evokes the unconditioned response, and hence serves as the reinforcing agent. (Syn. **unconditional stimulus; conditioning stimulus** [Razran]; **original stimulus** [Guthrie])

voluntary response. A response largely under the control of instructions or substitutes for instructions, so that the experimental stimulus acts merely as an occasion for the response, and is of much less importance than instructions in determining whether or not the response occurs, or the form of the response when it occurs. (Cf. **involuntary response; semi-voluntary response**)

References and Author Index

The numbers in italics following each reference refer to the text pages on which the paper is cited. The following list is not intended as a complete bibliography; it is fairly complete for the years following the publication of Razran's (1937) extensive bibliography. Articles in Russian have been cited only when adequate abstracts are available in another language. Abbreviations of journal titles are given in accordance with the conventions of the *World list of scientific periodicals*, 2d ed., Oxford University Press, 1934. Citations in the text are made by date of publication.

1. ADAMS, D. K. (1929) Experimental studies of adaptive behavior in cats. *Comp. Psychol. Monogr.*, 6, No. 27, 168 pp.—*253*
2. ADAMS, D. K. (1931) A restatement of the problem of learning. *Brit. J. Psychol.*, 22, 150-178.—*25, 101, 253*
3. ADAMS, D. K. (1937) Note on method. *Psychol. Rev.*, 44, 212-218.—*254*
   ADES, H. W., *see* No. 147.
4. ADES, H. W., METTLER, F. A., and CULLER, E. A. (1937) Distribution of acoustic pathways in the medial geniculate bodies. *Amer. J. Physiol.*, 119, 257-258.—*205*
   ALEXEJEV, W. A., *see* No. 684.
   ALLEN, M. K., *see* No. 309.
5. ALLEN, W. F. (1937) Olfactory and trigeminal conditioned reflexes in dogs. *Amer. J. Physiol.*, 118, 532-540.—*205*
6. ALLEN, W. F. (1938) Relationship of the conditioned olfactory-foreleg response to the motor centers of the brain. *Amer. J. Physiol.*, 121, 657-668. *205, 337*
7. ALLISON, L. W. (1932) An experimental study of reflex and voluntary eyelid responses. *J. exp. Psychol.*, 15, 56-72.—*131*
8. ALLPORT, F. H. (1924) *Social psychology*. Boston, Houghton Mifflin, xiv, 453 pp.—*14, 25*
9. ANDERSON, A. C. (1932) Time discrimination in the white rat. *J. comp. Psychol.*, 13, 27-55.—*174*

10. ANDERSON, A. C. (1933) Runway time and the goal gradient. *J. exp. Psychol.*, 16, 423-428.—*227*
   ANDERSON, B. O., *see* No. 849.
   ANDERSON, O. D., *see* Nos. 526, 528.

11. ANDERSON, O. D., and LIDDELL, H. S. (1935) Observations on experimental neurosis in sheep. *Arch. Neurol. Psychiat., Chicago*, 34, 330-354.—*306*

12. ANDREYEV, L. A. (1934a) Extreme limits of pitch discrimination with higher tones. *J. comp. Psychol.*, 18, 315-332.—*205*

13. ANDREYEV, L. A. (1934b) The effect of single and repeated doses of alcohol on conditioned reflexes in the dog. *Arch. int. Pharmacodyn.*, 48, 117-128.—*134*

14. ANDREYEV, L. A. (1935) Functional changes in the brain of the dog after reduction of the cerebral blood supply. II. Disturbances of conditioned reflexes after ligation of arteries. *Arch. Neurol. Psychiat., Chicago*, 34, 699-713.—*155*

15. ANDREYEV, L. A., and PUGSLEY, L. I. (1934) A study of the effects of hypercalcaemia produced by parathyroid hormone and irradiated ergosterol upon the activity of the cerebral cortex by means of conditioned reflexes. *Quart. J. exp. Physiol.*, 24, 189-206.—*156*

16. ANOKHIN, P. (1932) [Hypnotic stages in the normal balance between excitation and inhibition during formation and establishment of differential inhibition.] *Trud. Fiziol. Lab. Pavlov.*, 4, 339-349. (*Psychol. Abstr.*, 1932, 6, No. 4273.)—*131*

17. ANOKHIN, P., and STRAJ, E. (1937) A study of the dynamics of cortical nerve function: VI. Characteristics of the receptive function of the cerebral cortex following the unconditioned stimulus. *J. genet. Psychol.*, 51, 3-16.—*101*

18. ANREP, G. V. (1920) Pitch discrimination in the dog. *J. Physiol.*, 53, 367-385.—*28, 195, 205*

19. ANREP, G. V. (1923) The irradiation of conditioned reflexes. *Proc. roy. Soc.*, 94B, 404-426—*131, 179, 181*

20. ARAKELIAN, P. (1939) Cyclic oscillations in the extinction behavior of rats. *J. gen. Psychol.*, 21, 137-162.—*73, 130*

21. ARKHANGELSKY, V. M. (1929) [Complex higher nervous activity of underfed animals.] *Zh. Eksp. Biol. Med.*, 13, 5-13. (*Psychol. Abstr.*, 1934, 8, No. 955.)—*155*

22. ARKHANGELSKY, V. M. (1931a) [Conditioned reflexes in dogs after ligation and cutting of the spermatic cords.] *Fiziol. Zh. S.S.S.R.*, 14, 255-267. (*Psychol. Abstr.*, 1933, 7, No. 3733.)—*156*

23. ARKHANGELSKY, V. M. (1931b) [Conditioned reflexes in castrated dogs.] *Fiziol. Zh. S.S.S.R.*, 14, 268-279. (*Psychol. Abstr.*, 1933, 7, No. 3732.)—*156*

24. ARKHANGELSKY, V. M. (1935) Conditioned reflexes in a castrated dog during a long period following castration. *Eksp. Med., Kharkov*, 33-44. (*Psychol. Abstr.*, 1936, 10, No. 1892.)—*156*

25. ASIMOV, G. J. (1928) Bedingte Reflexe bei thyreoidektomierten Tieren. *Pflüg. Arch. ges. Physiol.*, 220, 350-355.—*156*
ASIMOV, G. J., *see also* No. 962.

26. ASRATIAN, E. (1935) [Defensive motor conditioned reflexes in dogs deprived of the motor areas of the large cerebral hemispheres.] *Dokl. Akad. Nauk S.S.S.R.*, 193-200. (*Psychol. Abstr.*, 1936, 10, No. 2410.)—*337*

27. BABKIN, B. P. (1938) Experimental neuroses in animals and their treatment with bromides. *Edinb. med. J.*, 45, part 1, 605-619.—*306*

28. BABSKIJ, E., and EIDINOVA, M. (1933) [Über den Einfluss des Hungerns auf die bedingten motorischen Reflexe.] *Fiziol. Zh. S.S.S.R.*, 16, 427-430. (*Zbl. ges. Neurol. Psychiat.*, 1934, 70, 329.)—*155*

29. BAIR, J. H. (1901) Development of voluntary control. *Psychol. Rev.*, 8, 474-510.—*278*

30. BAKER, L. E. (1938) The pupillary response conditioned to subliminal auditory stimuli. *Psychol. Monogr.*, 50, No. 223, 32 pp.—*123, 129, 134, 142, 205, 278*
BAKER, L. E., *see also* Nos. 590, 788.
BALL, J., *see* No. 507.
BALLACHEY, E. L., *see* Nos. 93, 94.

31. BALLACHEY, E. L., and BUEL, J. (1934a) Centrifugal swing as a determinant of choice-point behavior in the maze running of the white rat. *J. comp. Psychol.*, 17, 201-223.—*219, 227*

32. BALLACHEY, E. L., and BUEL, J. (1934b) Food orientation as a factor determining the distribution of errors in the maze running of the rat. *J. genet. Psychol.*, 45, 358-370.—*227*

33. BAM, L. (1937) [The effect of bromine upon differential inhibition in monkeys as determined by the physical strength of inhibitory stimuli.] *Arkh. Biol. Nauk*, 47, 24-52. (*Psychol. Abstr.*, 1938, 12, No. 4616.)—*134*

34. BARD, P. (1934) On emotional expression after decortication with some remarks on certain theoretical views. *Psychol. Rev.*, 41, 309-329, 424-449.—*314*

35. BASCHMURIN, A. E., and MULBERG, B. M. (1928) [The problem of the localization of neural centers in the cerebral hemispheres.] *Trud. Leningrad Vet. Inst.*, 2, 85-88. (Razran, 1939j, p. 287.)—*134*

36. BASS, M. J., and HULL, C. L. (1934) The irradiation of a tactile conditioned reflex in man. *J. comp. Psychol.*, 17, 47-65.—*131, 179*

37. BAYANDUROV, B. I. (1932) Zur Physiologie des Sehanalysators bei Vögeln. Z. vergl. Physiol., 18, 298-306.—306
BAYNE, T. L., see Nos. 527, 530.
38. BECK, L. H. (1939) Conditioning and the coordination of movements. J. gen. Psychol., 20, 375-397.—226
39. BEER, T., BETHE, A., and v. UEXKÜLL, J. (1899) Vorschläge zu einer objektivierenden Nomenklatur in der Physiologie des Nervensystems. Biol. Zbl., 19, 517-521.—6
40. BEKHTEREV, V. M. (1908) Die objective Untersuchung der neuropsychischen Tätigkeit. Congr. int. Psychiat. Neurol., Amsterdam, 20-27.—306
41. BEKHTEREV, V. M. (1909) Die objektive Untersuchung der neuropsychischen Sphäre der Geisteskranken. Z. Psychother. med. Psychol., 1, 257-290.—306
42. BEKHTEREV, V. M. (1912) Die Anwendung der Methode der motorischen Assoziations-reflexe zur Aufdeckung der Simulation. Z. ges. Neurol. Psychiat., 13, 183-191.—296, 307, 320
43. BEKHTEREV, V. M. (1913a) La psychologie objective. Paris, Alcan, iii, 478 pp.—9, 23
44. BEKHTEREV, V. M. (1913b) Objektive Psychologie oder Psychoreflexologie. Die Lehre von den Assoziationsreflexen. Leipzig, Teubner, xiii, 468 pp.—9, 23
45. BEKHTEREV, V. M. (1923a) Die Perversitäten und Inversitäten vom Standpunkt der Reflexologie. Arch. Psychiat. Nervenkr., 68, 100-213.—307
46. BEKHTEREV, V. M. (1923b) Studium der Funktionen der Praefrontal und anderer Gebiete der Hirnrinde vermittelst der assoziativ-motorischen Reflexe. Schweiz. Arch. Neurol. Psychiat., 13, 61-76. —316, 337
47. BEKHTEREV, V. M. (1923c) Die Krankheiten der Persönlichkeit vom Standpunkt der Reflexologie. Z. ges. Neurol. Psychiat., 80, 265-309.—307
48. BEKHTEREV, V. M. (1932) General principles of human reflexology. New York, International, 467 pp.—9, 23, 156, 184, 306, 307, 336
49. BELIALEV, M., and LUKINA, A. M. (1930) [Social types of problem children in individual reflexological experimentation.] Vopr. Izuch. Vospit. Lichn., 27-40. (Psychol. Abstr., 1935, 9, No. 4849.) —308
50. BENDER, L., and SCHILDER, P. (1930) Unconditioned and conditioned reactions to pain in schizophrenia. Amer. J. Psychiat., 87, 365-384.—308
51. BERITOV, I. S. (1924) On the fundamental nervous processes in the cortex of the cerebral hemispheres. Brain, 47, 109-148; 358-376. —182, 318, 336, 338

52. BERITOV, I. S. (1927) Über die individuell-erworbene Tätigkeit des Zentralnervensystems. *J. Psychol. Neurol., Lpz.*, 33, 113-335.— *132, 204, 336, 338*

53. BERITOV, I. S. (1932) [*Individually-acquired activity of the central nervous system.*] Tiflis, GIZ, 470 pp. (*Psychol. Abstr.*, 1934, 8, No. 132.)—*73, 132, 199*

54. BERNSTEIN, A. L. (1934) Temporal factors in the formation of conditioned eyelid reactions in human subjects. *J. gen. Psychol.*, 10, 173-197.—*43, 49, 119, 160, 174*
BERNSTONE, A. H., *see* No. 626.

55. BERREMAN, J. V., and HILGARD, E. R. (1936) The effects of personal heterosuggestion and two forms of autosuggestion upon postural movement. *J. soc. Psychol.*, 7, 289-300.—*308*
BETHE, A., *see* No. 39.
BIEL, W. C., *see* No. 310.

56. BLAGOVESHCHENSKAYA, W. (1929) [Formation of associations in animals with but one hemisphere.] *Nov. Refl. Fiziol. Nerv. Sist.*, 3, 333-378. (*Psychol. Abstr.*, 1930, 4, No. 4221.)—*337*

57. BLODGETT, H. C. (1929) The effect of the introduction of reward upon the maze performance of rats. *Univ. Calif. Publ. Psychol.*, 4, 113-134.—*04*

58. BOGOSLOVSKI, A. I. (1937) An attempt at creating sensory conditioned reflexes in humans. *J. exp. Psychol.*, 21, 403-422.—*50, 205*

59. BOGOSLOVSKI, A. I. (1938) Changements de la fréquence critique des papillotements lumineux à caractère de réflexe conditionné. *Arch. Ophthal., Paris*, 2, 219-227.—*205*
BOOHER, W. T., *see* No. 140.

60. BORING, E. G. (1929) *A history of experimental psychology.* New York, Appleton-Century, xvi, 699 pp.—*23*

61. BORING, E. G. (1933) *The physical dimensions of consciousness.* New York, Appleton-Century, xii, 251 pp.—*205*

62. BOROVSKI, V. (1929) An attempt at building a theory of conditioned reflexes on spinal reflexes. *J. gen. Psychol.*, 2, 3 11. *336*

63. BOWDITCH, H. P., and WARREN, J. W. (1890) The knee-jerk and its physiological modifications. *J. Physiol.*, 11, 25-64.—*131*

64. BRANDT, H. (1935) The spread of the influence of reward to bonds remote in sequence and time. *Arch. Psychol., N.Y.*, 27, No. 180, 45 pp.—*174*

65. BREGMAN, E. O. (1934) An attempt to modify the emotional attitudes of infants by the conditioned response technique. *J. genet. Psychol.*, 45, 169-198.—*293, 307*

66. BRIDGES, K. M. B. (1932) Emotional development in early infancy. *Child Developm.*, 3, 324-341.—*295*

67. BRITT, S. H. (1935) Tonal sensitivity in the white rat. *J. comp. Psychol.*, 19, 243-264.—*205*

68. Britt, S. H. (1936) Theories of retroactive inhibition. *Psychol. Rev.,* 43, 207-216.—*127*

69. Brogden, W. J. (1939a) The effect of frequency of reinforcement upon the level of conditioning. *J. exp. Psychol.,* 24, 419-431.—*149*

70. Brogden, W. J. (1939b) Unconditioned stimulus-substitution in the conditioning process. *Amer. J. Psychol.,* 52, 46-55.—*86, 101*

71. Brogden, W. J. (1939c) Sensory pre-conditioning. *J. exp. Psychol.,* 25, 323-332.—*94, 229*
   Brogden, W. J., *see also* No. 150.

72. Brogden, W. J., and Culler, E. (1935) Experimental extinction of higher-order responses. *Amer. J. Psychol.,* 47, 663-669.—*157*

73. Brogden, W. J., and Culler, E. (1936) Device for the motor conditioning of small animals. *Science,* 83, 269-270.—*49*

74. Brogden, W. J., and Culler, E. (1937) Increased acoustic sensitivity in dogs following Roentgen-radiation of the hypophysis. *Amer. J. Physiol.,* 119, 13-23.—*156, 205*

75. Brogden, W. J., and Gantt, W. H. (1937) Cerebellar conditioned reflexes. *Amer. J. Physiol.,* 119, 277-278.—*321*

76. Brogden, W. J., Girden, E., Mettler, F. A., and Culler, E. (1936) Acoustic value of the several components of the auditory system in cats. *Amer. J. Physiol.,* 116, 252-261.—*205*

77. Brogden, W. J., Lipman, E. A., and Culler, E. (1938) The rôle of incentive in conditioning and extinction. *Amer. J. Psychol.,* 51, 109-117.—*58, 59, 89, 106, 118, 125, 153, 156, 157*
   Brown, C. W., *see* No. 768.

78. Brown, C. W., and Searle, L. V. (1938) The effect of variation in the dose of benzedrine sulfate on the activity of white rats. *J. exp. Psychol.,* 22, 555-563.—*134*

79. Brown, H. C. (1916) Language and the associative reflex. *J. Phil. Psychol. sci. Meth.,* 13, 645-649.—*12*

80. Brown, J. S. (1939) A note on a temporal gradient of reinforcement. *J. exp. Psychol.,* 25, 221-227.—*170*
   Brown, M. A., *see* No. 736.

81. Brown, R. H. (1936a) The dim visibility curve of the rabbit. *J. gen. Psychol.,* 14, 62-82.—*196, 205*

82. Brown, R. H. (1936b) Color vision in the rabbit. *J. gen. Psychol.,* 14, 83-97.—*196, 205*

83. Brown, R. H. (1937) The bright visibility curve of the rabbit. *J. gen. Psychol.,* 17, 323-337.—*196, 205*

84. Brown, W. (1939) The positive effect of punishment. *J. comp. Psychol.,* 28, 17-22.—*125*

85. Bruce, R. H. (1932) The effect of removal of reward on the maze performance of rats. III. *Univ. Calif. Publ. Psychol.,* 6, 75-82.—*74*

86. BRUCE, R. H. (1937) An experimental investigation of the thirst drive in rats with especial reference to the goal gradient hypothesis. *J. gen. Psychol.*, 17, 49-62.—*227, 253*

87. BRUCE, R. H. (1938) The effect of lessening the drive upon performance by white rats in a maze. *J. comp. Psychol.*, 25, 225-248. —*227, 253*

88. BRUNSWIK, E. (1939) Probability as a determiner of rat behavior. *J. exp. Psychol.*, 25, 175-197.—*193, 194, 204*

89. BUEL, J. (1934) The linear maze. I. "Choice-point expectancy," "Correctness," and the goal gradient. *J. comp. Psychol.*, 17, 185-199.—*227*

90. BUEL, J. (1935) Differential errors in animal mazes. *Psychol. Bull.*, 32, 67-99.—*227*

91. BUEL, J. (1938) A criticism of Hull's goal gradient hypothesis. *Psychol. Rev.*, 45, 395-413.—*227*

92. BUEL, J. (1939) A correction to 'A criticism of Hull's goal gradient hypothesis.' *Psychol. Rev.*, 46, 86-87.—*227*
    BUEL, J., *see also* Nos. 31, 32.

93. BUEL, J., and BALLACHEY, E. L. (1934) Choice-point expectancy in the maze running of the rat. *J. genet. Psychol.*, 45, 145-168.—*227*

94. BUEL, J., and BALLACHEY, E. L. (1935) Limiting factors in the effect of the reward upon the distribution of errors in mazes. *Psychol. Rev.*, 42, 28-42.—*227*

95. BUGELSKI, R. (1938) Extinction with and without sub-goal reinforcement. *J. comp. Psychol*, 26, 121-134.—*64, 65*

96. BUGELSKI, R., and MILLER, N. E. (1938) A spatial gradient in the strength of avoidance responses. *J. exp. Psychol.*, 23, 494-505.—*170, 245*

97. BULL, H. O. (1928) Studies on conditioned responses in fishes. I. *J. Mar. biol. Ass. U.K.*, 15, 485-533.—*205*

98. BULL, H. O. (1930) Studies on conditioned responses in fishes. II. *J. Mar. biol. Ass. U.K.*, 16, 615-637.—*205*

99. BULL, H. O. (1935) Studies on conditioned responses in fishes. III. Wave-length discrimination in Blennius pholis L. *J. Mar. biol. Ass. U.K.*, 20, 317-364.—*205*

100. BULL, H. O. (1936) Studies on conditioned responses in fishes. VII. Temperature perception in teleosts. *J. Mar. biol. Ass. U.K.*, 21, 1-27.—*205*

101. BUNCH, M. E. (1939) Transfer of training in the mastery of an antagonistic habit after varying intervals of time. *J. comp. Psychol.*, 28, 189-200.—*131*

102. BURNHAM, W. H. (1917) Mental hygiene and the conditioned reflex. *J. genet. Psychol.*, 24, 449-488.—*11, 13, 306, 307*

103. BURNHAM, W. H. (1921) The significance of the conditioned reflex in mental hygiene. *Ment. Hyg., N.Y.*, 5, 673-706.—*11, 307*

104. BURNHAM, W. H. (1924) *The normal mind.* New York, Appleton, xx, 702 pp.—*11, 14, 25*
105. BUYTENDIJK, F. J. J. (1930) Über das Umlernen. *Arch. néerl. Physiol.,* 15, 283-310.—*131*

106. CALVIN, J. S. (1939) Decremental factors in conditioned response learning. Ph.D. dissertation, Yale University.—*133, 148, 149, 156*
    CALVIN, J. S., *see also* No. 319.
107. CAMPBELL, A. A. (1938) The interrelations of two measures of conditioning in man. *J. exp. Psychol.,* 22, 225-243.—*119, 138, 143 154, 308*
108. CAMPBELL, A. A. (1939) A reply to Dr. Razran. *J. exp. Psychol.,* 24, 227-233.—*308*
    CAMPBELL, A. A., *see also* Nos. 311, 312, 313.
109. CAMPBELL, A. A., and HILGARD, E. R. (1936) Individual differences in ease of conditioning. *J. exp. Psychol.,* 19, 561-571.—*138, 143, 302, 308*
    CAMPBELL, R. K., *see* No. 314.
110. CANNON, W. B. (1932) *The wisdom of the body.* New York, Norton, xv, 312 pp.—*82*
111. CARR, H. A. (1925) *Psychology, a study of mental activity.* New York, Longmans Green, v, 432 pp.—*82*
112. CARR, H. A., and FREEMAN, A. S. (1919) Time relationships in the formation of associations. *Psychol. Rev.,* 26, 465-473.—*164*
113. CARR, H. A., TOLMAN, E. C., THORNDIKE, E. L., CULLER, E. A., DASHIELL, J. F., and MUENZINGER, K. F. (1938) The law of effect. *Psychol. Rev.,* 45, 191-218.—*101*
114. CARTER, L. F. (1936) Maze learning with a differential proprioceptive cue. *J. exp. Psychol.,* 19, 758-762.—*226*
115. CASON, H. (1922a) The conditioned pupillary reaction. *J. exp. Psychol.,* 5, 108-146.—*14, 278*
116. CASON, H. (1922b) The conditioned eyelid reaction. *J. exp. Psychol.,* 5, 153-196.—*14, 174*
117. CASON, H. (1925a) The conditioned reflex or conditioned response as a common activity of living organisms. *Psychol. Bull.,* 22, 445-472.—*23*
118. CASON, H. (1925b) The physical basis of the conditioned response. *Amer. J. Psychol.,* 36, 371-393.—*328*
119. CASON, H. (1932) The pleasure-pain theory of learning. *Psychol. Rev.,* 39, 440-466.—*101*
120. CASON, H. (1934a) Dr. Hilgard on the conditioned eyelid reaction. *J. exp. Psychol.,* 17, 894-899.—*174*
121. CASON, H. (1934b) The rôle of verbal activities in the conditioning of human subjects. *Psychol. Rev.,* 41, 563-571.—*277*

122. CASON, H. (1935) Backward conditioned eyelid reactions. *J. exp. Psychol.*, 18, 599-611.—*174*

123. CASON, H. (1936) Sensory conditioning. *J. exp. Psychol.*, 19, 572-591.—*50*

124. CASON, H., and KATCHER, N. (1933) An attempt to condition breathing and eyelid responses to a subliminal electric stimulus. *J. exp. Psychol.*, 16, 831-842.—*205*

CATE, J. TEN, *see* TEN CATE, J.

125. CATTELL, J. McK. (1904) The conceptions and methods of psychology. *Pop. Sci. Mon.*, 66, 176-186.—*6*

CHARITONOV, S. A., *see* No. 224.

126. CHECHULIN, S. I. (1929) [Conditioned motor reflexes in thyroid-parathyroid deficiency.] *Vyssh. Nerv. Deyat.*, 405-439. (*Psychol. Abstr.*, 1934, 8, No. 2482.)—*156*

127. CLEMENTS, F. E. (1928) The effect of time on distance discrimination in the albino rat. *J. comp. Psychol.*, 8, 317-324.—*174*

COAKLEY, J. D., *see* No. 147.

COBB, S., *see* No. 757.

COHEN, L. H., *see* No. 772.

128. COHEN, L. H., HILGARD, E. R., and WENDT, G. R. (1933) Sensitivity to light in a case of hysterical blindness studied by reinforcement-inhibition and conditioning methods. *Yale J. Biol. Med.*, 6, 61-67.—*156, 277, 296, 307*

129. COLE, L. E. (1939) A comparison of the factors of practice and knowledge of experimental procedure in conditioning the eyelid response of human subjects. *J. gen. Psychol.*, 20, 349-373.—*149, 157, 205, 266, 277*

COLE, L. E., *see also* No. 597.

COLLE, J., *see* No. 612.

130. COOK, S. W. (1939a) A survey of methods used to produce "experimental neurosis." *Amer. J. Psychiat.*, 95, 1259-1276.—*307*

131. COOK, S. W. (1939b) The production of "experimental neurosis" in the white rat. *Psychosom. Med.*, 1, 293-308.—*285, 306*

COOK, S. W., *see also* No. 699.

132. COOK, S. W., and HARRIS, R. E. (1937) The verbal conditioning of the galvanic skin reflex. *J. exp. Psychol.*, 21, 202-210.—*267, 277*

133. COOMBS, C. H. (1938) Adaptation of the galvanic response to auditory stimuli. *J. exp. Psychol.*, 22, 244-268.—*107*

COPELMANN, L., *see* No. 575.

134. COWAN, E. A., and FOULKE, M. (1934) Variation in susceptibility to the conditioning of inhibition as an index of constitutional type. *Child Developm.*, 5, 201-236.—*277, 308*

135. COWLES, J. T. (1937) Food-tokens as incentives for learning by chimpanzees. *Comp. Psychol. Monogr.*, 14, No. 71, 96 pp.—*63, 74*

136. Cowles, J. T., and Nissen, H. W. (1937) Reward-expectancy in delayed responses of chimpanzees. *J. comp. Psychol.*, 24, 345-358. —*95*

Crawford, M. P., *see* No. 638.

137. Creed, R. S., Denny-Brown, D., Eccles, J. C., Liddell, E. G. T., and Sherrington, C. S. (1932) *Reflex activity of the spinal cord*. London, Oxford Univ. Press, vi, 183 pp.—*109*

138. Crisler, G. (1930) Salivation is unnecessary for the establishment of the salivary conditioned reflex induced by morphine. *Amer. J. Physiol.*, 94, 553-556.—*323*

139. Crisler, G. (1936) Avitaminosis-A and the salivary conditioned reflex induced by morphine. *Amer. J. Physiol.*, 115, 215-218.—*155*

Crisler, G., *see also* No. 452.

140. Crisler, G., Booher, W. T., Van Liere, E. J., and Hall, J. C. (1933) The effect of feeding thyroid on the salivary conditioned reflex induced by morphine. *Amer. J. Physiol.*, 103, 68-72.—*156*

141. Crutchfield, R. S. (1939) The determiners of energy expenditure in string-pulling by the rat. *J. Psychol.*, 7, 163-178.—*253*

142. Culler, E. (1928) Nature of the learning curve. *Psychol. Bull.*, 25, 143-144.—*157*

143. Culler, E. (1936) The conditioned-reflex method in the study of hearing by bone conduction: the differentiation of tactile from auditory responses. *Ann. Otol., etc.*, St. Louis, 45, 837-840.—*205*

144. Culler, E. (1937) Observations on the spinal dog. *Psychol. Bull.*, 34, 742-743.—*338*

145. Culler, E. (1938a) Observations on direct cortical stimulation in the dog. *Psychol. Bull.*, 35, 687-688.—*325*

146. Culler, E. (1938b) Recent advances in some concepts of conditioning. *Psychol. Rev.*, 45, 134-153.—*49, 131, 132, 174*

Culler, E., *see also* Nos. 4, 72, 73, 74, 76, 77, 113, 210, 211, 250, 251, 252, 253, 787.

147. Culler, E., Coakley, J. D., Shurrager, P. S., and Ades, H. W. (1939) Differential effects of curare upon higher and lower levels of the central nervous system. *Amer. J. Psychol.*, 52, 266-273.—*324*

148. Culler, E., Finch, G., and Girden, E. (1934) Apparatus for motor conditioning in cats. *Science*, 79, 525-526.—*49*

149. Culler, E., Finch, G., and Girden, E. (1935) Function of the round window in hearing. *Amer. J. Physiol.*, 111, 416-425.—*205*

150. Culler, E., Finch, G., Girden, E., and Brogden, W. J. (1935) Measurements of acuity by the conditioned-response technique. *J. gen. Psychol.*, 12, 223-227.—*37, 60, 94, 205*

151. Culler, E., and Mettler, F. A. (1934) Conditioned behavior in a decorticate dog. *J. comp. Psychol.*, 18, 291-303.—*314, 316, 337*

152. Culler, E., Willmann, J., and Mettler, F. A. (1937) Mapping the cochlea. *Amer. J. Physiol.*, 119, 292.—*196, 205*

153. Curtis, Q. F. (1938) Frustration as an experimental problem. IV. Some physiological consequences of frustration. *Character & Pers.*, 7, 140-144.—*306*

154. Darrow, C. W., and Heath, L. L. (1932) Reaction tendencies relating to personality. In K. S. Lashley, edit., *Studies in the dynamics of behavior.* Chicago, Univ. Chicago Press, 57-261.—*308*

155. Dashiell, J. F. (1930) Direction orientation in maze running by the white rat. *Comp. Psychol. Monogr.*, 7, No. 32, 72 pp.—*242*

156. Dashiell, J. F. (1935) A survey and synthesis of learning theories. *Psychol. Bull.*, 32, 261-275.—*71*

Dashiell, J. F., *see also* No. 113.

Davis, H., *see* No. 836.

157. Davis, H., Derbyshire, A. J., Kemp, E. H., Lurie, M. H., and Upton, M. (1935) Functional and histological changes in the cochlea of the guinea-pig resulting from prolonged stimulation. *J. gen. Psychol.*, 12, 251-278.—*205*

158. Davis, H., and Forbes, A. (1936) Chronaxie. *Physiol. Rev.*, 16, 407-441.—*338*

Davis, R. C., *see* No. 441.

Deese, L., *see* No. 660.

159. Delmas, A. (1930) Les réflexes conditionnels en psychiatrie. *Encéphale*, 25, 318-323.—*307*

Denisova, M. P., *see* No. 204.

160. Denisova, M. P., and Figurin, N. L. (1929) The problem of the first associated food reflexes in infants. *Vopr. Genet. Refl. Pedol. Mladen.*, 1, 81-88. (Razran, 1933b, pp. 73-75.)—*116*

161. Dennis, W. (1935) Goal gradient or entrance gradient? *Psychol. Rev.*, 42, 117-121.—*227*

162. Dennis, W., and Sollenberger, R. T. (1934) Negative adaptation in the maze exploration of albino rats. *J. comp. Psychol.*, 18, 197-206.—*227*

163. Denny-Brown, D. (1932) Theoretical deductions from the physiology of the cerebral cortex. *J. Neurol. Psychopath.*, 13, 52-67.—*336*

Denny-Brown, D., *see also* No. 137.

Derbyshire, A. J., *see* No. 157.

164. Derbyshire, A. J., Rempel, B., Forbes, A., and Lambert, E. F. (1936) The effects of anesthetics on action potentials in the cerebral cortex of the cat. *Amer. J. Physiol.*, 116, 577-596.—*330*

165. Dice, L. R. (1935) Inheritance of waltzing and of epilepsy in mice of the genus Peromyscus. *J. Mammal.*, 16, 25-35.—*286*

166. Dimmick, F. L., Ludlow, N., and Whiteman, A. (1939) A study of "experimental neurosis" in cats. *J. comp. Psychol.*, 28, 39-43.—*306*

167. DODGE, R. (1923) Habituation to rotation. *J. exp. Psychol.*, 6, 1-35.—
    130
168. DODGE, R. (1933) Anticipatory reaction. *Science*, 78, 197-203.—*25*
    DODGE, R., *see also* No. 911.
    DOMINGUEZ, K., *see* Nos. 403, 404.
    DOVE, C. C., *see* Nos. 625, 626.
169. DRABOVITCH, W. (1931) Pavlov et sa doctrine des réflexes condition-
    nels. *Psychol. et Vie*, 5, 88-92.—*307*
170. DRABOVITCH, W. (1935) Freud et Pavlov. *Évolut. psychiat.*, 21-35.—
    307
171. DRABOVITCH, W. (1937) La formation des réflexes conditionnés et la
    chronaxie. *Encéphale*, 32, 93-99.—*338*
172. DRABOVITCH, W., and WEGER, P. (1937) Deux cas de névrose expéri-
    mentale chez le chien. *C. R. Acad. Sci., Paris*, 204, 902-905.—
    302, 306
173. DREW, G. C. (1939) The speed of locomotion gradient and its rela-
    tion to the goal gradient. *J. comp. Psychol.*, 27, 333-372.—*227*
174. DUSSER DE BARENNE, J. G. (1919) Recherches expérimentales sur
    les fonctions du système nerveux central, faites en particulier
    sur deux chats dont le néopallium avait été enlevé. *Arch. néerl.
    Physiol.*, 4, 31-123.—*314*
175. DUSSER DE BARENNE, J. G., and McCULLOCH, W. S. (1937) Local
    stimulatory inactivation within the cerebral cortex, the factor
    for extinction. *Amer. J. Physiol.*, 118, 510-524.—*334*
176. DUSSER DE BARENNE, J. G., and McCULLOCH, W. S. (1938) Func-
    tional organization in the sensory cortex of the monkey (Macaca
    mulatta). *J. Neurophysiol.*, 1, 69-85.—*312*
177. DUSSER DE BARENNE, J. G., and McCULLOCH, W. S. (1939) Factors
    for facilitation and extinction in the central nervous system.
    J. Neurophysiol., 2, 319-355.—*334*
178. DWORKIN, S. (1934a) Conditioned motor reflexes in cats. *Amer. J.
    Physiol.*, 109, 31.—*73*
179. DWORKIN, S. (1934b) Hearing tests in normal and operated dogs
    and cats. *Trans. Amer. otol. Soc.*, 24, 143-151.—*205*
180. DWORKIN, S. (1935a) Pitch and intensity discrimination by cats.
    Amer. J. Physiol., 112, 1-4.—*205*
181. DWORKIN, S. (1935b) Alimentary motor conditioning and pitch dis-
    crimination in dogs. *Amer. J. Physiol.*, 112, 323-328.—*205*
182. DWORKIN, S. (1939) Conditioning neuroses in dog and cat. *Psy-
    chosom. Med.*, 1, 388-396.—*306*
    DWORKIN, S., *see also* No. 838.
183. DWORKIN, S., SEYMOUR, S. L., and SUTHERLAND, G. F. (1934) A
    conditioned reflex method of testing hearing in cats. *Quart. J.
    exp. Physiol.*, 24, 23-30.—*205*

184. EATON, M. T. (1937) The conditioned reflex technique applied to a less specialized type of learning. *J. exp. Educ.*, 6, 68-83.—*277*

185. ECCLES, J. C. (1935) Slow potential waves in the superior cervical ganglion. *J. Physiol.*, 85, 464-501.—*327*
    ECCLES, J. C., *see also* No. 137.

186. ECCLES, J. C., and SHERRINGTON, C. S. (1931) Studies on the flexor reflex. II. The reflex response evoked by two centripetal volleys. *Proc. roy. Soc.*, 107B, 535-556.—*131*
    EIDINOVA, M., *see* No. 28.

187. ELDER, J. H. (1934) Auditory acuity of the chimpanzee. *J. comp. Psychol.*, 17, 157-183.—*186, 205*

188. ELDER, J. H. (1935) The upper limit of hearing in chimpanzee. *Amer. J. Physiol.*, 112, 109-115.—*186, 205*

189. ELLIOTT, M. H., and TREAT, W. C. (1935) Hunger-contractions and rate of conditioning. *Proc. Nat. Acad. Sci., Wash.*, 21, 514-516.—*155*

190. ELLSON, D. G. (1937) The acquisition of a token-reward habit in dogs. *J. comp. Psychol.*, 24, 505-522.—*74*

191. ELLSON, D. G. (1938) Quantitative studies of the interaction of simple habits. I. Recovery from specific and generalized effects of extinction. *J. exp. Psychol.*, 23, 339-358.—*73, 131*

192. ELLSON, D. G. (1939a) Spontaneous recovery of the galvanic skin response as a function of the recovery interval. *J. exp. Psychol.*, 25, 586-600.—*133*

193. ELLSON, D. G. (1939b) The concept of reflex reserve. *Psychol. Rev.*, 46, 566-575.—*155*

194. ELLSON, D. G. (1940) Successive extinctions of a bar-pressing response in rats. *J. gen. Psychol.*, 22, (in press)—*153*

195. ENGELMANN, W. (1928) Untersuchungen über die Schallokalisation bei Tieren. *Z. Psychol.*, 105, 317-370.—*205*

196. ENGLISH, H. B. (1929) Three cases of the "conditioned fear response." *J. abnorm. (soc.) Psychol.*, 24, 221-225.—*293, 307*

197. ERICKSON, M. H. (1938a) A study of clinical and experimental findings on hypnotic deafness: I. Clinical experimentation and findings. *J. gen. Psychol.*, 19, 127-150.—*156*

198. ERICKSON, M. H. (1938b) A study of clinical and experimental findings on hypnotic deafness: II. Experimental findings with a conditioned response technique. *J. gen. Psychol.*, 19, 151-167.—*156, 320*

199. EROFÉEVA, M. (1916) Contributions à l'etude des réflexes conditionnels déstructifs. *C. R. Soc. Biol. Paris*, 79, 239-240.—*73, 113*

200. EVERALL, E. E. (1935) Perseveration in the rat. *J. comp. Psychol.*, 19, 343-369.—*114*

201. FAIRLIE, C. W. (1937) The effect of shock at the 'moment of choice' on the formation of a visual discrimination habit. *J. exp. Psychol.*, 21, 662-669.—*204*

202. FEARING, F. (1930) *Reflex action; a study in the history of physiological psychology.* Baltimore, Williams and Wilkins, xiii, 350 pp.—*130*
    FEARING, F., see also No. 280.

203. FIEANDT, K. (1938) Ein neues Invarianzphänomen der Farbenwahrnehmung. *Ann. Acad. Sci. fenn.*, B41, No. 2, 245 pp.—*204*
    FIELDS, P. E., see No. 615.
    FIGURIN, N. L., see No. 160.

204. FIGURIN, N. L., and DENISOVA, M. P. (1929) [The physiology of the differentiation of external stimuli. Based upon experimental data on the formation of differentiations in infants under one year.] *Vopr. Genet. Refl. Pedol. Mladen.*, 1, 131-165. (Razran, 1933b, p. 75.)—*140*

205. FINAN, J. L. (1939) Effects of frontal lobe lesions on temporally organized behavior in monkeys. *J. Neurophysiol.*, 2, 208-226.—*174*

206. FINCH, G. (1936) "Hunger" as a factor determining the magnitude of conditioned and unconditioned salivary responses. *Amer. J. Physiol.*, 116, 49.—*155*

207. FINCH, G. (1938a) Hunger as a determinant of conditional and unconditional salivary response magnitude. *Amer. J. Physiol.*, 123, 379-382.—*155*

208. FINCH, G. (1938b) Pilocarpine conditioning. *Amer. J. Physiol.*, 124, 679-682.—*322*

209. FINCH, G. (1938c) Salivary conditioning in atropinized dogs. *Amer. J. Physiol.*, 124, 136-141.—*323*
    FINCH, G., see also Nos. 148, 149, 150, 253.

210. FINCH, G., and CULLER, E. (1934) Higher order conditioning with constant motivation, *Amer. J. Psychol.*, 46, 596-602.—*60, 132, 206*

211. FINCH, G., and CULLER, E. (1935) Relation of forgetting to experimental extinction. *Amer. J. Psychol.*, 47, 656-662.—*25, 61, 62, 65, 71, 153, 156, 157*

212. FISHER, V. E. (1932) Hypnotic suggestion and the conditioned reflex. *J. exp. Psychol.*, 15, 212-217.—*156*
    FITCH, E. E., see No. 808.
    FITCH, F. B., see No. 369.
    FLETCHER, F. M., see No. 627.
    FORBES, A., see Nos. 158, 164.
    FOULKE, M., see No. 134.

213. FRANK, L. K. (1923) Suggestion for a theory of learning. *Psychol. Rev.*, 30, 145-148.—*24*

214. FRANKLIN, M. E. (1928) Die bedingten Reflexe bei Epilepsie und der Wiederholungszwang. *Imago, Lpz.*, 14, 364-376.—*308*
215. FRANZ, S. I. (1907) On the functions of the cerebrum: the frontal lobes. *Arch. Psychol., N.Y.*, 1, No. 2, 64 pp.—*316*
    FREEMAN, A. S., *see* No. 112.
216. FREEMAN, G. L. (1930) The galvanic phenomenon and conditioned responses. *J. gen. Psychol.*, 3, 529-539.—*277*
217. FREEMAN, G. L. (1933) The facilitative and inhibitory effects of muscular tension upon performance. *Amer. J. Psychol.*, 45, 17-52. —*109*
218. FRENCH, T. M. (1933) Interrelations between psychoanalysis and the experimental work of Pavlov. *Amer. J. Psychiat.*, 89, 1165-1203. —*290, 307*
219. FRITZ, M. F. (1930) Long time training of white rats on antagonistic visual habits. *J. comp. Psychol.*, 11, 171-184.—*131*
220. FROLOV, J. P. (1924) Differenzierung der Intensität bedingter Lichtreize. *Pflüg. Arch. ges. Physiol.*, 206, 20-28.—*205*
221. FROLOV, J. P. (1925a) Bedingte Reflexe bei Fischen. I Mitteilung. *Pflüg. Arch. ges. Physiol.*, 208, 261-271.—*31, 205*
222. FROLOV, J. P. (1925b) Über den Einfluss langedauernder Unterernährung auf die bedingten Speichelreflexe. *Pflüg. Arch. ges. Physiol.*, 207, 343-350.—*155*
223. FROLOV, J. P. (1937) *Pavlov and his school: the theory of conditioned reflexes.* New York, Oxford Univ. Press, xix, 291 pp.—*23, 308*
224. FROLOV, J. P., and CHARITONOV, S. A. (1931) Über die Grenzen und die Merkmale der biologischen Resistenz der Typen der höheren Nerventätigkeit der Tiere. *Pflüg. Arch. ges. Physiol.*, 228, 17-29. —*155, 308*
    FULCHIGNONI, E., *see* No. 584.
225. FULTON, J. F. (1938) *Physiology of the nervous system.* New York, Oxford Univ. Press, xv, 675 pp.—*339*
    FULTON, J. F., *see also* Nos. 750, 751.

226. GACKELL, L. (1928) [An investigation of conditioned inhibition in hysterical children.] *Zh. Nevropatol. Psikhiat*, 21, 682-690. (Razran, 1933b, p. 52.)—*307*
227. GANTT, W. H. (1935) Effect of alcohol on cortical and subcortical activity measured by the conditioned reflex method. *Johns Hopk. Hosp. Bull.*, 56, 61-83.—*134*
228. GANTT, W. H. (1936) An experimental approach to psychiatry. *Amer. J. Psychiat.*, 92, 1007-1021.—*280, 306*
229. GANTT, W. H. (1937) Essential anatomical structures of the reflex arc for establishment of conditioned reflexes. *Amer. J. Physiol.*, 119, 313-314.—*320*

230. GANTT, W. H. (1938a) Adaptation to a conditioned reflex pattern. (English.) *Fiziol. Zh. S.S.S.R.*, 24, 423-430.—*156*

231. GANTT, W. H. (1938b) Extension of a conflict based upon food to other physiological systems and its reciprocal relations with sexual functions. *Amer. J. Physiol.*, 123, 73-74.—*306*

232. GANTT, W. H. (1938c) A method of testing cortical function and sensitivity of the skin. *Arch. Neurol. Psychiat.*, *Chicago*, 40, 79-85.—*277, 307*

    GANTT, W. H., *see also* Nos. 75, 436, 492, 531, 547, 937.

233. GANTT, W. H., KATZENELBOGEN, S., and LOUCKS, R. B. (1937) An attempt to condition adrenalin hyperglycemia. *Johns Hopk. Hosp. Bull.*, 60, 400-411.—*323*

234. GARVEY, C. R. (1933) A study of conditioned respiratory changes. *J. exp. Psychol.*, 16, 471-503.—*109, 156*

235. GASSER, H. S. (1937) The control of excitation in the nervous system. *Harvey Lectures*, 32, 169-193.—*339*

236. GAUGER, M. E. (1929) The modifiability of response to taste stimuli in the preschool child. *Teach. Coll. Contrib. Educ.*, No. 348, 53 pp.—*307*

237. GEMELLI, A. (1937) I riflessi condizionali in psichiatria infantile. *Riv. Psicol. norm. pat.*, 33, 133-148.—*307*

238. GENGERELLI, J. A. (1928) Preliminary experiments on the causal factors in animal learning. *J. comp. Psychol.*, 8, 435-457.—*102, 253*

239. GENGERELLI, J. A. (1934) Brain fields and the learning process. *Psychol. Monogr.*, 45, No. 203, 115 pp.—*331*

    GENTRY, E., *see* No. 628.

    GERMAN, W. J., *see* No. 751.

240. GESELL, A. (1938) The conditioned reflex and the psychiatry of infancy. *Amer. J. Orthopsychiat.*, 8, 19-30.—*307*

241. GIBSON, E. J. (1938) A systematic application of the concept of generalization and differentiation to verbal learning. Ph.D. dissertation, Yale University.—*225, 227*

242. GIBSON, E. J. (1939) Sensory generalization with voluntary reactions. *J. exp. Psychol.*, 24, 237-253.—*181, 277*

243. GIBSON, J. J. (1936) A note on conditioning of voluntary reactions. *J. exp. Psychol.*, 19, 397-399.—*277*

244. GIBSON, J. J., and HUDSON, L. (1935) Bilateral transfer of the conditioned knee-jerk. *J. exp. Psychol.*, 18, 774-783.—*244*

245. GIBSON, J. J., JACK, E. G., and RAFFEL, G. (1932) Bilateral transfer of the conditioned response in the human subject. *J. exp. Psychol.*, 15, 416-421.—*243*

246. GILHOUSEN, H. C. (1938) Temporal relations in anticipatory reactions of the white rat in a maze. *J. comp. Psychol.*, 26, 163-175.—*227*

247. GIRDEN, E. (1935) Effect of Roentgen rays upon hearing in dogs. *J. comp. Psychol.*, 20, 263-290.—*156, 205*

248. GIRDEN, E. (1938) Conditioning and problem-solving behavior. *Amer. J. Psychol.*, 51, 677-686.—*185, 205*

249. GIRDEN, E. (1939) Cerebral determinants of auditory localization. *Amer. J. Psychol.*, 52, 1-15.—*205*
    GIRDEN, E., see also Nos. 76, 148, 149, 150.

250. GIRDEN, E., and CULLER, E. (1933) Auditory effects of Roentgen rays in dogs. I. *Amer. J. Roentgenol.*, 30, 215-220.—*156*

251. GIRDEN, E., and CULLER, E. (1934) Auditory effects of Roentgen rays in dogs. II. *Amer. J. Roentgenol.*, 32, 675-679.—*156*

252. GIRDEN, E., and CULLER, E. (1937) Conditioned responses in curarized striate muscle in dogs. *J. comp. Psychol.*, 23, 261-274.—*324*

253. GIRDEN, E., METTLER, F. A., FINCH, G., and CULLER, E. (1936) Conditioned responses in a decorticate dog to acoustic, thermal, and tactile stimulation. *J. comp. Psychol.*, 21, 367-385.—*156, 314*

254. GLASER, O. C. (1910) The formation of habits at high speed. *J. comp. Neurol.*, 20, 165-184.—*73*

255. GOLLA, F. L. (1921) The objective study of neurosis. *Lancet*, 201, 215-221.—*307*

256. GOODENOUGH, F. L. (1932) Expression of the emotions in a blind-deaf child. *J. abnorm. (soc.) Psychol.*, 27, 328-333.—*295*

257. GORHAM, T. J. (1937) Temporal factors in external inhibition. M.S. thesis, Yale University.—*110, 131*

258. GOS, M. (1935) Les réflexes conditionnels chez l'embryon d'oiseau. *Bull. Soc. Sci. Liége*, 4, 194-199; 246-250.—*140*

259. GRANT, D. A. (1939a) The influence of attitude on the conditioned eyelid response. *J. exp. Psychol.*, 25, 333-346.—*277*

260. GRANT, D. A. (1939b) A study of patterning in the conditioned eyelid response. *J. exp. Psychol.*, 25, 445-461.—*49*

261. GRETHER, W. F. (1938) Pseudo-conditioning without paired stimulation encountered in attempted backward conditioning. *J. comp. Psychol.*, 25, 91-96.—*41, 174*

262. GRINDLEY, G. C. (1929) Experiments on the influence of the amount of reward on learning in young chickens. *Brit. J. Psychol.*, 20, 173-180.—*64, 74, 94*

263. GRINDLEY, G. C. (1932) The formation of a simple habit in guinea pigs. *Brit. J. Psychol.*, 23, 127-147.—*52, 157*

264. GUK, E. D. (1934) [The conditioned reflex activity of schizophrenics.] *Sovetsk. Nevropatol.*, 76-84. (*Psychol. Abstr.*, 1935, 9, No. 717.) —*308*

265. GULLIKSEN, H. (1932) Studies of transfer of response. I. Relative versus absolute factors in the discrimination of size by the white rat. *J. genet. Psychol.*, 40, 37-51.—*192*

266. GULLIKSEN, H. and WOLFLE, D. L. (1938a) A theory of learning and transfer: I. *Psychometrika*, 3, 127-149.—*192, 204*

267. GULLIKSEN, H. and WOLFLE, D. L. (1938b) A theory of learning and transfer. II. *Psychometrika*, 3, 225-251.—*192, 204*

GUNDLACH, R. H., *see* No. 299.

268. GUSTAV, L., and WOLF, K. (1937) Kinderpsychologische Experimente mit bedingten Reflexen. *Z. Kinderforsch*, 1937, 46, 307-336.—*25*

269. GUTHRIE, E. R. (1930) Conditioning as a principle of learning. *Psychol. Rev.*, 37, 412-428.—*24*

270. GUTHRIE, E. R. (1933) Association as a function of time interval. *Psychol. Rev.*, 40, 355-367.—*171, 175*

271. GUTHRIE, E. R. (1934) Pavlov's theory of conditioning. *Psychol. Rev.*, 41, 199-206.—*25, 101, 133*

272. GUTHRIE, E. R. (1935) *The psychology of learning*. New York, Harper, viii, 258 pp.—*24, 77, 79, 89, 93, 116, 117, 131, 132, 226, 228, 254*

273. GUTHRIE, E. R. (1937) Tolman on associative learning. *Psychol. Rev.*, 44, 525-528.—*247*

274. GUTHRIE, E. R. (1938) *The psychology of human conflict*. New York, Harper, ix, 408 pp.—*24, 254, 293, 307*

275. GUTHRIE, E. R. (1939) The effect of outcome on learning. *Psychol. Rev.*, 46, 480-484.—*92*

GUTHRIE, E. R., *see also* Nos. 809, 946.

276. GUTHRIE, E. R., and HORTON, G. P. (1937) A study of the cat in the puzzle-box. *Psychol. Bull.*, 34, 774.—*91*

HAAS, E. L., *see* No. 887.

277. HAIRE, M. (1939a) A note concerning McCulloch's discussion of discrimination habits. *Psychol. Rev.*, 46, 298-303.—*204*

278. HAIRE, M. (1939b) Some factors influencing repetitive errors in discrimination learning. *J. comp. Psychol.*, 27, 79-91.—*204*

HALL, J. C., *see* No. 140.

HALL, M., *see* No. 369.

279. HALSTEAD, W. (1935) The effects of cerebellar lesions upon the habituation of post-rotational nystagmus. *Comp. Psychol. Monogr.*, 12, No. 56, 130 pp.—*130*

280. HALSTEAD, W., YACORZYNSKI, G. K., and FEARING, F. (1937) Further evidence of cerebellar influence in the habituation of after-nystagmus in pigeons. *Amer. J. Physiol.*, 120, 350-355.—*130*

281. HAMBURGER, F. (1914) Über Psychotherapie im Kindesalter. *Wien. med. Wschr.*, 64, 1313-1320.—*307*

282. HAMBURGER, F. (1933) Unterschwelligkeit und bedingter Reflex in der Neurose. *Wien. med. Wschr.*, 83, 776.—*306, 307*

283. HAMEL, I. A. (1919) A study and analysis of the conditioned reflex. *Psychol. Monogr.*, 27, No. 118, 65 pp.—*13, 277*

284. HAMILTON, E. L. (1929) The effect of delayed incentive on the hunger drive in the white rat. *Genet. Psychol. Monogr.*, 5, 131-207. —*174*

285. HAMILTON, J. A., and KRECHEVSKY, I. (1933) Studies in the effect of shock upon behavior plasticity in the rat. *J. comp. Psychol.*, 16, 237-253.—*114*

286. HANFORD, H. M., and MORGAN, C. T. (1939) A simplified lever-operated feeding device for conditioning studies in rats. *J. gen. Psychol.*, 21, 229-232.—*49*

287. HARDCASTLE, D. N. (1935) A suggested approach to the problems of neuro-psychiatry. *J. ment. Sci.*, 81, 317-331.—*307*

288. HARLOW, H. F. (1936) The neuro-physiological correlates of learning and intelligence. *Psychol. Bull.*, 33, 479-525.—*25, 317*

289. HARLOW, H. F. (1937) Experimental analysis of the rôle of the original stimulus in conditioned responses in monkeys. *Psychol. Rec.*, 1, 62-68.—*123, 134, 322*

290. HARLOW, H. F. (1939) Forward conditioning, backward conditioning, and pseudo-conditioning in the goldfish. *J. genet. Psychol.*, 55, 49-58.—*50*

HARLOW, H. F., *see also* No. 776.

291. HARLOW, H F., and SETTLAGE, P. H. (1936) The effect of application of anaesthetic agents on circumscribed motor and sensory areas of the cortex. *J. Psychol.*, 2, 193-200.—*337*

292. HARLOW, H. F., and SETTLAGE, P. H. (1939) The effect of curarization of the fore part of the body upon the retention of conditioned responses in cats. *J. comp. Psychol.*, 27, 45-48.—*324*

293. HARLOW, H. F., and STAGNER, R. (1933) Effect of complete striate muscle paralysis upon the learning process. *J. exp. Psychol.*, 16, 283-294.—*134, 278, 324*

294. HARRINGTON, M. (1938) *A biological approach to the problem of abnormal behavior.* Lancaster, Pa., Science Press, 459 pp.—*307*

295. HARRIS, H. (1934) Anxiety: its nature and treatment. *J. ment. Sci.*, 80, 482-512.—*307*

HARRIS, R. E., *see* No. 132.

HARTMAN, F. A., *see* No. 526.

HEATH, L. L., *see* No. 154.

296. HEILBRONNER, K. (1912) Über Gewöhnung auf normalem und pathologischem Gebiete. *Grenzfr. Nerv.-u. Seelenleb.*, 13, No. 87, 51 pp.—*13*

297. HELSON, H. (1927) Insight in the white rat. *J. exp. Psychol.*, 10, 378-396.—*253*

298. HENRY, F. M. (1938) Audition in the white rat. III. Absolute and relative intensity thresholds. *J. comp. Psychol.*, 26, 45-62.—*205*

299. HERINGTON, G. B., and GUNDLACH, R. H. (1933) How well can

guinea pigs and cats hear tones? *J. comp. Psychol.*, 16, 287-303.—*205*

HERON, W. T., *see* No. 800.

300. HILDEN, A. H. (1937) An action current study of the conditioned hand withdrawal. *Psychol. Monogr.*, 49, No. 217, 173-204.—*58, 106*

301. HILGARD, E. R. (1921) Conditioned eyelid reactions to a light stimulus based on the reflex wink to sound. *Psychol. Monogr.*, 41, No. 184, 50 pp.—*49, 109, 156, 162, 174*

302. HILGARD, E. R. (1933a) Modification of reflexes and conditioned reactions. *J. gen. Psychol.*, 9, 210-215.—*124, 156*

303. HILGARD, E. R. (1933b) Reinforcement and inhibition of eyelid reflexes. *J. gen. Psychol.*, 8, 85-113.—*131, 144*

304. HILGARD, E. R. (1934) The latency of conditioned eyelid reactions: a reply to Dr. Cason. *J. exp. Psychol.*, 17, 899-908.—*174*

305. HILGARD, E. R. (1936a) The nature of the conditioned response. I. The case for and against stimulus substitution. *Psychol. Rev.*, 43, 366-385.—*39, 49*

306. HILGARD, E. R. (1936b) The nature of the conditioned response: II. Alternatives to stimulus-substitution. *Psychol. Rev.*, 43, 547-564.—*49*

307. HILGARD, E. R. (1937) The relationship between the conditioned response and conventional learning experiments. *Psychol. Bull.*, 34, 61-102.—*18*

308. HILGARD, E. R. (1938) An algebraic analysis of conditioned discrimination in man. *Psychol. Rev.*, 45, 472-496.—*204, 264, 277*

HILGARD, E. R. *see also* Nos. 55, 109, 128, 578, 579.

309. HILGARD, E. R., and ALLEN, M. K. (1938) An attempt to condition finger reactions based on motor point stimulation. *J. gen. Psychol.*, 18, 203-207.—*322*

310. HILGARD, E. R., and BIEL, W. C. (1937) Reflex sensitization and conditioning of eyelid responses at intervals near simultaneity. *J. gen. Psychol.*, 16, 223-234.—*49, 174*

311. HILGARD, E. R., and CAMPBELL, A. A. (1936) The course of acquisition and retention of conditioned eyelid responses in man. *J. exp. Psychol.*, 19, 227-247.—*32, 124, 129, 133, 156*

312. HILGARD, E. R., and CAMPBELL, A. A. (1937) Vincent curves of conditioning. *J. exp. Psychol.*, 21, 310-319.—*156*

313. HILGARD, E. R., CAMPBELL, A. A., and SEARS, W. N. (1937) Conditioned discrimination: the development of discrimination with and without verbal report. *Amer. J. Psychol.*, 49, 564-580.—*205*

314. HILGARD, E. R., CAMPBELL, R. K., and SEARS, W. N. (1938) Conditioned discrimination: the effect of knowledge of stimulus-relationships. *Amer. J. Psychol.*, 51, 498-506.—*126, 186, 205, 267, 277*

315. HILGARD, E. R., and HUMPHREYS, L. G. (1938a) The effect of supporting and antagonistic voluntary instructions on conditioned discrimination. *J. exp. Psychol.*, 22, 291-304.—*265, 267, 277*

316. HILGARD, E. R., and HUMPHREYS, L. G. (1938b) The retention of conditioned discrimination in man. *J. gen. Psychol.*, 19, 111-125.—*126, 129, 130*

317. HILGARD, E. R., and MARQUIS, D. G. (1935) Acquisition, extinction, and retention of conditioned lid responses to light in dogs. *J. comp. Psychol.*, 19, 29-58.—*32, 111, 112, 124, 133, 153, 156, 157*

318. HILGARD, E. R., and MARQUIS, D. G. (1936) Conditioned eyelid responses in monkeys, with a comparison of dog, monkey, and man. *Psychol. Monogr.*, 47, No. 212, 186-198.—*32, 122, 124, 134, 156*

319. HILL, C. J., and CALVIN, J. S. (1939) The joint extinction of two simple excitatory tendencies. *J. comp. Psychol.*, 27, 215-232.—*131*

320. HOAGLAND, H. (1930) The Weber-Fechner law and the all-or-none theory. *J. gen. Psychol.*, 3, 351-373.—*333*

321. HOBHOUSE, L. T. (1901) *Mind in evolution.* New York, Macmillan, xiv, 415 pp.—*101*

322. HOFBAUER, L. (1897) Interferenz zwischen verschiedenen Impulsen im Centralnervensystem. *Pflüg. Arch ges. Physiol.*, 68, 546-595.—*131*

323. HOLLINGWORTH, H. L. (1928) General laws of redintegration. *J. gen. Psychol.*, 1, 79-90.—*24, 101*

324. HOLMES, F. B. (1936) An experimental investigation of a method of overcoming children's fears. *Child Developm.*, 7, 6-30.—*307*

325. HOLMES, S. J. (1911) *The evolution of animal intelligence.* New York, Holt, v, 296 pp.—*101*

326. HOLT, E. B. (1914) *The concept of consciousness.* New York, Macmillan, xvi, 343 pp.—*6*

327. HOLT, E. B. (1931) *Animal drive and the learning process.* New York, Holt, vii, 307 pp.—*2, 101, 102, 210, 327, 332*

328. HONZIK, C. H. (1936) The sensory basis of maze learning in rats. *Comp. Psychol. Monogr.*, 13, No. 64, 113 pp.—*227*

329. HONZIK, C. H., and TOLMAN, E. C. (1936) The perception of spatial relations by the rat: A type of response not easily explained by conditioning. *J. comp. Psychol.*, 22, 287-318.—*227*

330. HONZIK, C. H., and TOLMAN, E. C. (1938) The action of punishment in accelerating learning. *J. comp. Psychol.*, 26, 187-200.—*204*

331. HORTON, G. P. (1933) A quantitative study of hearing in the guinea pig (cavia cobaya.) *J. comp. Psychol.*, 15, 59-73.—*205*

332. HORTON, G. P. (1934) The effect of intense and prolonged acoustical stimulation on the auditory sensitivity of guinea pigs. *J. comp. Psychol.*, 18, 405-417.—*205*

333. Horton, G. P. (1935) An experimental study of stimulation deafness in guinea pigs. *Ann. Otol., etc., St. Louis,* 44, 252-259.—*205*
Horton, G. P., *see also* No. 276.

334. Householder, A. S. (1938a) Excitation of a chain of neurones. *Psychometrika,* 3, 69-73.—*339*

335. Householder, A. S. (1938b) Conditioning circuits. *Psychometrika,* 3, 273-289.—*339*

336. Householder, A. S. (1939) A neural mechanism for discrimination. *Psychometrika,* 4, 45-58.—*204*

337. Hovland, C. I. (1936) "Inhibition of reinforcement" and phenomena of experimental extinction. *Proc. nat. Acad. Sci.,* Wash., 22, 430-433.—*146, 147, 157*

338. Hovland, C. I. (1937a) The generalization of conditioned responses. I. The sensory generalization of conditioned responses with varying frequencies of tone. *J. gen. Psychol.,* 17, 125-148.—*131, 177, 178*

339. Hovland, C. I. (1937b) The generalization of conditioned responses. II. The sensory generalization of conditioned responses with varying intensities of tone. *J. genet. Psychol.,* 51, 279-291.—*142, 178, 179*

340. Hovland, C. I. (1937c) The generalization of conditioned responses. III. Extinction, spontaneous recovery, and disinhibition of conditioned and of generalized responses. *J. exp. Psychol.,* 21, 47-62.—*133, 142, 182*

341. Hovland, C. I. (1937d) The generalization of conditioned responses. IV. The effects of varying amounts of reinforcement upon the degree of generalization of conditioned responses. *J. exp. Psychol.,* 21, 261-276.—*142, 156, 180, 182*

342. Hovland, C. I. (1938a) Experimental studies in rote-learning theory. I. Reminiscence following learning by massed and by distributed practice. *J. exp. Psychol.,* 22, 201-224.—*227*

343. Hovland, C. I. (1938b) Experimental studies in rote-learning theory. II. Reminiscence with varying speeds of syllable presentation. *J. exp. Psychol.,* 22, 338-353.—*227*

344. Hovland, C. I. (1938c) Experimental studies in rote-learning theory. III. Distribution of practice with varying speeds of syllable presentation. *J. exp. Psychol.,* 23, 172-190.—*227*

345. Hovland, C. I. (1939) Experimental studies in rote-learning theory. IV. Comparison of reminiscence in serial and paired-associate learning. *J. exp. Psychol.,* 24, 466-484.—*224, 227*

346. Hovland, C. I. (1940) Experimental studies in rote-learning theory. VI. Comparison of retention following learning to same criterion by massed and distributed practice. *J. exp. Psychol.,* 26 (in press).—*225, 227*
Hovland, C. I., *see also* No. 369.

347. HOVLAND, C. I., and SEARS, R. R. (1938) Experiments on motor conflict. I. Types of conflict and their modes of resolution. *J. exp. Psychol.*, 23, 477-493.—*111*

348. HUDGINS, C. V. (1933) Conditioning and the voluntary control of the pupillary light reflex. *J. gen. Psychol.*, 8, 3-51.—*123, 134, 157, 226, 273, 277, 278*

349. HUDGINS, C. V. (1935) Steckle and Renshaw on the conditioned iridic reflex: a discussion. *J. gen. Psychol.*, 12, 208-214.—*277, 278*
   HUDGINS, C. V., *see also* No. 394.
   HUDSON, L., *see* No. 244.

350. HUGHES, B., and SCHLOSBERG, H. (1938) Conditioning in the white rat. IV. The conditioned lid reflex. *J. exp. Psychol.*, 23, 641-650.—*32, 140*

351. HULL, C. L. (1929) A functional interpretation of the conditioned reflex. *Psychol. Rev.*, 36, 498-511.—*174*

352. HULL, C. L. (1930a) Knowledge and purpose as habit mechanisms. *Psychol. Rev.*, 37, 511-525.—*211, 214, 215*

353. HULL, C. L. (1930b) Simple trial and error learning: a study in psychological theory. *Psychol. Rev.*, 37, 241-256.—*253*

354. HULL, C. L. (1931) Goal attraction and directing ideas conceived as habit phenomena. *Psychol. Rev.*, 38, 487-506.—*93, 215*

355. HULL, C. L. (1932) The goal gradient hypothesis and maze learning. *Psychol. Rev.*, 39, 25-43.—*174, 213, 216, 217*

356. HULL, C. L. (1933) Differential habituation to internal stimuli in the albino rat. *J. comp. Psychol.*, 16, 255-273.—*67, 241, 253*

357. HULL, C. L. (1934a) The concept of the habit-family hierarchy and maze learning. *Psychol. Rev.*, 41, 33-54, 134-152.—*216, 221, 227, 241, 242*

358. HULL, C. L. (1934b) The rat's speed-of-locomotion gradient in the approach to food. *J. comp. Psychol.*, 17, 393-422.—*114, 169, 213, 227*

359. HULL, C. L. (1934c) Learning: II. The factor of the conditioned reflex. In C. Murchison, edit., *A handbook of general experimental psychology*. Worcester, Mass., Clark Univ. Press, 382-455.—*23, 49, 226, 338*

360. HULL, C. L. (1935a) The conflicting psychologies of learning—a way out. *Psychol. Rev.*, 42, 491-516.—*223, 225, 227*

361. HULL, C. L. (1935b) The influence of caffeine and other factors on certain phenomena of rote learning. *J. gen. Psychol.*, 13, 249-274.—*224, 227*

362. HULL, C. L. (1935c) The mechanism of the assembly of behavior segments in novel combinations suitable for problem solution. *Psychol. Rev.*, 42, 219-245.—*208, 237, 238*

363. HULL, C. L. (1935d) Thorndike's Fundamentals of learning. *Psychol. Bull.*, 32, 807-823.—*174*

364. HULL, C. L. (1937) Mind, mechanism, and adaptive behavior. *Psychol. Rev.*, 44, 1-32.—*16, 25, 102, 172, 174, 227, 253*

365. HULL, C. L. (1938) The goal-gradient hypothesis applied to some "field-force" problems in the behavior of young children. *Psychol. Rev.*, 45, 271-299.—*242, 248, 254*

366. HULL, C. L. (1939a) Modern behaviorism and psychoanalysis. *Trans. N. Y. Acad. Sci.*, Ser. II, 1, 78-82.—*307*

367. HULL, C. L. (1939b) The problem of stimulus equivalence in behavior theory. *Psychol. Rev.*, 46, 9-30.—*192, 194, 203, 204, 205*

368. HULL, C. L. (1939c) Simple trial-and-error learning. *J. comp. Psychol.*, 27, 233-258.—*253*
    HULL, C. L., *see also* No. 36.

369. HULL, C. L., HOVLAND, C. I., ROSS, R. T., HALL, M., PERKINS, D. T., and FITCH, F. B. (1940) *Mathematico-deductive theory of rote learning.* New Haven, Yale Univ. Press, xii, 329 pp.—*25, 224, 227*

370. HULL, C. L., and SPENCE, K. W. (1938) "Correction" vs. "non-correction" method of trial-and-error learning in rats. *J. comp. Psychol.*, 25, 127-145.—*131, 227*

371. HUMPHREY, G. (1920) The conditioned reflex and the Freudian wish. *J. abnorm. (soc.) Psychol.*, 14, 389-392.—*307*

372. HUMPHREY, G. (1921) Education and Freudianism: I. The Freudian mechanisms and the conditioned reflex. *J. abnorm. (soc.) Psychol.*, 15, 350-386.—*307*

373. HUMPHREY, G. (1928a) The conditioned reflex and the laws of learning. *J. educ. Psychol.*, 19, 424-430.—*25*

374. HUMPHREY, G. (1928b) The effect of sequences of indifferent stimuli on a reaction of the conditioned response type. *J. abnorm. (soc.) Psychol.*, 22, 194-212.—*200*

375. HUMPHREY, G. (1930) Extinction and negative adaptation. *Psychol. Rev.*, 37, 361-363.—*130*

376. HUMPHREY, G. (1933) *The nature of learning in its relation to the living system.* New York, Harcourt Brace, vii, 296 pp.—*25, 101, 128, 130, 133*

377. HUMPHREY, G., and MARCUSE, F. (1939) New methods of obtaining neurotic behavior in rats. *Amer. J. Psychol.*, 52, 616-619.—*286, 306*

378. HUMPHREYS, L. G. (1939a) The effect of random alternation of reinforcement on the acquisition and extinction of conditioned eyelid reactions. *J. exp. Psychol.*, 25, 141-158.—*121, 149, 157, 194, 204*

379. HUMPHREYS, L. G. (1939b) Acquisition and extinction of verbal expectations in a situation analogous to conditioning. *J. exp. Psychol.*, 25, 294-301.—*150, 194*

380. HUMPHREYS, L. G. (1939c) Generalization as a function of method of reinforcement. *J. exp. Psychol.*, 25, 361-372.—*149, 178, 200, 204*
381. HUMPHREYS, L. G. (1940a) Distributed practice in the development of the conditioned eyelid reaction. *J. gen. Psychol.*, 22 (in press). —*148*
382. HUMPHREYS, L. G. (1940b) Measures of strength of conditioned responses. (In preparation.)—*154*
383. HUMPHREYS, L. G. (1940c) The strength of a Thorndikian response as a function of the number of practice trials. (In preparation.) —*121, 150, 204*
    HUMPHREYS, L. G., see also Nos. 315, 316.
384. HUNTER, W. S. (1933) Basic phenomena in learning. *J. gen. Psychol.*, 8, 299-317.—*25*
385. HUNTER, W. S. (1934) Learning: IV. Experimental studies of learning. In C. Murchison, edit., *A handbook of general experimental psychology*. Worcester, Mass., Clark Univ. Press, 497-570.—*227*
386. HUNTER, W. S. (1935a) Conditioning and extinction in the rat. *Brit. J. Psychol.*, 26, 135-148.—*119, 157*
387. HUNTER, W. S. (1935b) Conditioning and maze learning in the rat. *J. comp. Psychol.*, 19, 417-424.—*227*
388. HUNTER, W. S. (1935c) The disinhibition of experimental extinction in the white rat. *Science*, 81, 77-78.—*133*
389. HUNTER, W. S. (1935d) A curve of experimental extinction in the white rat. *Science*, 82, 374-376.—*157*
390. HUNTER, W. S. (1936a) Gradients in the establishment and extinction of conditioned locomotor responses to serial stimulation in the rat. *Kwart. psychol.*, 8, 1-8.—*168*
391. HUNTER, W. S. (1936b) Learning curves for conditioning and maze learning. *J. exp. Psychol.*, 19, 121-128.—*156, 227*
392. HUNTER, W. S. (1937) Muscle potentials and conditioning in the rat. *J. exp. Psychol.*, 21, 611-624.—*42, 133, 333*
393. HUNTER, W. S. (1938) An experiment on the disinhibition of voluntary responses. *J. exp. Psychol.*, 22, 419-428.—*133, 268, 277*
    HUNTER, W. S., see also No. 695.
394. HUNTER, W. S., and HUDGINS, C. V. (1934) Voluntary activity from the standpoint of behaviorism. *J. gen. Psychol.*, 10, 198-204.—*277*

395. ICHOK, G. (1934) Les réflexes conditionnels et le traitement de l'alcoolique. *Progr. méd.*, Paris, 2, 1742-1745.—*307*
396. IRWIN, O. C. (1939) Toward a theory of conditioning. *Psychol. Rev.*, 46, 425-444.—*155*
397. ISCHLONDSKY, N. E. (1930) *Neuropsyche und Hirnrinde. Vol. I: Der bedingte Reflex*, xviii, 328 pp.; *Vol. II: Physiologische Grundlagen der Tiefenpsychologie*, xv, 356 pp. Berlin and Vienna, Urban und Schwarzenberg.—*307*

398. IVANOV-SMOLENSKY, A. G. (1925) Über die bedingten Reflexe in der depressiven Phase des manisch-depressiven Irreseins. *Mschr. Psychiat. Neurol.*, 58, 376-388.—*308*

399. IVANOV-SMOLENSKY, A. G. (1927a) Études expérimentales sur les enfants et les aliénés selon la méthode des réflexes conditionnels. *Ann. méd.-psychol.*, 12, 140-150.—*306*

400. IVANOV-SMOLENSKY, A. G. (1927b) Neurotic behavior and the teaching of conditioned reflexes, *Amer. J. Psychiat.*, 84, 483-488.—*306*

401. IVANOV-SMOLENSKY, A. G. (1927c) On the methods of examining the conditioned food reflexes in children and in mental disorders. *Brain*, 50, 138-141.—*54, 307*

402. IVANOV-SMOLENSKY, A. G. (1928) The pathology of conditioned reflexes and the so-called psychogenic depression. *J. nerv. ment. Dis.*, 67, 346-350.—*307*

JACK, E. G., *see* No. 245.

403. JACKSON, T. A., and DOMINGUEZ, K. (1939) Studies in the transposition of learning by children: II. Relative vs. absolute choice with multi-dimensional stimuli. *J. exp. Psychol.*, 24, 630-639.—*204*

404. JACKSON, T. A., STONEX, E., LANE, E., and DOMINGUEZ, K. (1938) Studies in the transposition of learning by children. I. Relative vs. absolute response as a function of the amount of training. *J. exp. Psychol.*, 23, 578-600.—*204*

405. JACOBSEN, C. F. (1934) Influence of motor and premotor area lesions upon the retention of skilled movements in monkeys and chimpanzees. *Res. Publ. Ass. nerv. ment. Dis.*, 13, 225-247.—*337*

406. JACOBSEN, C. F. (1936) Studies of cerebral function in primates. I. The functions of the frontal association areas in monkeys. *Comp. Psychol. Monogr.*, 13, No. 63, 3-60.—*316*

407. JAMES, W. (1890) *Principles of psychology.* New York, Holt, I, xii, 689 pp; II, vi, 704 pp.—*4, 5, 259*

408. JAMES, W. T. (1933) The effect of reward on the response to painful experience in the conditioned reflex. *Amer. J. Physiol.*, 106, 71-79. —*101, 126*

409. JAMES, W. T. (1934a) A conditioned response of two escape reflex systems of the guinea pig and the significance of the study for comparative work. *J. genet. Psychol.*, 44, 449-453.—*101*

410. JAMES, W. T. (1934b) Morphological form and its relation to reflex action and behavior. *Res. Publ. Ass. nerv. ment. Dis.*, 14, 28-54.—*301, 308*

411. JAMES, W. T. (1936) The effect of the presence of a second individual on the conditioned salivary response in dogs of different constitutional types. *J. genet. Psychol.*, 49, 437-449.—*251, 303*

412. JAMES, W. T. (1937) An experimental study of the defense mechanism in the opossum, with emphasis on natural behavior and its relation to mode of life. *J. genet. Psychol.*, 51, 95-100.—*139*

413. JAMES, W. T. (1938) Constitutional differences between contrasted physical types among dogs. *Psychol. Bull.*, 35, 704-705.—*301, 308*

414. JAMES, W. T. (1939) Further experiments in social behavior among dogs. *J. genet. Psychol.*, 54, 151-164.—*251, 303*
JAMES, W. T., *see also* No. 528.

415. JOHNSON, H. M. (1913) Audition and habit formation in the dog. *Behav. Monogr.*, 2, No. 3, iv, 78 pp.—*196*

416. JOHNSON, H. M. (1927) A simpler principle of explanation of imaginative and ideational behavior, and of learning. *J. comp. Psychol.*, 7, 187-235.—*329*

417. JONES, F. N. (1939a) The "stepwise phenomenon" in rats. *J. comp. Psychol.*, 27, 39-44.—*204*

418. JONES, F. N. (1939b) The stepwise phenomenon. *Amer. J. Psychol.*, 52, 125-127.—*204*

419. JONES, F. N., and TAYLOR, F. E. (1938) The relative effects of goal orientation and direction of the last turn on maze learning in the rat. *J. comp. Psychol.*, 26, 19-26.—*219, 220, 227*

420. JONES, H. E. (1930) The retention of conditioned emotional responses in infancy. *J. genet. Psychol.*, 37, 485-498.—*148*

421. JONES, II. E. (1931) The conditioning of overt emotional responses. *J. educ. Psychol.*, 22, 127-130.—*307*

422. JONES, H. E., and JONES, M. C. (1928) Fear. *Childhood Educ.*, 5, 136-143.—*295*

423. JONES, L. F. (1939) A study of human salivary conditioning. *J. exp. Psychol.*, 24, 305-317.—*261*

424. JONES, M. C. (1924a) The elimination of children's fears. *J. exp. Psychol.*, 7, 382-390.—*307*

425. JONES, M. C. (1924b) A laboratory study of fear. The case of Peter. *J. genet. Psychol.*, 31, 308-315.—*307*

426. JONES, M. C. (1933) Emotional development. In C. Murchison, edit., *A handbook of child psychology*. Worcester, Mass., Clark Univ. Press, 271-302.—*307*
JONES, M. C., *see also* No. 422.

KADYKOV, B. I., *see* No. 969.

427. KALISCHER, O. (1909) Weitere Mitteilung über die Ergebnisse der Dressur als physiologischer Untersuchungsmethode auf den Gebieten des Gehör-, Geruchs-, und Farbensinns. *Arch. Anat. Physiol., Lpz., (Physiol. Abt.,)* 303-322.—*337*
KANTOR, R., *see* No. 930.

428. KANTOROVICH, N. V. (1929) [An attempt at associative-reflex therapy in alcoholism.] *Nov. Refl. Fiziol. Nerv. Sist.*, 3, 436-447. (Psychol. Abstr., 1930, 4, No. 4282.)—*298, 307*

429. KANTOROVICH, N. V., and LUKINA, A. M. (1926) [The formation of association reflexes in progressive paralysis.] *Nov. Refl. Fiziol. Nerv. Sist.*, 2, 369-380. (Psychol. Abstr., 1928, 2, No. 146.)—*308*

430. KANTROW, R. W. (1937) An investigation of conditioned feeding responses and concomitant adaptive behavior in young infants. *Univ. Ia Stud. Child Welf.*, 13, No. 337, 64 pp.—*116, 124, 140, 155, 156*

431. KAPPAUF, W. E., and SCHLOSBERG, H. (1937) Conditioned responses in the white rat. III. Conditioning as a function of the length of the period of delay. *J. genet. Psychol.*, 50, 27-45.—*160, 161*

431a. KAPPERS, C. U. A. (1917) Further contributions on neurobiotaxis. IX. An attempt to compare the phenomena of neurobiotaxis with other phenomena of taxis and tropism. The dynamic polarization of the neurone. *J. comp. Neurol.*, 27, 261-298.—*327*

432. KARGER, P. (1923) Suggestivbehandlung und heilpädagogischer Bedingungsreflex. *Mschr. Kinderheilk.*, 25, 306-313.—*307*

433. KASATKIN, N. I. (1932) Pavlov's theory of schizophrenia. *Arch. Neurol. Psychiat., Chicago*, 28, 210-218.—*308*

434. KASATKIN, N. I., and LEVIKOVA, A. M. (1935) On the development of early conditioned reflexes and differentiations of auditory stimuli in infants. *J. exp. Psychol.*, 18, 1-19.—*205*

KATCHER, N., *see* No. 124.

435. KATTSOFF, L. O. (1939) Philosophy, psychology, and postulational technique. *Psychol. Rev.*, 46, 62-74.—*254*

KATZENELBOGEN, S., *see* No. 233.

436. KATZENELBOGEN, S., LOUCKS, R. B., and GANTT, W. H. (1939) An attempt to condition gastric secretion to histamin. *Amer. J. Physiol.*, 128, 10-12.—*323*

437. KELLOGG, W. N. (1938a) Evidence for both stimulus-substitution and original anticipatory responses in the conditioning of dogs. *J. exp. Psychol.*, 22, 186-192.—*37, 49*

438. KELLOGG, W. N. (1938b) An eclectic view of some theories of learning. *Psychol. Rev.*, 45, 165-184.—*71*

439. KELLOGG, W. N. (1939a) The relationship between ambiguous conditioning and experimental extinction in dogs. A follow-up report. *J. comp. Psychol.*, 27, 283-287.—*131*

440. KELLOGG, W. N. (1939b) "Positive" and "negative" conditioning, without contraction of the essential muscles during the period of training. *Psychol. Bull.*, 36, 575.—*184*

KELLOGG, W. N., *see also* No. 885.

441. KELLOGG, W. N., DAVIS, R. C., and SCOTT, V. B. (1939) Refinements in technique for the conditioning of motor reflexes in dogs. *J. exp. Psychol.*, 24, 318-331.—*49*

442. KELLOGG, W. N., and WALKER, E. L. (1938a) "Ambiguous conditioning," a phenomenon of bilateral transfer. *J. comp. Psychol.*, 26, 63-77.—*113, 131, 244*

443. KELLOGG, W. N., and WALKER, E. L. (1938b) An analysis of the bilateral transfer of conditioning in dogs, in terms of the frequency, amplitude, and latency of the responses. *J. gen. Psychol.*, 18, 253-265.—*131, 138, 154*

444. KELLOGG, W. N., and WOLF, I. S. (1939) The nature of the response retained after several varieties of conditioning in the same subjects. *J. exp. Psychol.*, 24, 366-383.—*118, 129, 131*

445. KELLY, E. L. (1934) An experimental attempt to produce artificial chromaesthesia by the technique of the conditioned response. *J. exp. Psychol.*, 17, 315-341.—*50*

446. KEMP, E. H. (1936) An experimental investigation of the problem of stimulation deafness. *J. exp. Psychol.*, 19, 159-171.—*205*
    KEMP, E. H., *see also* No. 157.

447. KENNEDY, J. L. (1939) The effects of complete and partial occipital lobectomy upon thresholds of visual real movement discrimination in the cat. *J. genet. Psychol.*, 54, 119-149.—*337*

448. KENNEDY, J. L., and SMITH, K. U. (1935) Visual thresholds of real movement in the cat. *J. genet. Psychol.*, 46, 470 476.—*205*

449. KHOZAK, L. E. (1934) [An attempt to change the verbal reactions of children by an experimental organization of their actions.] *Na Put. Izuch. Vyssh. Form Neirodin. Reb.*, 405-414. (*Psychol. Abstr.*, 1935, 9, No. 1140.)—*307*

450. KLEITMAN, N. (1927) The influence of starvation on the rate of secretion of saliva elicited by pilocarpine, and its bearing on conditioned salivation. *Amer. J. Physiol.*, 82, 686-692.—*155, 322*

451. KLEITMAN, N. (1930) The effect of conditioned stimulation and of sleep upon conditioned salivation. *Amer. J. Physiol.*, 94, 215-219.—*156*

452. KLEITMAN, N., and CRISLER, G. (1927) A quantitative study of a salivary conditioned reflex. *Amer. J. Physiol.*, 79, 571-614.—*15, 37, 68, 157, 322*

453. KLEITMAN, N., and TITELBAUM, S. (1936) The effect of thyroid administration upon the differentiating ability of dogs. *Amer. J. Physiol.*, 115, 162-167.—*156*

454. KLESHCHOV, S. (1932a) Phylogenetische Vorstufen des musikalischen Gehörs, *Z. Sinnesphysiol.*, 62, 315-325.—*198, 205*

455. KLESHCHOV, S. (1932b) Phylogenetische Vorstufen des musikalischen Gehörs. *Z. Sinnesphysiol.*, 63, 188-196.—*198, 205*

456. KLESHCHOV, S. (1933) Phylogenetische Vorstufen des musikalischen Gehörs. Z. *Sinnephysiol.*, 64, 177-191.—*198, 205*
457. KLESHCHOV, S. (1936) Phylogenetische Vorstufen des musikalischen Gehörs. Z. *Sinnesphysiol.*, 66, 235-246.—*198, 205*
458. KLINE, L. W., and KOHLER, H. M. (1935) A comparison of the conditioning of muscular responses which vary in their degree of voluntary control. *Amer. J. Psychol.*, 47, 129-138.—*277*
459. KLÜVER, H. (1933) *Behavior mechanisms in monkeys.* Chicago, Univ. Chicago Press, xvii, 387 pp.—*187, 192*
460. KLÜVER, H. (1936) An analysis of the effects of the removal of the occipital lobes in monkeys. *J. Psychol.*, 2, 49-61.—*317, 337*
461. KOFFKA, K. (1924) *The growth of the mind.* New York, Harcourt Brace, xvi, 382 pp.—*15, 247*
    KOHLER, H. M., *see* No. 458.
462. KÖHLER, W. (1925) *The mentality of apes.* New York, Harcourt Brace, viii, 342 pp.—*14, 204, 243*
463. KÖHLER, W. (1929) *Gestalt psychology.* New York, Liveright, x, 403 pp.—*25, 313, 331*
    KONORSKI, J., *see* No. 603.
464. KONORSKI, J., and MILLER, S. (1930) Méthode d'examen de l'analysateur moteur par les réactions salivomotrices. *C. R. Soc. Biol. Paris,* 104, 907-910.—*101*
465. KONORSKI, J., and MILLER, S. (1936) [Conditioned reflexes of the motor analyzer.] *Trud. Fiziol. Lab. Pavlov.,* 6, 119-288. (Razran, 1939 i, p. 446).—*101*
466. KONORSKI, J., and MILLER, S. (1937a) On two types of conditioned reflex. *J. gen. Psychol.*, 16, 264-272.—*71, 101*
467. KONORSKI, J., and MILLER, S. (1937b) Further remarks on two types of conditioned reflex. *J. gen. Psychol.*, 17, 405-407.—*71, 101*
468. KOROTKIN, I. I. (1938) [The mechanism of the so-called "ratio" phenomenon in the physiology of the highest nervous system.] *Fiziol. Zh. S.S.S.R.,* 24, 696-714. (*Psychol. Abstr.,* 1939, 13, No. 4045.) —*204*
469. KOSTYLEFF, N. (1927) L'inversion sexuelle expliquée par la réflexologie. *Psychol. et Vie,* 1, No. 6, 8-12.—*307*
470. KOTLIAREVSKY, L. I. (1935) [The formation of pupillary conditioned reflexes and of a differentiation in response to both direct and verbal stimuli.] *Arkh. Biol. Nauk,* 39, 477-489. (*Biol. Abstr.,* 1937, 11, No. 13724.)—*278*
471. KOTLIAREVSKY, L. I. (1936) [Cardio-vascular conditioned reflexes to direct and to verbal stimuli.] *Fiziol. Zh. S.S.S.R.,* 20, 228-242. (*Psychol. Abstr.,* 1939, 13, No. 4046.)—*278*
    KOTYUKA, E., *see* No. 526.
472. KOVSHAROVA, V. (1934) [A study in experimentally influencing the verbal choice reactions of children.] *Na Put. Izuch. Vyssh. Form*

Neirodin. Reb., 415-435. (*Psychol. Abstr.*, 1935, 9, No. 1144.)—
307

473. KRASNOGORSKI, N. I. (1909) Über die Bedingungsreflexe im Kindesalter. *Jb. Kinderheilk.*, 69, 1-24.—*10*

474. KRASNOGORSKI, N. I. (1913) Über die Grundmechanismen der Arbeit der Grosshirnrinde bei Kindern. *Jb. Kinderheilk.*, 78, 373-398.—*10*

475. KRASNOGORSKI, N. I. (1923) Du processus de concentration dans l'écorce des grands hémisphères. *Rev. méd., Paris*, 40, 294-310.—*131*

476. KRASNOGORSKI, N. I. (1925) The conditioned reflexes and children's neuroses. *Amer. J. Dis. Child.*, 30, 753-768.—*286, 306, 307*

477. KRASNOGORSKI, N. I. (1930) Psychology and psychopathology in childhood as a branch of pediatric investigation. *Acta paediatr., Stockh.*, 11, 481-502.—*307*

478. KRASNOGORSKI, N. I. (1931) Bedingte und unbedingte Reflexe im Kindesalter und ihre Bedeutung für die Klinik. *Ergebn. inn. Med. Kinderheilk.*, 39, 613-730.—*155, 306, 307*

479. KRASNOGORSKI, N. I. (1933a) Die neue Behandlung der Enuresis nocturna. *Mschr. Kinderheilk.*, 57, 252-254.—*307*

480. KRASNOGORSKI, N. I. (1933b) Physiology of cerebral activity in children as a new subject of pediatric investigation. *Amer. J. Dis. Child.*, 46, 473-494.—*306*

481. KRASNOGORSKI, N. I. (1935) Neue Ergebnisse der Erforschung der physiologischen Tätigkeit des Gehirns im Kindesalter. *Jb. Kinderheilk.*, 144, 255-277.—*307*

482. KRECHEVSKY, I. (1932a) "Hypotheses" in rats. *Psychol. Rev.*, 39, 516-532.—*88, 204*

483. KRECHEVSKY, I. (1932b) "Hypotheses" versus "chance" in the presolution period in sensory discrimination-learning. *Univ. Calif. Publ. Psychol.*, 6, 27-44.—*131, 189, 204*

484. KRECHEVSKY, I. (1933a) Hereditary nature of "hypotheses." *J. comp. Psychol.*, 16, 99-116.—*204*

485. KRECHEVSKY, I. (1933b) The docile nature of "hypotheses." *J. comp. Psychol.*, 15, 429-443.—*204*

486. KRECHEVSKY, I. (1937) A note concerning "The nature of discrimination learning in animals." *Psychol. Rev.*, 44, 97-104.—*204*

487. KRECHEVSKY, I. (1938) A study of the continuity of the problem-solving process. *Psychol. Rev.*, 45, 107-133.—*190, 204*

KRECHEVSKY, I., *see also* No. 285.

KREINDLER, A., *see* Nos. 574, 575.

488. KRIAZHEV, V. I. (1929a) [The objective investigation of the higher nervous activity in a collective experiment.] *Vyssh. Nerv. Deyat.*, 247-291. (*Psychol. Abstr.*, 1934, 8, No. 2532.)—*134*

489. KRIAZHEV, V. I. (1929b) [The nature of the conditioned reflex ac-

tivity of a dog in the prodromal stage of rabies.] *Vyssh. Nerv. Deyat.*, 292-296. (*Psychol. Abstr.*, 1934, 8, No. 2489.)—*155*

490. KRIAZHEV, V. I. (1933) Der Charakter der bedingten Reflexe von hypophysektomierten Hunden. *Pflüg. Arch. ges. Physiol.*, 232, 389-401.—*156*

491. KUBIE, L. S. (1934) Relation of the conditioned reflex to psychoanalytic technic. *Arch. Neurol. Psychiat.*, Chicago, 32, 1137-1142.—*307*

KUPALOV, P. S., *see* No. 554.

492. KUPALOV, P. S., and GANTT, W. H. (1927) The relationship between the strength of the conditioned stimulus and the size of the resulting conditioned reflex. *Brain*, 50, 44-52.—*141*

493. KUPALOV, P. S., LYMAN, R. S., and LUKOV, B. N. (1931) The relationship between the intensity of tone-stimuli and the size of the resulting conditioned reflexes. *Brain*, 54, 85-98.—*156*

LAMBERT, E. F., *see* No. 164.

494. LANDAHL, H. D. (1938a) A contribution to the mathematical biophysics of psychophysical discrimination. *Psychometrika*, 3, 107-125.—*339*

495. LANDAHL, H. D. (1938b) Contribution to the mathematical biophysics of error elimination. *Psychometrika*, 3, 169-180.—*339*

496. LANDKOF, B. L. (1938) [Unconditioned and conditioned vascular reflexes in schizophrenics.] *Trud. Tsentral. Psikhonevrol. Inst.*, 10, 37-63. (*Psychol. Abstr.* 1938, 12, No. 5343.)—*308*

LANE, E., *see* No. 404.

497. LANG, J. M., and OLMSTED, J. M. D. (1923) Conditioned reflexes and pathways in the spinal cord. *Amer. J. Physiol.*, 65, 603-611.—*321*

498. LASHLEY, K. S. (1916a) The human salivary reflex and its use in psychology. *Psychol. Rev.*, 23, 446-464.—*13, 25*

499. LASHLEY, K. S. (1916b) Reflex secretion of the human parotid gland. *J. exp. Psychol.*, 1, 461-493.—*13*

500. LASHLEY, K. S. (1922) Studies of cerebral function in learning. IV. Vicarious function after destruction of the visual areas. *Amer. J. Physiol.*, 59, 44-71.—*315*

501. LASHLEY, K. S. (1924) Studies of cerebral function in learning. V. The retention of motor habits after destruction of the so-called motor area in primates. *Arch. Neurol. Psychiat.*, Chicago, 12, 249-276.—*184, 337*

502. LASHLEY, K. S. (1929) *Brain mechanisms and intelligence.* Chicago, Univ. Chicago Press, xiv, 186 pp.—*337*

503. LASHLEY, K. S. (1930a) Basic neural mechanisms in behavior. *Psychol. Rev.*, 37, 1-24.—*331*

504. LASHLEY, K. S. (1930b) The mechanism of vision: I. A method for rapid analysis of pattern-vision in the rat. *J. genet. Psychol.*, 37, 453-460.—*188, 196*

505. LASHLEY, K. S. (1934) Learning: III. Nervous mechanisms in learning. In C. Murchison, edit., *A handbook of general experimental psychology*. Worcester, Mass., Clark Univ. Press, 456-496.—*25, 339*

506. LASHLEY, K. S. (1938) Conditional reactions in the rat. *J. Psychol.*, 6, 311-324.—*204*

507. LASHLEY, K. S., and BALL, J. (1929) Spinal conduction and kinesthetic sensitivity in the maze habit. *J. comp. Psychol.*, 9, 71-105. —*227*

508. LEBEDINSKAIA, S. I., and ROSENTHAL, J. S. (1935) Reactions of a dog after removal of the cerebral hemispheres. *Brain*, 58, 412-419.—*314*

509. LEEPER, R. (1935) The rôle of motivation in learning; a study of the phenomenon of differential motivational control of the utilization of habits. *J. genet. Psychol.*, 46, 3-40.—*67, 227, 241*

510. LEPLEY, W. M. (1932) A theory of serial learning and forgetting based upon conditioned reflex principles. *Psychol. Rev.*, 39, 279-288.—*222, 225, 227*

511. LEPLEY, W. M. (1934) Serial reactions considered as conditioned reactions. *Psychol. Monogr.*, 46, No. 205, 56 pp.—*227*

512. LEPLEY, W. M. (1936) The effect of distraction upon serial position values in retention. *J. exp. Psychol.*, 19, 467-474.—*227*

LEVIKOVA, A. M., *see* No. 434.

513. LEVIKOVA, A. M., and NEVYMAKOVA, G. A. (1929) [The problem of the formation and differentiation of associated reflexes to auditory stimuli in infants.] *Vopr. Genet. Refl. Pedol. Mladen.*, 1, 89-105. (Razran, 1933b, pp. 77-78.) *116*

514. LEVIN, M. (1934a) "Crowding" of inhibition and of excitation. *J. Neurol. Psychopath.*, 14, 345-348.—*131*

515. LEVIN, M. (1934b) Narcolepsy and the machine age; the recent increase in the incidence of narcolepsy. *J. Neurol. Psychopath.*, 15, 60-64.—*131, 307*

516. LEVIN, S. L. (1934) [Peculiarities of the conditioned-reflex activity during hypnosis in children. I.] *Fiziol. Zh. S.S.S.R.*, 17, 196-206. (*Biol. Abstr.*, 1937, 11, No. 11062.)—*131, 156*

517. LEVIN, S. L. (1935) [The action of chloral hydrate and other remedies on the conditioned reflex activity.] *Fiziol. Zh. S.S.S.R.*, 19, 804-813. (*Psychol. Abstr.*, 1936, 10, No. 3404.)—*134*

LEVIN, S. L., *see also* No. 636.

518. LEWIN, K. (1933) Environmental forces. In C. Murchison, edit., *A handbook of child psychology*. Worcester, Mass., Clark Univ. Press, 590-625.—*242, 254*

519. LEWIN, K. (1935) *A dynamic theory of personality.* New York, McGraw-Hill, ix, 286 pp.—*242, 254*

LIDDELL, E. G. T., *see* No. 137.

520. LIDDELL, H. S. (1926a) A laboratory for the study of conditioned motor reflexes. *Amer. J. Psychol.*, 37, 418-419.—*15*

521. LIDDELL, H. S. (1926b) The effect of thyroidectomy on some unconditioned responses of the sheep and goat. *Amer. J. Physiol.*, 75, 579-590.—*156*

522. LIDDELL, H. S. (1934) The conditioned reflex. In F. A. Moss, edit., *Comparative psychology.* New York, Prentice-Hall, 247-296.— *29, 30, 227*

523. LIDDELL, H. S. (1936a) Nervous strain in domesticated animals and man. *Cornell Vet.*, 26, 107-112.—*306, 307*

524. LIDDELL, H. S. (1936b) Pavlov, the psychiatrist of the future. *J. Mt. Sinai Hosp.*, 3, 101-104.—*304, 307*

525. LIDDELL, H. S. (1938) The experimental neurosis and the problem of mental disorder. *Amer. J. Psychiat.*, 94, 1035-1043.—*282, 283, 306*

LIDDELL, H. S., *see also* No. 11.

526. LIDDELL, H. S., ANDERSON, O. D., KOTYUKA, E., and HARTMAN, F. A. (1935) Effect of extract of adrenal cortex on experimental neurosis in sheep. *Arch. Neurol. Psychiat., Chicago*, 34, 973-993.— *156*

527. LIDDELL, H. S., and BAYNE, T. L. (1927) Auditory conditioned reflexes in the thyroidectomized sheep and goat. *Proc. Soc. exp. Biol., N.Y.*, 24, 289-291.—*156, 306*

528. LIDDELL, H. S., JAMES, W. T., and ANDERSON, O. D. (1934) The comparative physiology of the conditioned motor reflex: based on experiments with the pig, dog, sheep, goat, and rabbit. *Comp. Psychol. Monogr.*, 11, No. 51, 89 pp.—*49, 102, 129, 139, 184, 197, 306*

529. LIDDELL, H. S., and SIMPSON, E. D. (1926) A preliminary study of conditioned motor reflexes in thyroidectomized sheep. *Proc. Soc. exp. Biol., N.Y.*, 23, 720-722.—*156*

530. LIDDELL, H. S., SUTHERLAND, G. F., PARMENTER, R., and BAYNE, T. L. (1936) A study of the conditioned reflex method for producing experimental neurosis. *Amer. J. Physiol.*, 116, 95-96.—*306*

531. LIGHT, J. S., and GANTT, W. H. (1936) Essential part of reflex arc for establishment of conditioned reflex. Formation of conditioned reflex after exclusion of motor peripheral end. *J. comp. Psychol.*, 21, 19-36.—*323*

532. LINDBERG, A. A. (1933) The formation of negative conditioned reflexes by coincidence in time with the process of differential inhibition. *J. gen. Psychol.*, 8, 392-420.—*126*

533. LINDBERG, A. A. (1936) External inhibition or negative induction within the cerebral cortex. *J. gen. Psychol.*, 14, 466-472.—*131*

LIPMAN, E. A., *see* No. 77.

534. LORENTE DE NÓ, R. (1938a) Limits of variation of the synaptic delay of motoneurons. *J. Neurophysiol.*, 1, 187-194.—*327, 339*

535. LORENTE DE NÓ, R. (1938b) Synaptic stimulation of motoneurons as a local process. *J. Neurophysiol.*, 1, 195-206.—*329, 339*

536. LORENTE DE NÓ, R. (1938c) Analysis of the activity of the chains of internuncial neurons. *J. Neurophysiol.*, 1, 207-244.—*329, 339*

537. LOUCKS, R. B. (1931) Efficacy of the rat's motor cortex in delayed alternation. *J. comp. Neurol.*, 53, 511-567.—*232*

538. LOUCKS, R. B. (1932) An automatic technique for establishing conditioned reflexes. *Amer. J. Psychol.*, 44, 338-343.—*49*

539. LOUCKS, R. B. (1933) An appraisal of Pavlov's systematization of behavior from the experimental standpoint. *J. comp. Psychol.*, 15, 1-47.—*181, 203, 312*

540. LOUCKS, R. B. (1934) A technique for faradic stimulation of tissues beneath the integument in the absence of conductors penetrating the skin. *J. comp. Psychol.*, 18, 305-313.—*49, 319*

541. LOUCKS, R. B (1935) The experimental delimitation of neural structures essential for learning: the attempt to condition striped muscle responses with faradization of the sigmoid gyri. *J. Psychol.*, 1, 5-44.—*322*

542. LOUCKS, R. B. (1937a) Humoral conditioning in mammals. *J. Psychol.*, 4, 295-307.—*323, 338*

543. LOUCKS, R. B. (1937b) Reflexology and the psychobiological approach. *Psychol. Rev.*, 44, 320-338.—*203*

544. LOUCKS, R. B. (1938a) Preliminary note on a general purpose recording technique. *J. Psychol.*, 6, 243-245.—*49*

545. LOUCKS, R. B. (1938b) Studies of neural structures essential for learning. II. The conditioning of salivary and striped muscle responses to faradization of cortical sensory elements, and the action of sleep upon such mechanisms. *J. comp. Psychol.*, 25, 315-332.—*320*

546. LOUCKS, R. B. (1939) An experimental investigation of chained responses in indirect conditioning. *Psychol. Bull.*, 36, 575-576.—*233*

LOUCKS, R. B., *see also* Nos. 233, 436.

547. LOUCKS, R. B., and GANTT, W. H. (1938) The conditioning of striped muscle responses based upon faradic stimulation of dorsal roots and dorsal columns of the spinal cord. *J. comp. Psychol.*, 25, 415-426.—*321*

LUDLOW, N., *see* No. 166.

LUKINA, A. M., *see* Nos. 49, 429.

548. Lukina, A. M., and Matusova, S. A. (1929) [Characteristics of conditioning in epileptics.] *Nov. Refl. Fiziol. Nerv. Sist.*, 3, 419-436. (*Psychol. Abstr.*, 1930, 4, No. 4344.)—*308*

Lukov, B. N., *see* No. 493.

549. Lumley, F. H. (1932) Anticipation as a factor in serial and maze learning. *J. exp. Psychol.*, 15, 331-342.—*227*

550. Lumsdaine, A. A. (1939) Conditioned eyelid responses as mediating generalized conditioned finger reactions. *Psychol. Bull.*, 36, 650.—*230*

551. Lundholm, H. (1928) An experimental study of functional anesthesias as induced by suggestion in hypnosis. *J. abnorm. (soc.) Psychol.*, 23, 337-355.—*156, 201, 320*

552. Lundholm, H. (1932) A hormic theory of hallucinations. *Brit. J. med. Psychol.*, 11, 269-282.—*156, 201*

553. Luria, A. R. (1932) *The nature of human conflicts.* New York, Liveright, xvii, 431 pp.—*287*

Lurie, M. H., *see* Nos. 157, 836.

Lyman, R. S., *see* No. 493.

554. Lyman, R. S., Kupalov, P. S., and Scholz, W. (1933) Effect of Roentgen rays on the central nervous system. Results of large doses on the brains of adult dogs. *Arch. Neurol. Psychiat., Chicago*, 29, 56-87.—*156*

555. McCulloch, T. L. (1934) Performance preferentials of the white rat in force-resisting and spatial dimensions. *J. comp. Psychol.*, 18, 85-111.—*67*

556. McCulloch, T. L. (1939a) Comment on the formation of discrimination habits. *Psychol. Rev.*, 46, 75-85.—*204*

557. McCulloch, T. L. (1939b) Reply to a note on discrimination habits. *Psychol. Rev.*, 46, 304-307.—*204*

558. McCulloch, T. L. (1939c) The rôle of clasping activity in adaptive behavior of the infant chimpanzee: III. The mechanism of reinforcement. *J. Psychol.*, 7, 305-316.—*82, 92*

559. McCulloch, T. L., and Pratt, J. G. (1934) A study of the pre-solution period in weight discrimination by white rats. *J. comp. Psychol.*, 18, 271-290.—*190*

McCulloch, W. S., *see* Nos. 175, 176, 177.

McCurdy, H. G., *see* No. 971.

560. McDougall, W. (1923) *Outline of psychology.* New York, Scribner, xvi, 456 pp.—*101*

561. McDougall, W. (1927) An experiment for the testing of the hypothesis of Lamarck. *Brit. J. Psychol.*, 17, 267-304.—*73*

562. McDougall, W. (1929) The bearing of Professor Pavlov's work on the problem of inhibition. *J. gen. Psychol.*, 2, 231-262.—*308*

563. McGeoch, J. A. (1932) Forgetting and the law of disuse. *Psychol. Rev.*, 39, 352-370.—*127*

564. McGeoch, J. A. (1933) The psychology of human learning: a bibliography. *Psychol. Bull.*, 30, 1-62.—*227*

565. McGeoch, J. A. (1934) Learning and retention of verbal materials. *Psychol. Bull.*, 31, 381-407.—*227*

566. McGeoch, J. A. (1936) The direction and extent of intraserial associations at recall. *Amer. J. Psychol.*, 48, 221-245.—*225, 226*

567. Macfarlane, D. A. (1930) The rôle of kinesthesis in maze learning. *Univ. Calif. Publ. Psychol.*, 4, 277-305.—*73*

568. Machtinger, A. (1933) [Über den Einfluss der langzeitigen einseitigen Überernährung auf die bedingten Reflexe bei Kindern.] *Fiziol. Zh. S.S.S.R.*, 16, 421-426. (*Z. ges. Neurol. Psychiat.*, 1933, 69, 731.)—*155*

569. Maier, N. R. F. (1929) Reasoning in white rats. *Comp. Psychol. Monogr.*, 6, No. 29, 93 pp.—*236*

570. Maier, N. R. F. (1939a) Qualitative differences in the learning of rats in a discrimination situation. *J. comp. Psychol.*, 27, 289-332. —*204*

571. Maier, N. R. F. (1939b) *Studies of abnormal behavior in the rat.* New York, Harper, 81 pp.—*285, 306*

572. Maiorov, F. P. (1933) [Elimination of the hypnotic state in dogs by means of bromides.] *Trud. Fiziol. Lab. Pavlov.*, 5, 133-146. (*Psychol. Abstr.*, 1933, 7, No. 4448.)—*134*

Marcuse, F., *see* No. 377.

573. Marinesco, G. (1937) Contribution à l'étude des troubles sensitifs hystériques et le rôle des réflexes conditionnels dans la physiopathologie de l'hystérie. *Rev. neurol.*, 68, 585-600.—*307*

574. Marinesco, G., and Kreindler, A. (1935) *Des réflexes conditionnels, études de physiologie normale et pathologique.* Paris, Alcan, vii, 171 pp.—*307, 308, 329*

575. Marinesco, G., Kreindler, A., and Copelmann, L. (1935) Le test de Rorschach et la dynamique de l'écorce cérébrale d'après les lois des réflexes conditionnels de Pavlov. *Ann. méd.-psychol.*, 93, 614-623.—*308*

576. Marquis, D. G. (1934) Effects of removal of the visual cortex in mammals, with observations on the retention of light discrimination in dogs. *Res. Publ. Ass. nerv. ment. Dis.*, 13, 558-592.—*205, 317, 337*

577. Marquis, D. G. (1935) Phylogenetic interpretation of the functions of the visual cortex. *Arch. Neurol. Psychiat.*, Chicago, 33, 807-815.—*317*

Marquis, D. G., *see also* Nos. 317, 318.

578. MARQUIS, D. G., and HILGARD, E. R. (1936) Conditioned lid responses to light in dogs after removal of the visual cortex. *J. comp. Psychol.*, 22, 157-178.—*129, 156, 315, 316, 337*

579. MARQUIS, D. G., and HILGARD, E. R. (1937) Conditioned responses to light in monkeys after removal of the occipital lobes. *Brain*, 60, 1-12.—*156, 316, 337*

580. MARQUIS, D. G., and PORTER, J. M., JR. (1939) Differential characteristics of conditioned eyelid responses established by reflex and voluntary reinforcement. *J. exp. Psychol.*, 24, 347-365.—*123, 146, 164, 268, 271, 277*

581. MARQUIS, D. P. (1931) Can conditioned responses be established in the newborn infant? *J. genet. Psychol.*, 39, 479-492.—*37, 140, 156*

582. MARTINO, G. (1933) Epilepsia experimental e humana. *Rev. Ass. paulista med.*, 2, 128-239. (*Psychol. Abstr.*, 1934, 8, No. 5552.)— *308*

583. MARTINO, G. (1939) The conditioned reflex of blinking. *J. Neurophysiol.*, 2, 173-177.—*321*

584. MARTINO, G., and FULCHIGNONI, E. (1938) Über die Bedeutung bedingter Reize (für den Bahnungsprozess) bei der durch Strychninisierung der occipitalen Rinde reflektorisch erzeugten Epilepsie. *Pflüg. Arch. ges. Physiol.*, 240, 212-220.—*320*

585. MATEER, F. (1918) *Child behavior, a critical and experimental study of young children by the method of conditioned reflexes.* Boston, Badger, v, 239 pp.—*11, 13, 119, 140, 308*

MATUSOVA, S. A., *see* No. 548.

586. MAX, L. W. (1935) Breaking up a homosexual fixation by the conditioned reaction technique: a case study. *Psychol. Bull.*, 32, 734. —*307*

587. MEIGNANT, P. (1935) Réflexes conditionnels et psycho-pathologie: Quelques remarques concernant les perversions et les anomalies sexuelles. *Gaz. méd. Fr.*, 327-332.—*307*

588. MENZIES, R. (1937) Conditioned vasomotor responses in human subjects. *J. Psychol.*, 4, 75-120.—*123, 134, 226, 274, 277, 278*

589. METALNIKOV, S. (1934) *Rôle du système nerveux et des facteurs biologiques et psychiques dans l'immunité.* Paris, Masson, 166 pp. —*338*

METTLER, F. A., *see* Nos. 4, 76, 151, 152, 253.

590. METZNER, C. A., and BAKER, L. E. (1939) The pupillary response conditioned to subliminal auditory stimuli: a control experiment. *Psychol. Bull.*, 36, 625.—*278*

591. MEYER, M. F. (1908) The nervous correlate of pleasantness and unpleasantness. *Psychol. Rev.*, 15, 201-216; 292-322.—*24*

592. MEYER, M. F. (1934) Frequency, duration, and recency vs. double stimulation. *Psychol. Rev.*, 41, 177-183.—*24, 101*

MICHEL, J., *see* No. 746.

593. MIKHAÏLOFF, S. (1922) Expériences réflexologiques. Expériences nou-
velles sur Pagurus striatus. *Bull. Inst. océanogr. Monaco*, No.
418, 1-12.—*133*
MILES, W. R., *see* Nos. 600, 601.
594. MILLER, A. R. (1934) A failure to confirm Pavlov's hypothesis of
external inhibition. *Amer. J. Physiol.*, 108, 608-612.—*131*
595. MILLER, J. (1939a) The rate of conditioning of human subjects to
single and multiple conditioned stimuli. *J. gen. Psychol.*, 20, 399-
408.—*157*
596. MILLER, J. (1939b) The effect of facilitatory and inhibitory attitudes
on eyelid conditioning. Ph.D. dissertation, Yale University. (Abstr. in *Psychol. Bull.*, 1939, 36, 577-578.)—*157, 263, 264, 272, 277*
597. MILLER, J., and COLE, L. E. (1936) The influence of a "voluntary"
reaction upon the development and the extinction of the conditioned eyelid reaction. *J. genet. Psychol.*, 48, 405-440.—*157, 226,
232, 262, 277*
598. MILLER, J. G. (1939) Symbolic technique in psychological theory.
Psychol. Rev., 46, 464-479.—*254*
599. MILLER, N. E. (1935) A reply to 'Sign-Gestalt or conditioned reflex?'
Psychol. Rev., 42, 280-292.—*227, 233, 245*
MILLER, N. E., *see also* No. 96.
600. MILLER, N. E., and MILES, W. R. (1935) Effect of caffeine on the
running speed of hungry, satiated, and frustrated rats. *J. comp.
Psychol.*, 20, 397-412.—*134, 175, 227*
601. MILLER, N. E., and MILES, W. R. (1936) Alcohol and removal of
reward. An analytical study of rodent maze behavior. *J. comp.
Psychol.*, 21, 179-204.—*132, 134, 227*
602. MILLER, N. E., and STEVENSON, S. S. (1936) Agitated behavior of
rats during experimental extinction and a curve of spontaneous
recovery. *J. comp. Psychol.*, 21, 205-231.—*114, 130, 132, 227*
MILLER, S., *see* Nos. 464, 465, 466, 467.
603. MILLER, S., and KONORSKI, J. (1928) Sur une forme particulière des
réflexes conditionnels. *C. R. Soc. Biol. Paris*, 99, 1155-1157.—
54, 71, 101
604. MIROLYUBOV, N. G., and UGOL, N. B. (1933) [The problem of the
state of the process of excitation in schizophrenics.] *Sovrem.
Psikhonevrol.*, 69-82. (*Psychol. Abstr.*, 1935, 9, No. 1260.)—*308*
605. MISBACH, L. (1937) Reciprocal modifications in the patellar reflex
and a concomitant voluntary reaction. *J. Psychol.*, 3, 63-88.—*131*
606. MISHCHENKO, M. N. (1932) The pecularities of conditioned reflex
activity of hypnotics. *Sovrem. Psikhonevrol.*, 63-67. (*Psychol.
Abstr.*, 1934, 8, No. 4572.)—*156*
607. MISHCHENKO, M. N. (1935a) [The rate of formation of conditioned
reflexes in the hypnotic state.] *Eksp. Med., Kharkov*, 33-40.
(*Psychol. Abstr.*, 1936, 10, No. 245.)—*156*

608. MISHCHENKO, M. N. (1935b) [The relation between hypnosis and experimental sleep in man.] *Eksp. Med., Kharkov*, 175-191. (*Psychol. Abstr.*, 1936, 10, No. 1999.)—*156*

609. MISHCHENKO, M. N. (1936a) [Conditions of the development of experimental sleep in man.] *Eksp. Med., Kharkov*, 57-66. (*Psychol. Abstr.*, 1937, 11, No. 1744.)—*156*

610. MISHCHENKO, M. N. (1936b) [The relation between stimulus strength and the degree of response in man.] *Eksp. Med., Kharkov*, 67-79. (*Psychol. Abstr.*, 1937, 11, No. 1745.)—*156*

611. MITRANO, A. J. (1939) Principles of conditioning in human goal behavior. *Psychol. Monogr.*, 51, No. 230, 70 pp.—*74*

612. MONTPELLIER, G. DE, and COLLE, J. (1939) Réactions conditionnées volontaires et involontaires. *Arch. Psychol., Genève*, 27, 134-156.—*277*

613. MOORE, W. E. (1938) A conditioned reflex study of stuttering. *J. Speech Disorders*, 3, 163-183.—*307*

614. MORGAN, C. L. (1894) *Introduction to comparative psychology*. London, Scott, xiv, 382 pp.—*53*

MORGAN, C. T., *see* No. 286.

615. MORGAN, C. T., and FIELDS, P. E. (1938) The effect of variable preliminary feeding upon the rat's speed-of-locomotion. *J. comp. Psychol.*, 26, 331-348.—*227, 253*

616. MORGAN, C. T., and MORGAN, J. D. (1939) Auditory induction of an abnormal pattern of behavior in rats. *J. comp. Psychol.*, 27, 505-508.—*286, 306*

MORGAN, J. D., *see* No. 616.

MORGAN, J. J. B., *see* No. 903.

617. MORGAN, J. J. B., and WITMER, F. J. (1939) The treatment of enuresis by the conditioned reaction technique. *J. genet. Psychol.*, 55, 59-65.—*307*

MORGULIS, S., *see* No. 951.

618. MORHARDT, P.-E. (1930) Les réflexes conditionnels dans les névroses et dans les états allergiques. *Vie méd.*, 11, 825-828.—*307*

619. MOSS, F. A. (1924) Note on building likes and dislikes in children. *J. exp. Psychol.*, 7, 475-478.—*307*

620. MOWRER, O. H. (1934) The modification of vestibular nystagmus by means of repeated elicitation. *Comp. Psychol. Monogr.*, 9, No. 45, 48 pp.—*130*

621. MOWRER, O. H. (1938) Preparatory set (expectancy)—a determinant in motivation and learning. *Psychol. Rev.*, 45, 62-91.—*267*

622. MOWRER, O. H. (1939) A stimulus-response analysis of anxiety and its role as a reinforcing agent. *Psychol. Rev.*, 46, 553-565.—*246, 307*

623. MOWRER, O. H. (1940) An experimental analogue of "regression" with incidental observations on "reaction-formation." *J. abn. (soc.) Psychol.*, 35, 56-87.—*56, 307*

624. MOWRER, O. H., and MOWRER, W. M. (1938) Enuresis—a method for its study and treatment. *Amer. J. Orthopsychiat.*, 8, 436-459. —*307*

MOWRER, W. M., *see* No. 624.

MUENZINGER, K. F., *see* No. 113.

625. MUENZINGER, K. F., and DOVE, C. C. (1937) Serial learning: I. Gradients of uniformity and variability produced by success and failure of single responses. *J. gen. Psychol.*, 16, 403-413.—*84, 96, 203*

626. MUENZINGER, K. F., DOVE, C. C., and BERNSTONE, A. H. (1937) Serial learning: II. The bi-directional goal gradient in the endless maze. *J. genet. Psychol.*, 50, 229-241.—*96, 168, 174, 203*

627. MUENZINGER, K. F., and FLETCHER, F. M. (1936) Motivation in learning. VI. Escape from electric shock compared with hunger-food tension in the visual discrimination habit. *J. comp. Psychol.*, 22, 79-91.—*73, 83, 203, 204*

628. MUENZINGER, K. F., and GENTRY, E. (1931) Tone discrimination in white rats. *J. comp. Psychol.*, 12, 195-205.—*205*

629. MUENZINGER, K. F., and WOOD, A. (1935) Motivation in learning. IV. The function of punishment as determined by its temporal relation to the act of choice in the visual discrimination habit. *J. comp. Psychol.*, 20, 95-106.—*74, 203, 204*

MULDERG, B. M., *see* No. 35.

630. MUNN, N. L. (1931) An apparatus for testing visual discrimination in animals. *J. genet. Psychol.*, 39, 342-358.—*188*

631. MUNN, N. L. (1939) The relative effectiveness of two conditioning procedures. *J. gen. Psychol.*, 21, 119-136.—*58*

632. MURPHY, G. (1929) *An historical introduction to modern psychology.* New York, Harcourt Brace, xvii, 470 pp.—*23*

633. MYASISHCHEV, V. (1929) [Experimental evidence on the problem of objective indices in sensory disorders.] *Nov. Refl. Fiziol. Nerv. Sist.*, 3, 458-480. (*Psychol. Abstr.*, 1930, 4, No. 4349.)—*290, 307*

634. NEET, C. C. (1936) A comparison of verbal, manual, and conditioned-response methods in the determination of auditory intensity thresholds. *J. exp. Psychol.*, 19, 401-416.—*195, 205*

635. NEMENOW, M. I. (1934) The effect of Roentgen-ray exposures of the cerebral cortex on the activity of the cerebral hemispheres. *Radiology*, 23, 86-93.—*156*

636. NEVSKY, I. M., and LEVIN, S. L. (1932) [Unconditioned and conditioned secretory activity in children during hypnosis.] *Kazansk. Med. Zh.*, 28, 344-351. (Razran, 1933b, pp. 30-32.)—*156*

NEVYMAKOVA, G. A., *see* No. 513.

637. NEWHALL, S. M., and SEARS, R. R. (1933) Conditioning finger re-

traction to visual stimuli near the absolute threshold. *Comp. Psychol. Monogr.*, 9, No. 43, 25 pp.—*141, 195, 205*
NISSEN, H. W., *see* No. 136.
638. NISSEN, H. W., and CRAWFORD, M. P. (1936) A preliminary study of food-sharing behavior in young chimpanzees. *J. comp. Psychol.*, 22, 383-419.—*74*
639. NISSEN, H. W., RIESEN, A. H., and NOWLIS, V. (1938) Delayed response and discrimination learning by chimpanzees. *J. comp. Psychol.*, 26, 361-386.—*236*
NOWLIS, V., *see* No. 639.

640. OLDFIELD, R. C. (1937) Some recent experiments bearing on 'internal inhibition.' *Brit. J. Psychol.*, 28, 28-42.—*130*
OLMSTED, J. M. D., *see* No. 497.
641. OPPENHEIMER, M., and SPIEGEL, E. (1937) Static and kinetic conditioned reactions. *Proc. Soc. exp. Biol.*, N.Y., 36, 563-564.—*205*
642. OSIPOVA, V. N. (1926a) [The speed of formation of association reflexes in children of school age.] *Nov. Refl. Fiziol. Nerv. Sist.*, 2, 218-234. (*Psychol. Abstr.*, 1927, 1, No. 2275.)—*140*
643. OSIPOVA, V. N. (1926b) [Associative-stimulative and associative-inhibitive child types.] *Vopr. Izuch. Vospit. Lichn.*, 16-20. (*Psychol. Abstr.*, 1927, 1, No. 2276.)—*308*
644. OSIPOVA, V. N. (1927) Indissoluble association reflexes in children. *Vopr. Izuch. Vospit. Lichn.*, 33-46. (*Psychol. Abstr.*, 1927, 1, No. 2154.)—*134, 308*

645. PANNHORST, P. (1932) Beitrag zur Klinik der bedingten Reflexe. *Nervenarzt*, 5, 185-191.—*307*
PARMENTER, R., *see* No. 530.
646. PATTEN, E. F. (1938) The influence of distribution of repetitions on certain rote learning phenomena. *J. Psychol.*, 5, 359-374.—*227*
647. PAVLOV, I. P. (1906) The scientific investigation of the psychical faculties or processes in the higher animals. *Science*, 1906, 24, 613-619. (Also in *Lancet*, 1906, 2, 911-915.)—*3, 10*
648. PAVLOV, I. P. (1927) *Conditioned reflexes.* (Trans. by G. V. Anrep) London, Oxford Univ. Press, xv, 430 pp.—*8, 15, 19, 23, 35, 47, 108, 110, 126, 132, 149, 153, 163, 174, 179, 198, 200, 202, 279, 307, 316, 336, 337*
649. PAVLOV, I. P. (1928) *Lectures on conditioned reflexes.* (Trans. by W. H. Gantt) New York, International, 414 pp.—*23, 288, 307, 336, 337*
650. PAVLOV, I. P. (1932a) Neuroses in man and animals. *J. Amer. med. Ass.*, 99, 1012-1013.—*306, 308*
651. PAVLOV, I. P. (1932b) The reply of a physiologist to psychologists. *Psychol. Rev.*, 39, 91-127.—*24, 101, 112*

652. PAVLOV, I. P. (1933) Essai d'une interprétation physiologique de l'hystérie. *Encéphale*, 28, 285-293.—*308*

653. PAVLOV, I. P. (1934) An attempt at a physiological interpretation of obsessional neurosis and paranoia. *J. ment. Sci.*, 80, 187-197.— *79, 308*

654. PAVLOV, I. P. (1935) [*Experimental pathology of the highest nervous activity.*] Leningrad, Ogiz, 32 pp. (*Psychol. Abstr.*, 1936, 10, No. 248.)—*306, 308*

655. PAVLOVA, A. M. (1937) [Materials on the problem of the effect of castration upon the conditioned reflex activity of a dog.] *Trud. Fiziol. Lab. Pavlov.*, 7, 781-793. (*Psychol. Abstr.*, 1938, 12, No. 3428.)—*156*

656. PAVLOVA, V. I. (1933) [On the possibility of forming a conditioned reflex in a case in which the absolute stimulus precedes the indifferent stimulus.] *Trud. Fiziol. Lab. Pavlov.*, 5, 21-32. (*Psychol. Abstr.*, 1935, 9, No. 3661.)—*174*

657. PEAK, H. (1933a) Reflex and voluntary reactions of the eyelid. *J. gen. Psychol.*, 8, 130-156.—*257*

658. PEAK, H. (1933b) An evaluation of the concepts of reflex and voluntary action. *Psychol. Rev.*, 40, 71-89.—*257*

659. PEAK, H. (1936) Inhibition as a function of stimulus intensity. *Psychol. Monogr.*, 47, No. 212, 135-147.—*109*

660. PEAK, H., and DEESE, L. (1937) Experimental extinction of verbal material. *J. exp. Psychol.*, 20, 244-261.—*227, 277*

661. PEIPER, A. (1934) Die bedingten Reflexe im Kindesalter. *Kinderärztl. Prax.*, 5, 551-560.—*307*

662. PEN, R. M. (1933) [The problem of typological characteristics of the reflex activities of children.] *Eksp. Issl. Vyssh. Nerv. Deyat. Reb.*, 173-189. (*Psychol. Abstr.*, 1934, 8, No. 713.)—*308*

663. PENNINGTON, L. A. (1937a) The function of the brain in auditory localization. II. The effect of cortical operation upon original learning. *J. comp. Neurol.*, 66, 415-442.—*337*

664. PENNINGTON, L. A. (1937b) The function of the brain in auditory localization. III. Postoperative solution of an auditory spatial problem. *J. comp. Neurol.*, 67, 33-48.—*337*

PERKINS, D. T., *see* No. 369.

665. PERKINS, F. T., and WHEELER, R. H. (1930) Configurational learning in the goldfish. *Comp. Psychol. Monogr.*, 7, No. 31, 50 pp.—*204*

666. PETERSON, J. (1916) Completeness of response as an explanation principle in learning. *Psychol. Rev.*, 23, 153-162.—*101*

667. PETERSON, J. (1922) Learning when frequency and recency factors are negative. *J. exp. Psychol.*, 5, 270-300.—*102*

668. PETERSON, J. (1923) Frank's suggestion for a theory of learning. *Psychol. Rev.*, 30, 402-406.—*24*

669. PETERSON, J. (1935) Aspects of learning. *Psychol. Rev.*, 42, 1-27.—*25*

670. PETROVA, M. K. (1934a) [Experimental neurosis cured by bromide.] *Arkh. Biol. Nauk*, 34, 15-39. (*Psychol. Abstr.*, 1937, 11, No. 5733.)—*134, 306, 308*

671. PETROVA, M. K. (1934b) [Further studies on determination of the strength of the nervous system in experimental animals.] *Arkh. Biol. Nauk*, 34, 41-62. (*Psychol. Abstr.*, 1937, 11, No. 5734.)—*134, 308*

672. PETROVA, M. K. (1935) [*Latest data on the action of bromides on the highest nervous activity.*] Moscow, VIEM, 204 pp. (*Psychol. Abstr.*, 1936, 10, No. 309.)—*134, 308*

673. PETROVA, M. K. (1936) [Effect of castration upon the conditioned reflex activity and behavior of dogs belonging to different types of nervous systems.] *Trud. Fiziol. Lab. Pavlov.*, 6, 5-114. (*Psychol. Abstr.*, 1937, 11, No. 1198.)—*156, 308*

674. PETROVA, M. K. (1937a) [Bromides and their effect upon castrated dogs (further materials on the study of the mechanism of the action of bromides).] *Trud. Fiziol. Lab. Pavlov.*, 7, 5-105. (*Psychol. Abstr.*, 1938, 12, No. 3567.)—*134, 156, 308*

675. PETROVA, M. K. (1937b) [Curing a castrated dog of the strong well-equilibrated type of a prolonged (18 months) neurosis by means of caffein and bromide.] *Trud. Fiziol. Lab. Pavlov.*, 7, 105-131. (*Psychol., Abstr.*, 1938, 12, No. 3568.)—*134, 156, 306, 308*

676. PETROVA, M. K. (1937c) [The formation of conditioned neural connections in a castrated puppy.] *Trud. Fiziol. Lab. Pavlov.*, 7, 231-257. (*Psychol. Abstr.*, 1938, 12, No. 3431.)—*156, 308*

677. PETROVA, M. K. (1937d) [The ultra-paradoxical phase in conditioning and its mechanism.] *Trud. Fiziol. Lab. Pavlov.*, 7, 535-590. (*Psychol. Abstr.*, 1938, 12, No. 3435.)—*308*

678. PETROVA, M. K. (1937e) [The combined action of bromides and caffein in a case of a chronic ultra-paradoxical phase and a general explosiveness of the excitatory process in a castrated dog of a "medium" type of nervous system (2 cases of abortive catatonia).] *Trud. Fiziol. Lab. Pavlov.*, 7, 591-647. (*Psychol. Abstr.*, 1938, 12, No. 3571.)—*134, 156, 308*

679. PETROVA, M. K. (1937f) [The combined action of bromides and caffein in curing pathological states of weak inhibitable dogs, which were produced by attempts to transform negative conditioned stimuli into positive and positive into negative.] *Trud. Fiziol. Lab. Pavlov.*, 7, 649-728. (*Psychol. Abstr.*, 1938, 12, No. 3572.)—*134, 156, 308*

680. PFAFFMANN, C., and SCHLOSBERG, H. (1936) The conditioned knee jerk in psychotic and normal individuals. *J. Psychol.*, 1, 201-208.—*305, 308*

681. PLAVILSTCHIKOV, N. N. (1928) [Observations on excitability of in-

fusoria.] *Russ. Arkh. Protist.*, 7, 1-24. (*Biol. Abstr.*, 1930, 4, No. 6008.)—*30*

682. PODKOPAEV, N. A. (1926) *Die Methodik der Erforschung der bedingten Reflexe.* München, Bergmann, vi, 64 pp.—*49*

683. POLTYREV, S. S. (1936) Die Rolle der Rinde und Subrindeknoten in der Bildung der bedingten Reflexe. *Z. Biol.*, 97, 180-186.—*314*

684. POLTYREV, S. S., and ALEXEJEV, W. A. (1936) Über die Möglichkeit der Bildung bedingter Reflexe bei Hunden mit exstirpierter Hirnrinde von der der Hemisphäre gegenüberliegenden Körperoberfläche aus. *Z. Biol.*, 97, 297-305.—*337*

685. POLTYREV, S. S., and ZELIONY, G. P. (1930) Grosshirnrinde und Assoziationsfunktion. *Z. Biol.*, 90, 157-160.—*314*

686. PORTER, J. M., JR. (1938a) Adaptation of the galvanic skin response. *J. exp. Psychol.*, 23, 553-557.—*107*

687. PORTER, J. M., JR. (1938b) Backward conditioning of the eyelid response. *J. exp. Psychol.*, 23, 403-410.—*174*

688. PORTER, J. M., JR. (1938c) Extinction of an acquired response as a function of the interval between successive non-rewarded trials. *J. comp. Psychol.*, 26, 261-270.—*134*

689. PORTER, J. M., JR. (1938d) The modification of conditioned eyelid responses by successive series of non-reinforced elicitations. *J. gen. Psychol.*, 19, 307-323.—*123, 133, 277*

690. PORTER, J. M., JR. (1939) Experimental extinction as a function of the interval between successive non-reinforced elicitations. *J. gen. Psychol.*, 20, 109-134.—*133*

PORTER, J. M., JR., see also No. 580.

691. POSNANSKAYA, S. (1934) [The influence of chronic inhibition of the conditioned food reflexes on orientation-investigatory reflexes.] *Na Put. Izuch. Vyssh. Form Neirodin. Reb.*, 188-205. (*Psychol. Abstr.*, 1935, 9, No. 1153.)—*114*

PRATT, J. G., see No. 559.

692. PRESSMAN, J. M. (1934) [An attempt to form conditioned reflexes in children by reinforcing before the signal (backward conditioning).] *Na Put. Izuch. Vyssh. Form Neirodin. Reb.*, 131-165. (*Psychol. Abstr.*, 1935, 9, No. 1155.)—*174*

693. PRIBYTKOVA, G. N. (1936) [On the influence of various doses of thyroxin on higher nervous activity.] *Bull. Biol. Med. Exp.*, *U.R.S.S.*, 2, 114-116. (*Psychol. Abstr.*, 1938, 12, No. 5221.)—*156*

694. PRINCE, M. (1921) *The unconscious.* 2nd ed., New York, Macmillan, xvi, 654 pp.—*292*

695. PROSSER, C. L., and HUNTER, W. S. (1936) The extinction of startle responses and spinal reflexes in the white rat. *Amer. J. Physiol.*, 117, 609-618.—*42, 105, 107, 133*

PUGSLEY, L. I., see No. 15.

PUPKO, L. K., see No. 961.

696. RABINOWICH, P. H. DE (1932) Reflejos condicionados de Pavlov en paralíticos progresivos: estudio clínico experimental. *Sem. med., B. Aires*, 39, 1712-1728.—*308*

697. RAEVA, N. V., and RAPPOPORT, E. J. (1934) [The sensory pathways in motor activity.] *Fiziol. Zh. S.S.S.R.*, 17, 636-652. (*Psychol. Abstr.*, 1935, 9, No. 1691.)—*321*

RAFFEL, G., *see* No. 245.

RAPPOPORT, E. J., *see* No. 697.

698. RASHEVSKY, N. (1938) *Mathematical biophysics: Physicomathematical foundations of biology.* Chicago, Univ. Chicago Press, xviii, 340 pp.—*330, 339*

699. RASKIN, E., and COOK, S. W. (1937) The strength and direction of associations formed in the learning of nonsense syllables. *J. exp. Psychol.*, 20, 381-395.—*226*

700. RAUP, R. B. (1925) *Complacency, the foundation of human behavior.* New York, Macmillan, xii, 201 pp.—*82*

RAYNER, R., *see* No. 904.

701. RAZRAN, G. H. S. (1930) Theory of conditioning and related phenomena. *Psychol. Rev.*, 37, 25-43.—*132, 156, 318, 336*

702. RAZRAN, G. H. S. (1933a) Conditioned responses in animals other than dogs. *Psychol. Bull.*, 30, 261-324.—*30, 49, 129, 155, 204, 308, 338*

703. RAZRAN, G. H. S. (1933b) Conditioned responses in children. *Arch. Psychol., N.Y.*, 23, No. 148, 120 pp.—*49, 129, 155, 204, 277, 307, 308*

704. RAZRAN, G. H. S. (1934) Conditioned withdrawal responses with shock as the conditioning stimulus in adult human subjects. *Psychol. Bull.*, 31, 111-143.—*277*

705. RAZRAN, G. H. S. (1935) Conditioned responses: an experimental study and a theoretical analysis. *Arch. Psychol., N.Y.*, 28, No. 191, 124 pp.—*122, 134, 144, 155, 157, 261, 277, 301, 302, 308*

706. RAZRAN, G. H. S. (1936a) Attitudinal control of human conditioning. *J. Psychol.*, 2, 327-337.—*262, 277*

707. RAZRAN, G. H. S. (1936b) The conditioning of voluntary reactions. *J. exp. Psychol.*, 19, 653-654.—*277*

708. RAZRAN, G. H. S. (1937) Conditioned responses: a classified bibliography. *Psychol. Bull.*, 34, 191-256.—*49, 338*

709. RAZRAN, G. H. S. (1938a) Conditioning away social bias by the luncheon technique. *Psychol. Bull.*, 35, 693.—*296*

710. RAZRAN, G. H. S. (1938b) Music, art, and the conditioned response. Paper, Eastern Psychological Association, April 1-2, 1938.—*296*

711. RAZRAN, G. H. S. (1938c) Transposition of relational responses and generalization of conditioned responses. *Psychol. Rev.*, 45, 532-538.—*203, 204*

712. RAZRAN, G. H. S. (1938d) Studies in configural conditioning. VII.

Ratios and elements in salivary conditioning to various musical intervals. *Psychol. Rec.*, 2, 370-376.—*198, 199*

713. RAZRAN, G. H. S. (1939a) Studies in configural conditioning: I. Historical and preliminary experimentation. *J. gen. Psychol.*, 21, 307-330.—*198, 206*

714. RAZRAN, G. H. S. (1939b) Studies in configural conditioning. II. The effect of subjects' attitudes and of task-sets upon configural conditioning. *J. exp. Psychol.*, 24, 95-105.—*198*

715. RAZRAN, G. H. S. (1939c) Studies in configural conditioning: III. The factors of similarity, proximity, and continuity in configural conditioning. *J. exp. Psychol.*, 24, 202-210.—*198*

716. RAZRAN, G. H. S. (1939d) Studies in configural conditioning: IV. Gestalt organization and configural conditioning. *J. Psychol.*, 7, 3-16.—*198*

717. RAZRAN, G. H. S. (1939e) Studies in configural conditioning: V. Generalization and transposition. *J. genet. Psychol.* (in press).—*182, 183, 198, 204*

718. RAZRAN, G. H. S. (1939f) Studies in configural conditioning. VI. Comparative extinction and forgetting of pattern and of single-stimulus conditioning. *J. exp. Psychol.*, 24, 432-438.—*129, 198*

719. RAZRAN, G. H. S. (1939g) Decremental and incremental effects of distracting stimuli upon the salivary CRs of 24 adult human subjects (inhibition and disinhibition?) *J. exp. Psychol.*, 24, 647-652.—*131, 133*

720. RAZRAN, G. H. S. (1939h) Extinction, spontaneous recovery, and forgetting. *Amer. J. Psychol.*, 52, 100-102.—*133*

721. RAZRAN, G. H. S. (1939i) The law of effect or the law of qualitative conditioning. *Psychol. Rev.*, 46, 445-463.—*49, 55, 71*

722. RAZRAN, G. H. S. (1939j) The nature of the extinctive process. *Psychol. Rev.*, 46, 264-297.—*131, 132*

723. RAZRAN, G. H. S. (1939k) A quantitative study of meaning by a conditioned salivary technique (semantic conditioning). *Science*, 90, 89 90.—*277*

724. RAZRAN, G. H. S. (1939l) A simple technique for controlling subjective attitudes in salivary conditioning of adult human subjects. *Science*, 89, 160-161.—*122, 262, 271*

725. RAZRAN, G. H. S. (1939m) Conditioning and attitudes. *J. exp. Psychol.*, 24, 215-226.—*308*

726. RAZRAN, G. H. S., and WARDEN, C. J. (1929) The sensory capacities of the dog as studied by the conditioned reflex method (Russian schools). *Psychol. Bull.*, 26, 202-222.—*204*

REMPEL, B., *see* No. 164.

RENSHAW, S., *see* No. 827.

727. REXROAD, C. N. (1932) Outline of the conditions under which learning occurs. *Psychol. Rev.*, 39, 174-183.—*25*

728. REXROAD, C. N. (1933) An examination of conditioned reflex theory. *Psychol. Rev.*, 40, 457-466.—*25, 156*

729. REXROAD, C. N. (1936) Reaction time and conditioning: first studies. *J. exp. Psychol.*, 19, 144-158.—*268, 277*

730. REXROAD, C. N. (1937) Reaction time and conditioning: extinction, recovery, and disinhibition. *J. exp. Psychol.*, 20, 468-476.—*133, 268, 277*

731. REYNOLDS, H. E. (1936) The disinhibiting effect of an electric shock upon the maze performance of the white rat. *J. comp. Psychol.*, 22, 187-197.—*133, 227*

732. REYNOLDS, H. E. (1939) Further disinhibition phenomena in the maze behavior of the white rat. *J. comp. Psychol.*, 27, 271-282.—*133, 227*

RIESEN, A. H., *see* No. 639.

733. ROBERTS, W. H. (1930) The effect of delayed feeding on white rats in a problem cage. *J. genet. Psychol.*, 37, 35-58.—*174*

734. ROBINSON, E. S. (1932) *Association theory today.* New York, Appleton-Century, viii, 142 pp.—*22, 101, 171, 175*

735. ROBINSON, E. S. (1934) Work of the integrated organism. In C. Murchison, edit., *A handbook of general experimental psychology.* Worcester, Mass., Clark Univ. Press. 571-650.—*106, 133*

736. ROBINSON, E. S., and BROWN, M. A. (1926) Effect of serial position upon memorization. *Amer. J. Psychol.*, 37, 538-552.—*225*

737. RODNICK, E. H. (1937a) Characteristics of delayed and trace conditioned responses. *J. exp. Psychol.*, 20, 409-425.—*127, 133, 157, 163, 174, 225*

738. RODNICK, E. H. (1937b) Does the interval of delay of conditioned responses possess inhibitory properties? *J. exp. Psychol.*, 20, 507-527.—*127*

739. ROJANSKY, N. A. (1914) Matériaux pour servir à la physiologie du sommeil. *Arch. Sci. biol.*, St. Pétersb., 18, 15-115.—*131, 156*

ROKHLINA, M. L., *see* No. 963.

ROLLE, S. D., *see* No. 961.

740. ROSENTHAL, J. S. (1932) Typology in the light of the theory of conditioned reflexes. *Character and Pers.*, 1, 56-69.—*308*

741. ROSENTHAL, J. S. (1937) [The conditioned reflexes in dogs deprived of one hemisphere. II.] *Arkh. Biol. Nauk*, 47, 47-52. (*Psychol. Abstr.*, 1938, 12, No. 4652.)—*337*

742. ROSENTHAL, J. S. (1938) [The conditioned motor alimentary reflex in dogs without the motor or skin analyzer.] *Fiziol. Zh. S.S.S.R.*, 24, 345-351. (*Psychol. Abstr.*, 1938, 12, No. 4653.)—*337*

ROSENTHAL, J. S., *see also* No. 508.

743. ROSENZWEIG, B. M. (1935) Der Einfluss beiderseitiger Exstirpation der Occipitallappen des Gehirns auf bedingte Gesichtsreflexe. *Acta med. scand.*, 84, 386-400.—*337*

Ross, R. T., *see* No. 369.

744. Rothmann, H. (1923) Zusammenfassender Bericht über den Rothmannschen grosshirnlosen Hund nach klinischer und anatomischer Untersuchung. *Z. ges. Neurol. Psychiat.*, 87, 247-313.—*314*

745. Rothmann, M. (1908) Über die Ergebnisse der Hörprüfung an dressierten Hunde. *Arch. Anat. Physiol., Lpz. (Physiol. Abt.)*, 103-120.—*337*

746. Rouquier, A., and Michel, J. (1934) Anorexie pithiatique élective. *Encéphale*, 29, 277-283.—*307*

747. Rubenstein, C. (1931) The treatment of morphine addiction in tuberculosis by Pavlov's conditioning method. *Amer. Rev. Tuberc.*, 24, 682-685.—*307*

748. Ruch, F. L. (1930) Food-reward vs. escape-from-water as conditions motivating learning in the white rat. *J. genet. Psychol.*, 38, 127-145.—*73*

749. Ruch, F. L. (1934) Goal direction orientation, generalized turning habit and goal gradient as factors in maze learning in the rat. *J. comp. Psychol.*, 17, 225-232.—*227*

750. Ruch, T. C., and Fulton, J. F. (1935) Cortical localization of somatic sensibility. The effect of precentral, postcentral and posterior parietal lesions upon the performance of monkeys trained to discriminate weights. *Res. Publ. Ass. nerv. ment. Dis.*, 15, 289-330.—*337*

751. Ruch, T. C., Fulton, J. F., and German, W. J. (1938) Sensory discrimination in monkey, chimpanzee and man after lesions of the parietal lobe. *Arch. Neurol. Psychiat., Chicago*, 39, 919-937.—*337*

Sack, A. L., *see* No. 964.

752. Sackett, R. S. (1939) The effect of strength of drive at the time of extinction upon resistance to extinction in rats. *J. comp. Psychol.*, 27, 411-431.—*155*

Sakharov, W. R., *see* Nos. 962, 965.

753. Sams, C. F., and Tolman, E. C. (1925) Time discrimination in white rats. *J. comp. Psychol.*, 5, 255-263.—*174*

754. Sanders, M. J. (1937) An experimental demonstration of regression in the rat. *J. exp. Psychol.*, 21, 493-510.—*114*

755. Sandiford, P. (1928) *Educational psychology; an objective study.* New York, Longmans Green, xix, 406 pp. *25*

756. Schaeffer, H. (1936) Les réflexes conditionnels chez l'homme. *Pr. méd.*, 44, 405-410.—*307*

757. Schaltenbrand, G., and Cobb, S. (1931) Clinical and anatomical studies on two cats without neocortex. *Brain*, 53, 449-488.—*314*

758. Schilder, P. (1929) Conditioned reflexes. *Arch. Neurol. Psychiat., Chicago*, 22, 425-443.—*277, 307*

759. SCHILDER, P. (1935) Psychoanalyse und bedingte Reflexe. *Imago*, Lpz., 21, 50-66.—*307*

760. SCHILDER, P. (1937) Psychoanalysis and conditioned reflexes. *Psychoanal. Rev.*, 24, 1-17.—*307*
    SCHILDER, P., *see also* No. 50.

761. SCHLOSBERG, H. (1928) A study of the conditioned patellar reflex. *J. exp. Psychol.*, 11, 468-494.—*16, 174*

762. SCHLOSBERG, H. (1932) An investigation of certain factors related to ease of conditioning. *J. gen. Psychol.*, 7, 328-342.—*35, 143, 144, 155, 226, 277, 308*

763. SCHLOSBERG, H. (1934) Conditioned responses in the white rat. *J. genet. Psychol.*, 45, 303-335.—*58, 148*

764. SCHLOSBERG, H. (1936) Conditioned responses in the white rat: II. Conditioned responses based upon shock to the foreleg. *J. genet. Psychol.*, 49, 107-138.—*49, 58*

765. SCHLOSBERG, H. (1937) The relationship between success and the laws of conditioning. *Psychol. Rev.*, 44, 379-394.—*49, 71, 74*
    SCHLOSBERG, H., *see also* Nos. 350, 431, 680.

766. SCHNEIRLA, T. C. (1929) Learning and orientation in ants. *Comp. Psychol. Monogr.*, 6, No. 30, 143 pp.—*219*
    SCHOLZ, W., *see* No. 554.

767. SCOTT, H. D. (1930) Hypnosis and the conditioned reflex. *J. gen. Psychol.*, 4, 113-130.—*156, 157, 271*
    SCOTT, V. B., *see* No. 441.
    SEARLE, L. V., *see* No. 78.

768. SEARLE, L. V., and BROWN, C. W. (1938) The effect of subcutaneous injections of benzedrine sulfate on the activity of white rats. *J. exp. Psychol.*, 22, 480-490.—*134*

769. SEARS, R. R. (1934) Effect of optic lobe ablation on the visuo-motor behavior of goldfish. *J. comp. Psychol.*, 17, 233-265.—*41, 157*

770. SEARS, R. R. (1936) Functional abnormalities of memory with special reference to amnesia. *Psychol. Bull.*, 33, 229-274.—*227, 291, 307*

771. SEARS, R. R. (1937) Initiation of the repression sequence by experienced failure. *J. exp. Psychol.*, 20, 570-580.—*292*
    SEARS, R. R., *see also* Nos. 347, 637.

772. SEARS, R. R., and COHEN, L. H. (1933) Hysterical anesthesia, analgesia, and astereognosis. *Arch. Neurol. Psychiat.*, Chicago, 29, 260-271.—*296, 307, 320*
    SEARS, W. N., *see* Nos. 313, 314.

773. SECHENOV, I. (1935) *Selected works*. Moscow, State Publishing House, xxxvi, 489 pp.—*23*

774. SEHAM, M. (1932) The "conditioned reflex" in relation to functional disorders in children. *Amer. J. Dis. Child.*, 43, 163-186.—*307*

775. SETTLAGE, P. H. (1936) The effect of sodium amytal on the formation and elicitation of conditioned reflexes. *J. comp. Psychol.*, 22, 339-343.—*325*
SETTLAGE, P. H., *see also* Nos. 291, 292.

776. SETTLAGE, P. H., and HARLOW, H. F. (1936) Concerning the sensory pathway in the conditioned reflex. *J. comp. Psychol.*, 22, 279-282. —*321*
SEYMOUR, S. L., *see* No. 183.

777. SHAFFER, L. F. (1936) *The psychology of adjustment*. Boston, Houghton Mifflin, xix, 600 pp.—*83, 307*

778. SHASTIN, N. R. (1930a) [Unconditioned and conditioned reflexes in myxedema.] *Med. Biol. Zh., Moscow*, 6, 470-482. (Razran, 1933b, pp. 35-37.)—*156*

779. SHASTIN, N. R. (1930b) [Unconditioned and conditioned reflexes in myxedema.] *Fiziol. Zh. S.S.S.R.*, 13, 617-626. (*Psychol. Abstr.*, 1933, 7, No. 5321.)—*156*

780. SHASTIN, N. R. (1938) [The methodology of studying conditioned reflexes in children.] *Fiziol. Zh. S.S.S.R.*, 24, 1055-1062. (*Psychol. Abstr.*, 1939, 13, No. 4067.)—*49*

781. SHERRINGTON, C. S. (1906) *The integrative action of the nervous system*. New Haven, Yale Univ. Press, xvi, 411 pp.—*82, 105, 107, 109*
SHERRINGTON, C. S., *see also* Nos. 137, 186.

782. SHIPLEY, W. C. (1933) An apparent transfer of conditioning. *J. gen. Psychol.*, 8, 382-391.—*227, 230*

783. SHIPLEY, W. C. (1934a) Studies of catatonia. VI. Further investigation of the perseverational tendency. *Psychiat. Quart.*, 8, 736-744.—*305, 308*

784. SHIPLEY, W. C. (1934b) Studies of inhibitions in conditioned responses. *J. gen. Psychol.*, 11, 46-64.—*199*

785. SHIPLEY, W. C. (1935) Indirect conditioning. *J. gen. Psychol.*, 12, 337-357.—*227, 230*

786. SHIPLEY, W. C. (1939) The effect of a short rest pause on retention in rote series of different lengths. *J. gen. Psychol.*, 21, 99-117.—*227*
SHIPLEY, W. C., *see also* No. 820.
SHURRAGER, P. S., *see* No. 147.

787. SHURRAGER, P. S., and CULLER, F. A. (1938) Phenomena allied to conditioning in the spinal dog. *Amer. J. Physiol.*, 123, 186-187.—*338*

788. SILVERMAN, A., and BAKER, L. E. (1935) An attempt to condition various responses to subliminal electrical stimulation. *J. exp. Psychol.*, 18, 246-254.—*205*
SIMPSON, E. D., *see* No. 529.

789. SINGER, E. A. (1911) Mind as an observable object. *J. Phil. Psychol. sci. Meth.*, 8, 180-186.—*6*

790. SINKEVICH, Z. L. (1929) [Simultaneous application of food and defense conditioned stimulations in children.] *Zh. Eksp. Biol. Med.*, 13, 79-85. (*Psychol. Abstr.*, 1934, 8, No. 730).—*101, 111*

791. SKINNER, B. F. (1931) The concept of the reflex in the description of behavior. *J. gen. Psychol.*, 5, 427-458.—*336*

792. SKINNER, B. F. (1932) On the rate of formation of a conditioned reflex. *J. gen. Psychol.*, 7, 274-285.—*157*

793. SKINNER, B. F. (1933) The rate of establishment of a discrimination. *J. gen. Psychol.*, 9, 302-350.—*187*

794. SKINNER, B. F. (1934) The extinction of chained reflexes. *Proc. nat. Acad. Sci., Wash.*, 20, 234-237.—*227*

795. SKINNER, B. F. (1935a) A discrimination based upon a change in the properties of a stimulus. *J. gen. Psychol.*, 12, 313-336.—*69*

796. SKINNER, B. F. (1935b) Two types of conditioned reflex and a pseudo type. *J. gen. Psychol.*, 12, 66-77.—*71, 72*

797. SKINNER, B. F. (1936) A failure to obtain "disinhibition." *J. gen. Psychol.*, 14, 127-135.—*133*

798. SKINNER, B. F. (1937) Two types of conditioned reflex: a reply to Konorski and Miller. *J. gen. Psychol.*, 16, 272-279.—*71*

799. SKINNER, B. F. (1938) *The behavior of organisms; an experimental analysis.* New York, Appleton-Century, ix, 457 pp.—*25, 55, 64, 66, 72, 74, 100, 121, 129, 130, 133, 137, 146, 149, 150, 151, 152, 153, 155, 157, 165, 166, 187, 226, 274, 277*

800. SKINNER, B. F., and HERON, W. T. (1937) Effects of caffeine and benzedrine upon conditioning and extinction. *Psychol. Rec.*, 1, 340-346.—*134*

SLOTOV, M. S., *see* Nos. 965, 966.

801. SLUTSKAYA, M. M. (1928) [Converting defensive into food reflexes in oligophrenics and in normal children.] *Zh. Nevropatol.*, 21, 195-210. (Razran, 1933b, p. 86.)—*113*

802. SMITH, D. E. (1939) Cerebral localization in somaesthetic discrimination in the rat. *J. comp. Psychol.*, 28, 161-188.—*337*

803. SMITH, K. U. (1934) Visual discrimination in the cat: I. The capacity of the cat for visual figure discrimination. *J. genet. Psychol.*, 44, 301-320.—*205*

804. SMITH, K. U. (1935) Apparatus for the study of sensory discrimination in mammals. *Science*, 82, 423-425.—*205*

805. SMITH, K. U. (1937) Visual discrimination in the cat: V. The postoperative effects of removal of the striate cortex upon intensity discrimination. *J. genet. Psychol.*, 51, 329-369.—*317, 337*

SMITH, K. U., *see also* No. 448.

806. SMITH, M. F. (1939) The establishment and extinction of the token-reward habit in the cat. *J. gen. Psychol.*, 20, 475-486.—*74*

807. SMITH, S. (1935) The principle of specific conditioners. *J. genet. Psychol.*, 46, 296-302.—*226*

808. SMITH, S., and FITCH, E. E. (1935) Skill and proprioceptor pattern. *J. genet. Psychol.*, 46, 303-310.—*226*

809. SMITH, S., and GUTHRIE, E. R. (1921) *General psychology in terms of behavior.* New York, Appleton, xii, 270 pp.—*14, 18, 82, 226*

810. SMOLENSKAYA, E. P. (1934) [Verbal symbols of conditioned and differential stimuli.] *Na Put. Izuch. Vyssh. Form Neirodin. Reb.*, 304-315. (*Psychol. Abstr.*, 1935, 9, No. 1163.)—*201*

811. SNYGG, D. (1936) Mazes in which rats take the longer path to food. *J. Psychol.*, 1, 153-166.—*227*

SOLLENBERGER, R. T., *see* No. 162.

812. SPELT, D. K. (1938) Conditioned responses in the human fetus in utero. *Psychol. Bull.*, 35, 712-713.—*140*

813. SPENCE, K. W. (1932) The order of eliminating blinds in maze learning by the rat. *J. comp. Psychol.*, 14, 9-27.—*227*

814. SPENCE, K. W. (1934) Visual acuity and its relation to brightness in chimpanzee and man. *J. comp. Psychol.*, 18, 333-361.—*187, 205*

815. SPENCE, K. W. (1936) The nature of discrimination learning in animals. *Psychol. Rev.*, 43, 427-449.—*189, 194, 204, 226*

816. SPENCE, K. W. (1937a) Analysis of the formation of visual discrimination habits in chimpanzee. *J. comp. Psychol.*, 23, 77-100.—*192*

817. SPENCE, K. W. (1937b) The differential response in animals to stimuli varying within a single dimension. *Psychol. Rev.*, 44, 430-444.—*191, 204*

818. SPENCE, K. W. (1938) Gradual vs. sudden solution of discrimination problems by chimpanzees. *J. comp. Psychol.*, 25, 213-224.—*190, 204*

819. SPENCE, K. W. (1939) A reply to Dr. Razran on the transposition of response in discrimination experiments. *Psychol. Rev.*, 46, 88-91.—*203, 204*

SPENCE, K. W., *see also* No. 370.

820. SPENCE, K. W., and SHIPLEY, W. C. (1934) The factors determining the difficulty of blind alleys in maze learning by the white rat. *J. comp. Psychol.*, 17, 423-436.—*219, 227*

SPIEGEL, E., *see* No. 641.

821. SPRAGG, S. D. S. (1933) Anticipation as a factor in maze errors. *J. comp. Psychol.*, 15, 313-329.—*227*

822. SPRAGG, S. D. S. (1934) Anticipatory responses in the maze. *J. comp. Psychol.*, 18, 51-73.—*227*

823. SPRAGG, S. D. S. (1936) Anticipatory responses in serial learning by chimpanzee. *Comp. Psychol. Monogr.*, 13, No. 62, 72 pp.—*96, 227*

824. STAGNER, R. (1931) Conditioned reflex theories of learning. *Psychol. Rev.*, 38, 42-59.—*25*

STAGNER, R., *see also* No. 293.

825. Steckle, L. C. (1933) A trace conditioning of the galvanic reflex. *J. gen. Psychol.*, 9, 475-480.—*174*

826. Steckle, L. C. (1936) Two additional attempts to condition the pupillary reflex. *J. gen. Psychol.*, 15, 369-377.—*277, 278*

827. Steckle, L. C., and Renshaw, S. (1934) An investigation of the conditioned iridic reflex. *J. gen. Psychol.*, 11, 3-23.—*277, 278*

828. Stephens, J. M. (1931a) The influence of different stimuli upon preceding bonds. An examination of the law of effect. *Teach. Coll. Contr. Educ.*, No. 493, vii, 83 pp.—*101*

829. Stephens, J. M. (1931b) Some weaknesses in the explanation of habit fixation as conditioning. *Psychol. Rev.*, 38, 137-152.—*25*

830. Stephens, J. M. (1934a) The conditioned reflex as the explanation of habit formation: I. The essential factors in the establishment of the conditioned reflex. *J. gen. Psychol.*, 10, 110-136.—*156, 277*

831. Stephens, J. M. (1934b) The conditioned reflex as the explanation of habit formation: II. The operation of a higher-order reaction and a lower-order reaction in close succession. *J. gen. Psychol.*, 10, 219-227.—*277*

832. Stephens, J. M. (1936a) The conditioned reflex as the explanation of habit formation: III. The operation of two higher-order reactions in close succession. *J. exp. Psychol.*, 19, 77-90.—*277*

833. Stephens, J. M. (1936b) Reply. *J. exp. Psychol.*, 19, 399-400.—*277*

834. Stephens, J. M. (1937) Data bearing on the conditioning of voluntary reactions. *J. exp. Psychol.*, 21, 236-239.—*277*

835. Stetter, H. (1929) Untersuchungen über den Gehörsinn der Fische. *Z. vergl. Physiol.*, 9, 339-477.—*302*

836. Stevens, S. S., Davis, H., and Lurie, M. H. (1935) The localization of pitch perception on the basilar membrane. *J. gen. Psychol.*, 13, 297-315.—*195*

Stevenson, S. S., *see* No. 602.

Stonex, E., *see* No. 404.

837. Storey, R. T. (1937) Proprioceptive discrimination in the cat and its cortical representation. Ph.D. dissertation, Stanford University.—*337*

Straj, E., *see* No. 17.

Sutherland, G. F., *see* Nos. 183, 530.

838. Sutherland, G. F., and Dworkin, S. (1932) Conditioned responses to sound and vibrations. *Amer. J. Physiol.*, 101, 97-89.—*205, 337*

839. Swann, H. G. (1935) The function of the brain in olfaction: The effects of large cortical lesions on olfactory discrimination. *Amer. J. Physiol.*, 111, 257-262.—*337*

840. Swift, W. B. (1912) Demonstration of dog Louisa who reacts to acoustic stimuli after extirpation of both temporal lobes. *Boston med. surg. J.*, 166, 56-57.—*337*

841. SWITZER, S. A. (1930) Backward conditioning of the lid reflex. *J. exp. Psychol.*, 13, 76-97.—*157, 174*

842. SWITZER, S. A. (1933) Disinhibition of the conditioned galvanic skin response. *J. gen. Psychol.*, 9, 77-100.—*133, 157, 163, 174*

843. SWITZER, S. A. (1934) Anticipatory and inhibitory characteristics of delayed conditioned reactions. *J. exp. Psychol.*, 17, 603-620.—*127*

844. SWITZER, S. A. (1935a) The effect of caffeine on experimental extinction of conditioned reactions. *J. gen. Psychol.*, 12, 78-94.—*120, 134*

845. SWITZER, S. A. (1935b) The influence of caffeine upon "inhibition of delay." *J. comp. Psychol.*, 19, 155-175.—*134*

846. SYMONDS, P. M. (1927) Laws of learning. *J. educ. Psychol.*, 18, 405-413.—*20*

847. TATARENKO, N. P. (1934) [Disorders of the conditioned-reflex activity in patients with senile psychosis.] *Sovrem. Psikhonevrol.*, 75-87. (*Psychol. Abstr.*, 1935, 9, No. 757.)—*308*

TAYLOR, F. E., *see* No. 419.

848. TELFORD, C. W. (1931) The refractory phase of voluntary and associative responses. *J. exp. Psychol.*, 14, 1-36.—*131*

849. TELFORD, C. W., and ANDERSON, B. O. (1932) The normal wink reflex; its facilitation and inhibition. *J. exp. Psychol.*, 15, 235-266.—*131*

850. TELFORD, C. W., and THOMPSON, N. (1933) Some factors influencing voluntary and reflex eyelid responses. *J. exp. Psychol.*, 16, 524-539.—*131*

851. TEN CATE, J. (1934a) Akustische und optische Reaktionen der Katzen nach teilweisen und totalen Exstirpationen des Neopalliums. *Arch. néerl. Physiol.*, 19, 191-264.—*205, 337*

852. TEN CATE, J. (1934b) Die Pupillenverengerung, als bedingter Reflex auf akustische Reize und ihre Beziehung zu der Grosshirnrinde. *Arch. néerl. Physiol.*, 19, 417-425.—*205, 278*

853. TEN CATE, J. (1934c) Können die bedingten Reaktionen sich auch ausserhalb der Grosshirnrinde bilden? *Arch. néerl. Physiol.*, 19, 469-481.—*314*

854. TEN CATE, J. (1938) Bedingte Reflexe bei Hunden nach beiderseitiger Exstirpation der Regio occipitalis der Grosshirnrinde. *Arch. néerl. Physiol.*, 23, 219-253.—*315, 316, 337*

855. TEN CATE, J. (1939) Bedingte Reflexe auf Lichtreize bei einer Katze nach beiderseitigen Exstirpation der Area striata. *Arch. néerl. Physiol.*, 24, 61-66.—*337*

856. THOMPSON, E. L. (1917) An analysis of the learning process in the snail, Physa Gyrina Say. *Behav. Monogr.*, 3, No. 3, iii, 97 pp.—*31*

857. THOMPSON, N., *see* No. 850.
    THORNDIKE, E. L. (1898) Animal intelligence. An experimental study
        of the associative processes in animals. *Psychol. Monogr.*, 2, No.
        8, 109 pp.—*6, 53*
858. THORNDIKE, E. L. (1911) *Animal intelligence; experimental studies.*
        New York, Macmillan, viii, 297 pp.—*71, 81, 82, 101*
859. THORNDIKE, E. L. (1932a) *The fundamentals of learning.* New York,
        Teachers College, xvii, 638 pp.—*25, 125, 271*
860. THORNDIKE, E. L. (1932b) Reward and punishment in animal learn-
        ing. *Comp. Psychol., Monogr.*, 8, No. 39, 65 pp.—*125*
861. THORNDIKE, E. L. (1933a) A proof of the law of effect. *Science*, 77,
        173-175.—*174*
862. THORNDIKE, E. L. (1933b) An experimental study of rewards. *Teach.
        Coll. Contr. Educ.*, No. 580, 72 pp.—*174*
863. THORNDIKE, E. L. (1935) *The psychology of wants, interests, and
        attitudes.* New York, Appleton-Century, x, 301 pp.—*25, 71, 81,
        102, 167, 174*
    THORNDIKE, E. L., *see also* No. 113.
864. THUMA, B. D. (1932) The response of the white rat to tonal stimuli.
        J. comp. Psychol., 13, 57-86.—*205*
865. TILTON, J. W. (1939) The effect of "right" and "wrong" upon the
        learning of nonsense syllables in multiple choice arrangement.
        J. educ. Psychol., 30, 95-115.—*125*
866. TIMMER, A. P. (1931) Die schizothymen und cyclothymen Tempera-
        mente Kretschmers im Lichte der Pawlowschen bedingten Re-
        flexe betrachtet. *Z. ges. Neurol. Psychiat.*, 133, 329-351.—*308*
867. TINEL, J. (1930) Les réflexes conditionnels dans les états névropa-
        thiques. *Encéphale*, 25, 65-81.—*307*
868. TINKLEPAUGH, O. L. (1928) An experimental study of representative
        factors in monkeys. *J. comp. Psychol.*, 8, 197-236.—*95*
869. TITCHENER, E. B. (1909) *A textbook of psychology.* New York, Mac-
        millan, 2 vols., xvi, 558 pp.—*4*
    TITELBAUM, S., *see* No. 453.
870. TOLMAN, E. C. (1932) *Purposive behavior in animals and men.* New
        York, Appleton-Century, xiv, 463 pp.—*25, 101, 248, 253*
871. TOLMAN, E. C. (1933) Sign-gestalt or conditioned reflex? *Psychol.
        Rev.*, 40, 246-255.—*227, 233*
872. TOLMAN, E. C. (1934) Theories of learning. In F. A. Moss, edit.,
        Comparative psychology. New York, Prentice-Hall, 367-408.—
        17, 71, 88
873. TOLMAN, E. C. (1937) The acquisition of string-pulling by rats—con-
        ditioned response or sign-gestalt? *Psychol. Rev.*, 44, 195-211.—
        103, 247
874. TOLMAN, E. C. (1938a) The determiners of behavior at a choice point.
        Psychol. Rev., 45, 1-41.—*204*

875. TOLMAN, E. C. (1938b) A reply to Professor Guthrie. *Psychol. Rev.*, 45, 163-164.—*247*

876. TOLMAN, E. C. (1939) Prediction of vicarious trial and error by means of the schematic sowbug. *Psychol. Rev.*, 46, 318-336.—*204*

TOLMAN, E. C., *see also* Nos. 113, 329, 330, 753.

877. TRACY, F. W. (1927) Experiments on the establishment of conditioned motor responses. M.A. thesis, Ohio State University.—*322*

TREAT, W. C., *see* No. 189.

878. TROLAND, L. T. (1928) *The fundamentals of human motivation.* New York, Van Nostrand, xiv, 521 pp.—*81, 82, 332*

879. TWITMYER, E. B. (1902) *A study of the knee-jerk.* Philadelphia, Winston, 36 pp.—*3*

VON UEXKÜLL, J., *see* No. 39.

UGOL, N. B., *see* No. 604.

880. UKHTOMSKI, A. A. (1926) [Concerning the condition of excitation in dominance.] *Nov. Refl. Fiziol. Nerv. Sist.*, 2, 3-15. (*Psychol. Abstr.*, 1927, 1, No. 2388.)—*50, 156*

881. UKHTOMSKI, A. A. (1938) [On conditioned reflex action.] *Fiziol. Zh. S.S.S.R.*, 24, 379-385. (*Psychol. Abstr.*, 1938, 12, No. 4661.)—*50, 156*

882. UPTON, M. (1929) The auditory sensitivity of guinea pigs. *Amer. J. Psychol.*, 41, 412-421.—*16, 40, 205*

UPTON, M., *see* No. 157.

883. VANDERPLANK, F. L. (1938) Sex hormones and their effect upon conditioned responses in the rudd (Leuciscus leuciscus). *J. exp. Biol.*, 15, 385-393.—*156*

VAN LIERE, E. J., *see* No. 140.

884. VOROBYOV, A. M. (1932) [Specific food excitability in relation to various diets.] *Trud. Ukrain. Psikhonevrol. Inst.*, 21, 161-169. (*Psychol. Abstr.*, 1933, 7, No. 3263.)—*155*

WALKER, E. L., *see* Nos. 442, 443.

885. WALKER, E. L., and KELLOGG, W. N. (1939) Conditioned respiration and the conditioned flexion response in dogs. *J. comp. Psychol.*, 27, 393-409.—*80*

886. WARD, L. B. (1937) Reminiscence and rote learning. *Psychol. Monogr.*, 49, No. 220, 64 pp.—*224, 227*

WARDEN, C. J., *see* Nos. 726, 930.

887. WARDEN, C. J., and HAAS, E. L. (1927) The effect of short intervals of delay in feeding upon speed of maze learning. *J. comp. Psychol.*, 7, 107-116.—*174*

888. WARNER, L. H. (1932a) The association span of the white rat. *J. genet. Psychol.*, 41, 57-90.—*164*

889. WARNER, L. H. (1932b) An experimental search for the "conditioned response." *J. genet. Psychol.*, 41, 91-115.—*25, 49*

890. WARREN, H. C. (1921) *A history of the association psychology.* New York, Scribner, ix, 328 pp.—*23, 101*
WARREN, J. W., *see* No. 63.

891. WASHBURN, M. F. (1916) *Movement and mental imagery.* Boston, Houghton Mifflin, xv, 252 pp.—*24*

892. WASHBURNE, J. N. (1935) An electro-chemical theory of learning. *J. educ. Psychol.*, 26, 99-122.—*329, 331*

893. WATERS, R. H. (1934) The law of effect as a principle of learning. *Psychol. Bull.*, 31, 408-425.—*101*

894. WATSON, J. B. (1907) Kinesthetic and organic sensations: their rôle in the reactions of the white rat to the maze. *Psychol. Monogr.*, 8, No. 33, vi, 100 pp.—*226*

895. WATSON, J. B. (1913) Psychology as the behaviorist views it. *Psychol. Rev.*, 20, 158-177.—*7*

896. WATSON, J. B. (1914) *Behavior. An introduction to comparative psychology.* New York, Holt, xii, 439 pp.—*3, 102, 328*

897. WATSON, J. B. (1916a) The place of the conditioned-reflex in psychology. *Psychol. Rev.*, 23, 89-116.—*12*

898. WATSON, J. B. (1916b) Behavior and the concept of mental disease. *J. Philos. Psychol. sci. Meth.*, 13, 589-597.—*13, 306*

899. WATSON, J. B. (1917) The effect of delayed feeding upon learning. *Psychobiology*, 1, 51-60.—*174*

900. WATSON, J. B. (1919) *Psychology from the standpoint of a behaviorist.* Philadelphia, Lippincott, ix, 429 pp.—*13, 25*

901. WATSON, J. B. (1925) *Behaviorism.* New York, Norton, 251 pp.—*13*

902. WATSON, J. B. (1926) Behaviorism: a psychology based on reflexes. *Arch. Neurol. Psychiat., Chicago*, 15, 185-204.—*25*
WATSON, J. B., *see also* No. 952.

903. WATSON, J. B., and MORGAN, J. J. B. (1917) Emotional reactions and psychological experimentation. *Amer. J. Psychol.*, 28, 163-174.—*13, 25*

904. WATSON, J. B., and RAYNER, R. (1920) Conditioned emotional reactions. *J. exp. Psychol.*, 3, 1-14.—*13, 293, 307*
WEGER, P., *see* No. 172.

905. WELLS, F. L. (1916) Von Bechterew and Übertragung. *J. Phil. Psychol. sci. Meth.*, 13, 354-356.—*12, 13*

906. WENDT, G. R. (1930) An analytical study of the conditioned knee-jerk. *Arch. Psychol., N.Y.*, 19, No. 123, 97 pp.—*42, 49, 109, 124, 131, 157, 174, 277*

907. WENDT, G. R. (1934) Auditory acuity of monkeys. *Comp. Psychol. Monogr.*, 10, No. 49, 51 pp.—*73, 186, 205*

908. WENDT, G. R. (1936) An interpretation of inhibition of conditioned reflexes as competition between reaction systems. *Psychol. Rev.*, 43, 258-281.—*116, 131, 132*

909. WENDT, G. R. (1937) Two and one-half year retention of a conditioned response. *J. gen. Psychol.*, 17, 178-180.—*129*

910. WENDT, G. R. (1938) Methods of recording action. *Arch. Psychol.*, *N.Y.*, 32, No. 228, 83 pp.—*49*
     WENDT, G. R., *see also* No. 128.

911. WENDT, G. R., and DODGE, R. (1938) Practical directions for stimulating and for photographically recording eye-movements of animals. *J. comp. Psychol.*, 25, 9-49.—*49*

912. WENGER, M. A. (1936a) External inhibition and disinhibition produced by duplicate stimuli. *Amer. J. Psychol.*, 48, 446-456.—*131, 133*

913. WENGER, M. A. (1936b) An investigation of conditioned responses in human infants. *Univ. Ia. Stud. Child Welf.*, 12, No. 318, 7-90.—*155*

914. WENGER, M. A. (1937) A criticism of Pavlov's concept of internal inhibition. *Psychol. Rev.*, 44, 297-312.—*132*

915. WENRICK, J. E. (1933) The conundrum of the conditioned response. *Psychol. Rev.*, 40, 549-559.—*175*

916. WENTINK, E. A. (1938) The effects of certain drugs and hormones upon conditioning. *J. exp. Psychol.*, 22, 150-163.—*134*

917. WEVER, E. G. (1930) The upper limit of hearing in the cat. *J. comp. Psychol.*, 10, 221-233.—*205*

918. WHEELER, R. H. (1929) *The science of psychology*. New York, Crowell, xvii, 556 pp.—*25, 253*
     WHEELER, R. H., *see also* No. 665.

919. WHITE, R. K. (1936) The completion hypothesis and reinforcement. *Psychol. Rev.*, 43, 396-404.—*88, 101, 244*
     WHITEMAN, A., *see* No. 166.

920. WICKENS, D. D. (1938) The transference of conditioned excitation and conditioned inhibition from one muscle group to the antagonistic muscle group. *J. exp. Psychol.*, 22, 101-123.—*244*

921. WICKENS, D. D. (1939a) A study of voluntary and involuntary finger conditioning. *J. exp. Psychol.*, 25, 127-140.—*269, 270, 277*

922. WICKENS, D. D. (1939b) The simultaneous transfer of conditioned excitation and conditioned inhibition. *J. exp. Psychol.*, 24, 332-338.—*244*

923. WILEY, L. E. (1932) The function of the brain in audition. *J. comp. Neurol.*, 54, 109-142.—*337*

924. WILLIAMS, K. A. (1929a) The reward value of a conditioned stimulus. *Univ. Calif. Publ. Psychol.*, 4, 31-55.—*74*

925. WILLIAMS, K. A. (1929b) The conditioned reflex and the sign function in learning. *Psychol. Rev.*, 36, 481-497.—*25*

926. WILLIAMS, S. B. (1938) Resistance to extinction as a function of the number of reinforcements. *J. exp. Psychol.*, 23, 506-522.—*73, 146*

WILLMANN, J., *see* No. 152.

927. WILSON, W. R. (1924) Selection in "trial and error" learning. *Psychol. Rev.*, 31, 150-160.—*24*

928. WINSLOW, C. N. (1938) The irradiation of extinction of conditioned responses within a pattern of multiple stimuli. *J. comp. Psychol.*, 26, 397-412.—*206*

929. WINSLOW, C. N. (1939) An experiment in the use of multiple conditioned stimuli and extinction in tests of hearing. *J. gen. Psychol.*, 21, 331-337.—*206*

930. WINSLOW, C. N., KANTOR, R., and WARDEN, C. J. (1938) An investigation of conditioning in cats to multiple stimuli. *J. genet. Psychol.*, 52, 211-225.—*206*

931. WINSOR, A. L. (1930a) Experimental extinction and negative adaptation. *Psychol. Rev.*, 37, 174-178.—*132*

932. WINSOR, A. L. (1930b) Observations on the nature and mechanism of secretory inhibition. *Psychol. Rev.*, 37, 399-411.—*132*

WITMER, F. J., *see* No. 617.

933. WITMER, L. R. (1935) Retention of intra-serial associations. *Psychol. Bull.*, 32, 690.—*227*

WOLF, I. S., *see* No. 444.

WOLF, K., *see* No. 268.

934. WOLFE, J. B. (1934) The effect of delayed reward upon learning in the white rat. *J. comp. Psychol.*, 17, 1-21.—*166, 174*

935. WOLFE, J. B. (1936) Effectiveness of token-rewards for chimpanzees. *Comp. Psychol. Monogr.*, 12, No. 60, 72 pp.—*62, 74, 89*

936. WOLFF, H. G. (1937) Die bedingte Reaktion. In P. Bumke and O. Foerster, *Handbuch der Neurologie*. Berlin, Springer, 2, 320-358. —*49*

937. WOLFF, H. G., and GANTT, W. H. (1935) Caffeine sodiobenzoate, sodium isoamylethyl barbiturate, sodium bromide and chloral hydrate: effect on the highest integrative functions. *Arch. Neurol. Psychiat., Chicago*, 33, 1030-1057.—*102, 134*

WOLFLE, D. L., *see* Nos. 266, 267.

938. WOLFLE, H. M. (1930) Time factors in conditioning finger-withdrawal. *J. gen. Psychol.*, 4, 372-378.—*164, 165*

939. WOLFLE, H. M. (1932) Conditioning as a function of the interval between the conditioned and the original stimulus. *J. gen. Psychol.*, 7, 80-103.—*164, 165, 269*

940. WOLFLE, H. M. (1933) The optimal time order for conditioning. *Psychol. Bull.*, 30, 677.—*174*

941. WOLOWICK, A. B. (1930) [The effect of diet on the activity of the higher nervous system in children.] *Mosk. Med. Zh.*, 10, 1-6. (Razran, 1933b, p. 23.)—*155*

Wood, A., *see* No. 629.

942. Wood, A. B. (1933) A comparison of delayed reward and delayed punishment in the formation of a brightness discrimination habit in the chick. *Arch. Psychol., N.Y.*, 24, No. 157, 40 pp.—*174*

943. Woodger, J. H. (1938) The formalization of a psychological theory. *Erkenntnis*, 7, 195-198.—*254*

944. Woodworth, R. S. (1918) *Dynamic psychology*. New York, Columbia Univ. Press, 210 pp.—*82*

945. Woodworth, R. S. (1938) *Experimental psychology*. New York, Holt, xi, 889 pp.—*49, 74*

Yacorzynski, G. K., *see* No. 280.

946. Yacorzynski, G. K., and Guthrie, E. R. (1937) A comparative study of involuntary and voluntary conditioned responses. *J. gen. Psychol.*, 16, 235-257.—*146, 269, 277, 322*

947. Yarborough, J. U. (1921) The influence of the time interval upon the rate of learning in the white rat. *Psychol. Monogr.*, 30, No. 135, 52 pp.—*164*

948. Yerkes, R. M. (1905) Bahnung und Hemmung der Reaktionen auf tactile Reize durch akustische Reize beim Frosche. *Pflüg. Arch. ges. Physiol.*, 107, 207-237.—*23, 131*

949. Yerkes, R. M. (1906) The mutual relation of stimuli in the frog Rana Clamata Daudin. *Harv. psychol. Stud.*, 2, 545-574.—*23*

950. Yerkes, R. M. (1934) Modes of behavioral adaptation in chimpanzee to multiple-choice problems. *Comp. Psychol. Monogr.*, 10, No. 47, 108 pp.—*243*

951. Yerkes, R. M., and Morgulis, S. (1909) The method of Pawlow in animal psychology. *Psychol. Bull.*, 6, 257-273.—*3, 10, 204*

952. Yerkes, R. M., and Watson, J. B. (1911) Methods of studying vision in animals. *Behav. Monogr.*, 1, No. 2, iv, 90 pp.—*195*

953. Yoshioka, J. G. (1929) Weber's law in the discrimination of maze distance by the white rat. *Univ. Calif. Publ. Psychol.*, 4, 155-184.—*217*

954. Young, P. T. (1936) *Motivation of behavior*. New York, Wiley, xviii, 562 pp.—*155*

955. Youtz, R. E. P. (1938a) Reinforcement, extinction, and spontaneous recovery in a non-Pavlovian reaction. *J. exp. Psychol.*, 22, 305-318.—*73, 146, 148, 157*

956. Youtz, R. E. P. (1938b) The change with time of a Thorndikian response in the rat. *J. exp. Psychol.*, 23, 128-140.—*73*

957. Youtz, R. E. P. (1939) The weakening of one Thorndikian response following the extinction of another. *J. exp. Psychol.*, 24, 294-304.—*73, 131*

958. Yurnan, M. N. (1929) [The effect of the removal of the suprarenals upon the conditioned defensive reflexes of the dog.] *Vyssh.*

Nerv. Deyat., 314-342. (*Psychol. Abstr.*, 1934, 8, No. 2509.)—*156*

959. YUSHCHENKO, A. (1927) Über die wirkung der einseitigen Ernahrung auf die bedingten Reflexe bei Kindern. *Jb. Kinderheilk.*, 115, 261-270.—*155*

960. YUSHCHENKO, A. (1928) Über die äussere erlöschende Hemmung bedingter Reflexe bei Kindern. *Jb. Kinderheilk.*, 122, 132-150.—*131*

961. YUSHCHENKO, A., ROLLE, S. D., and PUPKO, L. K. (1934) [The conditioned reflex with a temporary disorder of conduction in the ascending part of the unconditioned reflex arc.] *Arkh. biol. Nauk*, 34, 559-568. (*Psychol. Abstr.*, 1935, 9, No. 1711.)—*321*

962. ZAVADOVSKY, B. M., ASIMOV, G. J., and SAKHAROV, W. R. (1929) Über den Einfluss der Schilddrüse auf die höheren Nervenfunktionen der Hunde. II. *Pflüg. Arch. ges. Physiol.*, 223, 534-547.—*156*

963. ZAVADOVSKY, B. M., and ROKHLINA, M. L. (1929) Bedingte Reflexe bei normalen und hyperthyreoidisierten Hühnern. *Z. vergl. Physiol.*, 9, 114-144.—*156*

964. ZAVADOVSKY, B. M., and SACK, A. L. (1928) Über den Einfluss der Schilddrüse auf die höheren Nervenfunktionen der Hunde. I. *Pflüg. Arch. ges. Physiol.*, 220, 155-175.—*156*

965. ZAVADOVSKY, B. M., SAKHAROV, W. R., and SLOTOV, M. S. (1929) Über den Einfluss der Schilddrüse auf die höheren Nervenfunktionen der Hunde. III. *Pflüg. Arch. ges. Physiol.*, 223, 548-560. —*156*

966. ZAVADOVSKY, B. M., and SLOTOV, M. (1932) Über den Einfluss der Schilddrüse auf die höhere Nerventätigkeit bei Hunden. IV. *Z. vergl. Physiol.*, 16, 89-110.—*156*

967. ZAVADSKY, I. V. (1910) Circonvolution piriforme et odorat du chien. *Arch. Sci. biol.*, St. *Pétersb.*, 15, 223-257.—*337*

968. ZELIONY, G. P. (1929) Effets de l'ablation des hémisphères cérébraux. *Rev. méd.*, Paris, 46, 191-214.—*314*
ZELIONY, G. P., *see* No. 685.

969. ZELIONY, G. P., and KADYKOV, B. I. (1938) [Contribution to the study of conditioned reflexes in the dog after cortical extirpation.] *Eksp. Med., Kharkov*, 31-34. (*Psychol. Abstr.*, 1938, 12, No. 5829.)—*314*

970. ZENER, K. (1937) The significance of behavior accompanying conditioned salivary secretion for theories of the conditioned response. *Amer. J. Psychol.*, 50, 384-403.—*39, 40, 49, 90, 102, 116*

971. ZENER, K., and McCURDY, H. G. (1939) Analysis of motivational factors in conditioned behavior: I. The differential effect of changes in hunger upon conditioned, unconditioned, and spontaneous salivary secretion. *J. Psychol.*, 8, 321-350.—*155*

972. ZEVALD, L. O. (1933) [On the dependence of the value of the conditioned reflex on the physical force of the stimulus, and on the equilibrium of the exciting and hypnotic influences exercised on the cerebral hemispheres.] *Trud. Fiziol. Lab. Pavlov.*, 5, 193-198. (*Psychol. Abstr.*, 1935, 9, No. 3680.)—*156*

973. ZIEVE, L. (1937) Experimental study of visual perception and of Hull's conditioning theory. *J. comp Psychol.*, 24, 487-494.—*227*

Subject Index